THE PHILBY FILES

THE PHILBY FILES

The Secret Life of
Master Spy Kim Philby

Genrikh Borovik

Edited and with an introduction by

Phillip Knightley

LITTLE, BROWN AND COMPANY

BOSTON   NEW YORK   TORONTO   LONDON

First American Edition

ISBN 0-316-19284-9

Library of Congress Catalog Card Number 94-78576

10 9 8 7 6 5 4 3 2 1

MV–NY

*Published simultaneously in Canada
by Little, Brown & Company (Canada) Limited*

Printed in the United States of America

'I truly was incredibly lucky all my life. In the most difficult situations when I was sure this was it, the end, no way out, suddenly some stroke of luck would come my way. It was amazing how lucky I was . . . A lucky life!'

Harold Adrian Russell (Kim) Philby, 'spy of the century', not long before his death, in conversation with the author in Moscow.

Contents

INTRODUCTION

One evening early in February 1988, I sat in a darkened monitoring studio at the BBC Centre in London watching a Soviet television show coming live from Moscow. The Russians had been running trailers for the programme throughout the day. The notorious spy Kim Philby (Order of Lenin, Order of the Red Banner) had agreed to emerge from his Moscow cloisters to appear on screen and talk about his days as a KGB penetration agent in the British Secret Intelligence Service.

Although it was twenty-five years since Philby had defected to Moscow, public interest in him remained intense. Why had he betrayed his country, his service, his class, his colleagues, his friends, his wives? Many books had attempted an answer, but here was Philby himself, on camera, perhaps prepared to reveal all. The BBC had asked me to watch the programme with an interpreter and advise it of the newsworthiness of the interview.

I agreed with trepidation. A few weeks earlier I had spent six days with Philby at his Moscow apartment and had just finished writing a 20,000-word article on him which the London *Sunday Times* was soon to serialise. It now looked as if, for reasons known only to himself, Philby had decided to scoop me. But as the programme began I did not need the interpreter's whispered translation to know that it was not about Philby at all – it was a tribute to Graham Greene, who, in the last years of his life, had taken to visiting the Soviet Union frequently. There were scenes of Greene wandering the streets of Moscow, of him reading from his books, answering questions from students at Moscow University, and, towards the end, of Philby sitting in his study, looking severe and donnish, talking about his time with Greene when they were colleagues in SIS.

Although there was nothing newsworthy about Philby in the programme, once home again I sent Philby a telegram saying the *Sunday Times* would start the serialisation on 20 March, 'providing

you postpone your blossoming television career'. He cabled back
on 21 February saying, 'Television totally terminated'. He kept his
word. When the articles appeared I sent him a list of publications
around the world which had reproduced them and a sample of
clippings illustrating the sensation they had caused. He replied,
'Congratulations. Astonishing.'

Since I had already planned a new biography of Philby, I made
arrangements to return to Moscow at the end of May to put to
him the hundreds of new questions prompted by my earlier visit.
Then on 11 May came the news that Philby was dead. The end of
the masterspy brought an outpouring of adulation and hate around
the world. For every intelligence officer who opened a bottle of
champagne to mark the passing of 'a traitor to his country and the
free world', there was another who mourned the passing of 'the best
intelligence officer this century, a truly remarkable man'.

I began my biography anyway, deeply disappointed that Philby
had taken to his grave many of the secrets that could have illuminated
his life and times, some of the most earth-shaking in history. Or had
he? Throughout the writing of my book, I would have occasional
moments of recall, flashbacks to the Moscow TV documentary on
Greene. I remembered the presenter and interviewer, a well-tailored,
cosmopolitan Russian who would not have been out-of-place on any
British or American programme, turning to the camera and saying,
'Kim Philby. What a remarkable man. I know him well. I have been
collecting material on him for years and one day I will write a book
about him.' And I would think, 'Now that would be interesting – a
Russian view of Philby. Perhaps it needs a Russian to find the way
to Philby's soul.'

The Russian was, of course, Genrikh Borovik, TV star, novelist,
playwright, and now, author of this book. But it was not until
recently that I learned the intriguing story of his relationship with
Philby and the series of fortuitous events that have enabled him not
only to uncover the real Philby, but to reveal the sharpest picture
yet of the workings of the KGB, one of the three great players in
the espionage Cold War.

In the mid 1960s, Borovik had written a novel about spies but
the KGB had killed it without explanation. He was justifiably bitter
about this and when Gorbachev ushered in the new era of glasnost,
Borovik did not hesitate to remind the KGB that it owed him.
'I want to meet a Soviet spy,' he said, 'and I want to be able to

write about him.' In June 1985, Borovik's persistence paid off. He was told he would be allowed to meet Kim Philby, 'the spy of the century', to tape-record interviews with him, and then to make a film, or write a play or a book; the decision would be his.

Over the next three years, Borovik's tapes of his meetings with Philby expanded into 500 pages of typed transcripts. Before Borovik could find the time to do anything with this wealth of material, Philby died. But Graham Greene was still around and, discussing Borovik's dilemma one day, he came up with an idea. 'Why don't you juxtapose Kim's own story with the archives?' he asked. 'That'd be an amusing thing to do.' Without much hope, Borovik wrote to the KGB asking for access to Philby's personal file.

To his surprise he received a prompt letter assenting to his request and a few days later found himself in the Lubyanka sitting in front of a large cardboard box labelled, in Russian, 'Case File No. 5581. Volume 1. Top Secret. Committee on State Security of the Council of Ministers of the USSR'. On the first page was a list of those officers who had had access to the file over the years. There were remarkably few. In fact, the KGB archivist detailed to supervise Borovik's research told him that no one had seen the whole of file 5581. Philby certainly had not, both because it would have been against KGB practice to show an agent his file and because, as we shall see, it would have caused him great distress.

Access to Philby's file was the stimulation Borovik needed to write this book because it enabled him to move beyond Philby's own version of his life, which Borovik felt had already been told, into a story with several layers. First there is Philby's account, told in the twilight of his life, and seen through the rosy glow of memory and ego. Then there are the same events as seen by the KGB, both in the field and in Moscow. The two are often very different and Borovik offers his own view on which is true. And there is a third layer, perhaps the most important of all. An intelligence agency cannot lay bare its files in the manner the KGB has done with Philby without revealing a great deal about its operating procedures and thus its philosophy. So Borovik's reconstruction of the way the KGB ran Philby is the most comprehensive account yet of how the KGB actually functioned, and leads inexorably to a conclusion of enormous importance about the world intelligence community and the value of espionage.

The wealth of the material in the file stunned Borovik and it took him three years to digest and order it. The reader should be prepared to have his views about the KGB and Philby shattered for ever. I know that some of mine have been. For instance, the KGB took on Philby not through a brilliant, long-term plan to recruit British university students who would one day hold positions of power, but simply because it believed – mistakenly – that his father, St John Philby, was in British intelligence. This belief appeared to be confirmed when St John introduced Kim to that *bête noire* of the communists, 'the famous Anglo spy [Robert Bruce] Lockhart', one of the organisers in 1918 of a British conspiracy to overthrow the infant Bolshevik government.

And how did the KGB treat this tender ideological recruit? It lied to him about who he was actually working for and it threw him into the deep end of the dirty espionage pool by giving him as his first assignment the distasteful task of spying on his own father – and Philby did it. Desperate to prove himself to his his new masters, he carried out their every order. He made a list of his friends who might be recruited – the beginnings of the Cambridge ring – and he began to construct a Fascist front so as to distance himself from his left-wing past and his left-wing friends, painful though this must have been for him.

He became involved in a Stalin plot to assassinate the Spanish leader, General Franco, but won only the contempt of his controller, who reported to Moscow: '. . . even if he had been able to get close to F[ranco] . . . then he . . . would not be able to do what was expected of him. For all his loyalty and willingness to sacrifice himself, he does not have the physical courage and other qualities necessary.'

Philby gave his KGB bosses unquestioning loyalty, forming close personal relationships with them. In turn, they nurtured and supported him. Then, all of a sudden, they vanished, leaving him bereft. The explanation in File 5581 makes grim reading. There is a list of the names of Philby's controllers and, alongside, what happened to them and why:

'MAR', real surname Reif. Resident of OGPU in London 1934–36. Shot. German and Polish spy.

'MAN', Maly, Teodor Stepanovich. Resident of OGPU in London 1936–37. Shot in 1938. German spy.

'KAP', Gorsky. Resident of OGPU. Shot. German spy.

And so on. Borovik, fascinated by the list, cursory and incomplete though it was, writes that of those Moscow men who had responsible posts and who dealt with Philby, he could not find a single one who managed to survive Stalin's slaughterhouse of 1937–39.

They were replaced by a new wave of intelligence officers – bright, ambitious people determined not to make the same mistakes as their unfortunate predecessors. They insisted on a universal clean-up, a start from scratch. Some authors of earlier Philby biographies noted that Stalin's purges extended to the KGB but, until now, no one knew what effect this had on Philby's career as a spy.

The new officers read the files, came across Philby's name and went to their bosses. And the reformed KGB, to which Philby had agreed to devote his life, did not even know who he was. They had never heard of him. Who is he? Where is he? Who recruited him? Mar! But Mar has been executed as an enemy of the people. Who has been running him? Alexander Orlov! The traitor who defected to the West! They decided that it was all very suspicious. Philby could be a plant from British intelligence. Philby would have to be watched all the time. And so entered the splinter of suspicion that was to fester for the rest of Philby's active life with Moscow.

He was aware of it and resented it. In his own book, *My Silent War*, and in his interviews with me, he presented his career with the KGB as one seamless web of dedicated service, with never a moment of doubt until the stultifying years in Moscow under Brezhnev. Borovik reveals that this was not so. There were periods when his contact with his controller was irregular. Philby would disappear from time to time. He admitted later to withholding information from Moscow because it could easily be traced to him and he could not trust the KGB to protect him. He complained that no 'political education work' was done with him – he wanted explanations about what had been happening in the Soviet Union.

But the loss of his controllers in whom he had placed so much trust was nothing compared to his disillusionment over the Nazi–Soviet Pact of August 1939. This was shattering news for the Left around the world but it had a special significance for Philby. He demanded of his controller, 'What's going to happen to the single-front struggle against Fascism now?' In Moscow he told me that he considered that his work for the KGB 'had not harmed my own Britain at all'. But in 1939–40 he had to face the possibility that it did.

Philby, a war correspondent in France with the British Expeditionary Force, was spying for the Soviet Union – his controller reported to Moscow that Philby had provided valuable material on the BEF and the French army, including their strength, dispositions and 'some data on the Maginot line'. Since Stalin and Hitler were now buddies, how could Philby be certain that the information he was providing Moscow was not being passed straight to Berlin for use against the Allies on the Western front? He had joined the KGB to fight Fascism. Was he now working for the Fascists?

There is evidence that Philby thought so. In December 1939, after complaining that he had become disillusioned, he vanished. On 20 February, 1940, the London resident of the KGB reported to Moscow that their Paris man, 'Karp', had lost contact with Philby and in spite of his best efforts had not been able to re-establish it. Three days later Moscow ordered 'Karp' to cease trying. Philby was finished. He was to be left out in the cold.

It was not until a year later that the KGB changed its mind. Then, to its surprise, Moscow learnt that without its orders, without its help, suddenly and unexpectedly and all on his own, Philby had got into the British Secret Intelligence Service. The agent Moscow had cast aside had accomplished the impossible. It hastened to get in touch with him again.

Borovik is able to tell us for the first time who really brought Philby into the British service, a name entirely new even to spy buffs, how Moscow learnt of Philby's success, and the means it employed to, as it were, re-recruit him. He reveals that the initial elation in Moscow soon turned sour. Philby tried to slur over this in his own book by joking about it. 'My first factual reports on the secret service inclined [my Soviet contact] seriously to the view that I had got into the wrong organisation . . . and that somewhere, lurking in deep shadow, there must be another service, really secret and really powerful . . .' But the truth was much harsher. From the Lubyanka, Philby's entry into SIS looked too easy, suspiciously easy. It ordered him to write a detailed report about it. Borovik found it in the KGB file.

All right, said the KGB bosses, if you are really in British intelligence then give us a list of names of British agents who are going to be sent to work against us in the Soviet Union. When Philby replied, 'There aren't any', Moscow underlined this sentence twice in red ink and put two large question marks against it. They did not believe him.

As a result, Philby's career with the KGB now entered a surreal period. He was again emotionally ready for anything Moscow wanted of him because the German invasion of the Soviet Union in June 1942 meant that he could resume the anti-Fascist fight with a clear conscience. But, to his dismay, Moscow seemed uninterested in his material. Yes, they kept him busy – busy writing reports about himself, his father, his wife, his friends, his colleagues. Please write your autobiography again. How do you spend your time? Who are your closest friends? What do you talk about with the other Soviet agents you know? Tell us again how you managed to join SIS. We are sorry your wife is ill but when she is well again you must question her more closely about her past.

With the Germans at the gates of Moscow, the KGB was more intent on trying to trip up its best British agent, to get proof that he was an SIS plant, than in exploiting his privileged access to British secrets. Even the patient Philby – who, Borovik notes, never said a bad word to him about the KGB in all their time together – got fed up. 'We've recently raised the issue with "S" [Philby] about his submitting a summarising, complete, and detailed autobiography with notes on all his contacts, all his work with us, the English institutions, and the like,' reported his controller. 'But S says that unfortunately he doesn't have the time, that, in his opinion, now is the time that attention should be paid primarily to getting information, and not to writing various biographies. We pointed out the error of his conclusions to S.'

And when Philby was not writing and re-writing reports about himself, what did the KGB want him to do? Find out the names of Soviet citizens recruited by the SIS station chief, then living with his British embassy colleagues in Kuibyshev after being evacuated from Moscow. He hasn't recruited anybody yet, Philby said. And when another Soviet agent, Anthony Blunt, confirmed this, instead of lifting suspicion from Philby, it only made the Moscow spy bosses believe that Blunt too, might be a British plant, and that the SIS conspiracy to penetrate the KGB could be more widespread than they had imagined.

So the KGB did what all intelligence services do when doubtful about an agent – it handed his entire file to a trusted desk officer for an evaluation. Unusually, the officer in Philby's case was a woman and Borovik has even determined her name – Elena Modrzhinskaya. In the great history of espionage she will go down as the Russian version of James Angleton, the American counter-intelligence officer whose paranoid suspicions about KGB penetration nearly destroyed the CIA.

Elena Modrzhinskaya's orders were to examine Philby's file, and, if she considered it necessary, those of the others members of the Cambridge ring, and decide whether they were genuine recruits to the Soviet cause or British penetration agents cleverly planted on the KGB. Borovik rightly looks at her report at length because here we have the flaw at the heart of all espionage and confirmation of a theory I have long held – that most spying is useless because the better the information a spy produces, the less likely he is to be believed.

And this indeed was the first point Elena Modrzhinskaya raised. The very volume and value of the material that Kim Philby and the Cambridge ring had been sending to Moscow was suspicious. Could the British intelligence service really be run by such fools that no one had noticed that precious information was leaking to Moscow? Was it really possible that Philby, with his communist views, his work for the communists in Vienna and his Austrian communist wife, had been recruited for SIS and had sailed through its vetting procedures?

Steadily she developed the case against Philby. He had got little from his father; he had failed his mission in Spain; his controllers had been shot for being either German or Polish spies; or, in the case of Orlov, had defected to the West. Above all, Philby had failed to identify English agents working against the USSR, insisting, contrary to his bosses' views, that there were none. Philby's controllers were alerted to look for further evidence against him. It was easy to find. One of Philby's colleagues had related the contents of a report he had seen. Philby, who had trained his memory, wrote down all he could remember about the report and passed it to Moscow. Moscow already had an actual copy of the report and compared it with Philby's version. They were too alike. Philby could not have done his from memory and got it so nearly right. Conclusion: 'He is lying to us in a most insolent manner.'

The British intercepted and decoded a telegram from the Japanese ambassador in Berlin to his Foreign Ministry in Tokyo. Philby copied it and passed it to his controller. But Moscow already had a copy from another source. In comparing the two, the KGB noticed that the final paragraph, one suggesting that Hitler might soon try to make a separate peace with the Soviet Union – a vital piece of information for the British and Americans – was missing from Philby's version. Why? Philby had an explanation. Because of poor radio reception at the time the British intercepted the message, the last part of it was garbled and could not be decoded. But the KGB simply refused to accept this, preferring to believe that Philby had deliberately withheld this information. As far as it was concerned, it now had final proof that Philby was really working for the British.

And if Philby was a plant, then all the others probably were too. So the KGB London station was told that Philby, Guy Burgess, Anthony Blunt and John Cairncross were agents of British intelligence who had been inserted into the KGB agent network. Only Donald Maclean escaped. It was possible, Moscow said, that Maclean was a genuine recruit and sincerely believed that he was helping the communist cause, but he was being secretly manipulated by the others.

This is an astounding conclusion and, of course, totally wrong. But having reached it, the KGB bosses now proceeded to cover their backs and justify continuing to use the Cambridge spies. You can see the twisted intelligence logic at work: Elena Modrzhinskaya has made out such a powerful case against Philby and his colleagues that we will have to act on it. But what if, in the end, she turns out to be wrong? We might be blamed. We might be shot. So let's not cut off contact with the English agents altogether. In order to maintain their credibility, these agents will have to give us some genuine material and that will be valuable to us. Also, if we break off contact with them, the British will know they have been rumbled and will intensify their search for our other agents. So we will pretend nothing has happened and do our best to reinforce Philby's conviction that we trust him and his ring completely.

And so the game of deceit and double-dealing continued. The Cambridge spies were deceiving their colleagues, their service, their families and their country in the sincere belief that they were serving a greater cause through an elite intelligence service, the KGB, which fathered them, mothered them, and appeared to trust them totally. But, in turn, they were being deceived by the KGB because it really believed that they were playing a treble game and were all traitors to the communist cause.

Borovik draws the startling – but, I believe correct – conclusion from this, that the main threat to intelligence agents comes not from the counter-intelligence service in the country where they are working, but from their *own* centre, their *own* people. Take, for example, the incident that brought Philby down – the flight of Donald Maclean and Guy Burgess from Britain to Moscow in 1951. Here, at last, we have an answer to the question that has puzzled everyone – why did Burgess go too?

Readers of previous books on this topic will remember that the FBI and MI5 had been closing in on Maclean and that he was due to be interrogated by MI5 on Monday, 28 May. Tipped off by Philby that he was in danger, Maclean fled on the Friday, accompanied by Burgess who had arranged the get-away. Other accounts have suggested that Burgess's role was simply to get Maclean out of Britain on the cross-Channel steamer, and be back before Maclean was missed. But Burgess went all the way to Moscow, never to return. His disappearance immediately threw suspicion on Philby, because they were friends and had shared a house in Washington. SIS recalled Philby to London and, while agreeing that there was no real evidence against him, forced him to retire. Thus his career as a KGB penetration agent was over.

In my talks with Philby about this, he placed all the blame on Burgess. 'The unplanned part was that Burgess went too. We knew that Burgess's going put us at risk but Blunt and I decided to stay and stick it out. The whole thing was a mess, an intelligence nightmare, and it was all due to that bloody man Burgess. The KGB never forgave him. They kept us apart in Moscow to avoid recriminations over what had happened. I could understand that but I was sorry about it when I heard that he had died. He'd been a good friend.'

Borovik tells a vastly different story. Burgess was ordered to accompany Maclean to Moscow but was assured that he would soon be back in London. But when he arrived in the USSR, the KGB kept him there. And in doing so it ruined the career of its best agent, Philby, a man who could have become head of SIS. Borovik writes that in his many conversations with Philby about this, he could not bring Philby to blame the KGB. Donald Maclean had no such inhibitions. When he realised what Moscow had done he wrote a furious letter accusing the KGB of betraying Philby, of throwing him to the lions. As far as Borovik could discover, the KGB did not deign to reply.

This is a lucky book, in the sense that it is the result of a confluence of events that seemed unlikely, if not impossible. In the early days of glasnost, the KGB gave Borovik unlimited access to Philby; Graham Greene suggested a way of tackling the writing; Philby died, opening the way for Borovik to obtain access to his file. Did the new bosses of the old KGB realise how devastating this would be? For as Borovik has constructed it, Philby's story goes beyond the biography of one spy, outstanding though he was, and raises vital questions about espionage in general – for let us not pretend that the flaws this book reveals in the KGB are unknown in other intelligence services.

In a dirty, bogus business riddled with deceit, manipulation and betrayal, an intelligence agency maintains its sanity by developing its own concept of what it believes to be the truth. Those agents who confirm this concept – even if it is wrong – prosper. Those who deny it – even if they are right – fall under suspicion. From that moment on, the better that agent's information, the greater the suspicion. When other agents offer confirmation, the suspicion spreads, until the whole corrupt concern collapses – only for a new generation of paranoid personalities to start afresh.

The many revelations and insights in this book will help us reflect on the moral problems of espionage and, of more importance, will enable us to consider whether it has all been a waste of time and that we have been the victims of a vast international confidence trick to deceive us about the necessity and value of the world's second oldest profession.

Phillip Knightley
London, May 1994

A Few Words to the Reader

Before you begin this book, may I explain that it is built on a foundation of three layers. The first consists of the unprecedently open conversations that I had with Kim Philby about himself. I recorded these in the summer of 1985 – fifty hours of talk (about 500 pages of transcripts) to which I added whenever I met Kim on various occasions, mostly social, right up to his death in 1988.

Next come the documents from the secret Philby files which the KGB made available to me for my work on this book.

And, finally, the third layer – my own thoughts, conjectures and conclusions.

I did not clear my manuscript with anyone. I did not ask for advice from the Russian Foreign Intelligence Service, which took over from the KGB, or from anyone else. My reason was simple – I did not want any outside influence (much less pressure) on my own understanding of the essence and meaning of the events described. Therefore I alone am responsible for my suppositions and inferences.

One thing more. The book you are holding is not a history of Soviet intelligence, nor a biographical reference work about my hero. As a writer, what interested me was the personality of a legendary KGB agent and the character and psychology of his relationship with Moscow Centre. These were revealed largely in his conversations about himself and in the unique opportunity afforded me later to compare these observations with KGB documents about Philby which, incidentally, he himself was never able to see. These opportunities had never been presented to any other writer or journalist.

This is why I have not concerned myself with detail – when and where someone was a member of the GPU/NKVD/NKGB/KGB, when and what duty they carried out in the Soviet intelligence service. I did not have the knowledge to do so and I considered it impossible to ask for help, for the reasons I have already given.

This is all I wanted to say before you open the first page of this work. And now, as they wrote in novels of old, 'Over to you, dear reader.'

The Author
Moscow, May 1994

The Philby Files

PROLOGUE

The phone call was completely ordinary. There had been many during his illness.

Kim went on reading, lying on the cot. He read and dozed. He had flu and bronchitis together – and severe cases of both. The book fell from his hands, but sleep didn't come. He'd either read in a daze, or dozed through the book. He didn't answer the phone when he was sick. But this call alerted him somehow.

His wife picked up the phone. He heard her categorical reply: 'No, no, he can't, not at all. It's absolutely out of the question! The doctor says he can't go out. He doesn't even walk around the apartment.'

After a pause, she added, 'Maybe next week . . . But no sooner.'

Kim smiled to himself: defending his presence in the house, defending her nest. But the phone call still troubled him.

She hung up and came over to Kim. She was still annoyed, as she explained: 'From the British Embassy. Some woman. Demanding a meeting with you immediately. I told her, he's sick, but she insisted, she needs you urgently.' She lifted her shoulders, 'How urgent can it be? You're sick. I don't understand women like that! Do you know her?'

The anxiety became palpable. He knew the woman who could call from the British Embassy and demand an urgent meeting. She was secretary to the head of SIS in Beirut.

The news she or her chief was planning to give Kim was unlikely to be pleasant. They wouldn't be so insistent if it were pleasant. An urgent assignment? He doubted it: nothing special was going on, as far as he knew.

'They're always in a hurry, they panic everyone, and then it turns out to be nothing,' he agreed with his wife. 'It'll wait. That woman is a secretary in one of the sections. They're always in a rush.'

Sighing, she went back to her work. He picked up his book. It was up to Evelyn Waugh to chase away his anxious thoughts.

He called the woman four days later, when he really was feeling better.

'Well, at last,' she said with reproach.

'What's up?'

'We have to meet as soon as possible. It's urgent.'

'I can come to the embassy tomorrow.'

'Fine. But how about my place instead of the embassy?'

That was a strange suggestion and made Kim even more wary. A business meeting at the apartment of the chief's secretary? He'd been there before, but never on business.

'Of course, with even greater pleasure. What time?'

'How about three o'clock?'

At three he was at her apartment, bearing a bouquet of flowers. Flowers never hurt in any situation.

She opened the door, smiled gratefully as she took the bouquet, and led him into the living room.

'He's waiting for you.'

Rising from a chair to greet him was none other than Nicholas Elliott, an old colleague and friend, to some degree even an ally in the all the perturbations of the last few years.

'Well, thank God, you've recovered!' Elliott said, shaking his hand. 'I was getting worried. Hello, Kim.'

'What a pleasant surprise!' Kim was completely sincere. 'Too bad I couldn't see you earlier. But I'm on bad terms both with flu and bronchitis. And they were both against me.'

'How are you now?'

'Perfectly tolerable.'

'Then we can talk seriously?'

'I think so. What about?'

Elliott looked at their hostess. She was setting the table for tea for two.

'You're not having tea?' Kim asked her.

'A girlfriend is expecting me, unfortunately. I won't disturb you,' she said and left. Kim saw her front door shut.

'Wonderful tea. She brewed it well,' Elliott said, taking a sip and moving the other cup closer to Kim.

'I always prefer Scotch.'

'So do I, at times. Unfortunately, this isn't a conversation for Scotch. Rather, Scotch isn't for this conversation.' He looked into Philby's eyes. 'Kim, I don't have time to postpone this. And we've known each other forever, so, if you don't mind, I'll get right to the point. Unfortunately, it's not very pleasant.'

. . . So, I was right to feel anxiety when the phone rang . . .

'That is to be expected. You haven't come here with the Order of the Garter, to reward an old veteran.'

Elliott took a pen from the pocket of his light grey jacket. He put it on the table, covered it with the palm of his hand, and rolled it back and forth.

A fine fellow, thought Kim. He doesn't drink whisky. He has the same wife. He writes with an old-fashioned, fat Mont Blanc. He's steady and dependable even in that. Well, come on, what are you waiting for?

'Sorry for getting right on with it, but I don't have time. I've been here for several days as it is.'

'Nick, you haven't even started and you've already apologised twice. What's happened? Don't tell me you flew all the way here just to see me?'

Elliott nodded, pushed away the cup still full of tea, and left his pen alone: 'I came to tell you that your past has caught up with you.'

Kim laughed naturally. 'Have you all gone mad once again? You want to start all that? After all these years? You've lost your sense of humour! You'll be laughing-stocks!'

'No, we haven't lost anything. On the contrary. We've found additional information about you. And it puts everything in its place.'

'What information? And what is there to put in its place?'

Elliott stood up, paced the room, went to the window and looked out. Without turning, he said: 'Listen, Kim, you know I was on your side all the time from the moment there were suspicions about you. But now there is new information. They've shown it to me. And now even I am convinced, absolutely convinced, that you worked for the Soviet special services. You worked for them right up until forty-nine . . .'

Elliott said the word without emphasis, calmly and confidently, as if informing Kim of something insignificant, say, that it was raining. There he was, Nicholas Elliott, standing by the window and he could see that it was raining. The puddles were bubbling. No doubt about it. Like two times two.

'Who told you that nonsense?'

'It doesn't matter. A man who is very well informed about the whole case.'

'But it's totally absurd! You know yourself that it's absurd.'

Elliott returned to the table and went back to rolling his Mont Blanc the way you handle a rolling pin when you stretch out pizza dough. He rolled and said nothing. His silence was accusatory. As if to say, he hadn't expected Kim to hide anything from an old friend who had defended him in difficult times.

. . . *That's why they sent you. An old friend won't be able to take it, he'll start crying and say, yes, I worked for them, can't lie to you, thought Kim. But the old friend will first learn what information you have in your hands now. And how incontrovertible it is.*

Kim forced himself to smile. 'Look how stupid this seems. Astonishing! A man is suspected for a long time of mortal sins, they can't prove a thing, they're embarrassed in front of the whole world. They apologise. And then ten years later, some chief is struck by the old idea again. They decided to send an old friend, a wise and decent man, with only one goal, to persuade an innocent man to confess that he's a Russian spy, that he raped an old lady, murdered her, and lost her money at the roulette table. Along with embezzled funds. Is that why you're here?'

Elliott stopped rolling his pizza. He said very softly, amicably: 'Kim, if you were in my place, if you knew what I know, if you . . .'

'Yes, yes, if I had been given the assignment to do you in, would I do it? Do you really think so?'

'How could it be any other way?'

. . . *What did they know? What? From whom? . . .*

Kim spread his hands. 'Nicholas, dear Elliott! Maybe I would have flown to see you in Beirut, simply in order to see you. But I wouldn't talk to you the way you're talking to me.'

'And how would you talk to me?' Elliott asked curiously.

'I would offer you a drink instead of this lousy tea and laugh with you at the stupidity of our bosses.'

'Kim, they're not so stupid . . .'

. . . *He's speaking with some superiority. They really did find out something. Nicholas knows it too. What? Why is he so sure that I worked only until 1949? Where did that come from? It's stupid, but where did it come from . . .?*

'Can I ask you just one question? It may not destroy your faith in our bosses completely, but it may shake it.'

Elliott said nothing.

. . . Easy now. Carefully . . .

Kim went on with a laugh. 'Why, in the name of all that's holy, did I work for the Russians until forty-nine and not, say, until fifty-one, when this whole mess began? Why aren't I gambling or buying whisky on Soviet roubles to this day?'

. . . Easy . . . Not so sharp . . . He's not stupid, not at all . . . Watch yourself . . .

Elliott didn't flinch.

'I don't know. But you worked until forty-nine.'

'And when did I start, may I ask?' Kim put in as much kindliness as possible and only a crumb of irony.

Elliott heard only the kindliness. 'Don't laugh at me. You must agree that I'm the one who should be asking the question.'

'Sorry. I forgot. After all, this is an interrogation. You came here to interrogate me. And I keep thinking that I'm talking with a friend.'

'Now what does this have to do with an interrogation?' Elliott rejected the attack. 'There's no stenographer. No tape recorder. I'm not taking notes. It's a business discussion in a relaxed, friendly setting. Why an interrogation?'

'But doesn't your visit mean that our colleagues are planning to accuse me of what they already once accused me of with a resounding lack of success?'

Elliott looked at Kim closely and asked: 'Do you want me to give you my version of your work for the Russians?'

'Nicholas, are you serious?'

'I am.'

'I don't even want to discuss it.'

'You're upset, Kim. You'll have to hear me out. This may be a friendly talk, but you realise it's business, and I'm here not on my own whim.'

'So it is an interrogation. Then it has to be done properly. We can play only according to the rules. That's what they taught you, and me, Elliott,' Kim said.

. . . You're being too preachy. Elliott may react. You want him friendly.

At least at the beginning. After all, he could make this a formal interrogation. And it won't make it any better. But he hasn't received permission for a formal interrogation yet. That's the point. He wants to make the conversation close to an interrogation, but he can't start a real interrogation yet. If he could, he wouldn't spin all that nonsense about a friendly chat. And there would be a stenographer in the room. And he wouldn't need his Mont Blanc. It would all be done according to the rules. So it's not in the final stretch yet. They sent him to feel me out. But I'm not a woman. I know how to feel people too. And Elliott knows that. That's why he made a mistake – he told me too soon that it was a friendly talk and apologised twice. They need me for something. What . . .?

Out loud, Kim said: 'I understand: a friendly chat between professionals, or a business chat between friends. You must learn the truth. I am ready to help all I can. I need the truth no less than the people who made you fly from London to Beirut to see me.'

Elliott stopped rolling out his dough.

'I didn't expect to hear anything else from you. We're both professionals. And speaking seriously, I'm certain that if you had been given the same assignment . . .'

'Well, all right, if we're being serious,' Kim said helpfully. 'Of course, I'd have done the same thing. I'd even use the same words with you that you are using with me.'

Elliott looked at him, searching for a hidden meaning in his words. But he didn't seem to find them and smiled.

'Now that's better.' He went on smiling, and his smile was very natural, even dazzling. He asked: 'Then tell me, what would be the first question you'd ask in my place?'

. . . Bravo, Nicholas! You haven't aged. There's still pepper in the pot. You're smoothing over the unpleasantness. You want to look simple. A crummy journalist who doesn't know how to start the interview. But you know very well how to start it. And I'll start it the way you'd like to . . .

'I'd ask you, Nicholas, straight out: when and under what circumstances were you recruited by Soviet intelligence. And knowing you, I'd be certain that you had not been recruited and that you would tell me the honest truth. How's that?'

Elliott stopped smiling.

'No, I won't ask you that. What for? That's for the investigator. It's enough for me to know that you worked for a long time, many years, for Soviet intelligence and that you broke off in 1949.

What difference does it make when you were recruited: thirty-three, thirty-seven, or forty-one?'

. . . Does he not know or is he pretending not to know . . .?

'Do you want me to tell you what you were thinking?' Elliott asked.

'What?'

'You thought, "Does he not know or is he pretending not to know?" Right?'

. . . Clever devil! So sure of himself! . . .

'You know it's not true. I couldn't think that because no one ever recruited me. Who taught you to be such a clever interrogator?'

'No one taught me how to interrogate. It was your suggestion to ask about the recruitment.'

. . . Maybe that question isn't important for them? thought Kim. He realised that the question made him sad.

1

'THE SPY LIVES ONE FLIGHT UP'

Moscow, May 1985

'And this,' Ivan Afanasyevich said, 'is the Dynamo training camp.'

'Is he a Dynamo fan?'

'Crazy about them. Ever since Dynamo played in London after the war, remember?'

'Of course I do, it was Chelsea and some other team.'

'Arsenal. They played in the fog. I was just a kid then,' Ivan Afanasyevich recalled. 'He gives lectures to them sometimes. On the international situation. And criticises them harshly when they lose. His dacha is nearby. Beyond those woods.'

The car had turned off from the Leningrad Chaussee. The Dynamo training camp, a few low grey buildings, was on our left. We passed the woods and were now travelling along a wooden fence beyond which stood light, one-storey summer dachas, the dream of every Muscovite.

We reached the gates. Ivan Afanasyevich took out his red leather-bound KGB identification card and showed it to the gatekeeper, an elderly man in a greenish-blue uniform. Actually, the uniform was dark blue, and only the buttonholes on the crumpled collar were green, but it was enough to bring a green accent into the faded blue, and green was the colour of all the security services of our country. The gatekeeper was a strict man. He looked over our car, gave Ivan Afanasyevich a stern look, checked his ID closely and at length, and only then gave us a marshal-like wave to let us in. The gates were closed, however, and to give his wave any meaning, he first had to unhook the chain and open the gates with a terrible creak.

Ivan Afanasyevich gave the guard a little wave and sent him a kiss, and we drove down a paved road between a series of plots, which weren't separated by fences but were still clearly distinguished, holding wooden houses of the type called 'Finnish' here, even though I doubt you would find such monotonously shabby and monotonously colourless houses, especially in such concentration, anywhere in Finland. But the birches were lovely. The sun beat down on their leaves honestly and brightly. The grass was a juicy green, and ahead lay my meeting with the legendary Soviet agent Kim Philby.

I had applied to the KGB press centre several times with a request to meet a Soviet spy in order to write about him.

Many writers and journalists approached the press centre with such requests. And sometimes they got extremely interesting material.

I felt I had a score to settle with this organisation: long ago, in the mid-sixties, they quashed my first novel about spies. They killed it without explanation: 'inappropriate for the times' was all they said.

So they owed me, as far as I was concerned. And since we were in a period of change – 1985, the start of perestroika – I decided that it would be just to demand some 'compensation'.

Finally, I was informed that there was an opportunity to be introduced to Kim Philby. The KGB had discussed the matter with him and he had reacted with great interest. If I agreed, they would introduce us, and then I would negotiate our schedule of meetings and work. Whether this would be a play, a book, or a film – that was up to me. A film would be good. There was so little known about him. A few imaginative types published books in the West, but they made Philby laugh when he got hold of them. His own book, *My Silent War*, was the only serious source. But it was tiny, it did not cover even one hundredth of what he knew. The man was quite modest. But he would enjoy seeing a film about himself or reading a truthful book. That was the information I got from the man who was charged with telling me that I had received permission to meet Philby.

The generous choice of genres was probably explained by the fact that my literary interests extended to documentary prose, movies (I've made about two dozen documentaries and two or three feature films), and the theatre (I had plays running in the Soviet Union and in a dozen or so other countries). I had written about foreign intelligence quite a bit, too – I had done a series on the CIA for Moscow Central Television.

This is how I ended up in June 1985 in an official black Volga, which had picked me up at the offices of the monthly magazine *Teatr*, of which I was then editor-in-chief, to go to my first meeting with Kim Philby at his dacha outside Moscow. The short, energetic and talkative Ivan Afanasyevich, who accompanied me, was apparently attached to Philby, and was involved in all his affairs. Including his literary ones, I saw.

We stopped, got out of the car (Ivan Afanasyevich took a bag out of the boot) and headed down the narrow sandy path to one of those shabby colourless dachas. We were twenty metres away when the door of the glass veranda opened and a grey-haired man of medium height in wrinkled flannel trousers and a light pullover over a blue-checked shirt came out and walked towards us with a smile. His face was familiar to me from the many photographs in the books I had read in preparation for our conversations. Of course, in them he was much younger.

'Is that him?' I asked stupidly.

'It's him,' my companion answered with complete seriousness and a certain pride.

Confirmation that it really was 'him' were the blue eyes, a shy smile, and a light stutter with which he said his first words to us in Russian: 'Welcome . . .'

'Do you have a Slavic wardrobe and night stand for sale?' I asked.

He got the reference to the old joke right away and said: 'The spy lives one flight up. I'm an ordinary retired Soviet clerk.'

'Since I don't see a second storey, let me ask another question: you wouldn't be Kim Philby, would you?'

'You wouldn't be Genrikh Borovik, would you? I know your face more than you know mine. Big Brother watches you on TV.'

We went up onto the terrace, where Rufina Ivanova, Kim's wife, was setting the table for tea.

'I prefer Scotch,' Kim said with a laugh, but with a look at his wife added, 'but not first thing in the morning and, of course, only with Rufina's permission.'

Ivan Afanasyevich bent over his bag, unzipped it, rummaged

inside, and took out something heavy and rectangular that gurgled appetisingly. He announced heartily: 'Everything's under control. Ballantine's.'

Rufina Ivanova gave Kim a stern look. He raised his hands, calling on either the Almighty or Ivan Afanasyevich as witness to his weakness.

'And your order is filled, too,' my companion said to Rufina Ivanova.

She thanked him, took her parcel, and went inside.

'Well, I've done my job,' Ivan Afanasyevich summed up. 'I'm off. How long will you talk?'

Kim looked at me.

'For the first time, maybe three hours?' I proposed.

'Do you have enough tape?' Ivan Afanasyevich asked.

'I hope so.'

'I'll be back in three hours, don't be lonely.' Ivan Afanasyevich gave us his little wave and strode through the sunny meadow to his car.

'A good man,' Philby said, watching him go. 'Kind.' Rufina Ivanova served napoleons with the coffee. 'She bakes them herself,' Kim said proudly.

However, there were only two cups on the table.

'I have a lot of things to do. And I don't want to be in the way,' Rufina Ivanova explained and left us alone.

The sun's rays came through the window and birds watched us. There were a lot of birds here. They sat on the birch branches and watched the famous spy.

'They're waiting to be fed,' Kim said. He took out a piece of white bread from the basket on the table and a red Swiss army knife from his pocket. He opened it and set it down next to his plate. The bird community outside fluttered its wings in anticipation.

The coffee was steaming, the tape recorder was on, and I wanted to ask the first question.

'It's a banal question,' I said, 'but necessary: how did you come into the Soviet service?'

Kim cut off a few small pieces of bread for the birds, set aside his knife, and said nothing, as if following the old Russian custom of sitting in silence before heading out on a long journey.

He went off into himself, into the past. He was looking through his personal archives of memory, running a film on his personal screen. He folded his knife neatly, gathered up all the pieces and crumbs, put them on a plate, and covered it with a napkin – to the boisterous disapproval of his feathery friends who had been watching his every move. His movements were unhurried, decorous, practically planned.

Only when he was finished did Kim start his story. And he began with a promise: he was going to talk about his second life more fully than ever before. But did he know which life was his second and which was his first? Then he admitted: 'To tell the truth, I thought that by now the day when it happened wouldn't be of much interest to anyone . . .' His words seemed tinged with sadness. 'For you to be able to understand that day, I have to start much earlier.'

He gave me a questioning look – would I accept this turn in the conversation? It went without saying that I agreed. Philby cocked his head, turned his gaze inward, as if to see that day within the panorama of his entire life. He seemed to be planning an outline for his talk.

'It took me a long time to decide to work for the Communists, but the most important period was my last two years at Cambridge. Much has been written about the atmosphere there in the early thirties, and there is no need for me to go into it. Several factors influenced my decision – inner and external, emotional and rational. The study of Marxism and seeing the Depression in England. Books and lectures and the rise of fascism in Germany. Fascism was one of the deciding factors for me. I was becoming convinced that only the Communist movement could resist it. Of course, there were doubts and unfounded expectations. But there was also dissatisfaction with myself. I kept asking myself – why not give yourself totally to this movement? I had only one alternative: either I told myself, yes, or I gave up everything, betrayed myself, and dropped politics altogether.

'Once, I was sitting alone in my room in Cambridge. It was evening. No one with me. I sat in my armchair and thought . . . And I took my decision. It was a few days before the end of term. No one knew of my decision, naturally. I could have rejected it at any moment: I had not made any vows or promised anyone anything. But, as it turned out, it was a decision for life.'

Once you have a decision, you must act. Even before that evening he had been planning to go to Austria. Kim wanted to spend a year there, perfecting his German and getting to know the culture. Knowledge of both was required for government work.

'Kim, some might think it naive to plan to combine the two: becoming a Communist and getting a government job. What was your reasoning?'

'I had the example of my friend Donald Maclean, who by then had been a member of the Party at Cambridge for two years and nevertheless had started work at the Foreign Office.

'I did not plan to be a secret Communist, on the contrary, I planned to join the Party openly and openly announce it. Even though I was prepared to help Communists in any of their front organisations, too.'

Kim needed contacts with Austrian Communists. And he got advice from a very famous economist who was lecturing at Cambridge then, Maurice Dobb. Like Maclean, he was an open member of the Communist Party.

In those days people like that were not persecuted. Why? Perhaps because they represented a very strong trend among the intelligentsia. Things changed later. Take Peter Kapitsa, who worked in Cambridge and then decided to go to the Soviet Union. Many were surprised, of course, but no one criticised him. But when Bruno Pontecorvo did the same thing after the Second World War, it caused a great scandal. It must have been the effect of the Cold War.

The attitude in England towards Communists before the war and afterwards was quite different. Before, serious people, who should have been paying professional attention to the movement – for instance, M15, British intelligence – considered the interest in Communism a silly joke and treated it with great tolerance. I suggested to Kim that they were obviously acting in accordance with the old saw: 'If you are not a revolutionary in your youth, you have no heart. If you remain a revolutionary in old age, you have no head.'

'Unfortunately,' he replied, 'in many cases, they were right. In fact, quite a few young people who took up Communism at Cambridge dropped it rather quickly. Moreover, some became our fiercest enemies; for instance, Edward Crankshaw, Margaret Scepsler, and many more. Some were merely following fashion, others were romantic and seeking an outlet for their anarchic protests against everything in the world. But those feelings remained only feelings that led nowhere.'

Kim told Dobb that he was prepared to work for the Communist Party, and he replied: 'I've been observing you for several years and I've seen you move in that direction. I'm very pleased that you've taken this decision.'

Dobb himself was quite young. Later, he became a full professor, spent his whole life in Cambridge, remained a Communist to the end of his days, wrote many books about the Soviet economy, and often appeared both at Cambridge and outside, never hiding his Communist views. He enjoyed recognition in academia and great respect.

But Dobb may have been cautious with Kim then, because he said: 'Do not forget, young man, that there is a fascist regime in Austria. The Party is in an illegal situation there. None of my friends is there now, because the Communist leadership is in hiding. I can give you a letter of recommendation to the head of the International Organisation for Aid to Revolutionaries in Paris. He's Italian, but speaks good German, fair English, perfect French, and I am certain that he will introduce you to someone in Austria. The IOAR, as you know,' he explained, 'is not a directly Communist organisation, but it is connected with them.'

'Thank you very much,' was all Kim could say.

Dobb wrote a very warm letter of recommendation to that Italian. And he took it to Paris.

Kim had been to France many times as a boy with his father and as a student. 'I went to the man. Unfortunately, I do not remember his name or address. I do remember that he had a small office in a large establishment that looked like a newspaper office. Lots of telephones, typewriters, and people talking, typing, calling – they were all busy. I located him quickly and handed him the letter. The Italian was pleased. "Oh, this is my old friend!" He made the following suggestion.

'"Let's do this," he said. "I will give you a letter of recommendation to the head of the Austrian Committee for Relief from German Fascism, and you can develop your own contacts there."'

Kim agreed, and with the letter in hand left almost immediately for Vienna. He had £100 sterling in his pocket, a birthday gift from his father. It was a lot of money then, and he hoped to live modestly on it in Vienna for at least a year.

Once in Vienna, he rented a room he found in an advertisement, and headed straight for the committee to aid refugees.

It was run by George Neller, a pianist and composer by profession, and a Marxist and Communist by conviction. He worked for the committee without pay, and earned money by giving music lessons. After reading the letter from Paris, he asked Kim what he wanted to do.

'I'm ready to do whatever you need.'

'Oh, we need a lot!'

Neller explained that the committee helped all refugees from fascist Germany, especially workers, and it didn't matter whether they were Social Democrats or Communists. But later Kim realised that his organisation was Communist. The Social Democrats had their own committee to help 'their' refugees.

Neller suggested several kinds of work. 'You could collect money for us among your friends, help distribute clothing and financial aid, write leaflets and hand them out. To tell the truth, we have much more work than we have people, so that each one is worth his weight in gold.'

Kim asked him to recommend a place to rent a room, so as not to worry about the landlord's surveillance.

'Oh, we have a very close friend, a marvellous woman named Litzi Friedmann. A Communist. Last year she spent two weeks in jail for her activist work. Her apartment is in the centre of town. She will be happy to let you a room for a modest sum.'

Kim headed for the Latschkagasse in the ninth district of Vienna at the address Neller had given. He must have called ahead, because she offered him a very moderate rent for a good room in a quite civilised apartment in a large apartment building.

Kim soon learned that Litzi headed the IOAR in the ninth district, which was subordinated to the IOAR's city committee. The IOAR was illegal, but the Committee for Relief was totally official. Therefore, the Communist Party acted through the IOAR and the IOAR through the refugee committee.

At the district division, which Kim joined immediately, Litzi had a treasurer, an organisational secretary, an agitation secretary – all proper and accounted for.

At first Kim helped out only when there was an international aspect, but as his German improved, he took a more active part in all the activities of the cell. Soon the treasurer moved to another city, and he was given his job.

'It happened quite naturally, since I was a contributor to the

IOAR's treasury. That happened the day I met Litzi, when we started talking about the price of the room. A frank and direct person, she came out and asked me how much money I had. I replied: my father's gift of one hundred pounds, which I hoped would last me about a year in Vienna. She took a piece of paper, converted pounds to schillings, made some calculations, and announced, "You can live luxuriously on that much for a year! The rent will be very little, you need six schillings a day for food, and just pennies for transport. You don't need anything else. That will leave you an excess of twenty-five pounds. You can give that to the IOAR. We need it desperately."

'I liked her determination and I became a contributor to the IOAR.'

'What did you do?'

'Besides my work as treasurer I naturally participated in discussions and meetings, which took place once or twice a week. Many issues were discussed, even articles in Austrian and German newspapers. I also helped put together leaflets: I wrote drafts in English, friends translated them into German, and then we distributed our illegal products. We had a simple printing press. It was also in an "illegal situation", and we kept it hidden, but it worked perfectly.

'As treasurer, I phoned around to sympathisers to persuade them to donate money to help refugees from fascist Germany. I concentrated on the intelligentsia – doctors, lawyers, and so on. My English accent helped my work. If I were Austrian, I could have been more eloquent in dealing with our "clients", but it would have been easier for them to turn me down. When a young Englishman appealed to them to aid refugees from fascist Germany, they reacted sympathetically. And when I would hear, "All right, I'll give you ten schillings," I felt great satisfaction.'

In general, his British origins and passport in particular were extremely useful then. It is hard to imagine today what prestige a British passport had in countries like Austria, Czechoslovakia, Yugoslavia and so on in those years. Every travelling Englishman was taken for a lord or a diplomat with pockets full of pounds. Just showing your British passport would get you in wherever you wanted. A man with a Hungarian, Czech or Polish passport not only did not elicit respect from the police, but on the contrary, could find himself under suspicion for no other reason *than* his passport.

At that time there were quite a few Communists in Austria and

Czechoslovakia – from Yugoslavia, Bulgaria, Poland and Germany. Many had no papers and lived illegally, moving from house to house and trying to avoid the police. The question of regular contacts among them – that is, between Vienna and Prague, Vienna and Budapest, and Vienna and Belgrade – was critical. As soon as they learned that there was a man with a British passport working for the IOAR's ninth district, the administration of the organisation decided that he should be used for communications.

Kim's contact at the IOAR's city committee was a charming woman of fifty or so – Mitzi Frishau. She informed him of the decision to make him a courier.

He would receive a large sealed packet which could have held money, instructions, personal letters. Sometimes he was also given a package wrapped in brown paper. He had no idea at all what could be in these parcels, only that there were no legal methods of getting them from Vienna to Prague or to Budapest from one refugee to another or from one Communist organisation to another.

Mitzi Frishau would call, they would meet, she would give him the 'cargo' and instructions, and he would set off with his 'passe-partout' British passport in his pocket. For a small sum, Kim had obtained permanent visas to Prague and Budapest, and no one asked any questions.

I asked Kim if there had been any cloak-and-dagger routine. Along with the letters and packages, Mitzi gave him a spray of mimosa, which was the 'password' – he was supposed to hand it to the addressee. Of course, after several hours on the train from Vienna, the password looked pretty pathetic. And the contacts were rarely women. Handing a limp spray of mimosa to a man is not the most usual thing, and rather odd, in fact. He had no idea why they used mimosa for this. He didn't ask questions, he did what he was told.

'On my first trip to Prague I was supposed to deliver my cargo to a doctor named Novak. I came to the address given me, went up to the right floor, and rang the bell. I was very nervous: this was my first "secret" assignment. A man opened the door. I asked in German for Dr Novak.

"I am Doctor Novak," he replied.

'I took out the spray of mimosa from my pocket and handed it to him. I can imagine how ridiculous we must have looked to any of the neighbours. But luckily, no one was around. Novak chuckled and said: "Ai–ai–ai! Poor mimosa! I feel so sorry for it! Come in, come in."

"Thank God!" I thought. "Everything's all right."

'Inside the apartment, I gave him the package and the envelope. There were no oral messages for him. He asked about Mitzi Frishau and other mutual friends, and offered me coffee and cake. I spent a half-hour, we chatted about this and that, and then I went back to the station to catch the Vienna train.'

They had not given Philby a real cover story in case of arrest. It was felt that they would not dare arrest a man with a British passport. His plan, in case he was questioned about the contents of the envelope and package, was to reply that he was taking a package for friends and had no idea what was inside. If asked where he was taking it, he would have replied that the address was in his wallet. He would have taken out the wallet, searched, and then exclaimed in disappointment, 'Oh, what an idiot I am, I must have forgotten the address back in Vienna!' Philby realised that it was rather flimsy, but he consoled himself with the thought that people aren't always very convincing, even when they're innocent.

However, he couldn't recall a single incident in all his travels when he felt that he was in danger.

'And so I was a courier. I went to Czechoslovakia five times and to Hungary twice. This was the most interesting of all my jobs then. Naturally, I paid for the train tickets out of the £75 that Mitzi had left me for my "luxurious" life for a year in Vienna.

'At that time we were very stingy with money. If we could avoid spending a penny, we saved it and handed it over to the IOAR. They needed the money badly. It was distributed to the needy. I took part in that too. For instance, I would be told to go to such-and-such address with a sum of money or to take a carton of socks and warm gloves to distribute among the residents of a building. These were not only refugees from Germany but also Austrian workers who did not have enough to live on.'

In other words, there was a lot to do.

One grey February morning Litzi and Philby were at home. The lights were on. And suddenly, they went out. All over the apartment, not a single socket worked. He called a friend, Eric Gedye, the *Daily Telegraph* correspondent in Vienna. He was a sympathiser and was very well informed about everything happening in Central Europe.

Philby asked; 'Do you know what's happening? The lights went out in our neighbourhood.'

'There was shooting in Linz last night,' he replied. 'The power plant workers are on strike. There are rumours of an armed uprising against Dollfuss[1] and threats of fascism.'

Litzi had just started discussing what to do when the phone rang. It was one of the leaders of the central organisation of the Communist Party, whom Litzi knew. He asked them to be at a certain café and wait for orders there.

They went right away. About two hours later, the man came and told them that they had to set up a machine-gun post in one of the city's neighbourhoods very quickly. Would Litzi and Philby and the two others who had been waiting for him at the café take on this assignment? They expressed their readiness of course, but just in case, Philby asked: 'Does anyone here know how to fire a machine gun?'

'You just have to feed it shells,' the man said. 'We have someone to shoot it.'

The whole conversation only took a minute or two. The man told them to wait for further orders at the café and ran off. They spent almost the entire day there. He came back towards evening, around seven, and said: 'Nothing came of it today, but be here at eleven tomorrow morning.'

By that time there was sporadic shooting all over Vienna. People were using rifles, machine guns, and even mortars. The worker uprising was getting serious.

Dollfuss's army set up patrols and roadblocks at almost every street, but Philby and Litzi had no trouble getting home – his British passport helped, as usual. 'I walked with her on my arm, showing my passport to the patrols, and no one asked us anything. In the morning, carrying the passport before me like an icon, we went back to the café. However, our readiness to feed shells was of no use – around noon we were told that there were still troubles with setting up a machine-gun post. I remember talking about how strange it was that the Communists were always supportive of armed uprising, but when it came down to it, they had no arms to speak of.'

[1] *Dr Engelbert Dollfuss, Chancellor of Austria (1932–4), who brutally crushed the socialists and trade unionists in 1934, ordering his troops to fire on workers' housing estates. More than 1,000 civilians were killed. He was murdered the same year. (PK)*

The shooting in Vienna went on for two days. On the third day, the lights came back on in the apartment. Since the lamps had not been turned off, they switched on by themselves.

During the two days of shooting, Philby and others collected clothing and distributed food.

Eric Geyde describes in one of his books how Philby came to his house and asked him to open his closet. I asked Kim about the story.

'He was a good fellow. And he described things accurately. That is how it did happen. Eric saw my predatory look and realised what I was planning. He said, "Do you want me to go around naked?"

'"No," I replied. "You won't be naked, but you don't need this many suits. I'll take this one, this one, and that one. People need them more than you do."

'"Well, all right, take them."'

Kim chuckled as he remembered that episode.

'Our aid to the needy continued for ten days. I went to various addresses, seeking out the wounded, those who had fought in the battles, and helped as best I could. Of course, I do not remember any individuals, but I do remember telling each of them openly: I am a Communist. I remember that one or two of them replied in encouraging terms, it's good that you're a Communist, an armed uprising was long overdue. But most of them were depressed. It was a total defeat. Dollfuss dealt harshly with the rebels: they were shot or hanged. None of them could be sure of their future. It was difficult now to emigrate even to Czechoslovakia. And Hungary instantly returned all émigrés back to Austria. Some managed to get to the Soviet Union, I think there were about a hundred or 200 people like that. But their lives were not simple either.'

Philby and I were talking about this in 1987, and he mentioned that he had noticed that one of the Soviet figure skaters had an Austrian surname. He said that he wanted very much to believe that she was the daughter of one of the people he had helped then and who had managed to get to the Soviet Union.

Many Austrian Social Democrats had decided after those events that their only hope lay to the East and they joined the Communists.

For Philby, the economic depression and the growing threat of fascism was a serious emotional stimulus for Communist convictions. He had seen the Depression in England, and it was bad enough.

On the Continent – Germany, Austria, Hungary, and Yugoslavia – things were even worse. Austria then was a very poor country – not for the upper classes, of course, but for the people. The workers were in dire straits. Even if you had work, you could still be half-starved or starving. And if you lost your job, the situation was simply desperate. Even now we talk of unemployment as a big problem. But today the unemployed in Europe and America do not starve to death. Some own cars. In those days unemployment in Austria meant an almost certain death from hunger. Winters can be harsh there. Philby visited houses where they had only single windows with snow outside the panes. Two old people would be huddled around an iron stove. And often all he had for them was a pair of gloves or socks. And they would be so grateful!

In those days Austria was a centre for leftists, not many of whom were Communists, but there were many Marxists, who were sincerely and profoundly convinced of the righteousness of their philosophy. Meetings with people like Neller, Robert Brush and Hans Singer had great meaning for Philby. They discussed many issues, read books together and exchanged views on them. So along with the emotional power of the images of poverty in the midst of incredible wealth, there was the parallel growing influence of Marxism. They studied it in great depth and Philby was persuaded of its rightness. Theory and practice were joined naturally, nudging his thoughts in one direction.

They talked a lot about the Soviet Union, exaggerating its achievements, of course, but its example inspired them then. Added to that was the fascism in Germany. Information about it flowed into Austria, through the British, French, Austrian and Swiss press.

'I usually spent an hour or two every day in Vienna reading newspapers at the Herenhoff café,' Kim continued. 'I would take the café's copies of *The Times*, the *Daily Telegraph*. and *Le Temps* (which later became *Le Monde*), along with Austrian and Swiss newspapers, and read them.

'*The Times* was cautious, preparing the way for the future policy of appeasement. But the majority of the other papers spoke openly and frankly about fascism. This flow of information horrified me.'

He had a personal encounter with fascism. In the spring of 1933 he spent a month in Berlin. He went into a store that clearly belonged to a Jew because there were stormtroopers outside the door. Two followed him into the store and demanded to know what he was doing there, and why he wasn't boycotting a Jewish store.

He replied: 'This is your problem, not mine, these are your disagreements, not mine, so I will go to whichever stores I want.'

Back then he had a heavy English accent in German, and that must have added weight to his words. After that he made a point of going to Jewish stores: a naive action, of course. He wasn't helping anyone with his protest, and things could have ended with a beating. But he probably needed to do that, to prove to himself that he could stand up for his principles.

But in the spring of 1933 there were few people who had a sense of the true nature of Nazism or how far it would go. People told themselves that Italy was also a fascist country, but there was no comparison to Germany. There were many people in Austria, England and France who considered fascism more suitable for Europe than Communism and were ready to join the fascists if they would defend them from a possible socialist revolution in their own countries.

'And so, the rebellion had been quelled in three days. It was over by 15 February. My mood was low. Besides which, I was having trouble with money. I had given a lot away to the needy. I could no longer hope to stay in Vienna until June. Litzi and I added it up, and realised that I could stretch my funds only until April.

'We had started living as man and wife a long time before. I had liked her from the start, and we began an affair about ten days after we met. She had just turned twenty-three, she had been married and divorced. Even though the basis of our relationship was political to some extent, I truly loved her and she loved me. I did not want to leave her. Dollfuss had nipped social democracy in the bud, the only force that could have stood up to the Nazis in Austria. Many people were certain that they would soon come to power.

'That meant that Litzi would be marked: a Communist who had spent two weeks in prison for Communist activity and half-Jewish at that.

'I decided to marry her officially, give her a British passport, bring her to England, and continue the Party work together there.'

2

A Chat on a Bench
in Regent's Park

Philby and his wife left Vienna in April 1933. There were no
obstacles. They even shipped their furniture to London.

In London they lived in rather straitened conditions – one room in
a rooming house, 'the British equivalent to a Soviet communal flat: a
common bath, common kitchen, and so on,' Kim explained. On top
of that, there was a problem with work. It wasn't easy to find a job.
And he was still studying for the examination for the civil service.

'There was no work,' Kim told me. 'Many of my friends were
unemployed. And my decision to start working with the Communists, which was strengthened during the fighting in Austria, did not
weaken at home, on the contrary. I was full of determination to do
something that would help people. But what could I do in London,
what was I capable of? I didn't know. I'm not even talking about
international affairs: Hitler in Germany. All my friends knew that
he had been brought to power with only one goal: to destroy
Communist Russia. If someone had said to me then: go out on the
square and shout, Down with Capitalism, Long Live Communism!
I would have climbed up on Nelson without a second thought, raised
a red flag and shouted. Luckily no one suggested anything that stupid
and it didn't occur to me, either. The only public leftist action in
which I participated then was the May Day demonstration: 1 May
1934 in London. Luckily, it was the last. Not the last demonstration,'
he said with a smile, 'but my last participation in such things.'

'You could have been noticed by your future, how should I put
it, foes?'

'There were thirty or forty thousand participants. None of those
who knew me by sight in my circle then – that's who you meant
by "future foes", isn't it? – saw me marching enthusiastically.'

'Today, do you feel any irony for that enthusiasm?'

Kim leaned back in his chair and looked through the windows
into a world filled with sunshine, greenery and birds, as if looking

back into 1934, the streets of London and at himself, young and marching in a May Day parade.

'No, why? It's just that I now look at that period, as one of your poets put it, "from the grey heights of age".' He quoted in pretty good Russian, then ruffled his hair, smiled with that half-shy smile, and added: 'But without irony. Rather with sympathy and a certain amount of surprise, I suppose.'

'You're surprised by yourself as a young man?'

'No. I'm surprised by the enormous role that chance played in my life, good luck and fortune.' He laced his fingers. His hands were strong.

'You mean, that you weren't noticed in the parade?'

'Well, that's a detail. After all, I could have been in the parade simply out of curiosity. Doesn't a Cambridge graduate have the right to hear what British workers are saying on May Day . . .? No, I meant something else. I meant joining the Communist Party. I wasn't a member then. But I wanted to be. I went to their headquarters. To the British Communists. One of my friends, I don't remember who, warned them that I was coming, and they let me in. They asked me why I was there. I said that I wanted to join the Party.'

Kim laughed and spread his hands, as if in apology.

'That's what I was like then . . . The man talking to me must have been stunned. He looked at me suspiciously for a long time: I could have been a provocateur, a spy. But he didn't throw me out, he asked, "But who are you? Where did you come from? Why haven't I ever seen you before?"

'I replied, "I was in Austria, taking part in the events." I thought that would explain who I was much more than any document. He thought a bit and then said,

'"I believe you. But the Party, as you know, is illegal.[1] It is very difficult for us. And we must check you out. Name two or three people who can vouch for you."

'I did. And I said, "How long will it take?"

'"Five or six weeks."

'"So long?"

'He laughed. "Is that a long time? Come back in six weeks and we'll talk."

---

[1] *Philby's memory is at fault here. The Communist Party was never illegal in Britain. (PK)*

'I left. I wanted the six weeks to be over as soon as possible. But luckily before the time came, a man whom I had met in Austria sought me out. He talked about this and that, and at the end of the conversation asked, as if in passing, indifferently, as if about a cigarette, whether it would be good for me to meet a very serious person who could offer me important and interesting work relating to my desires. He didn't say who the "serious person" was or what the important and interesting work would be, but he hinted that the person was tied to international Communist and anti-fascist movements.

'It was exactly what I wanted and what I had been looking for. I knew that this acquaintance of mine tended to speak of the very important things very casually, like a mug of beer. And the shorter and more casual his conversation about something, the more serious that something was. So I agreed immediately, and with great joy, to meet this person.

'There's an example of luck: just imagine what would have happened if that acquaintance from Austria had not found me in time or it hadn't occurred to anyone to introduce me to that stranger . . . The six weeks would have passed, I would have come to Party headquarters in London, joined, and my whole life would have been very different. It's very unlikely that you would be talking with Kim Philby in a dacha outside Moscow. There . . . a lucky break . . . One of many in my life.'

'Are you a fatalist?'

He pondered the way he always did, as I later learned, whenever we talked about his own feelings and thoughts. He looked into himself, at his life and for the precise words. He didn't want to make a mistake.

'No, not in the mystical sense, or in the philosophical one, either. I'm simply stating a fact: luck played an enormous role in my life. But you have to know how to use luck, and that depends only on the person.'

'So, you accepted happily . . .'

'Yes, I accepted happily, and two or three days later we went off for that meeting.'

'Kim, please, don't rush. Details. Everything.'

He nodded seriously. 'I'm a journalist, I understand. More coffee?'

I refused.

'Then I have to feed that horde out there. I've broken their schedule.'

He picked up the breadcrumbs with the napkin, got up and went to the porch. There, so much joy and sunshine splashed him in the shape of two or three dozen little feathered creatures. They settled on his shoulders and arms. They circled his head. They sang his praises. They berated him for making them wait. They looked at me, too, in amazement, trying to understand why that stranger just sat and didn't share their stormy emotions. Kim finished the ritual of feeding calmly and with dignity, still thinking about that day, I could tell from his face. Back on the terrace, he sat down and continued:

'We went for that meeting in the morning. It took several hours to get there. It was a fanciful voyage around the city. We took a taxi . . . then my companion stopped it . . . Paid . . . Switched to another car . . . We went in the opposite direction . . . Stopped again. Went down into the Tube . . . Got on the train last, just as the doors were shutting . . . And then pretended to have made a mistake and got off just as the train was leaving . . . And alone on the platform, we would see if anyone else had got off . . . Or we'd get on at the last moment . . . Now all these tricks are known to every schoolboy who has seen two or three movies about Stierlitz[2] or James Bond . . . But these tricks, so stale now, were then new to me.' He smiled. 'By the way, I've never seen a James Bond movie . . .'

'Impossible!' I was astonished. 'You're pulling my leg!'

'Not at all. I just never had an opportunity. And now I'm not particularly interested.' He gestured impatiently. 'Well, I kept trying to guess where we were headed. It was only after three or four hours of suffering that my friend said at last, "Well, here we are." And do you know where we were? In the middle of London, in Regent's Park, just a mile away from where we had started our marathon that morning. We walked another several hundred metres down a path and stopped at a bench with a man on it. My guide said: "Here we are." He spoke very casually, as if we had come to visit a friend, not to a meeting with "an important person".'

'"Hello," I said. The man got up from the bench, offered his hand, and also said, "Hello."

'"My name is Kim Philby," I said.

'"I had figured that out," the man replied. "Pleased to meet you.

---

[2] *Stierlitz is the Russian version of James Bond. (PK)*

Sit down." He sat me down on the bench next to him. His eyes were laughing. I looked up to see why my Austrian friend was so quiet, but he was far away, walking swiftly down the lane.'

Philby sighed deeply and smiled, as I thought, to himself. No, he wasn't upset; these memories were pleasant. He liked thinking about the man whom he met on a bench in Regent's Park and he liked thinking about himself then.

'So we were left alone. I never saw my Austrian acquaintance again.'

'How did your new acquaintance introduce himself?'

'He said his name was Hallan.'

'Was that his real name?'

Kim shook his head. 'That was a name to be used with me. I was supposed to call him that. And only at first. Later he changed his pseudonym, and I called him Otto.'

'What was your first conversation about?'

'At first he asked me about my views and my activity. I told him who I was, what I was, how I had studied in Cambridge, had worked in a socialist club, fought in Austria and decided to become a Communist . . .'

'You told him all that openly?'

'Absolutely. I trusted him from the start. And there was my Austrian friend, who had added to my conviction that all this was extremely serious. At the very end of the conversation – which was rather long – he said, "I know that you want to join the Communist Party. I respect your decision, but listen to what I have to say. You will be accepted in the Party. Gladly. And you will become one of many thousands of Communists. You will be a good Communist, a loyal Communist. You will have ties with the working class. A direct tie. But by background, education, appearance and manners you are an intellectual to your bone marrow. A bourgeois, to put it bluntly. It's no trick to see that in you. You're a brave fellow, I was told how you behaved in Austria. But what will you do here in the Party? You will cut off your ties with your class, but it's unlikely that you'll blend into the working class. Let's say you will hand out leaflets on the street. But anyone can do that, you don't need your education for that. You came down from Cambridge. You have a marvellous career ahead of you. A bourgeois career. And if you want to help the anti-fascist movement, the Communist movement, you have to help us in that way. The anti-fascist movement needs people who can enter into the bourgeoisie. From our part, from the Communists. So much depends on that!"'

'Did he say who "we" were?'

'No, not then. And I didn't ask any questions about him. I saw that I must not do it. And to tell the truth, I never did learn who he was or whom he represented – the Soviet Union or the Comintern? But I caught his point immediately. I was being offered a very interesting future, a very interesting life. I had a life goal. And I was being offered the means to reach that goal. I could give the Communists and anti-fascists information that they couldn't get from anyone else.'

'What did you reply?'

'I said, "In other words you are simply asking me politely if I would be willing to become an infiltrator for the Communist anti-fascist movement?" And he replied, "That's just what I want to propose. The Party doesn't play a big part in British life. If you were to sell the *Daily Worker* in working-class neighbourhoods of London that would be a fine thing, of course. But you can help Communists in a much more real and palpable way. You can undertake a real and important job."

'I liked that very much. My future looked romantic. And even though later I realised that this was not the best word to describe the difficult, exhausting and often very ordinary, even boring, work that required enormous patience, will-power and control, I didn't know it then. And even if I had, I'm sure that I would have given the same answer: "I agree." '

'Did you discuss any terms?'

'Do you mean money?' Kim asked.

'Among other things.'

'No,' he said and shook his head resolutely. 'There was no discussion of that. And if he had offered me any money then, I would have refused. But I think he understood that and didn't start any talk of money.'

'Did you make a plan for your next meeting?'

'Yes, he told me that we would meet in two weeks and how it had to be organised. But he told me in a way that made me feel that we had developed the procedure together. He also told me what to do if the meeting didn't take place – whether he couldn't make it or I. He proposed special measures in case I discovered that I was being followed. We discussed all that.'

'Did he give you an assignment?'

'Don't be silly! What assignments could I have had then? The only possible assignment was to end all contact with Communists, reduce contacts with left-wing friends, and try to live the life of a decent and proper bourgeois, the son of a famous aristocrat of right-wing views, a young man who had finished Cambridge and dreamed of a good career.'

'Did you like the prospect?'

'Basically, yes, even though I knew that it would be hard to part with my friends. Besides which I had always despised the prospect of a bourgeois career. But now it had a completely different meaning. The path which I would never have taken in ordinary circumstances was illuminated by a new light.'

'Did you and Hallan talk at all on that bench in Regent's Park about how your career should develop?'

'In very general terms. The paths could be many. Diplomacy, journalism – which I found very attractive – or some government service. But neither he nor I went into detail at that first meeting.'

Kim stopped and thought. Then he said: 'It was an amazing conversation. And he was a marvellous man. Simply marvellous . . . I felt that immediately. And it never left me. We'll be coming back to him. I want him to be remembered well . . .'

'Did you speak English?'

'No, mostly German. I spoke German very well then. I've forgotten a lot now, without practice. But I spoke it well then. Very well.'

'What about him?'

'He spoke English and German fluently. But German better. And I preferred it. I think it was a language close to him. I decided then that he was either an Austrian or a Czech.'

'But was he a Soviet citizen? From the Soviet Union?'

'No, no, he was in an illegal situation. I can't swear that he wasn't a Soviet, but he behaved in a way that made me feel that he had come from Austria or Czechoslovakia. He knew Marx and Lenin brilliantly . . . He spoke of the revolution with enthusiasm. He was very well educated . . . You could talk on any topic with him . . . But I realised all that later, not that day . . .'

'Did he say anything about himself?'

'Almost nothing.'

'What did he look like?'

'He looked thirty-five. The first thing you noticed about him were his eyes. He looked at you as if nothing more important in life and more interesting than you and talking to you existed at that moment.'

'What that a practised style? A method?'

'No, that was his essence. I became convinced of that later. He loved people.'

'What was his real name?'

'I didn't know it then.'

'And now you do?'

'Yes. I learned it many years later, in the Soviet Union, when I went to our intelligence museum. His picture is there. He died during the war.'

'At the front?'

'He died on a ship headed for America. The ship was sunk by Germans. You could say that he died at the front. Definitely.'

Gradually my meetings with Kim Philby became ordinary and more or less regular, even if there were large intervals between them. They got used to my going to his dacha; I went there in the car that belonged to *Teatr* and without Ivan Afanasyevich. The strict guard at the creaking gates would open them as soon as he saw me. Even something like a friendly smile would appear on his face. He must have watched television, too, from time to time and got to know my face.

My conversations with Kim Philby moved in complicated ways.

At first, despite his own promises, he did not deviate much from his book, *My Silent War*. I gathered that he wanted to do no more than outline the main stages of life that were outside the scope of the book. But in time (and our talks went on for about three years, almost up to his death), he began returning without prompting to what we had already covered, recounting the same events in more detail and with more frankness, never repeating himself and always remembering what he had already told me. This did not apply to most of the episodes or periods of his life and work – he selected them as he pleased.

I will give but two examples.

In talking about his trip to Austria in one of our early meetings, he said that he had got a letter of recommendation to Paris 'from a lady in Cambridge'. Much later, returning to this topic, he clarified with disarming ease that the 'lady from Cambridge' was actually Maurice Dobb.

In his first description of the meeting in Regent's Park, a nameless 'Austrian friend' introduced Philby to the Soviet agent. Eighteen months later Kim decided to reveal her name.

'It was Edith Tudor-Hart. She brought me to the KGB.'

I do not know the reasons for such extensive revelations. Either it was a function of our improving relations, or it was the general situation in the country, moving, albeit not at top speed, towards glasnost and openness, or it might have been a sense of inevitability – impending death and the desire to tell what he had never told anyone.

Taken together, these factors turned our talks into a spiral, in which every new twist opened up on a wider panorama and new details.

However, I am certain that even on his deathbed he would not have told anyone what he could not tell or felt he should not tell. His self-discipline never left him.

What did Kim do in those first few months after that conversation on the bench in Regent's Park?

In our talks he recalled those days with warm nostalgia, which related more to his new friend than to his work. He considered the man a kindly alien from another more rational civilisation come to show the world the road to justice and universal happiness.

I wanted to learn as much as possible from Philby about his actual work, but whenever we talked about it, he would smile shyly, cut bread for the birds, and turn the conversation back to 'Otto'. He talked of his marvellous education, his humanity, his fidelity to building a new society with new human relations.

'But I was his main interest,' Kim said. 'At least, that was my impression every time I met Otto. He asked about my life, my plans, my difficulties, what I loved and what I hated. Of course, that is part of a good spy's professional interests when he finds an agent. I understood that. But for all that, I was certain that my life and I myself interested him not so much professionally as on a human level.'

'Did Dale Carnegie's *How To Win Friends* exist then?' I joked.

Kim shrugged. 'Carnegie always existed, I agree. Under various pseudonyms. But no Carnegie can ever put love and interest in people into anyone's heart. Otto's interest was sincere, unfeigned. If only because many of his actions were spontaneous and completely unpredictable. And his character traits were also unexpected and seemed to contradict one another. He was well brought up, composed, and yet a very immediate and sometimes quite simple man. And he had a marvellous sense of humour. Qualities like that cannot be learned, they must exist in you from birth. If you don't have them, it's for a long time, as they say . . .'

And Kim told me in detail how he once got orders from Otto to go to Paris on a Friday, stop at the Madison Hotel on the Left Bank, and wait for further orders. Kim thought something very important was happening. He bought a ticket, went to Paris, and found the Madison, after several hours of checking for a tail and making sure he was not followed. After that he took a cheap room and waited for 'further orders'. On Saturday morning Otto rang and invited him to lunch. Once again, Kim travelled carefully. Otto was waiting in a café. He was in a great mood and told funny stories. Kim couldn't wait for the serious conversation and asked quietly: 'Well then, what is it?'

'What are you talking about?' Otto asked.

'Why did you bring me to Paris?'

'What do you mean?' Otto seemed almost hurt. 'Why? What day is it?'

'Saturday.'

'And tomorrow?'

'Sunday.'

'And what does that mean?'

Kim could only shrug.

'It means that you are spending the weekend in Paris! I managed to get away for two whole days! I couldn't enjoy it alone. That's why I called you here.'

Kim leaned back in his chair, rested his forearms full-length on the table, looked sadly at the birds outside the window, and said softly, as if heaving a sigh: 'Wasn't that wonderful?'

He was lost in his memories. I did not want to interrupt, I couldn't ask the next question. I did not want to frighten those birds of memory, so I pretended to adjust my tape recorder.

He violated the silence himself, understanding what I needed, and went back to my question. 'As for my work then, I had almost none. Otto and I met regularly. And he taught me the rules of conspiracy. He hammered them into my head: how to call the necessary person on the phone, how to check, how to recognise a tail in a crowd, and other basics. I got sick of it once and said politely, "Otto, you are telling me this for the tenth time. In the same words. I have memorised it. Like poetry."

'"The tenth time?" he asked. "Well, that's only the beginning. When I get to one hundred, then you can consider the course complete."'

'What rules of caution did Otto follow in regard to you?' I asked. 'He couldn't be one hundred per cent sure that you weren't following someone else's orders, could he?'

'I am certain that he and his service had checked me thoroughly before our first meeting.'

'Through whom?'

'I think the British and Austrian Communists had noticed me. Surely Otto and his people maintained ties with them and could get the opinion of people they trusted.'

'Did Otto tell you anything about himself?'

'Never.'

'You mean, you knew nothing about his life?'

'Absolutely nothing.'

'That means that Otto performed his one hundred per cent of caution?'

'He did it three hundred per cent! But that was no obstacle to our personal relations. I sometimes felt that we had been friends since childhood.'

I kept pushing him with questions about his work. He avoided answering at first, replying that his real work began much later and that in 1934 there was nothing of importance, nor could there have been.

It was only some time later that he told me what he had been doing then. It turned out that in the first few months of his collaboration with an 'international anti-fascist organisation,' Kim performed several assignments which were fateful not only in his own life, but in the history of Soviet intelligence and to some degree in the history of the twentieth century.

His ability to speak intelligently and voluminously without saying anything or very little when he did not want to give something away was very impressive and even, I would say, overwhelming, lulling, soothing. While you we're talking to him, you had the impression that you'd got everything you wanted from him, but once you got home . . .

We would sit at a square table in the tiny glassed-in terrace of his government-issue dacha. I would do a simultaneous translation of what Kim said into my microphone. I would give the tapes for transcription the same day and by evening or the following morning I would get the typed text. I would start reading greedily only to find that I had been right on the brink of something sensational, just two centimetres from the secret, yet those two centimetres had remained uncrossed.

Your lessons, dear Master Otto, were not wasted. Your pupil learned them for life.

Of course, all Philby told me was extremely interesting. Some of his words, turns of phrase, details, reactions to others – it was sheer pleasure listening to him. But he preferred to say little about his concrete actions – what he reported to Moscow, how he reported, when he reported. In any case, at first. He was charmingly unforthcoming, at first.

Kim was a born writer. He proved it not only with his brilliant articles in the London *Times*, as special correspondent on Franco's side during the Civil War in Spain, but in his excellent book, *My Silent War*, published in 1968.

He knew how to structure a conversation, filling it with wise and entertaining details, each of which was the fruit of his observation and deep thought. His subtle, purely English sense of humour never ceased to delight me, and I realised bitterly that I lost a lot in my simultaneous and diligently accurate translation into my tape recorder.

As I have said, for some episodes in his life and work I had to get additional permission from his bosses. The authorities usually vacillated. After all, they were brought up on the same principles as Philby. The principles are international and accepted by all the intelligence services of the world: if you can keep quiet about it, do so.

But I had no intention of retreating: if they had given me permission to meet Kim Philby, then let me ask him whatever I thought would interest the reader and let Kim tell me about it as fully as possible. What possible threat could there be for our country in secrets half a century old and revealed by a man who had left the West a quarter century ago? I said all this to the people who had the power to open a new page in the biography of Kim Philby. As a result, I would get one okay after another. Of course, my main support came from glasnost (I would not have got anywhere ten years earlier). I cannot rule out this factor either: the liberal attitude of the top brass was fed by the hope that the author would respond by 'glorifying the home office' for which Kim Philby had worked. But I have no intention of condemning or applauding. I have only one goal – to tell the truth and to try to understand what it was like, what it meant, for Kim Philby to work for the KGB.

I must say that I always had the feeling that Kim enjoyed getting each okay to unbutton yet another secret, getting the opportunity to relax just a bit, to get out from under the pressure of the rules made over fifty years ago. I do not know how the permission was conveyed to Kim – whether by telephone or whether Ivan Afanasyevich brought it along with his packages of groceries from the KGB's special distributors with the mandatory bottle of Kim's favourite whisky (everyone who knew and esteemed him brought a 'bottle for Kim' from abroad, and there were many such people among the agents).

Philby was a modest man and two or three times during our meetings when the conversation inadvertently turned to his present life, he said that he lived very well and had plenty of everything. There was always a pack of imported cigarettes, which he would stealthily slip into his pocket whenever he heard Rufina Ivanova's steps on the terrace. Like a magician, he would make his lit cigarette vanish, too, and the evidence would dissipate over the table. An ordinary handkerchief was his helper, and he would greet his wife with an innocent and welcoming look in his blue eyes.

As I understood it, there were two sins which Rufina Ivanova would not forgive and allowed only occasionally with her 'official' permission: whisky and cigarettes. It was beyond her powers to ban them totally and categorically. Always disciplined and cautious, Kim in these cases allowed himself to break the rules (sometimes secretly, sometimes overtly – although with her permission), even though the rules were for his health and he could have paid more attention to her demands, whom he loved and treated with touching attention.

In time Kim became much more liberal about the old restrictions.

Our relationship moved from the official interviewer–interviewee one to a warm, human one – even friendship, I hope.

I will describe later how I managed to arrange a meeting for Kim with Graham Greene, who had worked in a section of the SIS headed by Kim. The two old men, known throughout the world, had not seen each other in several decades, and had maintained their mutual friendship, respect, and desire to meet. But all of Greene's attempts to see his former boss were met with refusal by the official authorities. Even their correspondence was made difficult. So my help in arranging the meeting in 1987 predisposed Kim towards me even more.

During one of our last meetings, he suddenly gave me a gift – he returned to the early months of his work in London, about which I had tried in vain to get some information in our earlier meetings, and told me the true story, which no one had known (with the exception of a very few people), about how Donald Maclean and Guy Burgess were brought into the Soviet intelligence system.

In his interviews with various journalists – right up to his death – he never touched on this theme, as far as I know. If he did talk about his friends, he always stressed that they were not connected among themselves and worked for the Soviets without knowing about the others' work. For instance, he told Phillip Knightley in 1987 that he had learned about Maclean and the KGB 'only after the start of the war' and that 'he doubted that he had been recruited while at the university'.

In fact, everything was quite different.

. . . He told me that he had not told anyone else about his life and work in such detail as he had told you.'

'I'm having trouble understanding my role. Retelling what's done on the tape? That doesn't interest me much.'

Greene thought a bit and spoke as if musing to himself. 'If you were to juxtapose his story with archival documents . . . That might lead to an amusing thing.'

That was the genesis of this idea.

The first years of perestroika were in full swing. Life tossed me into politics, into public works, into political editorial programming on television. My nature wouldn't let me sit on the sidelines.

But the idea suggested by Greene stayed in my head. When I saw a few relatively free weeks in the offing, I called the GPU, the main directorate of intelligence at the KGB, and told them my idea. I was asked to send my request in written form. A few days later I got a letter informing me that I would be assisted with the archives. A few days after that I was given a room for my work and on the table in front of me lay a thick file in a cardboard cover with the words: 'Case File No. 5581. Volume 1. Top Secret. Committee on State Security of the Council of Ministers of the USSR'.

Only a few people in the KGB were familiar with it or could have read it. The list covering many years was appended right on the first page and no one else had ever seen File 5581. At least that is what I was told by the lanky young officer, very polite and serious, who was to sit next to me in the room while I leafed through the file and made notes, written and dictated.

Among those who hadn't seen it was 'Söhnchen' (Sonny) himself, whose full name was written in ink on the line for 'Agent – Informer'. It bothered me to see that coarse word used for the man with the shy and slightly apologetic smile who had spent so many hours with me and who was no longer among the living.

The day after Kim Philby met 'Otto' in Regent's Park, a cipher telegram was received at the Lubyanka:[1]

No. 2696 from London, from 'Mar'[2] June 1934[3]

[1] Documents are presented with the original style intact. The only changes are to orthographic mistakes and typographical errors.
[2] Pseudonym of the Soviet resident in London in 1934.
[3] No day given.

PHILBY RECOMMENDS SEVEN

In three years of conversations and meetings with Philby, the file marked 'KIM', which stood on a shelf in the study of my Moscow apartment and contained transcriptions of his taped story of himself, kept growing, turning in time into two large files of over 500 pages of typed text.

Next to them were others, with material about him, clipped or copied from Western newspapers that I happened to see; and books that were published in England and in America, devoted to the activities of intelligence agencies, not only Soviet ones. In almost every book the name Philby was listed in the index along with many pages that dealt with him. There wasn't a book in which Kim wasn't called 'spy of the century,' and the work to which he had dedicated his life 'the greatest treason of the twentieth century'.

In our age of astonishing sensations, discoveries and revelations, he was still a mysterious figure, undiscovered, unrevealed, undescribed – no one, in essence. Heads of state and governments – from Winston Churchill to Ronald Reagan – spoke about him in their speeches and made guesses about his fate. Political scientists argued about him, and almost every correspondent visiting Moscow tried to get an interview with him.

For several years I couldn't find the time to undertake a book and did not publish a single excerpt from Philby's story. The only thing I did do was a television programme showing him talking about his friend Graham Greene. But Kim Philby was no longer with us. He died in the summer of 1988.

The last person to ask wonderingly, 'Haven't you finished that book yet?' was Graham Greene not long before *his* death. I replied that in our turbulent times few people would be interested even in such a great spy. Dozens of books and hundreds of articles had been written about him. Greene shook his head.

'You're mistaken. He will long remain the subject of awe or hatred, they will continue arguing about him for decades to come

We have recruited the son of an Anglo agent, advisor of Ibn-Saud, Philby. Mar

And after that communication, the residence sent a long letter to Moscow.

(From Mar's letter of June 22, 1934).
Philby. From now on we will call him 'Sonny' or 'Söhnchen'. Through 'Edith', whom you know and who worked at one time for Siegmund in Vienna, we established that an Austrian Party member with recommendations from Viennese comrades to 'Edith' arrived on the island with her English husband from Vienna. She is also known to Arnold.[4] 'Edith' checked the recommendation and got confirmation from all our Viennese friends. In Vienna the press reported on the happy marriage of a young Viennese woman with a prince from the court of Ibn-Saud (clippings will follow). According to the Viennese friends of Edith and the 'newlyweds' themselves no one knows about their sympathies and work for the Party either in Vienna or on the island (with a few exceptions). Sonny was never a member of the Party and tried to hide his sympathies for the Party, since he was planning a diplomatic career after Cambridge. Edith's references on Sonny are highly positive. I decided to recruit the fellow without delay (of course not for the organs directly, it's too soon for that) for anti-fascist work. Sonny was supposed to take over his father's apartment and his wife would stay with Edith temporarily. Arnold and Edith and I developed a plan for Arnold to meet Sonny before Sonny and his wife moved into his father's apartment. I knew about the colossal role played by the father with Ibn-Saud not only from the press but from the professor as a friend of Ross's (the school director). The meeting between Arnold and Sonny took place with all caution. The result is his complete readiness to work. Sonny made an excellent impression on Arnold. It turns out that Sonny's sympathy for the Party comes from the socialist club[5] at Cambridge University, that the sons

[4] Arnold Deutsch ('Hallan', 'Otto'), Soviet agent, in 1934 an assistant to the illegal resident of the GPU in London.
[5] *Actually the Cambridge University Socialist Society, founded by Harry Dawes and other leftists to replace the University Labour Club which had collapsed under the failures of the Ramsay MacDonald government (1931–5). Philby was the CUSS treasurer, 1932–3. (PK)*

of many important Anglo-functionaries sympathise with the club and did work for it. We will have the list of their names soon. Sonny understood everything and is prepared in the interests of the work completely to hide and separate from his Party friends. You will receive a separate report on all his friends. Incidentally, he mentioned Ross, who is prepared to do anything we want, among his father's friends. What are our tasks for the time being with Sonny? Get everything out of his father's apartment (if there is anything there). Get Sonny involved in work and test him. Then send him to Ross's school.

The telegram and letter about the recruitment of Kim Philby had a major effect at the Lubyanka. Evidence of that is the impatience with which Moscow immediately demanded a list of 'Sonny''s contacts from the residence. Of course, the new agent could have been used right away: for sifting through 'Father''s papers and for gathering information among his high-placed friends. But the far-seeing Centre realised that this could be done only with the greatest caution so as not to hinder 'Sonny''s future career, which promised serious and unusual prospects.

The Centre to London
(Excerpt from letter #2 to Swede-Mar,[6] 7 July, 1934)
We are waiting for you to send Sonny's report on his friends and connections. Only after you have checked them thoroughly will we be able to make a final decision on how best to use him. What are his prospects for a diplomatic career? Are they realistic? For which country and which language will he study at Ross's school?[7] Will he choose his own path or will his father 'suggest' he meet someone and discuss it? That would be good.
    Search the father's apartment only after you are certain that there is something interesting there for us.

[6] Swede was the pseudonym of Alexander Orlov, who was the 'wandering resident' for Western Europe, organising an agent network for the GPU there.
[7] Ross was principal of the School of Slavonic Languages and a known MI6 contact. (PK)

Thus Kim's first strategic assignment was to break off all contacts with the Left. That meant not only breaking off with people of left-wing interests, among whom he had many good friends, but also such 'trifles' as getting rid of the left-wing literature he owned – selling his books, ending subscriptions to leftist newspapers, not buying leftist publications in news kiosks – in a word, cover up all the channels that could establish or even suggest that Kim Philby retained left-wing views.

But in this general demand for a break in left-wing ties, Otto made one serious exception. In one of their first meetings he asked Kim to choose a convenient time and appropriate excuse to go to Cambridge and, without attracting undue attention, do an 'inventory' of his leftist friends – meet them and evaluate each from the point of view of collaborating with Otto. In other words, they were talking about possible recruitment.

Kim had not been at Cambridge for a long time. Much water had flowed under the bridge and much had happened. He had been doing underground work, had smelled gunpowder in Austria, had married an Austrian Communist and brought her to London (which was even mentioned in the newspapers). Many of his old crowd knew about parts of it: some knew some things, others other parts. To pretend that none of it had happened did not make sense. So he and Otto developed a rather logical strategy for the behaviour of the 'new' Philby.

The months spent in Austria did not have to mean that the graduate of Cambridge, the scion of an old aristocratic family, had moved even further left than the positions he had held in the university's Socialist Club. After all, he could have become disillusioned in the Communist movement. Dealing with English Communists after Austria could also have increased his doubts. Young Philby, after all he had seen, could easily have decided to leave politics completely for a while, to sort things out for himself, and then decide what course to take in life and which political shore to choose. And who was forcing the young man to make a political choice? He was married. He had to earn money. Why shouldn't he simply take care of his own affairs, his career, which would progress more smoothly if he had fewer responsibilities to any political group?

That was the Philby they created for Kim's trip to Cambridge. Still charming, witty, sweet, friendly and politically neutral, he would meet his friends. Naturally, he would not avoid conversations either about his former leftist enthusiasms, or about Austria or fascism, or Stalin, or Hitler.

As Kim said later, he went off to Cambridge in September 1934. He did everything demanded of him and when he returned to London he handed Otto a list of seven men. These seven, in Kim's opinion, were the most suitable of all his Cambridge friends for collaboration and they were the ones to be brought in to work in their common cause.

Kim gave each of the seven a long reference, with his opinions pro and contra, his views of their strong and weak points. He listed them in order of descending value.

First on the list was Donald Maclean.

Kim was certain that Maclean was the most serious of anyone he had met at Cambridge. Donald was convinced of the righteousness of socialism. Yet he was planning to take the exam for the Foreign Office.

In those days, Kim told me, leftist views were very popular among professors, and civil servants were tolerant towards them, seeing them as nothing more than a fad, especially since many of the left-wing students at Cambridge came from wealthy and often noble families. Quite a few professors delighted in teaching that Marxism was the only rational path of development for human society if it were not to want to lose all vestiges of humanity and turn the world into a jungle.

The fact that Maclean did not hide his convictions and at the same seriously intended to take the Foreign Office exam spoke not of his naivety but of his honesty. Moreover, the FO would have been hard put to find a formal excuse for rejecting Maclean: he came from a rich, conservative family, his father had been a Cabinet member, and Donald had a Cambridge degree with a first in foreign languages.

For Otto and his colleagues, Maclean was suitable in every way: a convinced Communist, smart, serious, and talented with a brilliant Foreign Office future.

And it would be easy for him to pretend that he had become disillusioned in the leftist movement and to break with it at any moment when the interests of the cause demanded it, a cause that Maclean would never betray, in Kim's opinion.

That is why Maclean headed Philby's list.

The last name on the list was Guy Burgess.

In our conversations, Kim described Burgess as a very gifted man with an astonishing intellect; not simply a Communist by conviction, but a Party member, an active member who boasted of his membership. This is a typical detail. At Cambridge he had a sporty two-seat roadster. Whenever he took part in a leftist demonstration, he would 'march' in his car, sometimes using it like a small tank against counter-demonstrators. For all his undeniable gifts, Guy was flamboyant, unable to control himself or his tongue. He got a kick out of shocking people and making them talk about him. It seemed to be his life's goal – to make himself the centre of attention. But there was a strong argument for Guy: if he could be persuaded to maintain discipline for the greater good of the Cause, he would keep it more stringently than anyone else on earth. For all his unpredictability, he had enormous will power and once he decided on something, he was implacable.

After his return from Cambridge, Kim met Otto and another man whom Kim was supposed to call 'Theo'. Kim thought that this second 'contact' was clearly Otto's boss. The three of them went over Kim's list thoroughly and then, Kim thought, Otto and Theo sent it to the Centre.

(Excerpt from Mar's letter, 7 October 1934)
Some more about Sonny. You already know the following news. His ability to get a situation here is very limited since his father is not here. He wants to work as a journalist and get a job on a monthly magazine. Besides which he has connections with the *Daily Telegraph*, *Manchester Guardian*, Reuters, and maybe he will later get a job there. He can take advantage of other opportunities, if necessary, through his father. If it's necessary, he is willing to go there.

Here he has many friends from the best homes who know nothing about his former political views. Among them, Martin Less, the chief geologist of Anglo-Persian [this must refer to Anglo-Persian Oil Company], thirty-five years old, politically neutral . . . very wealthy. Denizen Ross, head of the school (a very good friend of his father's). Vinogradov, foreign editor of the *Manchester Guardian*, son of Minister Runciman.[8]

Sonny participated here at the annual dinner of the Geographical and Central Asian Society. At that dinner he met

[8] The names in the document are given either in English or in Russian transliteration.

Lawrence and Lord Allenbis [sic].[9] The Swede and I decided
that he must work over all his friends from Cambridge who
shared his views, so that we could use some of them in our
work. Of course, we could be dealing with one of two people:
Burgess and Maclean. Burgess is the son of very wealthy
parents. He was a Party member for two years, very smart,
and dependable, but according to Sonny a bit superficial and
could let slip in some circumstances.

On the contrary, Sonny has high praise for Maclean
('Orphan' from now on). He is the son of the late minister
of education. Twenty-two, he is studying foreign languages
and literatures. He is very serious and aloof (according to Sonny
he has very good connections: Clery, secretary of the Minister
of Education, Pelham, permanent secretary of the ministry
section, Evelyn Shukbugn [Shuckburgh] from the Foreign
Office, Blaise Gillie, minister of health, Lady Margot Asquitt
[Asquith], Wiolet [Violet] Bonham Carter, head of the civil
service, Maurice Bonham Carter, personal secretary of Lord
Asquitt [Asquith], John Simon, Foreign Office, Isaac Foot,
Lord Rader, Henry Gladstone, Sohn von Horace Rumboldt,
all from the Foreign Office).[10]

'Orphan' maintained that he had told the Party in Cambridge
that he could join the Foreign Office, but the Party was not
interested in that and so now he wants to go back to Cambridge
and do Party work. We had 'Sonny' ask him to refrain from
that, and if he agrees, we will come into direct contact with
him. He has already agreed not to do Party work and is
preparing to join the Foreign Office. Naturally, further work
will be conditional on his breaking all ties with the Party.

Burgess visited us at home[11] and is now going with the son
of Rothschild, a close friend, to the South of France, he wants

---

[9] *Viscount Allenby, British field marshal. As commander-in-chief of the Egyptian
Expeditionary Force in the First World War, he invaded Palestine, captured Jerusalem
and ended Turkish resistance by the battle of Samaria, 1918. (PK)*
[10] I am listing the names mentioned in the letter of the London resident of the
GPU because of my certainty that I will in no way thereby discredit the people
named (except perhaps in the misspellings of their names, for which apologies
are due not from me but from the letter's author): none of them can be held
responsible for knowing Kim Philby, Donald Maclean or Guy Burgess.
[11] A reference to Guy Burgess's trip to Moscow in the summer of 1934.

to get money from him for the Party. Maybe the Swede has already told you all this. We would like to know your opinion – should we use him?

'Sonny' is going to become a student at the 'Professor''s school, and then starting in October he will have a real opportunity to work with the Professor.

Summation: 'Sonny' will connect us with 'Orphan', while Burgess goes off to one side.

A short time later Kim again met his colleagues. They told him of the Centre's high estimation of his work and informed him that it was considered best to leave the final negotiations with Maclean to Kim.

The year 1934 was coming to a close. It was time for the Christmas vacation at Cambridge. Rather than have Kim draw attention by a second trip to Cambridge, they decided to use Maclean's planned trip to London.

Kim invited him to his place for an important conversation. A quick study, Kim tried to talk to his friend in the same manner as Otto had talked to him six months earlier in Regent's Park.

But there were differences, of which Kim was aware. First of all, this had not been Otto's first such talk. Secondly, the talk with Maclean would be both simpler and harder, for the very same reason: Kim had reason to worry before such an important meeting.

He tried to make it as relaxed as possible. No one else was at home. A modest table was set. After preliminary chitchat they moved to business. Kim began by assuring his friend that he did not doubt Maclean's intentions to follow the convictions that they had both reached at Cambridge. Nor did he doubt that a brilliant career at the Foreign Office awaited his friend. Proof of that was his extraordinary abilities. But how did Maclean plan to combine his convictions with work in the Foreign Office of Great Britain, which exemplified the worst, the most hypocritical and the most cruel aspects of the British Empire, built on the oppression of colonial peoples?

'I hope to find opportunities to defend my principles there, too,' Maclean replied with a chuckle.

'Are you certain that selling the *Daily Worker* in the front hall or even passing it out gratis to everyone at the Foreign Office is the best way to move up the ladder there?'

Without any sense of guilt for plagiarising Otto's talk, Kim followed the scenario from Regent's Park. He told Maclean that being a legal or even illegal member of the English Communist Party with his background, manners and education was honest but useless. Handing out leaflets at the Foreign Office calling for a change in British imperialist policies was the best way to strengthen them. But there was a way out. He could serve the Communist movement without leaving the Foreign Office, moving swiftly up the ladder, having a brilliant career and not despising himself for it.

Kim told me that Maclean heard out his well-prepared tirade calmly, even without apparent interest, and when Kim finished asked only one question: 'Do you mean Soviet intelligence or the Comintern?'

He could have been asking about tomorrow's weather.

Kim was stunned. Maclean's question was much too direct. Kim still had an arsenal of arguments and approaches. It was a shame to leave them unused. But he replied just as directly. 'To tell the truth, I don't know. But the people I could introduce you to are very serious, they work in a very serious international anti-fascist organisation, which may be tied to Moscow.'

Maclean was silent and then asked: 'Do you need an answer immediately?'

'Do you want to think it over?'

'I would like to discuss it with Klugman. Before giving you a final decision. You know that they have certain hopes for me, too.'

Kim naturally knew James Klugman, Maclean's friend, and an activist in the British Communist Party. He replied with an unequivocal refusal. 'That is categorically impossible.'

Maclean was a bit put out, but Kim said: 'Go home and think about it. Let's meet in a few days. But if you intend to speak of this with Klugman or anyone else, then it's all off and this conversation never happened.'

Their talk petered out. Maclean said good-bye and left.

Two days later he found Kim and said simply: 'All right, I agree.'

'Good. I'll set up a meeting with those people.'

And he went to Otto. Theo was still in London (even though Kim continued to call the man Theo when talking with me, I suspect that it was Orlov). The three of them worked out a way for Maclean to meet Otto.

Kim told it to Maclean. It was simple. Approximately an hour before the meeting Maclean would go to a railway station, named by Kim, synchronise his watch with the clock, and at the precise designated time, enter the café that Kim would tell him about. In his left hand he would be carrying a certain book with a bright yellow jacket, and in his right, a newspaper or something.

Kim did not remember whether Maclean met only Otto that first time or whether both Otto and Theo were at the café.

After the meeting at the café, Otto told Kim that his friend was already officially 'one of us'.

And so Donald Maclean, the son of a British Cabinet minister, a man of brilliant abilities, the first on Kim's list of seven recommendations, became an agent in December 1934, and perhaps like Kim was still not quite sure whose agent he was – the Comintern's, or the GPU's.

The recruitment of Guy Burgess went differently.

The description of Burgess by Kim naturally led to grave doubts. There were many arguments and discussions. The Centre took a long time before approving the recruitment. It might never have taken place if Alexander Orlov had not returned to London. He was fated to play a rather strange, not completely explicable but significant role in Kim Philby's life. Of course, he also played a serious role in the history of Soviet espionage and, therefore, in the history of the country.

Orlov did not work permanently in London then. He was a 'roving forward' for Soviet intelligence in Western Europe, but he was familiar with the operation with Kim, Maclean, and all the other men on the list. Orlov was a man of action, who did not like hesitation and who believed like Napoleon that is it better to take a wrong decision than none at all. He was of the firm belief that Guy Burgess should be recruited as quickly as possible. Without knowing him personally, Orlov may have felt a sympathetic kinship to him, according to Kim. Both men had something in common, even though Orlov was quite 'macho', and Burgess a homosexual.

Otto's attitude towards Burgess's recruitment was much more cautious and doubt-filled. Mar was also ambivalent. As for Kim, he quite properly considered himself a novice and felt that having provided his list, he had played his part. But he did not manage to maintain his neutrality.

A rather difficult situation had arisen. The Centre, after all, would accept the recommendations of the London residence, and was waiting for them. But there was no agreement in London.

The indecisiveness could have continued for quite a while if the problem had not solved itself. The solution was dictated by the object of the debates, Burgess himself, in a manner typical of him and without his knowing it.

He had been a close friend of Maclean's at Cambridge and had worked with the British Communists; and of course he had noticed the changes in the behaviour of his friend. Maclean, who was following the same recommendations given to Kim, began cutting himself off gradually from the leftist movement, avoiding his leftist friends, no longer buying leftist newspapers, and avoiding conversations that used to interest him.

But Burgess knew the strength of Maclean's convictions and was not deceived.

'Burgess would not have been Burgess,' Philby told me, 'if he had believed Maclean's switch and if he had not expressed his doubts in the most outrageous way. Anyone who wants to understand Burgess must remember that if the fellow had decided to do something, no angels in heaven or devils in hell could stop him. And so that disgusting hooligan' – Kim spoke with a smile that indicated that the actions, at least this time, of the hooligan suited him – 'began pursuing Maclean. No one could have predicted that. At every meeting, he said to Donald, "Do you think that I believe even for one jot that you have stopped being a Communist? And do you think that you can convince me of that? Me? You're simply up to something! I know you, you old liar and sneak. You expect me to believe that you would betray yourself? Never in your life!"

'And he would pester Maclean not only when they were alone, but even if there were others about. Guy could have ruined the whole operation about Maclean's departure from the left.'

One day when Maclean could no longer take the attacks, he said to Burgess: 'Listen, shut up, damn you! All right, I am still who I was. But I can say no more, I don't have the right.'

Guy was delighted and said that he had known from the very start that Maclean was working for the Comintern or for Moscow.

Maclean almost fell over from the shock. 'What makes you say that? Nonsense! Utter nonsense!'

But Guy merely nodded and said, ironically, 'Of course, of course . . . total nonsense.'

The situation was made worse and much more dangerous. There was only one way out – to recruit Burgess. And as quickly as possible.

The three conferred once again, Philby told me. Kim stayed in touch with Maclean. They decided that Burgess would accept the offer to work for them, if not with delight, then at least as a natural development of events. It should appeal to his adventurous nature. They also thought that the offer to work for the intelligence service and Guy's agreement would put him inside a framework of discipline that he could perceive romantically. And if he decided to be disciplined, he would be. The way was obvious: Guy would leave Maclean alone and stop blabbing.

And Kim brought one more argument to bear. 'If we do not take him with us, we could end up with a scandal. Among his Communist friends, and out of the best intentions, he will start defending Donald Maclean and saying that he is not lost to the Party, not a traitor, and that he knows a thing or two that he cannot reveal. And he'll wink and nudge and smile significantly. And he'll tell only his most trusted friends, and soon everyone will know. That will ruin our work.'

They all came to the same conclusion: there was no time to waste and Burgess must be recruited immediately.

And so that 'disgusting hooligan,' that eternal *enfant terrible*, dictated to Soviet intelligence how to deal with him.

The preliminary conversation with Burgess must have been held by Maclean, Kim thought. He also arranged for a rendezvous between his Soviet colleagues and his incorrigible friend. But the actual process of recruitment was done without Kim's knowledge.

At that time Burgess, according to Kim, was not told about Kim Philby's ties with Moscow. Philby insisted that Guy learned about Kim's work with Moscow only during the Civil War in Spain. The Soviet colleagues sent him then to Gibraltar to give 'a needed man' money and a cipher code. The 'needed man' turned out, unexpectedly for Burgess, to be Kim Philby.

That is what Kim told me at first.

Later, it turned out to have happened quite differently, including the meeting in Gibraltar. But that meeting took place later and there were several years of turbulent events before it.

4

DEUTSCHLAND ÜBER ALLES

Kim's statement to me during one of our early conversations that in the first months of his work for Soviet intelligence he had done 'nothing important, nothing serious was happening, just a few trifles of the espionage life' did not, to put it mildly, correspond with reality. It was thanks to 'Sonny' that the foundation was laid for the formation of a group of brilliant young men from Cambridge (and not only from there), who worked with Soviet intelligence out of ideological considerations. Fate prepared a noticeable role in history for them, no matter how we may regard them today.

There were other rather important projects for him in his early career with Soviet intelligence. He was told not only to break his former leftist ties but also to create an opinion of himself in society that would help him attain a position that would allow him to accomplish whatever Soviet intelligence needed.

That meant first of all changing his relationship with his father. In 1934 the latter was in the Middle East and was not particularly interested in seeing his 'left-wing' son. Kim's marriage to an Austrian Communist, which was reported in the Viennese papers, had not thrilled the elder Philby either.

On the advice of his Soviet colleagues, Philby began working his father over patiently with letters.

Quite quickly the London residence could inform Moscow that as a result of his correspondence with his father, Sonny seemed to have convinced him that he had ended his leftist enthusiasms. The father began to trust him more, and even allowed him and his wife to move into his London flat. Moreover, he entrusted Kim with the publication of his articles and began recommending him to his friends. In September 1934, thanks to his father's efforts, Kim was recommended by an editor of *The Times*, whom Sonny did not know personally, to the Minister of Internal Affairs of India for the position of director of the press bureau of the Indian government. The minister even sent Kim a personal invitation to take this position. However, on orders from the residence, Sonny refused the Indian offer. Instead in October 1934 he entered the School of Slavonic Languages to learn Russian. His father helped him too. The head of the school was his old friend Ross, who had great respect for the elder Philby and which extended to the son. Ross even taught Kim Russian himself.

Of course it was no secret to the residence that Ross's school prepared students of a 'broad profile', including people for the British intelligence services. Therefore the Centre kept reminding 'Sonny' to be extremely careful.

> The fact that the head of a certain school has suddenly shown great friendship for 'Sonny' has interested us. Is this not proof that, knowing 'Sonny''s former leftist views, certain circles are attempting to test him . . .? Therefore 'Sonny' must not in any case manifest any activity toward getting closer to the school's director.

This was from a letter to the London resident from Moscow.

In order to direct any possible test, the residence decided to try Kim as a journalist, 'so that he can prove his loyalty to the government through the press', wrote the resident to Moscow. In February 1935 the residence informed Moscow that 'Sonny' had got a job as a correspondent and later as deputy editor of the magazine *Review of Reviews*.

In the spring of 1935 they learned that Philby senior was planning to come to London. The news elicited great interest at the Centre. There they stubbornly persisted in considering 'father' part of the Secret Service. And they still treated Kim like the little boy who could be used to get at the father. The documents of the time call Philby senior a 'famous Anglo spy'. The Centre urged the resident 'to use the father's visit to the full 100 per cent'.

He arrived in London in June 1935. Kim's assignment was to look through all his documents and photograph 'the most interesting', which he did. However, to the disappointment of Kim's Soviet colleagues, his father's papers revealed no secret or even important political documents. Alexander Orlov ('Swede') reported to Moscow about this unexpected failure.

It surprises us and seems highly unlikely that his father, who according to Söhnchen saw Ibn-Saud daily and besides which is the Standard Oil representative in Arabia, would not be a close and intimate collaborator with the Intelligence Service.

Orlov, who was quick to judge, was quite unhappy with 'Father's behaviour. He did not fit any of the preconceived notions. He was supposed to present documentary evidence of his work with the Secret Service – and he did not. According to Orlov, he should have been trying to get important political posts for his son, and instead, he was satisfied with his son's career in journalism. Philby senior did not know that the position Kim held in journalism was not good enough for the GPU. Orlov wrote to Moscow:

'Söhnchen' will insist that his father use his connections to get him another political job (as secretary to some politician, for instance). But 'Father' is quite pleased with his son's journalism career and is not inclined to help him. However, Söhnchen hopes to force his father to do something for him.

And his father finally was of some use to Soviet intelligence. Of course, it was in an unexpected way, not where Orlov had expected. The resident reported a sensational bit of news to Moscow:

Through his father, 'Söhnchen' has met the famous Anglo spy Lockhart, who is editor of the *Evening Standard*. Lockhart offered him a job at his newspaper, and 'Söhnchen' accepted.

News of the meeting created a furore at the Lubyanka. Lockhart was by then the symbol in the USSR of the worst of British intelligence. Every schoolchild knew that 'in 1913 that agent of British imperialism began working in Russia in the guise of a British diplomat. Obeying his masters and himself a fierce enemy of Soviet power, he was one of the organisers in 1918 of a conspiracy to overthrow the government (the Lockhart conspiracy). But his treacherous plans were exposed in time by the glorious Cheka.' This is how Lockhart was described in popular Soviet brochures.

Naturally the Centre grabbed at the thread leading to the famous English spy. They gave him the code name 'Anna', and suggested to the London residence that they 'under no circumstances refuse to play with "Anna" and to pay particular attention to this question'.

However, this line of Kim's work made no noticeable developments in the future.

Around the middle of 1935, one of Kim's university chums began to play a prominent role. The documents call him 'Genrikh' [or Henry] and he worked as permanent assistant to some 'famous person'. The residence announced that '"Sonny" would keep up ties with him and carefully gain his confidence. It is premature to speak of where this connection might lead, but we feel that we cannot miss this opportunity.'

The Centre agreed to this plan and also focused on 'Sonny''s ties with Poles (in particular with Ambassador Raczhinski, whom the Centre felt could be of interest later. 'Bear in mind,' the Centre warned, 'that the Poles spy among other things, and some, primarily. As sophisticates in the field, they could unmask "Sonny", who lacks experience as an agent, if he shows his curiosity too strongly.'

By the autumn of 1935 'Genrikh' was of great interest to the Centre. They sent orders 'to pay exceptional attention to working on "G" ["H"]' because Lubyanka expected him to 'open the curtain to the place we have been trying fruitlessly to reach all this time – the Intelligence Service'.

'G' is a man with no restraints – and blatantly amoral (a drunkard and a homosexual), who leads a double life with an amplitude of vacillation from low dives to the Intelligence Service. Therefore we fell that you will have a comparatively easy time working on 'G'. We think that you should not raise the question of recruiting 'G'. A better approach is: 'Sonny' obtains 'G''s trust, gets him drunk (without skimping on expenses), and unobtrusively sucks out what we want to know about the work of the Service. 'G' could fall into our hands another way – through 'Mädchen'. Since 'Mädchen' is a homosexual and, we presume, acquainted with 'G' since Cambridge, he would have no trouble approaching him.

A while later, a new subject appears – a certain 'K'. The residence reported on him to the Centre:

'Sonny' has visited 'K' at work several times and spent the night there. Once 'K' read several letters from the Ambassador to him. For these cases we should have a good and swift-acting sleeping drug. I've assigned 'Sonny' to steal 'K''s private love letters, which the latter keeps. Then I asked him to try to get as many addresses of his mistresses as possible. The next time 'K' is drunk, 'Sonny' will try to get his address book, which must have the addresses, and copy the necessary ones. He might find other interesting things there. Naturally he will replace the book so that 'K' will never know.

The Centre corrected him.

Bear in mind that 'K' could be exceptionally important for us . . . That is why we think it harmful to use sleeping pills and the like, which will not give you 'K' but could spoil all the work that has been done. Use 'Mädchen' or 'Sonny' as the key to 'K'. Do not rush, work methodically.

In other words, 'Sonny' was being used in the first months after his recruitment. He had many assignments, including the usual espionage dirty work. Obviously, they did not avoid it and trained 'Sonny' to accept it, sinking him in it up to his neck. At that time, Kim's first mentor, Otto, wrote about his student to the Centre:

It's amazing that such a young man is so widely and deeply knowledgeable. In conversation with him, you always sense the patrician in him. He is very modest, even too modest. In discussing plans of work, he never raises any doubts about his personal life. The question simply does not exist for him. He is so serious that he forgets that he is only 25. He has only one flaw: he stutters severely . . . 'Sonny' is very shy, indecisive, and physically clumsy. His stutter makes him even more insecure . . . 'Sonny' has studied Marxist teaching quite deeply. In general, he studies everything thoroughly, but always says that he knows little. By nature he is gentle and kind . . . 'Sonny''s moods fluctuate significantly sometimes.

How did the filth and cynicism of daily espionage coexist with the character described above? Only the story of Kim Philby's entire life can answer that question.

★   ★   ★

Moulding the image of a young man from a respectable family who had had his fling with leftist, perhaps even radical, ideas in his early youth and had now matured went well for Kim. He tried to feel like a mature man whose biography proved that he had both a warm heart and a pretty good head on his shoulders. People tend to treat you as the person you think you are.

Philby and Otto often discussed his professional future, what field he should select. There were three factors to consider. First, it had to be a field in which he could achieve great success. Second, the success should be of interest to Soviet intelligence. And the third factor was to temper their desires to their abilities.

When all three factors were put together and after some efforts were made, Philby became a journalist. His first position was not very important. At first he was an assistant to the editor of a small monthly. The publication had few prospects of winning a large audience. But Otto was encouraging, as usual.

'Don't worry,' he told Kim, 'that the work isn't very interesting or important. The main thing now is to open the door, to take the step and get inside the house. Once you're inside, you'll look around and then decide which way to go. But if you're outside on the street, you'll never have any opportunity to get ahead in your work.'

Even though his modest start disappointed Philby, he knew that he was right.

In following Otto's orders to create a new image, Kim not only broke off with his leftist friends, but assiduously cultivated old and new acquaintances who were conservatives. An old school chum turned out to be a permanent secretary to the deputy minister at the War Ministry.

As a source of information he was not particularly valuable to the Soviets, but he had quite a few good and useful contacts. It was he who introduced Philby to his friend, an older man named Talbott.

This Talbott played a role in Philby's advancement in the world of journalism. For several years he had been the editor and owner of a magazine called *The Anglo-Russian Trade Gazette*. The edition was intended to serve the financial figures and businessmen who had had business interests in Russia before the Revolution and who wanted to get back their investments. They formed a special association around the magazine to pressurise the British government in that direction. Talbott's magazine was the association's publication.

However, neither the association nor the magazine had any

success. The old capitalists and financiers gradually lost all hope of getting anything from the Bolsheviks and eventually died out. Talbott did not know what to do or where to get funding for his magazine.

'I don't know if he came up with this himself or not, but one fine day he shared his new idea with me,' said Philby.

'"My magazine is dying," he told me. "But unlike the magazine, I have no intention of dying and I would like to live for a while yet. However, in order to fulfil this natural human desire, I need money. And so I have decided to publish a new magazine. Not on an Anglo-Russian base, but on an Anglo-German one. To activate Anglo-German trade. What do you think?"

'I thought the idea very interesting, and told him so.

'"Excellent," he continued. "I'm telling you about it not simply to keep you informed of my plans, you know. You might have noticed that even though I plan to live a long time, I am no longer young. But journalism demands youth and energy. Especially for starting up a new magazine; even more so, if you have to start a new magazine before the old one has died. Therefore I need a young, energetic and talented editor. I don't need to explain why he must be energetic and talented, but I will answer the question why must he be young: so he will not ask for too much money. Since you have all three qualities, my young friend, I intend to offer you the job of editor with enormous prospects and modest salary."

'I asked him to name the sum. He did.'

'Was it a lot?'

'Not at all. But I recalled Otto's words that it is better to be inside the house than on the street, and I replied that I would probably accept, but I needed a few days to think about it. Talbott shrugged, but gave me several days.'

Philby needed the time not so much for his own thoughts, as to let Otto know. As expected, Otto gave his approval on the spot.

The moment he began working at the Anglo-German magazine Philby started his practical work for the Soviet Union.

Everything he had done before was natural and simple work that did not demand any special effort. At Cambridge he acted in a milieu that was familiar and he had been prepared to make that list. But now, editing a magazine, Philby was starting on a totally new stage, both as an editor and, if you will, a politician. He joined the Anglo-German Fellowship – an organisation that existed in England to improve relations between England and Nazi Germany. He made friends at the German Embassy in London, first in the press department, and later in others. Quite quickly he obtained some little-known information about unofficial contacts between England and Nazi Germany among financiers, industrialists, specialists in export and import, and other people interested in a closer alliance between England and Nazi Germany. It was then that he began to feel like a spy, like a man gathering information. His contacts grew quickly. New acquaintances even introduced him to Ribbentrop, who was then German Ambassador to England. As editor of the Anglo-German magazine he met him frequently in London and later, when Ribbentrop became minister of foreign affairs, saw him in Berlin.

He began travelling there regularly – spending at least one week a month in the German capital. Philby negotiated with Ribbentrop's various experts and advisors, and made solid contacts in the Ministry of Propaganda, which was headed by Goebbels.

(From Man's letter to the Centre)
. . . 4. 'Sonny.' He returned just a few days ago from Berlin, where he was taken around for two weeks as a foreign VIP. They showed him 'achievements' and the 'new spirit'. He saw people from the Ministry of Propaganda and people from Ribbentrop's bureau. Talks touched on future work, the magazine, and related technical questions.

The magazine will begin publication only in October. I am sending you the July issue of *Geopolitik* with his article. The first goal we set ourselves with 'Söhnchen' – making him into a major journalist – has been met, since he is editor of a magazine. Undoubtedly, this work has strengthened his ties with Germany and local Germanophiles, and will give him new ties. The future will show which of these ties we will use and in which way. Let us not forget that he is hindered in developing those ties and turning business relations into personal ones by the fact that his wife is Jewish.

'This was the basic course of my work for the Soviets in 1935 and 1936. I can't say that the work was particularly engrossing, but I realised that it had its importance. Germany was arming itself wildly. Hitler spoke openly of his military plans in the East. And every trifle, every detail of possible plans and in particular facts about the collaboration of British and American industrialists with Hitler, had to be useful to the Soviet Union.

'I had told you that the work was not particularly engrossing. That's putting it mildly. If you put aside whatever results could have been useful to us, the rest of my work as mouthpiece for Anglo-German friendship was profoundly repulsive to me. In the eyes of my friends, not even my leftist friends but simply acquaintances, even conservative ones, but honest conservatives, I looked pro-Nazi. I realised that, and it was a very bitter realisation, especially since at that time, on Otto's orders, I was moving further and further way from the Left, from Communists, from people who sympathised with them. Finally I found myself unexpectedly surrounded by people whom I hated, now in friendly relations with them. The situation was paradoxical. It was out of hatred of fascism that I took the decision to do what I was doing – that is, working for the Soviet Union – but I had to pretend to be a friend of fascists or pro-fascists. And I had to break off with the friends I loved.'

I could see Kim give a small shudder.

'That must have been very difficult.'

'I remember how I once came to the library, went up to the desk to ask for a book, and suddenly saw my old chum, an Englishman who had also taken part in the events in Austria. I couldn't help offering my hand to him and saying how glad I was to see him. But he did not take my hand. Instead, he asked coldly, "Tell me, please, had you started working as a police informer back in Austria? Or did you take on for that job later?"

'The worst part was that there was nothing I could say. What could I say? I simply turned and left.

'I did not tell Otto about this meeting, but he was a very sensitive man and always cheered me up, telling me that he knew how difficult it is to leave old friends, how hard it was to seem a traitor in their eyes. But my conscience was clear, he reminded me.

'My conscience was clear, in fact. And those words made me feel better. But, to tell the truth, not for long.'

Otto warned Kim about something else, as well. He said: 'You have to have a sense of measure. Yes, there will be a war, and to keep Hitler from winning, you have to pretend now to be an ally of the Anglo-German alliance. But you do not have the right to look like a Nazi in the eyes of your friends. Your image is of an independent-minded Englishman who accepts Hitler's Germany as a fact of European life in the middle of the 1930s. You can have a positive or negative attitude towards that fact, but it is impossible to "ban" Germany or "exclude" it from today's Europe. As a true Englishman you are trying to gain some benefit, economic and cultural, for your country out of the situation. Moreover, by supporting Anglo-German closeness, you are trying to avert war in Europe.'

Otto also said that serious changes could occur unexpectedly and swiftly in the fate of the Anglo-German society and magazine, as well as in the balance of power in Europe. If war broke out, it would be hard and long. But fascism would be destroyed, and even for that reason alone, Kim could not look like a hundred per cent Nazi now.

'I remembered all his advice and suggestions and obeyed as precisely as I could, trying to be independent and not taking the position of a proponent of the German order. Otto, of course, was clairvoyant. All his predictions came true. And the first was his prediction about a sharp change in the fate of the magazine.'

One day in Berlin, Philby dropped in on a friend in the Ministry of Propaganda. To his surprise he heard: 'I think, Herr Philby, that this will be your last visit to us.'

'Why?' he asked warily.

'You see, we've decided to change the financing of our magazine. We want to deal with another banking group in England and from now on we will carry all the expenses for publishing the magazine.'

Here I must explain that the magazine was financed equally by the British and the Germans. A switch to unilateral financing meant that Berlin would be the owner of the publication.

Philby asked: 'Are you trying to say that you intend to publish a one-hundred-per-cent Nazi magazine in England?'

'Yes, precisely,' he replied. 'It will be more convenient and more honest.'

'But you will achieve very little,' Philby said, quite sincerely.

'That is our business. We have decided and we will act in accordance with that decision. In any case, you will not be receiving any more money from us.'

'What was your reaction to this?' I asked Kim.

'To tell the truth, I was disappointed. For two reasons. First of all, I was losing a chance to help the Soviet Union. And secondly, I was losing my job and my salary. It may have been low, but it was my only source of income.

'At my next meeting with Otto I told him all about this. I said I was disappointed and that I would have to look for another job or other Germans who could share in financing the magazine.

'To my surprise, Otto was not in the least upset. "The hell with them. Good. Just in time."

'"What do you mean? Why just in time?"

'"Because you are leaving London."

'"Where am I going?"

'"To Spain, where else!" Otto replied. "How can a talented young journalist sit around in London when there is a civil war in Spain, when the first battle against fascism is being fought?"

'I was terribly pleased and asked right away, "Where will I be working? Madrid? Barcelona? Valencia?"

'"You won't be going to any of those cities. You will go to the other side. You will go to Franco."

'"Me – to Franco? I will be in Spain, on his side?"

'"A fine question," Otto said with a smile. "And what other side could journalist Kim Philby, a proponent of Anglo-German unity, be on in Spain?"'

Philby's fate took another sharp turn.

He was supposed to go to Spain as a freelance journalist, not with any particular publication, but at his own risk, on his own funding. The financing would come from the Soviets, but he had to find a way of 'earning' the money, that is, laundering it. So he sold his books and records.

Naturally, he would have preferred going to Madrid, Barcelona or Valencia, or to any place that belonged to the Republicans. It was hard going to Franco. But Philby understood that he could be of more use there.

Another of Otto's predictions came to pass very quickly. The Nazi magazine that Philby's friend in Hitler's Ministry of Propaganda had told him about was published in England. The new editor was a man named Carroll – a real Nazi. On the day the war with Germany started, he was arrested and spent the entire war in prison. If Philby had stayed with the magazine, he too would have ended up behind bars.

And he concluded: 'I wouldn't have been much use then!'

5

SPECIAL ASSIGNMENT

It was 1937, a year that brought sorrow and the death of innocent people. The old folk in Russia said: you can't divide the number 1937 by anything, not a single numeral – and that meant trouble. And trouble there was.

But for Kim it was, in his words, a romantic time. Until then he had not felt like a real spy, but only a preparatory one. Rummaging in his father's papers, recommending friends from Cambridge for recruitment, even collecting information about Anglo-German ties and, contrary to his own feelings, taking part in them, developing them – all that was perhaps not always pleasant, but not very difficult. Now he was off to meet danger, to the front, whose slithering, constantly bending and changing line was watched with interest and hope not only in England, but in the whole world. The first battle against fascism was being fought in Spain. He fired, and was fired upon. The future of Europe depended in many ways on what happened there. Kim planned to go there in the hope of being some help to the people he supported with all his heart. After all, wasn't it for their sake that he had entrusted his fate to people he had never known, to a country where he had never been?

In a word, his Big Work lay ahead.

Apparently the idea to send 'Sonny' to Spain on Franco's side came up in mid-December 1936. It was then – in a telegram to the Centre – that the resident Man wrote:

We must consider the newspaper question to have been a fiasco. The reason: lack of money from the German Ministry of Propaganda and failure to fulfil their latest promises, which outrages Talbott and cools off his pro-German feelings ('I never had this unclean feeling with the Russians. They like to drag things out, but once they sign something, it's sacred.') He keeps complaining that the Germans are spreading rumours that he is a Bolshevik agent. I don't rule out the possibility that the newspaper failed because of that sort of suspicion on the part of the Germans.

There is a possibility of shifting 'Söhnchen' to other work, which I will refrain from doing because of the special assignment. A separate report on the special assignment follows.

The special assignment was Spain. Apparently the idea of sending Kim there did not come from the Centre. The resident actually had to postpone Kim's trip by two weeks. At last a telegraphed answer came from Moscow. The Centre gave its approval for the trip, but expressed great concern over communications. Here is an extract from the coded telegram from the Centre, sent in the middle of January 1937 to Man:

As for Söhnchen. We sent a telegram saying that we agreed to his trip. In your telegram you told us that he hopes to maintain communications through your people. Tell us from whom you got these people and how you plan to organise ties with them. Secret writing should be used only in the most extreme cases, otherwise it could lead to a failure of Söhnchen.

Getting ready for Spain was a rush, no more than two weeks. Neither Otto nor Theo had been there and they couldn't tell Kim much about the country. He hadn't received many instructions, either, he later said.

They told him what should interest him: the location and movements of troops, their arms, number, communications systems; the mood of the government and the officer corps; aid from Germany and Italy; the relations between the Spanish military and the Germans and Italians; the commanders, headquarters, Franco, his bodyguards, and so on.

Otto handed him a rather simple secret code. On a large sheet of very thin but very strong paper was a list of objects in which he was supposed to be interested in Spain: cannon, tank, airport, battalion, regiment, truck with infantry, watchman etc. Each had a codeword: 'when', 'what', 'if', 'since' and so on.

He was told that every week or two he should mail a letter to a certain address. Every fifth word in the letter had to be a codeword. If he had to tell them about ten planes at some airport, the fifth word after the number '10' would be 'that,' which stood for 'plane' and four more words after that would be 'there,' which stood for a small airfield under construction.

This very simple code was easy to learn, and Kim was soon writing cleverly constructed secret letters. He never achieved great heights stylistically, but the letters read like ordinary epistles to a relative or girlfriend from a not very highly educated loafer.

His unknown 'relative or girlfriend' was called 'Mlle Dupont' and she lived in Paris. He didn't ask any questions about her, that wasn't done. But many years later, when he happened to be on business in France's capital, Kim went to the street in the address, found the house and was very surprised – more of which later.

Otto told Kim that besides the postal communications, he could in an extreme emergency meet personally in Spain or the South of France with a 'contact'. The bosses did not plan to meet Kim: he would be there a short time, only two or three months.

Kim was a bit upset: such a responsible assignment and no meeting with Otto or Theo. They reassured him: he would like his contact if he had to have a meeting in Spain. They would have a preliminary meeting in London.

Soon after that conversation, the bosses introduced Kim to his future contact on a Soho street. She was a woman of twenty-five or twenty-six. Kim could tell she was Russian from her accent and looks. But she was better dressed than an ordinary Soviet woman abroad could afford. Most probably she was a white émigrée who sympathised with the Soviet cause, Kim decided. (His bosses called all non-Soviet Russians 'white,' no matter their political views.)

Following espionage etiquette, Kim did not ask any questions about her. He was supposed to memorise her features. That was the point, so that if necessary, they could find each other in the future meeting place.

Kim knew how to memorise people's faces by then. He looked at her closely, listened to her voice, asked her to walk for him (a person's gait was very important). She observed and listened to him just as closely. He took a few steps for her, too. They had both been trained by the same teachers. They must have looked very silly; at least Kim felt that way. Moreover, his new acquaintance chuckled as she watched him. She was easy to remember, a good-looking woman, slender, lively. Her charming smile, with sparks of mockery, let him assume that she had a sense of humour. Almost half her pale, slightly nervous face was filled with her large, anxiously attentive, grey eyes, which did not correspond to her smile. Her English was quite acceptable, with a slight Russian accent that was 'Scandinavianised', as Kim described it. Could she be 'Mlle Dupont', he wondered. She told him to call her 'Mary'. His name as far as she was concerned was 'Tom'.

The four of them stood on a Soho street corner for ten or fifteen minutes, chatted about this and that, and then parted, all of them pleased, it seemed, by the 'exhibition'.

'You'll ask for a meeting with her only under the most urgent circumstances,' Theo reiterated at their next meeting. 'By mail. All the necessary words in the code.'

During our conversations, Kim often smiled with condescension, recalling the lack of security of those days. To think that two major Soviet agents — one chief of the espionage network in London, the other, as Kim correctly assumed, in charge of secret agents throughout Western Europe — met in broad daylight on a London street. They could already be under surveillance, yet they calmly met a Cambridge man, on whom Moscow was pinning such great hopes, and a pretty woman whose Russian accent was obvious to any passersby.

In those days, Kim was not surprised at the ease with which his patrons, usually quite demanding in terms of conspiracy and cover, suddenly permitted themselves such lapses. The patriarchal measures of security used by Soviet intelligence in those days corresponded to the naive and light-hearted level of British counter-intelligence work. In any case, his Soviet colleagues had very few failures in England then. The complicated rules and methods for both sides came much later.

Among Kim's instructions was one to which he paid particular attention. His bosses told him that even though his mission was very important for today's intelligence needs, it might be even more important for his work — he should use the trip to establish himself as a journalist, 'to come out onto the big arena', as Otto put it.

In fact, it was a unique opportunity. Spain was the centre of the world's attention. News from there was front-page stuff; and there was more than enough coming from Republican Spain, and a lack of news from Franco's side. Journalists were not particularly drawn to Franco: his rebellion did not have popular support, and the censorship of the Generalissimo worked shamelessly. Later Kim saw that the Francoists did not make any effort to woo the press and considered military success, destroying the Republican army, their main goal. Recognition would come after the victory – that was the Generalissimo's postulate.

Kim Philby headed for Spain, the pleasant weight of a marshal's staff in his neophyte journalist's backpack. Had he any room in his backpack then for a spy's staff as well?

He travelled by boat from Southampton to Lisbon. From there he was to go to Seville, the largest city in Franco-held territory. He was to spend four or five days there, waiting for a visa. He couldn't get it in England, because London did not have diplomatic ties with the Franco regime.

He got the visa without any difficulties at the so-called Franco Agency (the Francoists did not have an embassy in Lisbon then: cautious Salazar, who helped Franco secretly in every way he could, nevertheless continued to maintain diplomatic relations with the Republicans), and got on the train for Merida.

Salazar's Portugal was wholly on Franco's side and gave him considerable help, but covertly, unlike Hitler and Mussolini.

In Merida Kim got off the train in order to get on another one four hours later, headed for Seville via Salamanca. Those hours of waiting were his first hours in the war: at just that time the Republicans were bombing Merida.

The first bomb blew up away from the railway station, in town. The passengers immediately heard the rumour about a brave Italian officer who refused to take shelter and to the delight of the oohing ladies fearlessly stood in the middle of a square with a Republican plane circling overhead. The madman was the only casualty of the bomb. The ladies' delight cost him both legs.

Soon a plane flew over the station. Everyone raced out of the station building to see what kind it was: was it one of our own, belonging to Franco, come to save the city? Kim thought nothing would be more stupid than dying or losing his legs on the first day in Spain, especially from friendly fire. So he did not run out with the others to identify the plane. When the passengers rushed back in a panic, shouting '*Rojo! Rojo!*' – 'Red!' – Kim was already under cover, shamelessly. He did not thirst for the awe of ladies, he had more important things to do. The plane dropped a bomb very close to the station and headed back for Republican territory.

That was the only time Kim went through an air raid. But he would be threatened more than once by the *Rojos*.

His first hours on Spanish soil passed in this manner. The tracks were not damaged by the bombing and the train came on time. At the appointed hour the young journalist got in and set off for Seville.

All the good hotels in Seville were filled with army officers, government offices, clerks, and wealthy Spaniards fleeing the Republicans. Kim had to settle for a tiny room in a hotel whose name he could not remember. He made his first visit to the British-South American bank, where he deposited his modest funds – a completely logical step for a young but serious journalist who had come to the city of his own will and on his own money. Only after that did Kim visit the press centre of the Franco government. Though he couldn't get any useful information – the Franco bureaucrats kept their mouths shut – he met several Spanish journalists.

It can't be said that the young British journalist won the hearts of the Franco people. At the time, their attitude towards the British was very negative. They hated the Republicans and anyone who did not speak out against the reds. Britain and France were biding their time: they maintained diplomatic relations with the Republicans and were in no hurry to recognise Franco. Therefore the first reaction of the government clerks, army officers and especially those who had lost property behind the front lines was more than hostile when meeting any Englishman. Multiply that by the passionate nature of Spaniards, and it could become a real obstacle in his work.

Kim diligently tried to adapt himself to the circumstances. His image was still the one developed with Otto for the Anglo-German Society: an independent-minded Englishman. Within reason that Englishman expressed sympathy for Franco, and within reason he criticised the restrained attitude of the British government towards the Franco regime.

Philby managed to have a letter ready for Paris just two weeks after his arrival in Seville. Then he wrote weekly. He had visited Cordoba and a few other cities, and had been to the Madrid front. He had made quite a few good friends, and now, whenever he travelled outside Seville, he could take with him several serious letters of recommendation, which helped him establish more new contacts, which meant more new information for the Paris mademoiselle.

He learned fast. As it turned out (and he checked himself later) he was almost always correct about troop movements, he was good at distinguishing rank, he could estimate the amount of weapons, planes on an airfield and other 'objects of interest' he encountered on his trips. He made useful contacts with Italians, who were founts of information. They were so boastful of the successes of the Italian army near Casablanca and other fronts, they gave such detailed descriptions of the situation and their heroic exploits, that Kim didn't even have to ask leading questions – it was all he could do to write it all down (journalists were allowed to do that) or remember it.

Here I will interrupt the narrative based on the words of Kim Philby and attempt to compare his story with the documents.

First of all, Kim did not go to Spain without the support of the British press. He had letters of recommendation from influential people. They were intended to help him establish connections. On 24 January 1937 (before Kim left on 3 February for Lisbon), Man wrote to the Centre:

> 'Sohnchen' has received accreditation as a correspondent for two telegraph agencies, the London Central News and the London International News Service, as well as from the *Evening Standard* (Lord Beaverbrook's yellow newspaper). He has letters of recommendation from Haushofer and two letters from the Marquis Merry del Val, Franco's London representative: one to Franco's Lisbon representative and the other to the marquis's son, who is chief of military censorship in Talavera. His assignment: to establish the security system, particularly for Franco, and then of the other leaders, the means of access to them etc.

Moscow followed the movements of its agent in Spain with close, strangely close, attention. Man reported his every step to the Centre: 'Söhnchen left for . . .', 'Söhnchen should be in Lisbon today . . .', 'Söhnchen is headed for the meeting point . . .', 'In the next mail I hope to be able to tell you something . . .'

In the meantime the journalist-spy continued expanding his connections, expressing delight over the heroism of his new Italian friends and sending weekly letters to Paris, like an ardent suitor, to the unknown Mlle Dupont, whom he visualised as the grey-eyed Mary from Soho.

The Italians were not in fact as simple as Kim imagined. After his return from one of his trips, a young Spanish woman, whom he had befriended soon after his arrival in Seville, told him with a nervous laugh that during his absence two Italian officers had come to her. They had seen her with Philby before and warned her to break off her friendship, because the Englishman pretending to be a journalist was actually a spy.

'Whose spy?' Kim asked, rather stupidly.

'A British spy!' she whispered.

He blamed himself later for a long time both for the inappropriate question and for giving the Italians reason to suspect him. He didn't need to be thought of as anybody's spy.

He tried to let his 'mademoiselle' know about this right away, but the cipher did not have the right words for it. He did manage to hint at certain suspicions that certain irresponsible people were voicing. But there were no consequences from that conversation – at least none known to Philby.

However, suspicions about him were raised not only in Spain.

On 23 April 1937, Man wrote to the Centre that his colleagues in intelligence in London (he may have meant the GRU, the Soviet military intelligence) were suddenly interested in Kim Philby and his former boss in journalism, Talbott. Having learned rather belatedly about their ties, the colleagues came to the conclusion that Philby was 'a German spy in England'.

It happened this way: one of the many branches of Soviet intelligence had ties to a friend of Kim's who had been to his flat when Kim was in Spain. The friend, digging around (on orders from the Soviets) in the travelling journalist's papers, found a letter addressed to him from the German Ministry of Propaganda. That led to the conclusion that Kim Philby, son of the famous Arabic scholar with ties to the Intelligence Service, was working for the Germans. A fine family! The information was passed on to Moscow. Man, who learned about it somehow, hurried to inform his bosses of the suspicions of people who did not know about the younger Philby's ties with the NKVD. The resident reminded them that before leaving for Spain Kim had given him a copy of the letter from the Ministry of Propaganda, and it had been sent to Moscow immediately, where it was numbered and added to the 'Sonny' file.

Once Kim returned to London from Spain, Otto probably told him to be more careful in choosing his friends. He may have hinted that the friend who had visited his flat had the impolite habit of riffling through the owner's papers, reading them and drawing strange conclusions that he shared with ignorant people. The documents do not reflect this conversation I assume must have taken place. Nor did Kim mention the incident.

I don't know if Kim thought back to his own first assignment for the Soviets – going through his father's personal papers, making copies of the interesting ones and sending them to Moscow 'for study'. But that, too, was not the most decent behaviour. If Kim were religious, he could have seen in his friend's dirty deed a small mirror of fate which reflected the betrayal of his father.

But in those days, family ties were not considered important. Ideological ties were much more so. That was taught not only by his Soviet mentors, but some of his professors at Cambridge and by very respected authors. Therefore I doubt Kim felt any guilt.

Suspicions, suspicions . . . 'British spy', 'German spy'.

Of course, in 1937 no one called him a Soviet spy.

If you didn't count some extremely hostile or suspicious bureaucrats and officers, on the whole, as Philby told me, he did not have any particular difficulties in that first three-month trip to Spain, except for a famous episode in Cordoba, when he was arrested and had to swallow the paper with the secret code.

That episode, which happened in March 1937, is described in *My Silent War*, and Kim did not dwell on it in our conversations. I will remind the reader that Kim was arrested in Cordoba almost accidentally. The arrest was either the result of the hostility of local authorities towards the British, or simply a mistake. Whichever way, Kim was awakened in the middle of the night by Guardia Civil soldiers who burst into his hotel, and taken to the local police station. There would have been no problem except for the fact that the secret code, written on very thin, strong paper and given to him by Otto, was in his watch pocket. Kim remembered it when he was in the police station. If he hadn't been so sleepy, Kim told me, he would have had the sense to take the code out of his pocket and eat it on the way. But he hadn't thought of that. And when they asked him to empty his pockets and put everything on the table, he broke out in a cold sweat: it was only *then* that he remembered. But along with fear came a saving thought. He took his wallet out of his back pocket and tossed it on the table with a challenging air, and everyone in the room – two guards and the chief – rushed over to the leather distraction, leaving Kim unwatched for several seconds: they were enough for Kim to pull out the paper and swallow it.

Finding nothing suspicious, the police let the English journalist go with a reluctant apology. Kim replied that there were no hard feelings: it was their work, and times were complex.

When he returned to Seville, he started a letter to Paris with a request for a new code, but then he realised that there was no word for 'code' in their code, since no one had thought it might be needed. He had to tell Mlle Dupont that he had lost his Anglo-Spanish dictionary, which he had received from friends before he left for Spain, and he asked her to find a way to get him another copy – not of course, by post, since it could be lost once again.

The whole business upset him. He hadn't expected such a stupid and elementary mistake from himself, one that could endanger the whole operation. There was only one silver lining in the whole black mess: apparently, this was the emergency that would allow him to ask for a meeting with the pretty Soho contact.

He didn't need to wait long for an answer – in those days the mail went much faster, without the enormous amount of unneeded junk mail that travels all over the world today. But the handwriting on the envelope was a surprise. It wasn't that of 'Mary', it was none other than that of the charming loafer, Guy Burgess.

In the letter Guy announced that he was planning to be in Gibraltar and would be happy to see his old friend if he could come there on a certain day. They could have dinner at the Rock Hotel, where Guy would be staying.

Kim understood that a meeting with the grey-eyed, unknown friend would not now take place, but of course he was happy to see Guy. He didn't need to hide this meeting with an old college chum; they could talk openly. Kim appreciated this bold move on the part of his bosses. As for Mary, he never saw her again. He thought it was the morbid suspiciousness of his Soviet colleagues towards white émigrés. In the telegram quoted earlier, the Centre markedly expressed its concern over the methods of communication with Kim that the London resident had offered. Perhaps it was that telegram that put an end to Otto and Theo's plans for Mary.

On the appointed day Kim came to Gibraltar. That evening he and Guy dined at the restaurant and talked late into the night. Kim got a new sheet with the code (this time the word 'code' was on it) and £80 for expenses. Why £80, rather than £70 or £90, Kim did not know, but the question did not worry him. In any case, any amount of money was useful, because it made it easier for him to travel around Spain.

Seeing this manifestation of trust for Guy from his Soviet colleagues, Kim told him his Spanish observations in detail, especially those that he could not express in the letters to Paris. As Philby told me, he did not ask Guy anything, he simply told him what he thought was necessary and was certain that Guy would pass it on to the right place.

'Did he?' I asked.

'I don't know for sure. I never talked about it with him or with the Soviet colleagues, but I think he did,' Philby replied.

That is all that Kim told me about that meeting in Gibraltar. I did not ask any more. How was I to know several years ago during a conversation with Kim, long before I was allowed to see the archives, that in fact the meeting was at the centre of political and human passions, a knot of several confused plot lines and policy at the highest levels? How was I to know that over dinner at the Rock Hotel, Kim Philby would be given an assignment which could affect the history of Spain and perhaps of Europe?

I must return to the events leading up to the meeting at the Rock Hotel.

6

LICENCE TO KILL

S.M. Kirov, whom Stalin considered one of his most dangerous rivals in the Party, was killed in Leningrad in 1934. The killing heralded the start of mass terror in the country. In August 1936 Zinoviev and Kamenev were executed.

The destruction of the highest Party and state leadership, and of the not-so-very-old 'Old Bolsheviks', was in full swing. A new wave of killings was to come to the higher and middle levels of the Red Army command, of the KGB – in particular of the intelligence service – and to writers and other cultural figures. Millions of peasants were robbed and then sent to Siberia to perish.

While the world may not have known about the terror, millions of Soviet citizens knew or guessed, since their relatives and friends had already been its victims, and the apogee of the terror, 1937, was yet to come.

However, this bloodbath was not enough for Stalin. On 25 September 1936, Stalin and Zhdanov, who always vacationed in the south in this season, sent an urgent telegram to the Politburo:

> We consider it absolutely necessary and urgent to name comrade Yezhov to the post of People's Commissar of Internal Affairs. Yagoda is clearly not at his best in the task of exposing the Trotskyite–Zinovievite bloc. The OGPU is four years behind in this work. All the Party workers and the majority of the regional representatives of the Commissariat of Internal Affairs are talking about this. Agranov may remain as Yezhov's deputy.

Yezhov knew what was expected of him. The bloodletting increased. *Izvestia* published Boris Efimov's famous poster: tiny enemies of the people caught in the powerful grasp of the commissar of internal affairs' fist in a quill-covered glove. The caption read 'In Yezhov's gloves' (*yezh* is Russian for hedgehog).

Among the measures taken to fulfil the demands of the leader
of the peoples, Yezhov created a special group to commit terrorist
acts outside the borders of the first socialist state in the world. He
also took into account the experience of his predecessor, Genrikh
Yagoda, who foresaw many needs and created a department to
manufacture poisons. Nothing was spared in the development and
research and the purchase of exotic ingredients and recipes. The
group was within the ministry of state security and only a few
people knew of its existence. Stalin was one.

The events in Spain were working in Stalin's favour. They proved
that the enemy was not sleeping, that the class struggle was growing
more acute, and that the foreign enemy was working with the
domestic enemy. Therefore, the terror was not only justified, but
necessary. This led to the thought at the Lubyanka that not only
internal but some international problems could be solved in a simple
and radical way.

Everything was personified in Russia then. There were no plain
ideas. There were the bearers of those ideas. Good and evil all had
names and passports. Every problem was the fault of someone
specific. And someone had to be thanked for every achievement.
Therefore, it seemed obvious that if Franco were removed, the
rebellion would end.

In December 1936 Yezhov informed Stalin that the Lubyanka
was planning to send an agent to Spain, to Franco-held territory
– a talented young man from an aristocratic British family, who
served Moscow, and not out of fear but out of conscience. He told
him just for information, late at night, as his report to Stalin was
coming to an end.

Stalin shot a look at him, and spoke slowly, as if examining every
word. 'Not from fear? He's working for conscience . . . But can you
pay with fear for work? That would be immoral. And you can't
pay with conscience either. You can sell conscience. But you can't
pay for work with it.' He looked at the commissar with interest,
waiting to see what he would say.

'It's just . . . I meant . . . well,' Yezhov stammered. 'It's just a
folk saying.'

Stalin nodded, as he heard just what he had expected. He said
calmly: 'Some sayings that are called folk sayings were actually
forced onto the people by various scoundrels from the land-owning
classes. They were trying to force the people to work for them.

And they did not want to pay for that work. So they forced them to do slave labour either through threats or by getting blind obedience. And they called that blind obedience conscience . . . But a slave's obedience is not conscience. Only the proletariat has a real conscience. And it does not sell it. To anyone.'

Stalin finished and pushed a button. His study door opened and Poskrebyshev came in. Stalin nodded towards the papers on his desk. Poskrebyshev came over, picked them up, placed them deftly into a file, put it under his arm, gave the seated Yezhov a hostile look – it was almost four a.m.! – and left.

Yezhov got up. He felt a cold emptiness in his belly. He did not know what Stalin had meant, but he sensed that there was some sort of rebuke in it. Just in case, he whispered fervently, delighted by the leader's wisdom: 'I understand, Comrade Stalin,' and added one more, for veracity's sake, 'I understand.'

Stalin, reaching for other papers on his desk, said softly: 'Good. That's good, if you understand.' And he excluded the commissar from the field of his attention.

Yezhov turned silently and, trying not to let his boots squeak, went towards the door. Stalin's low voice stopped him. 'By the way, Yezhov, how are things going with the poisons? Are you working on it?'

Yezhov turned happily, grateful for the interest and the attention. He could tell a lot about it, much had been done . . .

But Stalin merely nodded, without looking up from his work. 'Fine, next time.'

In his car, Yezhov sighed with relief: everything seemed fine, he need not have worried.

The accuracy of all the details of this conversation between Stalin and Yezhov cannot be guaranteed, but I am certain that such a conversation took place.

The first paper then went to London, proposing to send Söhnchen to Franco, and also speaking very cautiously but firmly about the need to get as much information as possible about the system for Franco's personal security and that of other rebel leaders, about the routes their cars took, their licence numbers, the guards' home and office addresses, the way to get passes etc. Nothing more than information was demanded of Söhnchen, but that part of his assignment in Spain Moscow called 'special'. The residency paid great attention to it and it was characterised as being extremely important.

In his next report Yezhov began talking about the work on poisons, but Stalin listened indifferently and interrupted with a question on a different topic.

A new conversation about Philby came up with Stalin in March 1937. Stalin was in a good mood, smoking his pipe without inhaling, and kept turning his face upwards to blow smoke at the ceiling. They spoke of Spain. Suddenly he asked: 'How are things with that English aristocrat? Is he still working in Spain?'

Yezhov replied that he was there and working well, sending valuable information. The commanders of the Republican army and Soviet military advisors in Spain called it valuable more than once.

'He is working well, yet Franco keeps advancing. That's not logical,' said Stalin and leonine folds creased his face, making him seem grim and weary.

'I suppose we could solve the question of Franco himself, if there is a – '. Yezhov stopped, seeing the vulpine eyes flash at him.

But he was prepared for that. He had expected Stalin to ask about the Englishman. And he had prepared the neat phrase, as he thought it, about Franco ahead of time. He probably should not have said 'if there is a political decision'. He hadn't actually said it, but Stalin understood. What should he do now – retreat? Or wait?

He had an answer prepared. 'We were simply considering it, in case the need arose . . . to be ready. But we understand that the propaganda losses would be too great for us, if it were discovered that it was our agent . . . On the other hand, the agent we have in mind for this special assignment has not been discovered by anyone, according to our sources.' It was an answer in case Stalin refused.

But no refusal came. There was only a long pause and the eyes studying the commissar closely. Was this a provocation? Were they trying to set up Comrade Stalin? Did they want to compromise him with an international scandal? Of course, they could always say that even an English aristocrat who hated fascism could not control his hatred and had destroyed the vile fascist flunkey that was Franco . . . But Stalin had a great distrust of agents. They were hypocrites. Their profession was to deceive. It was just a question of whom they were deceiving. Today one person, tomorrow another. And the day after that, they would try to deceive Comrade Stalin. A deceiver's profession was a dangerous one. Where were the limits? He had noticed that actors whom he had seen on stage continued to playact in real life. The ladies clutched their breasts when they depicted love for him, for Comrade Stalin. But what they were really thinking, no one knew. Agents were also actors. Philby was a traitor to boot. He had betrayed his own people. Where was the guarantee that he would not betray others? But these were the kind of people Comrade Stalin had to deal with . . . What could he do . . .?

Yezhov waited for an answer.

Stalin slowly knocked the tobacco from his pipe into a thick crystal ashtray . . . without a word. He said nothing.

That was a sign to act, of course. And Yezhov decided to act.

Later, Yezhov would be removed, as everyone who had to pay for something that was in fact Stalin's fault. Perhaps the memory of the silent command that Stalin had given Yezhov and which he did not in fact obey became one of the many reasons Stalin decided to destroy Yezhov. But a year remained before Yezhov's execution. The commissar did not know he had only a year to live. He returned to the Lubyanka in excellent spirits, full of energy, even though it was four, the usual hour for a meeting with Stalin.

With swift strides, he went to his office and without sitting down asked his secretary to send for the person Man called 'Comrade Alexei' in his letters. He came in a few minutes later, spruce, ready for orders, understanding that he had been called in for an important job. Yezhov was seated at a big desk, and to his right, on the green baize, under his right hand, lay coloured pencils. He did not keep them in the crystal cup meant for pencils, but this way, like logs at a felling site. (Later the entire security building – all the clerks, agents, illegals on vacation in Moscow, all the employees – would keep their pencils the way their commissar did: lying on green baize, fake leather, or wooden surface, and not in a pencil holder.)

Paying no attention to his visitor, Yezhov continued writing. When he finished the last sentence, he neatly hid the page covered in his tiny script with another piece of paper. This was the rule at the interior ministry: no one, not even the highest official, could see what was written on a paper on someone else's desk – either of higher or lower rank.

Yezhov rose and paced his office, imagining that he was Stalin. 'Comrade Alexei' remained standing, not having been invited to sit down. Everyone knew the leader's habit of softly walking on the carpet during meetings. And so Yezhov also walked around his office. Just like Stalin he came up close to 'Comrade Alexei' and slowly lit a Russian cigarette, a papirosa (he would have smoked a pipe but he knew that they would laugh at him, or worse, tell on him to Stalin), staring at his face, and then blew smoke off to one side, so as not to get it in his eyes, and then smiled.

'What are you standing for? Sit down, make yourself comfortable.' With a broad gesture, he indicated the armchair near the small table set perpendicular to his large desk.

His visitor sat down, resting his hands on the polished surface of the table, like a schoolboy. He hated Yezhov, as did everyone else in the security forces, and he feared him, as did everyone else. The arrests had been going on for a year. After Yagoda's arrest, they had skimmed off the first layer of people who had worked directly for him. But that was a small layer, just ten or fifteen offices on the sixth floor. 'Comrade Alexei' worked on the eighth. He had been transferred to the sixth floor when Yezhov took over. He was moved down, but it was a move up. The promotion was pleasant but it did not make him happy. Everyone expected another round of arrests after the first 'test' run. Yezhov was hated for being the harbinger of future, radical changes. To move the deadly aim away from themselves, people sent long lists of 'Yagoda's cronies' to the new authorities.

Yezhov sat down in his armchair. He was so short he barely reached over the top of his desk. He sprawled comfortably. (You bastard, thought 'Comrade Alexei', you should be home in bed at this hour instead of making your co-workers stay up with you.) He started talking about the weather, spring's coming, it would be nice to go hunting at least once, but work was keeping him too busy, the international situation was complicated, and Comrade Stalin was devoting a lot of attention to the work of the Party organs. Therefore it wouldn't be so soon that he could hunt beast or bird.

'Our hunt is of a different nature,' he said, giving his visitor a significant look, which involved widening his tiny eyes and sticking out his lower lip.

'Come on, come on, get on with it. Why did you call me in?' thought 'Comrade Alexei' as he nodded sympathetically and said: 'Yes, we hunt a different quarry, a larger bird. That's very well put! But you have so much work, dear Comrade Yezhov, such a heavy burden on your shoulders!' (And he thought: 'And I can see that you've returned in good spirits from your visit to The Boss. And that means that The Boss is in a good mood. I have to be careful with you.')

Yezhov kept on talking about insignificant trifles. Then he looked at the large clock on his desk; it was four in the morning. He went to the curtained window, carefully moved the drapes a centimetre and looked outside into the dark. He moaned: 'Time flies. There's too much to do even in twenty-four hours.' And he dropped ever so casually: 'Oh, by the way, how are things going with your agent near Franco?'

'So that's the issue. I wonder if anything happened there?' worried 'Comrade Alexei'. He said aloud: 'He's working, Comrade Yezhov. We're in contact.'

'And is he really with Franco?'

'No, not with Franco himself, but on the territory of the Francoists.'

'Is he a Francoist?'

'We have no such information,' 'Alexei' replied cautiously.

Yezhov continued in a serious tone: 'Well, how can this be, the agent is working and working, but Franco keeps advancing? It's not logical, dear comrade.'

'It doesn't depend only on him,' said 'Comrade Alexei', and he mustered a smile.

'That's what I should have replied,' Yezhov thought bitterly. But he said: 'Well, then, why were you boasting about him so much to us; remember our conversation?'

'He got the approval,' thought 'Comrade Alexei'. 'We're awaiting orders,' he said.

'Everybody's always awaiting orders,' the commissar sighed. 'On every question. No one wants to take responsibility. That's why I have to stay here wearing out the seat of my pants until dawn.'

'The important thing is to say nothing now,' thought 'Comrade Alexei', and he simply looked at his boss loyally.

'Well, what are you looking at?' Yezhov said. 'All right, go on home. Get some sleep, and then think about what we should do. Report to me by evening.'

'Comrade Alexei' went through the streets of Moscow with gloomy thoughts. As he had left the fourth entrance of the state security building, he saw a Black Maria to the right, in front of the iron gates that led through the archway into the inner courtyard. Four a.m., the best time for arrests.

Later that morning he returned to work: sleepy, gaunt, with puffy eyes and a grim expression . . .

Quite a panic struck the Centre – or at least the small circle of the initiated. The 'bumping off' Franco scenario, which had only been discussed as a hypothetical possibility, had suddenly become a real assignment, and an assignment that had come from Stalin, or at least, had his approval.

That assignment had to be accomplished at any cost! And the machinery started up.

For the London residence it had started up at the most unfortunate time. We can see that from Man's letter to 'Comrade Alexei' at the Centre dated 9 March 1937.

Dear Comrade Alexei!

I understand the importance of the assignment you have given us and I will do everything I can. I am afraid that with the capabilities left at my disposal I will not achieve the goal. Söhnchen is in Seville at the present moment. His last letter was dated 20 February and did not arrive until 5 March. The censors hold on to the letters for a long time . . . He let us know in primitive cipher, part of which we could not unscramble, that . . . he wants to get to Malaga, but is encountering some kind of obstacle . . .

To pass him the assignment, I must send someone to him. Who? 'Intourist', whom Comrade Deutsch mentions, is not willing to go a second time. Please read her report and you will see that our 'Intourist' would, if she went again, if she could get through onto Spanish territory, bring suspicion not only upon herself, but on Söhnchen, too. Besides which, she does not know Söhnchen and Söhnchen does not know her.

That means we can only send his wife. She, however, does not know how to find him, for by the time she gets there, he could have moved on, but she could write or telegraph him to wait for her. She could give him the assignment – but then it must be in the form of a letter, because I cannot pass along the special assignment verbally, she would die of fright. I could write it in hints, after all, he and I had already discussed it. But how will she get the weapon there? I doubt that poison would yield anything. I do not know about this poison yet, I wrote to Peter, we'll see what can be done with it. Perhaps my 'Sailor' can do something, but he's at sea now, North Africa–Madeira–Lisbon, and won't be back until late March, around the 25th. And then there's the question of whether their ship will stop at a Spanish port (last time it did not), and even if it does, how do I let Söhnchen know to be in that city at that time? But, perhaps, I will be able to combine that with his wife's trip. I have one plan after another, but I will not settle on one until I get Söhnchen's next letter, because at the moment I do not know if he went to Malaga or not. In a day or two, maximum three, probably before this reaches you, I will let you know by telegraph about all the measures we are taking. I will always call the wife 'Anna'.

With my greetings. Yours, Man.

And so, the residence faced several problems at once. How to let Kim Philby know that the special assignment (which they had discussed in general terms before he left for Spain: gathering information on Franco's bodyguards for the possible liquidation of the head of the rebels, without naming Kim as the possible candidate for the killer) was to be done now? How to let him know that it had to be done completely, that is, including the act of terrorism? How would he react when he found out that he was supposed to do it – he, Kim Philby, aka 'Sonny', aka 'Söhnchen', the son of a famous Arabist, the twenty-six-year-old budding journalist and Cambridge man? Who could be sent to let him know? A letter, with 'hints', would be risky. And the person to tell him would have to be very trustworthy and very brave.

Let us say that it were done: someone tells Kim his assignment. Kim, as a disciplined and loyal man, agrees to liquidate Franco. But then the main questions come up: where, when, how? The Centre has proposed a poison. Are they crazy? Have they been watching too many movies about the Three Musketeers? How is he going to administer the poison? From Milady's ring into a goblet of wine? Idiots! And he, Teodor Stepanovich Maly, former priest, has to write politely to Moscow that he will try to do something with the poison . . . Total idiots! You have to have a weapon here.

And a weapon has a 99 per cent risk of failure, and in the case of success, the inevitable death or arrest of Philby and 'fame' throughout the world: a terrorist hired by Moscow killed General Franco! And that means the death of everyone connected to 'Sonny', the entire group, the entire network.

In other words, Man had more than enough reason for his gloomy thoughts. Add to that the almost comic but serious problem of the cipher that 'Sonny' had swallowed when arrested in Cordoba, and you can imagine the range of almost insoluble problems that the GPU resident in London had to deal with once he got the special assignment for the liquidation of Franco.

But Man quickly resolved the first question – he found a person who could get the special assignment to 'Sonny' with minimal risk.

On 9 April 1937, exactly a month after sending the letter cited above, Man wrote to 'Comrade Alexei' once more.

> I am including 'Söhnchen''s report, written on the basis of the information he gathered before he received our special assignment. All the data in the report are apparently obsolete. After the report, I received a telegram from him the day before yesterday saying that he is expecting money in Talavera, after which he will go to Burgos and Salamanca. The incident he describes, being searched in Cordoba, refers to our cipher, which he swallowed. Along with the assignment I sent him the new cipher. With greetings, Yours, Man.

So, Man had found someone to give 'Sonny' the 'Go' signal. And we finally have the answer to the question of who brought Kim Philby the licence to kill Franco. From Man's letter it is clear that it was none other than Guy Burgess. 'Along with the assignment I sent him the new cipher': we know that 'Sonny' got the new ciphers and £80 from Guy Burgess, that this happened in Gibraltar during a friendly dinner in the restaurant of the Rock Hotel. The Russian word for 'unfortunate fate' happens to be *rok*.

Burgess was not a man who would recoil from talking about a terrorist act. Blood flowed like water in Spain, not far from the Rock, on both sides of the front. The Francoists were killing Republicans, the Republicans were killing Francoists, as well as Trotskyites, and syndicalists, and anarchists. But did Burgess know the meaning of the assignment or was it passed in a letter using the new cipher? And if he did know, did he understand that the attempt on Franco's life almost certainly meant death for Philby and perhaps for his entire group? I do not have the answers to these questions.

The times were harsh. Thousands of people were dying on the front in Spain, no less worthy of living than the young scion of a noble British family, one of the most promising Kremlin agents. Jordan, the hero of Hemingway's *For Whom the Bell Tolls*, and with him dozens, perhaps hundreds of people would have sacrificed themselves if they had the chance to kill Franco. All that is true; however, as the poet said, 'But still, but still . . .'

I did not have these documents while Kim was alive. I wanted to know Guy Burgess's reaction to the news he brought to Kim along with the cipher and £80, and Kim's reaction to the order – 'execute the special assignment'. It is too late to ask him, but the official documents, the correspondence between the residence and the Centre, give us food for thought.

I did not ask Philby if he had been given the assignment to kill the head of the Spanish rebels. He himself never mentioned it, although he did briefly touch on the subject. We were talking about a later period in his life, when he was being questioned in London, suspected of being the 'third man' with Donald Maclean and Guy Burgess after their defection to the USSR.

At that time (1951) Kim already knew that a responsible executive in Soviet military intelligence in the Netherlands, Walter Krivitsky, who had defected to the West in 1937 (he was found dead in a Washington hotel in 1941), had told investigator Jane Archer in England about a young British journalist that the GPU had sent to kill Franco. Krivitsky, as Philby told me, had learned about it in a casual conversation at the GPU. Soviet intelligence had learned about the interrogation and what Krivitsky had said from their agent Anthony Blunt, a friend of Kim's.

Krivitsky had no other information, did not know the Englishman's name, nor what he looked like, nor the newspaper he represented. But in the early fifties, knowing what Krivitsky had said in 1937, Kim was certain that his interrogator would ask him about it. So he had prepared an answer.

This was it: 'First of all, I met Franco several times [these meetings took place during his second trip to Spain], I stood two feet away from him and, as you see, did not try to kill him. Second, take a look at me. Do I look like a man who would be given an assignment like that?'

I would like to return to Gibraltar and the meeting of the two friends at the Rock.

In accordance with his agreement with the Soviets, Kim prepared and carried out the recruitment of Donald Maclean on his own. Maclean and Philby knew about each other's work for the Soviets. As for Guy Burgess, Maclean prepared him for recruitment, and he was recruited by someone from the GPU residence in London. Maclean, in keeping with the rules of the game, was not supposed to tell Burgess that Philby was working for Soviet intelligence. In our conversations, Kim, telling the story of Maclean's recruitment for the first time, nevertheless maintained that Guy Burgess did not know about Kim's work for Moscow until he met him in Gibraltar to give him the code, the money, and as we now know, the order to kill Franco.

It is clear that Philby did not tell the entire truth.

Generally Kim did not like to speak about which of his agent friends knew of the others' work for Soviet intelligence. When he did address the issue, his statements were contradictory. He told me the whole story of how he had recruited Maclean, but in a later interview with Phillip Knightley, he maintained that he did not know until the end of the Second World War that Maclean had been working for Soviet intelligence. He allegedly learned of Burgess's work only because the latter wrote to Kim about it.

I can explain Kim's incoherent and contradictory stories only by the Centre's anxiety over connections and information among agents. It was one of the worst problems in the relationship between the Centre and the London residence.

The Centre had been expressing concern for a long time that all three agents (at a minimum!) knew that the others were working for the Soviets. Moreover, they seemed to be discussing every assignment they got individually. Philby had to know about this concern, since appropriate 'work' was done with all three on this subject by the residence, demanding from them what the Centre wanted – total isolation of the agents from one another and total conspiracy about their ties with Moscow. Here is an excerpt from a report written in Moscow about the relationship between the three agents.

(Notes for the personal files of Sonny, Orphan and Mädchen. 7 March 1936)

From the group's files it is clear that all three agents know about one another as working for Soviet intelligence, even though the files show that only 'Orphan' and 'Mädchen' were supposed to know about each other.

In response to a question about it, Mar explained that allegedly 'Sonny' was given instructions to be the organiser of a group of British young men for espionage. On that basis, 'Sonny' called a meeting at his place, with himself, 'Orphan', and 'Mädchen' present, and he told them about the assignment. Later, when Mar took 'Orphan' on, he told him to check 'Mädchen''s connections in Cambridge and told 'Orphan' that he, Mar, was working alone and was dropping them. 'Orphan', instead of doing Mar's assignment, met 'Mädchen' in Cambridge and confessed about his ties and work with Mar. Mar assumes that 'Orphan' made the confession because he was under the influence of 'Mädchen'.

Why did not Philby tell the truth? For a simple reason, I think. He was still holding on in his disciplined way to the old version, the old cover story that had been developed for him five years earlier. Perhaps he had the welfare of his friends, his Soviet colleagues, in mind. He did not want to let down any them, even those who had died long ago.

It was three months since Kim had arrived in Spain. He had written several articles for various British publications. He had gathered a lot of excellent material for a big article that he planned to write back in London, where he would be free of the Franco censors, for a major newspaper, perhaps *The Times*.

His first trip was coming to an end. Kim returned home bypassing Portugal, through Europe. In Southampton Litzi met him. In Kim's absence Otto had maintained constant contact with her, and so she could tell her husband when he could meet his Soviet colleague.

Kim was worried before the meeting, awaiting an evaluation of his *real* work, as he considered it. Otto came at the appointed hour to the appointed place and said: 'You should be ashamed of yourself, young man, writing such boring letters to the lovely lady in Paris!

You bored Mlle Dupont so much that she stopped opening your letters and turned them over to us immediately.'

Kim picked up the joke. 'Just try writing a single interesting letter to the beautiful lady if every fifth word in it is "tank" or "cannon".'

'Well,' said Otto, now seriously, 'even though you didn't turn Mlle Dupont's head, the people who got your letters were pleased by their contents and thank you for your work.' And then he added: 'You managed to convey a lot of truly valuable information. Thank you.'

It was high praise, and Kim could not hide his pleasure. Then Otto informed him that he would soon be returning to Spain, but it would be better if he were not a neophyte journalist, but a special correspondent for a major newspaper. For that he needed a good and balanced article somewhere prominent. He had to finish the article they had planned before his departure. They then had to interest a serious and influential newspaper or a popular magazine in his work.

Kim's story about his first trip to Spain can be divided into two parts. He spoke eagerly and in great detail about the period before his meeting with Burgess in Gibraltar, and almost nothing about the period afterwards – even though it was after that meeting that the countdown to the moment of truth began.

The moment never did come. The special assignment approved by Stalin was never executed. This heralded trouble, big trouble. And not only for Kim Philby. Did he think about that? I do not know. We never spoke about it. He took to his grave the truth about the most important part of his first mission to Spain – the liquidation of the Caudillo.

7

'RESPECTFULLY YOURS, MAN . . .'

Soon the 'big article' was ready. It had to be published. Otto suggested asking Kim's father for help.

'Start at the very top,' his father said. 'Send it to *The Times*.'

Kim did. He was in luck once again. *The Times* received the article just when they did not have their own correspondent on Franco territory. Kim's father was true to his word, too. A few days later he called his son and said: 'I just ran into Barrington-Ward, the assistant editor of *The Times*, at my club. He told me that you've written a good article and they will be happy to print it. Besides which, they are prepared to send you to Spain as their special correspondent.'

'I'm very pleased to accept their offer. Please tell them that I accept.'

'I don't need your acceptance. I've already told them that you'll set off as you as you get the word,' Philby senior grumbled into the phone and hung up: he did not like excess talk.

Kim related the news to his Soviet colleague and soon set off to the *Times* offices.

At that time *The Times* was the authoritative newspaper for England and the world. It wore a mantle of world fame and glory from the last century. So its editors were quite unimpressed by twentieth-century newspaper innovations. They pretended not to notice them at all. At least, the newspaper made almost no concessions to populism. The format did not change. The articles written by staff were not signed but bylined simply 'from our own correspondent' or 'from our special correspondent'. The newspaper building was proudly old-fashioned and a move to other quarters would have been considered heresy. No attempts were made at modernisation inside, either. The heavy furniture had not been changed in decades. People had to walk upstairs: a lift was considered a symbol of new-fangled technology and they decided not to waste money on it.

Kim was introduced to the editor of the foreign section, Ralph

Deakin, his future boss. Deakin was a colourful figure. A fifty-year-old bachelor, rather pompous and a bit of a snob, he was basically a fine fellow. He greeted the young journalist warmly.

'We thank you for your article,' he said. 'You understand that we have great difficulties in getting any information at all from the Franco side. The war has been going on for ten months, and you are the fourth correspondent we are sending there . . . The first was almost killed in a car crash. The second was there only four months before retiring, he couldn't take the struggle with the censors. He did nothing but fight with them. Then we sent our Berlin correspondent. We sent him simply to have someone there. But he couldn't adjust, either. Your job is to make friends with the Spaniards. Do not worry if you do not get important information for the newspaper right away. Wait. I think that respectability and objectivity will bear good fruit. You will be met by our correspondent, the Berlin one. He hates Spain and spent all his money on telephone calls asking us to send him back to Berlin. I can imagine how happy he will be to see you.'

Kim liked his new boss's reasoning. His sensible advice suited his main objectives, too. Deakin suggested that he spend two or three weeks at the newspaper to see how they handle foreign news, read it, edit it, and write headlines. ('At *The Times* subs are an art!' Deakin pointed out.)

'We do everything a special way, differently from other newspapers,' Deakin announced proudly, 'and you must be familiar with it.'

Before leaving for Spain, Kim was introduced to the editor, Geoffrey Dawson. He was an active supporter of Chamberlain's policies and had close ties to him. He was one of the movers of the Munich agreement. As an editor, he was quite firm, even harsh. Kim liked such people if they had an intellect to match their character. Dawson definitely had such an intellect, even if – stupidly, in Kim's opinion – he was behind Munich.

Kim recalled those several weeks at the newspaper with pleasure: interesting work, interesting people. It was his first experience of editorial life. Since the orders from his friends were 'to enter the great arena of journalism', he tried as hard as he could and quickly mastered many tricks of the trade that he would need as a correspondent in Spain.

Another view of the same period and the same events can be found in a letter sent by Man, the Soviet resident in London, to the Centre in Moscow on 24 May 1937, to 'dear Comrade Alexei'.

> I want to report to you on the situation with 'Söhnchen'. What I want to report consists of two parts: the first is very sad, because it tells that he did not do anything, and the second, which took place in the last few days, is very good and compensates us for the first part. I'll start with the bad.
>
> 'Söhnchen' came back on 12 or 13 May in a very depressed state . . . He had not even managed to reach interesting objectives (Burgos and Salamanca). I do not know whether it was because his legalisation was not solid enough, or because the Italians suspected him of being a British spy, or for some other reason. But I think, rather sense from my conversations with him, that even if he had been able to get to Salamanca and even if he had been able to get close to F[ranco], which is a separate matter, because only two or three journalists have been able to do that so far, then he, despite his willingness, would not be able to do what was expected of him. For all his loyalty and willingness to sacrifice himself, he does not have the physical courage and other qualities necessary.
>
> That is the first half of my report . . .

So, the mission approved by Stalin himself turned out to be 'impossible'. The special assignment was not completed. The trust from above was unjustified. Someone would have to pay, not necessarily the failed executor of the special assignment. In those days the top levels did not punish the 'shooter' (especially those shooters like Philby who were not easy to replace). The anger would be turned against the people who did not ensure his success.

That is why Man felt it necessary to write an explanation to someone higher up the chain of command. That is why he wrote about Söhnchen in gloomy tones ('Söhnchen came back in a very depressed state'), which is probably closer to the truth than the almost humorous story Kim told about his first meeting with Otto in London upon his return. That is why Man uses the anecdotal approach ('I have good news and bad news; I'll start with the bad'), hoping to mollify his superior. That is why he defends Kim so diligently: 'only two or three have managed it'; they have spread rumours about 'Sonny' being a spy; his credentials were not adequate – for these and many other reasons he could not even get to Salamanca and Burgos, much less to General Franco; and even if he had got close to him, he couldn't have done what they wanted anyway.

In other words, Man, who might have been privately opposed to the special assignment from its inception and who might have guessed that it did not come from 'Comrade Alexei', tried to show his superiors that the assignment was not completed for objective reasons.

It is to Man's credit that he never tries to blame Söhnchen. The lack of physical courage is after all another objective reason: his father did not bring him up to be brave, we can't sue the father! He couples this with assurances about Kim Philby's loyalty, his readiness to sacrifice himself. However, a terrorist act requires not only readiness to sacrifice oneself, but readiness to shoot or stab another person. Philby was not capable of that. He was perfectly sincere when he said to the investigator many years later: 'Take a look at me. Do I look like a man who would be given an assignment like that?'

Man, naturally, understood that in defending the young man whom he liked he was also defending himself. But he was also supplying Comrade Alexei with arguments for his talk with his superiors, who would have him on the carpet. Would Man manage to deflect the blow from himself? Reading the letter, it is hard not to believe that Man – Teodor Stepanovich Maly – already knew that he could not avoid his fate.

Confirmation of that is in the letter's final lines. But let us return to the letter where we broke off. Man had promised the good news that would compensate for the bad.

When Söhnchen returned, I decided to use his trip to maximum benefit for us, in order to make up at least in part for the failure. I wanted:

A) to deepen his acquaintances in German and Germanophile circles here. I had in mind F. Putlitz, the German government and Germanophile circles here with which he had had ties (Poggot et al.). And also Haushofer (*Geopolitik*) in Berlin. I told him to write another article for *Geopolitik*.

B) or to act in accordance with our old plan, i.e., to make him a major journalist so that later he could get on a respectable, major newspaper as a correspondent in a country that interests us: Germany, Poland, Italy.

For that goal I wanted him to write a book about post-rebellion Spain, in a dispassionate spirit with a slight list in Franco's direction. That idea had to be dropped, because it would have taken a lot of time and better materials than he had.

I must tell you that, as you could tell from his long report, which I sent to you the last time, when he was in Spain I wrote to him to send a few articles from there to *The Times* and ask to represent them. He wrote a letter asking them to hire him for Spain but he did not send an article and *The Times* turned him down. When he returned, I suggested that he write an article in the right spirit for *The Times* and then for the *Daily Telegraph* and the *Evening Standard*, and at the same time mobilise the aid of his father, who is here at present, to help him get a job at one of these papers. This line led to success. He first wrote an article for *The Times* (which I append for you) and told his father about it, so that the latter could help place it.

The article either just suited the paper, or the father's protection helped, but after that he was offered a job at *The Times* officially and as the only correspondent on Franco territory, with an excellent salary, per diem, and other perquisites and a car. He is to leave for there around 3–4 June via Paris and Hendaye, where 'they want to talk with him' (could it be a representative of the Intelligence Service?)[1] – and before that he is to spend about ten days at the editorial offices of *The Times* to learn about the paper, especially since he will be on a salary. Besides which, he must learn to drive a car and continue here with his teacher of Spanish . . . I feel that the goal which we set for ourselves regarding 'Söhnchen', that is to make him a major journalist with the possibility, upon his return from Spain, to go to a country of interest for us, for instance, Germany or Poland, and there under cover for *The Times* to work for us, has been achieved.

And then comes this:

[1] Philby told me that when he was the *Times* correspondent, he gave material he had gathered that was not of 'newspaper interest' to the British Embassy in France, with the knowledge of the paper.

> I think it would not be wise to give him future assignments
> that he is incapable of accomplishing and thereby demoralis-
> ing him.

Let us note once more Man's nobility, as he obliquely but quite
unambivalently criticises the special assignment placed on the young
agent's shoulders. In that bloody, hot summer of 1937, when heads
fell like chestnuts from a tree in autumn, Man had to realise that such
a phrase, on the one hand, is justification for himself, but on the other
hand, brings him closer to the abyss. Any failure to obey orders – be
it a poorly tightened screw at a factory or a crack in the foundation of
a house – could be branded with the fateful word 'sabotage' and the
person responsible an 'enemy of the people'. After that, there usually
came four more words – 'highest measure of punishment', usually
given in abbreviation, 'VMN'. It stood for execution by shooting.
Only a man who knew that he was doomed would allow himself
to express doubt about orders that had come from above.

The next phrase in the letter confirms that Man knew his fate
was sealed:

> I will not be able to give him communications while he is in
> Spain, nor will I have the time or possibility to take care of it,
> in view of my departure from here that you have arranged.

Man had been called back to Moscow. He could not have doubted
the reason why. He did not escape along the way. Perhaps he still
had hopes of justice.

This letter was the penultimate document Man sent to the Centre.
It ended with words that sounded like a will:

> Therefore I propose letting him have this opportunity to go
> to Spain, which will not cost us any money. And upon his
> return to use him with his new abilities in a direction that suits
> us. The place should be Germany, Poland, Italy, or, at worst,
> Austria, Hungary, any country that you can add to this list.
> Respectfully yours, Man. 24 May 1937.

Man sent his last letter to the Centre fifteen days later, on 9
June 1937.

'Söhnchen' has worked at *The Times* for a while and tomorrow leaves via Paris and Hendaye for Spain. Communication will be maintained with him during his trips from Spain to Hendaye for telephone conversations with his editors. He has received instructions from the newspaper that information of a secret nature that he manages to gather should be sent from Hendaye to the Imperial and Foreign News Department of the newspaper. I enclose his note, dealing with the question of Spanish gold . . . Respectfully yours, Man.

In 1938 Man was killed.

On one of the pages in the archives, dealing with a later period, 1940, I found a list of all the service staff who controlled Philby until 1940. Man was among them. To the right of this codename was typewritten:

1936–1937. Resident of London residence, Maly Teodor Stepanovich. Archive file 9705. Sentenced in 1938. German spy.

A German spy. How simple.

8

THIRD IN A DUET

His apprenticeship at *The Times* completed, the new special correspondent Kim Philby headed for Spain, via Paris. From there he
took a train to Hendaye in the South of France near the border
with Spain.

There, the *Times* Berlin correspondent Kim was to replace was
waiting for him. James Holburn was indescribably happy to meet
him. He was a frank man who shared the story of his conflicts
in Spain and told Kim many important things about the course of
Franco's attack on Bilbao. These conversations, which were more
expedient to hold outside Spain, took two or three days, and then
the future and former *Times* correspondents headed south, beyond
the Pyrenees, to the city of Vitoria, where Franco's headquarters
for the attack on Bilbao were located. Holburn did not hold back
and gave Kim all his connections – with the censors, the postal
service that would send Kim's telegrams, and everyone else he had
met in the brief time he had been stationed in Spain. Once he had
fulfilled his duties, he shook Kim's hand and said, with mixed
feelings of sympathy and delight, 'Well, I don't envy you,' wished
him success, and left with a happy smile to represent *The Times* in
his beloved Berlin.

In leaving London, Kim had armed himself with recommendations from the British press, influential Spaniards, and also from his
friends in the German Embassy. One letter was written by the German press attaché with the unexpectedly Irish name Fitzrandolph,
and another by an embassy advisor, who had a not very common
name, von Bismarck. Since it was written and spoken with its title,
Prince von Bismarck (the advisor was a direct descendant of the great
German), it was impressive.

Both letters served Kim well. Their authors wrote that they had
known Philby for a long time, that he was reliable and honest.
Prince von Bismarck felt it necessary to say that even though his
friend was basically positive about the Third Reich, he was not a

total apologist for it and permitted himself healthy criticism of its shortcomings.

Kim and Otto received that phrase happily, because it did not suit their plans in the least for Kim to be known as a supporter of Germany or of Franco. If he were, he would get no more from the Germans than condescending patronage. But everyone had to treat seriously an objective correspondent.

In earning a consequential reputation, Kim was helped by his position at *The Times*. He sensed that right away. On his last trip even an ordinary censor would not deign to meet him. Now, the clerks met him with respect, which was in part the function of his different financial situation. The salary and expenses for travel, car, petrol and engine oil were all generously paid by *The Times*. As Kim put it, it gave him great pleasure to know that his main work could be done at the newspaper's expense, not Moscow's.

In Philby's file there is a report from the London residence (mid-1937) which includes a Russian translation of a report he sent over with Guy Burgess. 'Mädchen' retold what he had heard from his friend Harold Nicolson about *The Times*'s attitude towards their new correspondent.

> Nicolson told me that he had lunch with Dawson [editor of *The Times*] and Princess Bibesco. Dawson said the following. Many people think that we people at *The Times* are old-fashioned. But what other newspaper would dare to do what we have done? We have made a very young man one of the most important foreign correspondents on the basis of a single brilliant article. Then Dawson said they are pleased with K, that they have the highest opinion of him, that is he is marvellous man, and so on. K is very successful. He has made a name for himself very quickly.

Then the chief of the residence (no longer Man, who had been recalled to Moscow) reported:

> Vaize (Donald Maclean) told me that he read Lord Cranborne's statement announcing his talk with Duke of Alba. During this talk Alba reproached Cranborne for England's hostile position toward Franco, and Cranborne replied that it was a reaction to

Franco's bad attitude towards British journalists. Alba assured him that now that *The Times* had sent such a brilliant young journalist, the situation would change.

In other words, the editors of *The Times*, one of the most influential newspapers in the world and the authorities on the territory held by Franco, treated the Soviet spy Kim Philby with great respect. Both sides (not to mention the third – Moscow) had great hopes for him.

Quite different ones, of course.

After the fall of Bilbao Kim spent two or three days there, reporting on the situation. The Francoists enjoyed their victory and Kim often thought of the vagaries of fate that forced him to seek the good will of people he hated and to be hostile to those he loved, and for whose sake he had embarked on a double life.

A lull followed the campaign, and Kim decided to go to Salamanca, to get to the goal that he could not reach on his last sojourn. Franco and his headquarters were there. His credentials from *The Times* worked flawlessly.

Salamanca is a charming, ancient city, and Kim fell in love with it. Despite the fact that all the hotels, pensions and palaces were filled, he had his usual luck – he got a private room. He was lucky in another way, too. A week before his visit to Salamanca the head of Franco's press department was replaced. The former one, known for his intolerant hostility towards journalists, was transferred, and in his place they appointed the very man to whom Kim had given a letter of recommendation on his last trip, written by his father: the Marquis Merry del Val, Franco's representative in London.

The new press department head had been educated in England. He and Kim quickly developed good relations. Pablo Merry del Val taught Kim his favourite Basque game, *pelota*. The Soviet spy and the Spanish aristocrat played it twice a week and chatted about politics. Kim quickly discovered that his partner hated the Falange quietly but strongly. He had negative feelings about the Caudillo too, assuming, not without reason, that he would be in no hurry to restore the monarchy. They turned into a friendly and harmonious duet. There was a third man in this duet – an agent of the GPU, who naturally brought dissonance into the melody and turned the duet into a trio, but more about that later.

Good relations with a press department are important for a

journalist. Six weeks after his arrival in Spain Kim obtained an interview with Franco.

At last 'Sonny' was completing the first part of his assignment from Moscow the year before – to be in close proximity to Franco, within five feet of him. But now that mission had been removed from his shoulders. Perhaps Teodor Stepanovich Maly's arguments had swayed Moscow?

Philby and I, naturally, did not discuss this and I saw no more references to special assignments in the documents relating to Kim's second sojourn in Spain.

There were many other things for which Kim should have been grateful to his friend, the lover of *pelota*. It was he who made sure that the *Times* correspondent, and none other, regularly received mail from the press department and the latest bulletins on troop movements of the Franco forces. It goes without saying that the third participant in the 'duet' used this permission to sing his unhasty song.

Kim's affairs during his second stay in Spain were going very well. But on the eve of 1938 a tragic event occurred which almost ended his life.

In late November-early December 1937 the Republicans launched a serious attack on Teruel. For several weeks the battle raged with varying success. It was decided that a group of foreign correspondents accredited under Franco, including Philby, would go to the battle zone. They arrived on 29 December 1937, and the next day headed out in cars from Saragossa towards Teruel. About eight kilometres away, they stopped the cars and wandered around the hills, examining the former battlefields. By evening, they returned to Saragossa to write their first reports. Two days later, on the 31st, they went to the area again. Kim was in a car with the Associated Press correspondent Eddie Neil and Reuters' Dick Sheepshanks. A man from the press department drove. Three or four cars followed them. Once they arrived at the spot, the reporters all got out. But it was cold and they quickly returned to their cars to warm up. Kim was pleased, because he always tried to stay behind, after the others left, to ask the officers some special questions that did not need to be overheard.

When he got back to the car, he saw that two of his fellow travellers were already in it. It was a two-door car, which meant that to get in the back seat, you must move the front seat forward, squeeze in, and then pull the front seat back into place. The windows were fogged over in the cold, and Kim was sure that two of his colleagues were already in the back seat. So he opened the door on the driver's side and found that Eddie Neil was at the wheel and Sheepshanks was next to him in the passenger seat.

'What are you doing?' Kim asked.

'Opening a bottle of rum. Come on in and warm up.'

What ensued made Kim believe once and for all in his luck. It would have been logical to ask Eddie Neil to move and climb into the back seat behind him. But for some reason, Kim shut the door on Eddie's side, went round, and opened the door on Sheepshanks's side. He offered to get in the back and leave the front seat for Kim. But the finger of fate pointed at the back seat for Kim. Kim pushed Sheepshanks and his seat forward, and got in at the back behind him.

They talked. Suddenly the door on the driver's side was flung open and the passengers saw Bradish Johnson, the *Newsweek* correspondent. According to Kim, none of the men in the car liked him very much.

'May I join you?' he asked.

Eddie Neil replied: 'The important thing is to shut the door quickly. It doesn't matter if you end up inside or outside.'

Johnson chose to see an invitation in those words and got in the front behind the wheel, while Eddie Neil moved to the back next to Philby. The conversation lagged a bit, as happens when someone unwanted intrudes. Bradish sensed this, and offered a box of chocolates to Kim to smooth things over.

'I remember thinking,' Philby told me, 'that offering a piece of candy was not the best way for a big lug of a man to make friends at the front line. But I thanked him and reached for the box. There was an explosion.

'My first reaction was outrage at the American. "What the hell!" I thought. "What a stupid joke." I must have been thinking of all the practical jokes with exploding cigars and billiard balls I had seen in American films. I turned to my friends for support and saw the grey-white face of Eddie Neil, who opened his eyes for a second and shut them again. Johnson lay under the steering column without moving, and I saw a terrible wound on Sheepshanks's face – the eye socket was empty.

'It was only then that I realised that it had not been a joke, that it was a real explosion, and that I had to act. I jumped out of the car. About twenty metres away I saw a low wall, about a metre high, and a dozen soldiers hiding near it from the shells. I shouted, "*Venga, venga, ayuda!* Come here!" They were simple, uneducated soldiers, peasants. They obeyed. I told them to pull my friends out of the car, not knowing if they were alive or if they would be pulling out corpses. Two press officers ran up to us. Once of them shouted, "Hey, what happened to you?"

'What do you mean?" I asked, but looked down at my hands and chest, and saw that I was covered with blood. Face, hands, clothing. I said I was all right, but there were three heavily wounded men.

'"You're wounded too, you're covered in blood. Come with me," said one of the press officers.

'"What about my friends?"

'"My comrade will take care of them, and you will come to the hospital."

'He dragged me there. At the field hospital two young doctors quickly found the small wound on my head. I kept trying to tell the man who brought me that the blood wasn't mine but that of my poor colleagues, but it turned out to be from my head wound. The doctors gave me a shot, bandaged my head, and kept clucking over me, asking what had happened.

'I told them it was Republican fire. But I knew that it wasn't simply Republican fire, but Soviet shells. And I saw a good omen in the fact that it blew up next to me, but did not touch me, and that it had happened on the eve of my birthday – the next day, 1 January 1938, I turned twenty-six.

'The shell had exploded two or three metres from the car and the angle of the shrapnel flight was such that I was the only one in a protected position. The greatest blow came to poor Johnson from *Newsweek*, who was at the wheel, where I would have sat, and to the other two.

'Johnson died instantly. Sheepshanks and Neil were taken to the hospital. Sheepshanks died a few hours later, but Neil, when I came to see him in his room a few hours later, looked pretty good. He hadn't lost his sense of humour and in a weak voice he said: "I saw you get out of the car and take over the command of the army."

'But the next day Neil grew worse, gangrene set in, and he died a day later.

'This tragedy had been caused by a shell shot from our side.

I was the only one to survive, who had been spared. If I had sat in front at the wheel or on the passenger side, if I had got in behind the driver, I would be dead now, like all my friends.'

Philby returned to the story of the exploding shell several times. The vision of death, which came to his friends and which merely blew its icy breath on him, remained forever. He never stopped being amazed at the chain of small random accidents that had saved him.

'When I returned to Salamanca,' he said, recalling more details, 'I looked so picturesque that I later read somewhere that someone had put a woman's fur coat on me after the explosion. In fact I was wearing the coat my father had given me, which he had received from one of his Arab princes. It was a very amusing piece of tailoring: bright green fabric on the outside and bright red fox fur on the inside. It was rather outrageous, I grant you. But there was nothing better in the world for the cold Spanish winter.'

9

'A Decoration for Señor Philbot'

That tragic incident changed Philby's life in Spain; and, strangely enough, for the better.

One day Merry del Val called and said: 'Listen, try to stay put in your crummy hotel tomorrow afternoon.'

'Why?' Kim asked.

'They will come for you,' he said grimly. 'And take you away.'

'Where?'

'To Franco.'

'Why?' Kim still did not understand.

'Because he has decided to bestow a decoration upon you for your heroic actions on the front in the struggle against Communism.'

'You're joking!'

'No, I'm not. He got a very colourful description of your behaviour at the battlefield, and has decided to encourage you to further exploits.'

The next day at exactly twelve noon, Kim was in his hotel, as ordered, waiting. An hour passed, then two, and three, and four, and he had begun to think it was a joke when Merry del Val appeared at the palace at six and took Kim to another palace, the most famous in Burgos: home of Franco and his headquarters.

Kim's friend showed his documents and they were taken to a small room, where a junior officer was waiting for them. He led them to another room, where they waited by the door for a few minutes until it opened and they were taken into yet another room . . . They saw an amazing picture.

The room was not very large, probably thirty square metres. It was filled with a round table. There were military maps on the table. Poring over them were three small men. Kim recognised one of them as Franco, another was head of the general staff, Davil, and the third was Minister of Foreign Affairs, Di Fortano. All three were midget-sized and all three were looking for some point on the map, which had forced them to climb up on the table.

When the guests entered the room, the three gnomes were practically lying on the table, engrossed in their search. There was also a photographer in the room, but Kim did not notice him right away. He coughed discreetly, to let them know they were there. At last one of the short men noticed them, whispered something, and all three climbed down from the table, adjusted their cuffs, ties, jackets and trousers – all three were in uniform.

The junior officer accompanying Kim came up to the Generalissimo and handed him a small box. Franco opened it, took out the decoration, looked at it, came up to Kim, stood on tiptoe and pinned it on his chest.

The photographer's camera clicked.

After pinning on the decoration, Franco stood firmly on his feet and made a small speech.

When it was over, he looked at the recipient. Kim made a brief speech of thanks in English. Pablo Merry del Val translated it into Spanish. The photographer took pictures. The Caudillo went over to Kim once more and shook his hand. The ceremony was finished. Before Kim and Pablo reached the door, the three dwarfs were back on the table covered with military maps.

As far as Kim's life in Spain was concerned, this was a stunning sensation. Everyone knew that the Francoists did not like the English, and suddenly there was a young English journalist, the correspondent of Britain's most important newspaper, receiving a decoration from Franco personally. News of this event was in all the Spanish and English papers, and in many others around the world. Philby was famous. He received a telegram from Dawson at *The Times*, congratulating him, approving his work, and wishing him well in continuing in the same spirit.

'There were a lot of funny things connected with that decoration. I told you how in the spring of 1934 I had planned to join the British Communist Party. I went to its Central Committee in King Street, number 16. I was taken in to see William Gallagher. He asked me questions for a long time and then said that the Party had to test me. While it was testing me, I met my first Soviet colleague, as you know, and never saw Gallagher again.

'He had forgotten me completely in the more than three years that had passed since our meeting. When it became known that a British journalist had received the Order of the Red Cross for military valour from the hands of Franco himself, the outraged Gallagher, who was a Member of Parliament then, got up in the House of Commons and asked Anthony Eden, Foreign Secretary, if he had given permission to a certain Mr Philbot, the correspondent of *The Times*, to wear a decoration handed to him by the fascist Franco.

'Eden replied that the honourable Member must have in mind Mr Harold Philby from *The Times*. If so, since Mr Philby had not applied to the Foreign Office for permission to wear that decoration, the question should properly be put to someone else, if it were to be put at all.

'The whole business was quite curious. The decoration itself meant nothing to me, but it opened many doors that I had never dreamed would open for my main work. Once I had the decoration, I could ask any question at practically any government level, and get the most detailed and frank replies.'

Besides that occasion, Kim met Franco for four interviews. Some were more successful than others. But one interview he never forgot, because it was significant for him as an agent.

Kim asked Franco: 'Germany and Italy are helping you in the struggle against Madrid. When the war ends, they could ask for something in return. To what degree will you consider yourself dependent on the Germans and Italians after the war?'

Unexpectedly, Franco blew up and answered, barely controlling his anger: 'We are extremely grateful for all the help we have received and are receiving from the Germans and the Italians in this war. But if anyone thinks that with that help anyone has bought even one centimetre of our independent Spanish policy, he is cruelly mistaken. No one has acquired anything here.'

He spoke in a way that made Kim understand that this small but sturdy man, for reasons best known to himself, hated Hitler and Mussolini. Kim naturally told his Soviet colleague about this and recalled the episode frequently during the Second World War. The British had been worried that Franco would allow German troops to cross Spain and Gibraltar to Africa. Kim's instinct told him that Franco would not agree. Philby had no proof, but the memory of the uncontrolled rage pouring out of the little volcano allowed him to maintain that Franco would not give German troops access to Africa through Spain. Kim was right.

Back to the decoration. The British were very unpopular with

Franco then. The logic of the Francoists was this: we can understand the behaviour of the Russians, they were our enemy. But these English, who keep trumpeting that they are the defenders of Western democracy, are not willing to move a finger to help us! Aren't they traitors?

And then, from among these traitors, comes a British journalist from the main British newspaper, and the Generalissimo decorates him.

After the decoration, Kim's usually difficult task of gathering information for his main work became simple. The difficulty was to select the most important nuggets from the huge slabs of information he now got.

Here is a picture of Philby's trips after the decoration. He goes to the front, accompanied by an officer from the press office. They visit the commander, say a colonel. The press officer introduces him with the obligatory addition: 'This is the British journalist who received a decoration from Franco's hands.'

The colonel immediately says; 'Oh, please, sit down. Hey, boy, bring a bottle of wine!'

And they have a friendly, frank talk, and the question always comes up; can the colonel help the journalist in any way?

Philby starts asking about the course of the military operation, naturally – 'for the newspaper'. The colonel readily brings out the map, spreads it on the table, and shows him, explains, and draws for him. His trust is absolute. All Philby has to do is make an effort to remember the number of regiments and divisions, which shower down upon him as if the colonel were not speaking to a journalist but reporting to Franco. He has to be careful here. As a journalist, he could write down what he hears. But he tries to avoid writing to keep people from being cautious.

Kim's memory was not the best and he could not remember everything he was told. He resorted to a primitive method at first, excusing himself to go to the toilet and make notes there. Later, he found a more polite and effective method. When the maps were taken away and the colonel would ask what else he could do for the journalist, he would pause to think and then say: 'If your people could show me all that in person, I would be very grateful. I'm not very good with maps.'

The colonel would call in a captain, who would take him to the theatre they had just seen on the map. Thus he saw and heard everything twice: first on the map and then at the site. That was enough to remember the main parts.

On the way back, the officer would chatter incessantly, feeling obliged to amuse the *Times* correspondent throughout the trip. It interfered with his thinking, sorting what he had seen and heard. No matter how Philby tried to shut him up, he kept talking!

But as soon as he got out of the car and into the hotel room, Philby sat down at the desk and wrote everything down.

The bottom line is that Philby's best material on Spain came from Franco himself. He helped Philby the most in his work – his main work, and his newspaper work.

Moscow was pleased by the information coming from 'Sonny'. Things were going well at *The Times* as well. The newspaper praised him from time to time. All the random occurrences, happy accidents – including the Soviet shell – came together and put Philby in a situation in which, as he said, it was not hard to be effective. Not without reason, he was considered an expert on Spain. When Britain decided to recognise Franco, the new British Ambassador called Kim to the Embassy, sat him down in an armchair and said: 'Well, tell me about Spain. You know this country better than anyone.'

His knowledge of Spain was quite good then, better than that of many Spaniards, who should have known their country and its problems.

Before leaving for Spain the second time, Kim got letters of recommendation from the Germany Embassy in London and the names of people at the German Embassy in Spain. In time, the German contacts in Spain took on special weight because the divisions were increasing between Spain and Germany. This was a result of military and political problems. The greatest disagreements were on strategy and aviation tactics.

The Times was worried about one thing: could there be some compromise in Spain? The newspaper stood for peace in Europe at any cost. Dawson was known as one of the inspirers of the Munich agreement, and the editors did not want any unpleasantness in Spain, Portugal, France or Austria. In conversations with Franco, Kim touched on the theme several times, approaching from different sides. Could there be a compromise between him and the Republicans? Could peace be established in Spain based on guarantees from the great powers? Would he be interested, say, in the mediation of the League of Nations? In general, he brought up the question of compromise at every opportunity. But Franco always replied categorically:

'No, we will fight to the end, to the complete capitulation of the Republicans!' Knowing him, Kim had not expected any other reply. But it was important to show British readers, and the whole world, that fascism would not compromise.

In Salamanca, Kim lived in the Maldonado Palace. All it takes to turn a palace into an ordinary apartment house that immediately becomes neglected is to place locks on all the rooms and put a bed in each – two, three, even four beds. And you get a residential building. A palace quickly turns into dingy ordinariness, a building with no distinction. But how hard it is to perform the reverse – to turn a grey building, dirty and neglected, into a palace. Perhaps that is why all revolutions deal so handily with palaces and their owners, and have so many difficulties and so little success in making the lives of millions happier.

The German Embassy was also in a palace. Kim did not remember its name, he told me, but could visualise where it was very well: a traditional Spanish palace with a large patio. The Germans tried to make the house open and hospitable, and in the evenings after work it came alive, with many guests. Kim, naturally, was a frequent visitor.

First Secretary Stille was a friend. He helped Kim with many contacts. The German Ambassador was von Vautel at first. But as Philby told me, it was impossible to deal with him. He was quite stupid, an open Nazi, and a man who flouted diplomatic conventions. He supported fascism in Spain, persecuted the royalists, and did it in a brazen manner. He had many enemies.

He was soon replaced by another ambassador – von Stern. He was a professional diplomat and quickly changed the atmosphere at the Embassy. He tried not to interfere in the Francoists' internal affairs, to improve relations with Franco, and to repair the damage done by von Vautel.

By that time Germany's participation in the war on Franco's side was no longer a secret, so there was no point in trying to get classified information about it from Stern – everyone knew everything.

But Kim had made a rule for himself – before turning in his monthly or bimonthly report to his Soviet colleague (going to the South of France for that), he visited Stern for a chat. The man would not tell him anything particularly important, but Soviet intelligence needed the German Ambassador's personal view of the situation. It was important to cultivate him, just in case Kim ever needed first-hand information on something important.

He never noticed any surveillance. But the *Abwehr* was very active. The Germans were interested in the number and make-up of the international brigades and the interrogated prisoners of war. They gathered information both on military matters and on international Communism. They were tough interrogators, frequently using physical violence. The press corps knew this.

Every war is hell. But a war where the people for whom you are working are losing and the people against whom you have been sent to work are winning is a bitter one. This is what Philby was experiencing. The Italians, Germans and Francoists had concentrated enormous forces. The Republicans were suffering defeat after defeat. Their internal divisiveness made it worse: anarchists, syndicalists, Trotskyites . . . Kim listened with heavy heart to tales of the splintering among the Republicans, about the battles among parties and factions. It was hard to explain why internal hostility, 'purity of the ranks', was more important to them than the struggle with fascism. The Communists were killing Trotskyites, the Trotskyites were killing anarchists, and so on. They were killing one another. The Republicans could not have a united front. The Francoists laughed and said that they did not need to fight; The Republicans would destroy themselves.

'Yes, this was a real trial for me,' Philby recalled, 'one of the hardest periods of my life: a paradox. On the one hand I did a lot for my main work and achieved success as a journalist; on the other, I felt a terrible weight. I would reach a battlefield soon after the shooting had died down and see the corpses of my comrades. I did not know any of them, of course, but they were the people whose cause I served, to which I was devoted. In Spain I read about the death of two of my friends from Cambridge – Cornford and Hayden-Guest. The British press wrote all about it. Both were marvellous people, close to the Communist Party. Hayden-Guest was a brilliant intellectual, John Cornford a talented poet. I knew both well and loved them. Naturally, they died on the Republican side.'

'Thinking of you as a traitor?'

'Perhaps . . .'

'Did you ever visit the Republicans?'

'No, never. It was unjustified and too risky. And they would not have given me permission – I mean our Soviet friends.'

'I read in one book that you wrote a rather pro-German article about the bombing of Guernica, practically maintaining that the Republicans themselves destroyed the town. Is that so?'

'I know that Patrick Seale wrote about that. But he confused things. I did not write anything at all about Guernica. That was written by my predecessor at *The Times*, Holburn. And since we were both in Spain for about two months, Seale must have confused which of us wrote the article.'

'Hemingway once said that fascism does not leave works of art behind. It leaves only violence and blood. There is an enormous difference between what was written by journalists in Franco-held territory and journalists on the Republican side. It is enough to list a few names to make things clear. Writers like Hemingway, Mikhail Koltsov, Ilya Ehrenburg, Alberto Moravia and documentary film-makers Roman Karmen and Joris Ivens. Many cultural celebrities came to the Republicans. But Franco had almost no one who was celebrated or respected in the world.'

'That is true. But it was easier writing about that side. There was no ambivalence. The sympathy of the world was with the Republicans. On the Franco side things were very different. Even those among us who sincerely sympathised with the Francoists – and there were a few – were not very eager to show their sympathies – except for the lowest scum, who had nothing to lose, or for the fools. On the Franco side the journalists were quite a motley crew. The composition changed often, because so many could not stand the struggle with the censors and gave up. Others would come in their place. I had to watch my relations with my fellow reporters. It was dangerous to fall out with them, even with the power of *The Times* behind me. That is why no one could accuse me of direct ties with the Nazis or the Francoists. I behaved modestly, 'hands down', as the English say. And of course, I was always ready to share information with my colleagues. They appreciated that. So on the whole, I had good relations with the press. I don't remember making any enemies. The people I did not like I tried to avoid.

'There were very few journalists who supported Franco whole-heartedly. The only one I can recall was Bill Carney of *The New York Times*. He was Irish Catholic and supported Franco with militant conviction. The rest tried to be objective.

'On the Republican side Ernst de Caux represented the London *Times*. He was a well-informed correspondent who wrote well and objectively. He had lived in Spain for a long time and spent most of it among liberal circles. He had a deep sympathy for the Republicans, but he could not overlook what was happening among the anarchists, syndicalists, Trotskyites and Communists. He wrote the truth.

'You mentioned names. I think the only journalist with a prominent name whom I met on the Franco side was Randolph Churchill, son of Sir Winston. Quite a colourful figure. He reminded me of Guy Burgess, but on the other side politically. Noisy and always arguing with everyone.

'Once in San Sebastian we were in a crowded restaurant in the centre of town. He had been drinking and he began a loud tirade about the Spaniards being bad soldiers. People tried to quieten him down, but he would not listen. A captain in uniform came up to him, tapped him on the shoulder, and said, "It might interest you to know that many people in this restaurant speak English. Could you at least speak more quietly?"

'Churchill, furious, turned around. "And who the hell are you?"

'"I am a Spanish officer."

'Randolph stared at him, as if he were a red flag, and shouted, "Then why aren't you at the front, damn you, Spanish officer?"

'We tried to shut him up, and apologised to the Spaniard, explaining that our friend was not well. Somebody described this scene later in a book. He was the most famous journalist on Franco's side. But he was famous primarily because of his father.'

10

CAPRICCIO ESPAGNOL

Once I told Kim Philby that I had read a few pages in Patrick Seale's book about his friendship in Spain with the film actress Frances Doble. Was that true?

He raised his hands in mock horror.

'I think it would be better if I told you the story. It will be more accurate.'

He looked around at the door leading to the house where Rufina Ivanova was pottering. She rarely disturbed us, but she brought us a smile and welcome as well as coffee and napoleons that she baked herself, or tea which she prepared to the taste and preferences of her husband and treated very seriously. I realised fairly quickly that her pleasant visits covered up another mission – to see if her husband had lit a cigarette. Philby, before giving in to smoking, which he did from time to time, would display the caution and circumspection worthy of a good agent with a quick look at the door. In spy jargon this is 'losing your tail'. When he was certain that there was no surveillance, he lit up a cigarette and started the promised story.

In the summer of 1937, when Philby was already the *Times* correspondent, he ran into Dick Sheepshanks on the street.

'Listen,' Sheepshanks said. 'I've invited a very interesting woman to lunch today, Frances Doble, the actress. Would like to join us?'

Kim knew about Doble; he had seen her on stage several times and in some movies. She was a well-known actress, and very pretty. Kim accepted the invitation.

Unfortunately, it was one of the most miserable occasions of his life. He and Dick drank more than they should have, and began an argument about which part of Spain was the real Spain. The argument was mainly between the actress and the *Times* reporter, which was not the best way to spend lunch with a beautiful woman. He left the restaurant in a foul mood.

Then, as usual, came a chain of coincidences. Soon after lunch the press department invited the foreign correspondents to visit Saragossa, the site of recent battles. Kim was working on an article and did not go. He decided to go alone later, when he could ask the questions he needed to ask. So he stayed behind in Salamanca. One day, heading for the press centre, he ran into Frances Doble.

'Oh, it's you,' she said. 'I'm happy to see you. I have the feeling that all my friends have abandoned the city and me with it. They're all off somewhere.'

Since this conversation was beginning on a very different note from the one on which the last had ended, Kim took a chance and invited her to lunch. This time, they avoided politics. Lunch blended into dinner, which in Spain begins late, around ten, and ends long after midnight.

They met again and again. Three or four days later, the inevitable happened.

'There was a lot written about our affair, truth and lies,' Kim told me. 'I think she wrote something about it herself. I was really very involved with her. She was not only beautiful and smart, she was pleasant. She was born in Canada and had lived in England. She had ties with the British royal family and adored Spain. These two circumstances guaranteed her the respect and even the awe of many people. Everyone was her friend. Of course, she was a royalist, of the most right-wing kind. She supported Franco, but at the same time did not trust him, just like my friend Pablo Merry del Val, because of his ambivalence towards the monarchy. She had come to Spain simply because she loved the country. She was interested in it. Perhaps it had begun with purely romantic urges – Don Quixote, Careen, and so on. She came in May of 1937, I believe. She had given up the stage about two years earlier. She came for a week to see what was going on, and stayed for three years.'

'Because of you?'

'Perhaps in part.'

'Did she know about your work for the Soviets?'

'Not in the slightest. Naturally, I felt rather uncomfortable around her. Not because we parted – that was bound to happen, she was ten years older – but because without knowing it, she was a great help in my work. One evening with her at some reception, some party at an embassy, gave me loads of valuable ties and contacts. She opened doors for me that would have taken me years to open otherwise. But I would be lying if I said that I started the affair only for the sake of my work. She was a charming woman, and I was young and lonely.'

'You lived together?'

'Yes.'

'And what about your letters to "Mlle Dupont" in invisible ink?'

'I wrote them with ordinary developer. First I would write an ordinary letter with ordinary ink and then on the back I would write with liquid developer. Simply ironing the page with a warm iron or holding it near fire would make the "secret" lines appear. Every schoolboy knew that trick by then. I still don't know why the ordinary military censors in the mail car of the trains didn't get me! It probably never occurred to them that a serious spy could stoop to a jar of developer. The jar was always in the house and did not arouse any suspicions. After all, I was a reporter and I even had a camera. I kept the jar of developer next to it, along with film, and it blended right in. When it was time to write a letter, I thought it through first, had it ready in my mind, so that I could write it down in a half-hour or at most an hour. For that hour I found reasons for Frances to leave the house. I would send her to the hairdresser, or to get the groceries, or arranged for her to have coffee with a girlfriend – I got her out. She never once asked me why I kept a jar of developer in the house, especially since I replaced it with new ones from time to time.'

'Did she love you?'

'I hope so . . . I think so. A traditional writer would say that we had a "dizzy affair". And he would be right. The age difference did not bother us then. She had many habits to which I had to accustom myself. She was used to living on a higher plane. She had the opportunity and liked socialising with aristocratic and monarchist families, which, I admit, was not something I did daily.

'The only thing I could offer her then was my company, interesting friends, and my car. She loved riding around with me in the car.'

Rufina Ivanova came out on the terrace, bustling about. Everything was fine on the terrace. The cigarette smoke had dissipated long ago. Kim turned to his wife with a smile and asked, daringly: 'Right, Rufina?'

'What are you talking about?'

Kim thought and replied quite seriously: 'Life.'

'Then, right,' she said and added to me, 'everything that Kim says about life is absolutely true.'

We waited for her to finish her chores and leave the terrace. Then we continued.

'Whom did you meet in Spain thanks to Frances?'

'Many people, too many to enumerate. Why don't I tell you about someone she met through me? Although it wasn't very successful.'

I settled down to listen to another Philby short story.

In Spain Kim had met the head of the German *Abwehr*, von Osten, who worked under the name 'Don Julio'. The initiative for the meeting came from him, because he must have received information from the German Embassy that Philby was friendly towards Germany.

Kim did not remember exactly when and how they first met. It must have been at some reception at the German Embassy in Franco's territory. It was located in Salamanca at first and then was moved to Burgos. Kim was a fairly frequent visitor. The Germans opened their Embassy right after the famous phrase was heard on the radio – 'A cloudless sky over all of Spain' – and Franco began his rebellion. Of course, it had all been worked out earlier.

Kim visited the German Embassy twice a week. Everyone knew him there as a friend of Ribbentrop, which naturally helped him. Kim dropped the names of his high-placed German friends as much as possible. Besides Bismarck's letter, he also had one from Marshal Liberstein and several other good names. He did it as tactfully as possible, so as not to cause annoyance or envy, but persistently. The Germans are disciplined, and when they form the impression that you have good connections in the highest spheres, they trust you almost completely. So they welcomed Philby, especially since by then many young Englishmen went to Germany to make friends with the Nazis. They went to the Nuremberg rallies and brought Oswald Mosley along with them. He was already active in England. Perhaps the Germans saw the *Times* correspondent as just such an Englishman. They believed what they wanted to believe, and he did not disillusion them, even though he never did say that he supported National Socialism.

Kim's new acquaintance was not a diehard Nazi, more a German nationalist, a patriot of military background. He was a good friend although perhaps not the smartest man in the world. He liked eating well, drinking well, living well. When he invited Kim for lunch, Kim always accepted, not only because it would lead to information but because he knew that it would be a good lunch. He was frank in his conversations with Kim, often inviting him to his office at headquarters with maps on the walls covered in pins, and spoke very freely with Philby. Kim continued:

'The *Abwehr* of the time was characterised by a certain easy-going attitude toward secrecy. I saw it later, too, when I worked for the Intelligence Service during the war. We discovered then, for instance, that the Germans told their agents much more than was necessary. And in the *Abwehr* ciphers we found terrible lapses: they would give an agent's codename and his real name in the same telegram. So I do not think that the boastful von Osten was too much of an exception for the *Abwehr*. Be that as it may, he was extremely useful for me. I suspect that he wanted to use me. He invited me to his office and showed his maps, in order to astonish me with his knowledge, hoping that I would tell some important people in the Third Reich what a good man he was. In his eyes I was a chum of Ribbentrop and Hess. The poor fellow had no idea that my real friends lived in a very different place.

'It would be a mistake to assume that von Osten sat around without work, and merely gave expensive lunches and boasted in front of the *Times* correspondent. He worked hard, but there was a playboy in him who considered himself irresistible and made him stupid. As a result, many of his plans collapsed. As proof I will tell you this story. When I came back from a trip, I found Frances in a furious state. What was the matter? While I was away von Osten had invited her to lunch, spoke charmingly, fed her well, and then suggested a trip to France, where she would meet Republican émigrés from Spain, get to know them, and then tell him which of them could be useful to the *Abwehr*.

'"He asked me to be a spy!" she told me in outrage. "And he made another proposition, the one the stupidest men make over lunch to women. I thanked him for the fine meal and went home."'

'Did you have to break off with him, too?'

'To his credit, he apologised, said that he had been tipsy. I did not want to lose such a good contact.'

'How did you break up with Frances?'

'We did not become husband and wife. But I remembered those two years with gratitude to her. We parted by the will of fate, as they say. The big war began. I was in the north of France then, she was in the south. When Hitler invaded France, she went to Spain and from there to Portugal, while I went to England . . . After the start of the war, I wrote to her in Spain, but did not receive an answer. Turbulent years separated us and we could not find each other.'

'And you never saw her again?'

'I did. In January 1952, I think. I was living in England, I was suspected of ties with Maclean and Burgess. I was being interrogated, they considered me the "Third Man". Those were difficult times – we'll get to that. Suddenly, the telephone rang in my country house, where I was living then, and a woman's voice said, "This is an old friend whom you forgot long ago." I recognised her instantly. "Frances!"

'We met in London. Just a friendly meeting. I was married. She had not got my letter in Spain. She wrote to me in France from Portugal, asking me what to do. But I was gone by then and did not get her letter. She wrote another one to *The Times*, but I was no longer at the paper and did not get that letter, either. The mails were not very good in those days. Planes were shot down, ships sunk . . .'

'Did Litzi know about your affair with Frances?'

'Yes. It was around that time that we separated.'

'Did she work with you?'

'Yes, she knew about my work for Soviet intelligence. She was a good friend. When we moved to London from Austria and I started working for the KGB, she was a in a delicate situation. She had to break her ties with the Left, like me, stop working with the Communists, otherwise she would compromise me. But it was too great a sacrifice for her. I understood. We discussed the whole problem calmly and decided that we would have to separate. Not right away, but as soon as there was a reasonable opportunity.

'That came when I went to Spain.

'When I left, she moved to Paris. She spoke French very well. She got an apartment, started university in Grenoble, and was quite happy. When the war started, I knew she would be better off in England. If the Germans took Paris, she would not survive. At that time any movement between France and England – except for military movements – could be made only with permission from the

Ministry of Foreign Affairs. I wrote a letter requesting permission for her to return to England. Legally she was still my wife, and they had no reason to refuse. The ministry gave its approval, and she moved back to London.

'Litzi was back in England and we still lived apart. We did not divorce officially until 1946. She married a German émigré and lived in East Germany, in Berlin. Fifteen years ago we exchanged greetings through a friend of hers who came to Moscow. I don't know if she's still alive, but it's probable that she is. It is not such an unusual age for a woman. She has a daughter who has been to Moscow several times, but I haven't seen her.'

What role in that triangle was played by 'Mlle Dupont', to whom Kim regularly sent 'love letters'? The level of developer in the jar dropped every week. He had to restock several times. But his 'love' was unrequited and gradually the Parisian lady began to irritate him. It got harder and harder to compose the 'legal' part of the letter. He did not want to seem a total idiot, even to the censors. And there was a danger: imagine an alert censor, who compared the necessarily simplistic letters with the articles in *The Times* – well, perhaps not a censor (few are subtle, the work leaves its imprint), but someone from Franco's counter-intelligence. That could have happened? Philby worried about it. But try as he could, he had trouble writing logical letters, and he grew more and more irritated with his addressee. Slowly she changed in his mind from a pretty young woman to someone grey and faceless. He began calling her 'Aunt Dupont' or just 'auntie' to himself. Of course, writing to an aunt, and an old maid (mademoiselle) at that, was just as boring as writing to the young beauty. 'Sonny' was clearly not made for platonic love.

It is amazing that this epistolary affair did not end tragically. There were at least two reasons for potential failure: the secret writing that even in those days was considered anachronistic; and the address where the letters were sent.

'Are you going to keep teasing me?' I asked Kim.

'You are a playwright, I am a journalist. Let's keep up the suspense to the end,' he replied with a laugh. 'I only learned much later what that address represented, after the war. When we get there, I'll reveal the secret.'

11

BIG BILL

During his second sojourn in Spain, Kim Philby regularly met his Soviet controller. For that he travelled to the South of France. Many journalists made such trips to rest from war life and to contact their newspapers without interference or to pass on material under a different name, one the Franco censors would not allow. Philby also made these trips, to talk with his editors, to deal with the British Embassy in France, or for rest and recreation. *The Times* always knew about his movements; he received a letter of permission from the editors for each trip. In France there existed a famous train, which travelled between Bayonne at the western end of the Franco-Spanish border and Narbonne at the eastern end. The train left Bayonne in the evening and returned the following morning, and it was celebrated for two reasons: the passengers could enjoy the Pyrenees, and the glorious cuisine. The train was very popular.

Before his second departure to Spain, Philby was told that he would now have regular meetings with his Soviet contacts. The first would take place rather quickly, just two or three weeks after his arrival, as Kim remembered it, on the first Sunday in June. He had to take the train from Bayonne to Narbonne and meet the man there.

Kim already knew him; they had met several times in London. But he did not know his real name. It was Alexander Orlov. Kim knew him as 'Big Bill'. Kim felt he needed to tell me about him in greater detail.

Before him, Kim had had two controllers, Otto and Theo. He felt that both were very good men who had taught him a lot. Otto introduced him to 'Big Bill', in the very same park where he had met Otto. Kim sensed right away – and was told – that Big Bill represented Moscow, the OGPU, directly. He could see it in his appearance and could feel his inner strength. To Kim, he was the Messiah who had come from the Promised Land. That does not mean that he thought any less of Otto or Theo. But they had come from Austria and Hungary respectively. Now he was dealing with a real Soviet, and he treated him like a hero. 'If I were to put it in political terms,' Philby said, 'Theo and Otto were Communists, but Big Bill was a Bolshevik.'

The 'Bolshevik' was very polite and charming, but Kim immediately sensed his will, cruelty and determination. He spoke decent German and weaker English, so they usually conversed in German. He treated Kim paternally, which emphasised his power. 'I do not remember whether he told me anything or taught me anything that I did not already know from Otto and Theo. But there was an aura about him. He was full of energy and the desire to act constantly. It was an expression of his desperately romantic attitude towards his profession.'

He was introduced to Big Bill in 1934 and until 1936 saw him no more than a dozen times in London. Their meetings came to an end in late 1936. Kim's understanding was that he had gone to Madrid to head the intelligence in Republican Spain. In the few weeks Kim spent in England between his two stints in Spain, he met only Otto. He instructed Kim in his coming meetings with Big Bill. They set up a schedule, once a month in southern France. At every meeting Kim was to give his contact a written report and an oral one. He would ask questions and give Kim instructions. Philby was very happy: the three months in Spain without contacts showed how hard it was to work alone.

Big Bill was probably still in his thirties then. He was a complicated man – a little of everything. But openness, sincerity and frankness predominated, even though Kim found him cruder than Otto and Theo. Once, when he had handed in his written report and given his oral explanation, Orlov read it, heard him out, and said: 'You know, when I met you in London the first time, I thought nothing would come of you. But I see I was mistaken. You're a good man.'

There was a rendezvous with him in Perpignan, in France. They both had come there from Spain, but Orlov had been on the other side, the Republican side. They were to meet at the railway-station square. Kim stood there, waiting. Suddenly a big car pulled up and Big Bill got out. He was dressed strangely – his raincoat was bulging on one side and the bottom of the coat was rolled up. They greeted each other, and Kim asked: 'What's the matter?'

'Why?'

'Your coat seems odd.'

'You noticed?'

'Of course. Anyone would.'

He spat in annoyance. 'Damn it!' And then he opened his coat proudly. 'Look! Isn't it nice?'

Kim saw a huge automatic rifle tied to his side. Big Bill patted it gently and then pulled the coat over it once more.

'Wait here, I'll be back soon.' He got in the car and drove off.

He returned half an hour later, got out of the car, walked around Kim and then asked: 'Well, is everything normal now?'

'Yes.'

'Too bad I had to leave it off. What a gun!'

He was a typical operative. Kim never asked him questions, but gathered a few things from the hints Orlov dropped – for instance, that he had played an active part in suppressing the Trotskyite organisations in Spain. He even told Kim that once in Madrid, on a hot day, he was resting on his bed, wearing only his underwear. A semi-automatic rifle was next to him. Suddenly two men burst into the room. Orlov picked up the semi-automatic and without asking any questions, killed both. He later learned that they had been sent to kill *him*. That's the way he was. Yet he was warm and sensitive. He valued courage. When Kim met him in January 1938, after the shell had exploded and he had told him all about it, Orlov exclaimed: 'Oh, I'll tell my daughter. She'll think you're the greatest hero in the world!'

He adored his wife and daughter. They lived in the South of France. The intelligence service in those days sometimes followed a patriarchal lifestyle – the head of the family had his wife and daughter with him even as he did his not very legal business. A lot seems funny now, hard to explain, a lot seems tragic and base, but a lot seems sacred.

At one of their regular meetings, Orlov suddenly asked Kim: 'Could you get leave from the newspaper for ten days or so?'

Kim said that he had been working long enough to be able to ask for time off. But why did he need the vacation?

Orlov casually replied: 'Need to pop over to Japan.'

Kim asked no more questions. They agreed how it would be done. Kim called the editor of the foreign desk of *The Times* from St-Jean-de-Luz and said that he had run into a friend who was going to Japan and had invited Kim to spend a few days there with him at his expense. Kim told the astonished editor that his reporter had a rare opportunity to see the Far East.

There was a pause at the other end of the line and then the editor got hold of himself and rather drily suggested weighing everything before taking a decision.

Kim told Orlov that the editor did not seem very happy about the proposed trip. But Orlov was determined: the trip was very important, he had to get the paper to agree. A second phone call got the editor to agree reluctantly, and he added that the whole project seemed strange to him.

Kim himself wanted to know why he was being sent to Japan. But one did not ask such questions. Orlov seemed very confident and Kim was sure that he knew what he was doing. They agreed that Kim would go back to Spain and wait for the signal to leave.

But a week passed, then another, then a month. Philby sat and waited, not going out on assignments, but no signal came from Orlov. At last the time came for their next meeting. Orlov did not bring up Japan. Kim asked what had happened. Orlov replied in his casual way: 'Oh, you mean Japan? I think it's off.' Without any explanations.

This put *The Times* correspondent in a tricky situation with his editors. He had not done any of his newspaper's assignments for a month, refusing to travel. Now the trip was off. How could he explain that to the editors? He looked irresponsible.

'And was it Orlov who was irresponsible?' I asked.

Kim replied cautiously: 'I don't know. It wasn't like him. Maybe something had not worked right.'

'But what could have been in the works? A meeting with Sorge, perhaps?'

'I thought about it, much later, when I learned of the existence of Richard Sorge. Perhaps they were planning to have me work with him. Of course, I was a total ignoramus in questions of Japan or the Far East, but I spoke German well, and I could have been of help to him. But these are just conjectures. In fact I know nothing about it. I tried to smooth things over at *The Times*, but subsequently, when the clouds started gathering above me and the questioning began, I always worried that this might come up and I would be in a difficult situation. Why was I planning to go to Japan? Who was the "friend" who had invited me? His name? Address? And so on. What could I have said? That we had lost touch? I should remember his name at least. Fortunately, my interrogators did not know or had forgotten about my planned trip.'

'Did you sense that Orlov could defect to the West?'

'No. I told you, for me he was the Messiah.'

'When did you learn of his defection?'

'Much later, during the war. Quite accidentally. And I was stunned. I could not believe that a real Bolshevik – and that's how I saw him – could betray . . . But he didn't betray. He never said a word in America about me or the others in the group. He was called to the Senate, he was interrogated by the FBI. He knew all of us, and others about whom we knew nothing.'

'How do you explain that?'

'People leave for various reasons. I am certain that he left out of fear that things would be bad for him when he returned to Moscow. I can't rule out that he had his reasons for thinking that. But he was no traitor. Leaving for the States, he must have decided to give them a certain amount of information, but far from everything that he knew. If he sold something for a sum of money or other benefits, why did he have to sell anything else? I know that in Russian "to sell" and "to betray" are very similar, but there is a difference. He must have drawn a line known only to himself between the two concepts and kept to it stringently.'

'When you later worked in Washington, were you afraid that you might bump into him? Say, in a café. Or in the corridors of the CIA. It could have happened at any time, couldn't it?'

'It could have.'

'What would you have done?'

'I think I would have walked past, without noticing him.'

'And he?'

'I think he would have done the same.'

'Another question. You did not know about Orlov's defection and you did not feel any danger from him. But the Centre knew that he had left, that the whole network of agents in England and Spain, and perhaps of all Western Europe, was in his memory. According to the rules, the Centre should have got you out of possible danger. But it did not do that. Moreover, you were not even informed of Orlov's departure, you were not warned to be careful, you were not given any advice or instructions. How do you explain that?'

'Orlov wrote a letter to Stalin with a promise not to expose anyone if Stalin did not harm his relatives still in the USSR.'

'How could Stalin with all his suspicions believe him?'

'You are asking me a question I cannot possibly answer.'

'Well, how about this: Orlov was a tricky game to get a Soviet agent inside America's secret service.'

'What for?'

'Well, for disinformation. To shuffle the deck, cover up traces, communications – to confuse things.'

'That was a theory for a while among specialists.'

'I'm basing it on a fairly simply idea. Walter Krivitsky, the OGPU agent, defected a year before Orlov, in Holland. In 1941 he was found shot dead in his hotel room in Washington. We can assume that the OGPU finished him off.[1] But Orlov was not harmed.'

'Krivitsky, unlike Orlov, betrayed many people, including me. It did not have tragic consequences for me, since he did not know my name or the newspaper where I worked. But if he had, he would have betrayed me totally. As for Orlov, here is what I can tell you. When I was already in Moscow, I guess in the mid-seventies, a man high up in the KGB, someone I knew well, said to me: "Kim, you were close to Orlov. What if we asked you to write him a letter in very friendly tones? About how you remember him well and esteem him highly, that you wish him all the best and so on . . . We will find a way to get it to him." I replied that I would write such a letter. But they never approached me about it again. I don't know what happened. Then, a few years later, I heard that Orlov was dead.'

According to the documents, when Philby came to Spain for the second time in the summer of 1937, he did not have a meeting with Orlov right away. His first contacts with the Centre were apparently through 'Pierre' (Ozolin-Haskin, from the French residence, later shot in Moscow). 'Pierre' would take the materials from Kim and bring them to Paris, from where they would be sent on to Madrid (sometimes via Moscow). The information Kim delivered would be obsolete by the time it reached its destination. Besides which, 'Pierre', coming from Paris, could not give Kim adequate instructions on what information Madrid needed. So in September, the Centre decided that it would be better to have a direct link between Kim and Madrid. For that they decided on the version that 'Man in his time had agreed upon with "Söhnchen"', as it said in the document. 'Stefan' would inform Kim of the date of their coming meeting. It had been arranged for them to meet in the lobby or café of the Miramar Hotel in Biarritz at noon. There 'Stefan' would tell Kim

---

[1] *The American police verdict was suicide and recent KGB statements have supported this. (PK)*

that he was going to be working with 'Big Bill'.

It was an operation like any other, nothing special about it. But the words 'Man in his time' are pertinent.

Man was being interrogated assiduously at the Lubyanka, a confession of collaboration with German espionage being beaten out of him, but the documents still referred to his plans with one of Moscow's most valuable agents. But the reference pointedly said 'in his time'. September 1937 was no longer his time.

Life in the USSR was full of contradictions. Outstanding scientists, condemned to death for 'espionage on behalf of. . . (fill in the blank)', were working in the *sharashkas*, closed scientific centre–prison camps. Poland was a favourite country in the court sentences. Germany, England and Japan followed. Poland had been a traditional enemy and the White Guards were concentrated in Poland. Moscow seemed to think that every Pole was a spy. Some scientists condemned for 'sabotage' would be shot while others, convicted of the same crimes, would later receive the Stalin Prize, be released, and showered with respect.

A few years later, when Hitler invaded the USSR, some of the generals and marshals arrested for 'espionage for Germany in order to overthrow Soviet power' would be released, no matter what they had been sentenced to. But others, with shorter sentences, would be executed a few months after Hitler's invasion. (Seeing General Rokossovsky after his sudden release from prison, Stalin asked: 'Why haven't I seen you for so long? Where have you been?' The general stood to attention and replied that he had been sentenced to prison and had been in the camps. Stalin puffed on his pipe, shook his head, and commented: 'A fine time to be inside.' And went on to business.)

Mikhail Koltsov, the Soviet Union's most popular journalist, who spent three years in Spain and wrote one of the best books about the Civil War, *Spanish Diary*, was a man of great courage, practically a national hero in the USSR. He served in Spain both as a correspondent for *Pravda* and as a political emissary for the Kremlin. He was arrested, convicted as a spy, and shot. His brother, Boris Efimov, whose cartoon 'In Yezhov's gloves' was published in *Izvestia* in 1937, remained popular and in the good graces of the authorities all his life. Ilya Ehrenburg survived, as he explained, only thanks to 'a lucky ticket in the bloody lottery'. There was no logical explanation as to who would be shot and who would survive.

Yezhov, who replaced Yagoda as head of the secret police, tripled the number of arrests and executions, following Stalin's orders, and created 'execution zones' around Moscow, where bodies were buried in ravines. A year later he was sacked and shot. He was replaced by Lavrenti Beria, who used the excuse of combating unjustified repressions to start a new wave of repressions against those who had initiated the earlier ones.

Offices at the Lubyanka kept emptying, on every floor, not just the executive one. New people came to fill the offices – young, happy, confident in the rightness of their being there. They received high titles and positions. The authorities did not skimp on buying souls and loyalty. A young man with two pips on his uniform could be promoted in a few days to wearing rhomboids, the equivalent of the old general's rank, and move into an office that still retained the smoke of the favourite tobacco of the previous tenant (a Polish spy, of course). He would have even greater love for the Leader, be ready to die for him, and desperately chase away the thought that his fate might be the same as his predecessor's. He would be happy.

It is useless trying to find logic in that satanic whirlwind. We can only seek tendencies.

I have mentioned the list of people who controlled Kim Philby, that is, those who met him regularly, passed on instructions, and received information. Some are still alive. But of those who headed residences, who held responsible posts, who were noticeable, I did not find one who lived through the slaughter of 1937–1939.

In Philby's archive file I found a list of people who had dealt with him in any capacity in local regions. The list, compiled in early 1940, is very cursory and incomplete.

1. 'Mar' – real surname Reif. Resident of OGPU in London in 1934–36. Shot. German and Polish spy.
2. 'Man' – Maly Teodor Stepanovich. Resident of OGPU in London in 1936–37. Shot in 1938. German spy.
3. 'Kap' – Gorsky. Resident of OGPU in——in——. Shot. Polish spy.
4. 'Paul' ('Pierre') – Ozolin-Haskin. Resident of OGPU in——in——. Shot. German spy.
6. 'Swede' – Orlov (Nikolsky) – traitor.

But let us return to our hero, whom Stefan (Man was back in Moscow by then) was supposed to meet and hand over to Orlov.

It was not easy to contact the *Times* correspondent in Salamanca. How was he supposed to call him out to France, how to agree on a meeting? Stefan looked for a solution and found the only possible way – working through Kim's legal wife, Litzi.

Soon after getting orders to pass 'Söhnchen' to Orlov, Stefan informed Moscow that he had sent Litzi, who had just returned from holiday, to *The Times*. She told them that she would like to see her husband. The editors telegraphed their correspondent to come to the border for a meeting. There was nothing unlikely about it. Stefan reported that he would go to the border at the same time as Litzi, that he would learn the date of the meeting in a day or two and tell 'Swede' about it, so that he would arrive at the border from the other side. 'The help of the newspaper and "Söhnchen"'s wife is the only way to get into contact with him,' Stefan wrote. He added: 'He is separated from his wife. He has a Spanish woman. The wife knows about it, but this circumstance does not complicate things.'

Stefan naturally knew that Kim had separated from Litzi (but not officially divorced her). Disciplined 'Sonny' kept his Soviet contact informed of changes in his personal life and, judging from other documents, asked for his advice and took it in this tangled love affair. I do not know if the residence asked permission from the Centre for its agent's romance with Frances. I can imagine the Centre's doubts: what if agent 'Mary' becomes jealous of her husband, agent 'Sonny'? And will the jealousy ruin the good work of the family spy cell? Apparently the residence decided that 'Mary' would not let them down and would not give in to her emotions.

'Mary' went on working for them, helping the residence when it lost contact with 'Sonny'. A wife looking for her husband, wanting to see him – what could be more natural? And who would suspect that the wife is moved not by love but by orders received from the capital of a country far to the east?

The episode of the trip to Japan does not look as simple in the documents as Philby had described it. But his supposition was correct: the trip was not Orlov's initiative. The assignment came from the Centre, and it was a categorical assignment. Big Bill apparently had no idea of its goal. He and Kim (Orlov stressed Kim's initiative here) developed a rather clever plan.

'Söhnchen' tells his circle that a good friend or friend of his father has proposed accompanying him to Tokyo and that he has decided to take up the offer of a free and interesting trip. The non-existent 'friend' would be travelling with his valet. An agent known as 'N6' will be Kim's valet. But 'N6' must not know that Philby is also an OGPU agent. So 'Söhnchen' will advertise for a valet in the newspaper and Orlov would send 'N6' to be hired without telling him that 'Söhnchen' is 'one of us'.

But Orlov was very concerned that the whole idea of the trip and its postponement were hurting Philby with his editors. '"Söhnchen" is not budging from the fascist capital, waiting for a very urgent reply from me: is he going, is the trip delayed, or completely off?' Orlov wrote to Moscow. 'In waiting for the reply, he cannot go to the front and do his assignments for the paper.'

Orlov's letter is interesting for many reasons. But the most interesting part is the date. Orlov signed the letter on 10 July 1938. Two days later, on 12 July, he broke with the Stalinist regime and defected to the West. But even on the even of his departure he worried about the fate and good name of his agent, Kim Philby.

The security of an agent was not always the concern of his mentors at the KGB. An example of this is the address to which 'Söhnchen' sent his secret letters to Mlle Dupont. Philby promised more than once to astonish me with the story, but he kept putting it off, keeping up the dramatic suspense. He told me about it, as promised, when the time came, that is, when our conversation had reached his work after the end of the Second World War. But here it is anyway.

Soon after the victory over Germany, Philby's work (he was by then head of SIS's Section 9) brought him to Paris and he had the nostalgic idea of finding the house of his 'lover'. In a spare moment, he went to the address he had written to so many times and which he knew by heart. According to Kim, he was prepared for almost anything – a luxurious mansion, an apartment building, a cellar in a old house, an artist's garret, a florist's shop, bakery, law office, bomb shelter, prison, bordello – anything; but not what he found.

The house to which he had been writing his top-secret letters was the USSR Embassy in France.

If any of the intelligence services in Spain – Francoist, German, Italian – or any of the censors had taken an interest in the address to which the *Times* correspondent sent his strange letters so regularly, Moscow's agent 'Söhnchen' would have ceased to exist.

He told me about it with a laugh: it was 1987. But I can imagine his feelings four decades earlier as he strolled along rue de Grenelle in Paris.

12

'WHO IS THIS "SONNY", ANYWAY?'

The archival documents – letters, cipher telegrams, notations, directives and so on, dealing with the period of our story, particularly from the middle of 1938 – begin to betray anxiety, if not bewilderment. All the names on the papers are different now, both recipients and senders. Even the signature to which I had grown accustomed, following the word 'Correct', certifying that the document is an original or an accurate copy, was different.

The new people who moved into the old offices at the Lubyanka in Moscow and in the residences abroad initiated a universal clean-up, demanding reports, clarifications and checks. The way it is always done in Russia – starting from scratch.

Who is this 'Söhnchen'? An aristocrat? From Cambridge? Is he a decoy? Who recruited him, Mar? Who is Mar? An enemy of the people? Executed? Check Söhnchen! Three times over! Four times!

The residence in Paris received a letter (1938, No. 15) with a demand to report urgently on the whereabouts of the source 'Sonny'. There is no communication with him, he has not reported in a long time. (Note that they call Kim by his old pseudonym, even though he had been 'Söhnchen', not 'Sonny', for quite a while.) In this letter the Centre suggested getting in touch with his wife, who might know where he is.

Fin, the new resident in Paris, replied in confusion that 'Sonny' was not known to the residence. He asked to be informed who he was. If they were referring to the wife of the source called 'Snag', he felt it better not to deal with her, she was 'alien to us'. Moreover, there was no agreed procedure between her and the residence.

On Fin's typed letter there is a notation made in ink, in Moscow: 'Comrade Bazarov, explain to Fin.' Bazarov explained who 'Sonny' and his wife were. But Fin still did not want the responsibility of meeting the unknown wife of an unknown source. Today Bazarov explained one thing, tomorrow the General Procurator of the USSR would explain something quite different. It was more prudent to say no.

It was only towards the end of September 1938 that the Centre determined the location of the prodigal 'Sonny'. He wasn't 'Sonny', they learned, but 'Söhnchen', and he had been sent to Spain by his newspaper. But there was no news from him, even though he was supposed to write regularly every two weeks. They had also found 'Mary', but she had no news from him either.

This letter, signed by 'Pierre' ('Fin' was gone, his caution had not saved him; he was replaced by 'Pierre', aka 'Paul', aka Ozolin-Khaskin) added fuel to the fire of confusion at the Centre. The Centre asked: when, where and under what circumstances did Pierre last see 'Söhnchen'? Who were all these people, 'Söhnchen', and his wife who is not his wife, and his strange friends, the 'interns', with their filthy homosexuality? Wasn't it suspicious that they had all been recruited by the London residence, which had been headed by enemies of the people and that the last person to work with them had been Alexander Orlov, aka 'Swede', aka 'Nikolsky', the traitor who defected to the West?

That may be why the people at the Lubyanka asked for references on the 'interns' from Paris and not London. The Centre did not know that 'Pierre' would soon be declared an enemy of the people and executed – as would many of the new people who had just moved into a prestigious Lubyanka position, since the purges had not yet scraped out all the layers there.

The bloody house was in an uproar. Communications were interrupted. No one trusted anyone. There were enemies of the people all around.

But Pierre was still alive. He had the opportunity to inform the Centre from Paris about the group of British 'interns' working for Soviet intelligence and the role of source 'Söhnchen'. His explanation is tinged with sarcasm at the expense of the Centre.

(From 'Pierre's letter of 25 December 1938)
The group consists of several sources, who are well known to you and therefore I will not dwell on them . . . [How brazen! Certainly 'Pierre' knew that the new people at the OGPU knew very little about the group, otherwise they would not have asked for information. But he would pay for his mockery later.] The group's composition:

1. 'Söhnchen'. You have the most detailed information on him and his work [more sarcasm]. The information we receive through him is very interesting, but it must be noted that his moods are subject to intense swings. For instance, recently, when the Czech conflict increased, he was in a great panic, demanding a passport and so on, but now he has calmed down. He is very proud of his fame as a journalist and so he reports to us less frequently and with less material than he could. I have not seen him personally in over two months, and so I will give you more details after our next meeting. 'V' knows him very well.

2. 'Mary'. 'Söhnchen'''s wife. You know about her too. [Really?] 'V' knows her, too. She works as a messenger. She is totally aware of the work of 'Söhnchen', 'Mädchen' (despite the fact that I meet 'Mädchen' separately), and many other people, whom she knows from her old work in England.

But 'Pierre'''s brief, sarcastic notation was not enough for the Centre. They needed to know what the so-called 'Sonny' was reporting to them. How valuable was his information? What was his morality like? His true political views? How much money was he getting? (That was an important issue: you can tell a lot about a man from the way he treats money.) They needed as many letters from various people as they could get so that the reports could be compared. This was the demand of the Centre. The reports started coming in to Moscow:

'Söhnchen' is an Englishman, correspondent of the English newspaper, *The Times*, in fascist Spain, the only foreign correspondent personally decorated by Franco. His father is an important British scholar of the Near East, allegedly works in the Near East for the Intelligence Service.

'Söhnchen' seems like a reasonable, morally stable person who is close to us politically. He works with great willingness. In work he exhibits initiative. He always knows what might be of interest to us, and is well-oriented at present on the military situation in Spain. All his materials on location and movements of fascist units were confirmed by data held by the Republican military command, and the latter always gave high marks to these materials . . . As for money questions,

'Söhnchen' is very modest. He never asks for money. He lives modestly. I want to add the following to his political characterisation: once he complained that because of his work in fascist Spain he was completely cut off from our political life, cannot follow the Party press and the current Party political life in general, and that recently as a result he has often felt doubts on some political events. In particular, he did not understand the problems of a united front, a popular front, and asked me to get him our political literature regularly. I had many long political talks with him and supplied him with the appropriate political literature, which he read in Paris before returning to fascist Spain. I must say that it was very successful . . .

In all the time I have worked with him I had doubts about him only once. It was when he suggested recruiting 'Flora'[1] and then two or three weeks later, in connection with the proposal 'Mädchen' received from the Intelligence Service about using Jewish organisations for their work, suggested placing 'Flora' in the Intelligence Service. At that moment he seemed a bit suspicious to me. It looked as if he was determined to foist 'Flora' on us and, to make it more interesting, offered us the combination with the Intelligence Service.

I do not know the story of the work of 'Söhnchen' and this group with us, so my report covers only my impressions of the year working with him.[2]

Worries about Kim continued despite the fact that the people who knew his work and had seen him in action gave him very good reports. Perhaps, in the view of the vigilant Lubyanka, the reports were too good.

Doubts lead to more doubts. Suspicions send out feelings to new victims. So it was with Kim. Added to the worry about lack of communication with him and the suspicions of his loyalty came a new concern.

In late March 1939 a fairly typical letter came to the Centre from the Paris residence:

[1] Flora Solomon.
[2] The author of this report is not given. The report must date to late 1938–very early 1939. It is probably by 'Pierre'.

At the last meeting 'A' communicated the following. 'Stuart'[3] has a friend here – a British journalist, allegedly tied to us in our work, loyal, and very valuable. Since 'Stuart' often meets this man and has his trust, he has often heard from him (the journalist) complaints about the irregularity of communications with him and his dissatisfaction with the work and his supervision. This journalist complained to 'Stuart' that the man with whom he is connected has never talked to him on general political topics and does not elicit self-respect [sic] and so on . . . Since 'A' said that the journalist's work deals directly with the work of the Construction,[4] we assume that this is one of 'Pierre''s sources, recently passed on by him to comrade 'Kap'.[5] This is for your information.

Across it was written the note:

This is about 'Söhnchen', who is connected to 'Pierre'. Ask 'Pierre' how recently and how frequently he meets 'Söhnchen' and about his mood. Why do we have no materials from 'Söhnchen? 3.04.39. Sudoplatov.

This was the opportunity to get back at 'Pierre'. He was not doing his work with his agent. The telegram went off to him immediately.

Let us recap: Orlov broke with the Stalinist regime on 12 July 1938. It is unlikely that Kim would see his disappearance as an ordinary change in controllers. He would have sensed that something was wrong; and newspapers on the Franco-held territories (including *The Times*) supplied him with information about what was happening in Moscow in those months and years. I do not know if he guessed about Orlov's defection, but he certainly could have assumed that 'Big Bill' had been called back to Moscow for reprisals. I do not know what kind of man 'Pierre' was. But anyone coming after Orlov would have seemed inadequate to 'Sonny'.

Could this be the source of Kim's disillusionment, which he shared with 'Stuart'? Could this explain his periodic disappearances, which

[3] Donald Maclean.
[4] 'Construction' means Spain.
[5] The new chief of the London residence, Gorsky.

so worried the Centre? Is this why he disliked Pierre, his new controller? And apparently his relations with 'Kap', who replaced 'Pierre' at the London residence, were no better.

In just a few months both new 'post-Orlov' controllers – 'Pierre' and 'Kap' – were shot: one for being a German spy, the other a Polish one. Did Kim's complaint, passed along by Maclean, about his Soviet colleague play a role in the investigation? Perhaps.

The world of espionage is cruel. Cruelty *per se* is always unpleasant. But cruelty smeared in the filth of denunciations and lies is even more terrible.

By mid-1939, after multi-layered arrests in the OGPU, there were only a few people left who had any idea of the condition of the agent network. The new people had to start learning about the agents from scratch, about their codenames, their contacts, their countries.

'Pierre' had to explain to the Centre that 'Mary' was 'Söhnchen''s wife, his connection with the residence, a woman with a British passport, an Austrian Jew by birth, who spoke good German and English and poor French, and that she was most easily reached through 'Mädchen'. It was easy enough to say 'through "Mädchen"' – but who was he, or she? It is not fair to mock this bewilderment. It is mixed with blood and death.

Telegrams, letters, questions. Who know the answers? The ones who did were either shot, or in the camps – and no one knew which ones. And the questions kept arising.

On 10 July 1939, the London resident reported:

'Mary' raised the question about paying 'Edith'. I asked her to write about it and I am sending you her letter. I know nothing about this case, and your instructions would be highly appreciated . . . 'Mary' announced that as a result of a four-month hiatus in communications with her, we owe her and 'Mädchen' £65. I promised to check at home and gave him £30 in advance, since she said they were in material need . . . 'Mary' continues to live in the 'Scythian''s[6] country and for some reason, she says on our orders, maintains a large apartment and so on there. I did not rescind those orders, since I do not know why they were given; however I would ask that you clarify this question. 'Kap'.

6 The OGPU residence in France.

Think of all the papers that had to be read through and all the people who had to be located – if they were not in prison or the grave – and all the time and effort expended to be able to scrawl in pencil the following conclusion a few days later:

> Inform 'Kap' that at one time, when it was necessary, 'Mary' was given orders to keep an apartment in Paris. That is no longer necessary. Have her get rid of the apartment and live more modestly, since we will not pay. 'Mary' should not be paid £65, since we do not feel that we owe her, *for anything*. We confirm the payment of £30. Tell her that we will pay no more.

How can the London residence be expected to deal with 'Mary', wife of 'Söhnchen', if they are not quite sure who 'Söhnchen' himself is in July 1939? All the reports on him were at the Centre. Now the Centre was telling its residence in London about him: how Philby had been at Cambridge, gone to Vienna, met his present wife there, come back to London, planned to join the British Communist Party, but on the recommendation of the 'Edith' who was the cause of the Lubyanka's debt to 'Mary' was recruited by 'Stefan' to work for 'an international anti-fascist organisation', and so on and so forth. Here's a letter dated 19 July 1939:

> 'Söhnchen' is a very serious, educated man. He is precise in financial questions. He is disciplined, so much so that he even turned to our people for resolution of family problems and followed their advice. Communications with him were very irregular, particularly of late. Meetings with him were organised only to pass on information and no political-educational work was done with him, which upsets him.

It looks as if everything was back in place. The Centre had sent a glowing character reference on him. May we consider all the questions and suspicions gone?

13

ON THE BRINK OF THE BIG WAR

The war in Spain was coming to an end, ending with the defeat of the Republicans, the victory of fascism, which had shown its strength here. Ending also was an era for Kim. He had come there, in his words, a beginner-journalist and an intern spy, and he left a famous and respected *Times* correspondent, a spy who had developed faith in himself, the confidence that he could handle things.

Now a new war was knocking at Europe's door.

In the summer of 1939 the Centre faced the question of what to do with Philby, how to use him. In June, 'Pierre', one of the few who knew Kim and his wife personally, sent his proposals for Kim to Moscow:

'Söhnchen' will finish up his work in Spain soon. He will have to decide what to do next – drop his journalistic activities to move to some office or continue them? He will turn to us with this question and we have to prepare an answer now.

In a recent meeting with 'Mary', she told me that in her opinion 'Söhnchen' would be much more useful if he worked in the Foreign Office.

His father could help him get a job in the Foreign Office. 'Mary' thinks that he is in England now, having arrived from Syria. 'Söhnchen''s father is a major British spy. ['Pierre' thought it better to inform the Centre of this, just in case.]

I think it would be best to use 'Söhnchen' in Italy. Since he knows French and Spanish, he could master the local language quickly. His old ties in Spain would help him in his work, especially since he could have a recommendation from Franco himself, since he was wounded during the Teruel operations and was decorated by Franco.

I would recommend that he try for a diplomatic or consular post, because he could be used more broadly and with greater interest for us.

In ink, the following recommendation is written on this report: 'Pierre, probably, is right. But it must be discussed with "Söhnchen" himself. Sudoplatov. 14 June, 39.'

A month later, on 10 July 1939, the new chief of the London residence, 'Kap', reported to the Centre:

> Very soon, 'S' will come here to resolve the question of his future work. While here, 'Mary' met one of her intimate friends, a certain 'Stuart', whom, she says, we knew nothing about.[1] She has written a detailed report on him. This 'Stuart' is now working on some top-secret project, probably for the illegal ministry of information and, in his words, has already recommended 'Söhnchen' for this work to his bosses. This question will be decided while 'Söhnchen' is here . . . According to 'Mary', 'Söhnchen' had formed numerous ties in the country where he presently is with very interesting people who have ties with the British Intelligence Service and has developed very good relations with them . . . Some of them have already given 'Söhnchen' individual, albeit rather strange assignments, like writing down the plate numbers of lorries.
>
> When you give us orders on what to do with 'Söhnchen' we would appreciate some orientation on him, for he is known to us only in the most general terms . . .

There are pencilled notations by the big chiefs on 'Kap''s letter. The new superiors were naturally looking for traitors and they posed questions in the margins of the letter: How did 'Stuart' (Maclean) know 'Söhnchen?' Why was he recommending 'Söhnchen' for work? To whom was he recommending him?

This situation would be funny if it were not tragic: upstairs, at the Lubyanka, they do not know 'Stuart'. Downstairs, at the residence, they do not know 'Stuart' or 'Söhnchen'.

In the margins, in another pencil and another handwriting, a middle manager tries to enlighten his bosses (obeying the boss's orders, embarrassed by his lack of knowledge). Diplomatically, the middle manager suggests preparing an orientation report on 'Söhnchen', including information about his past work in Spain, a character reference and a list of contacts.

[1] The new staff of the London residence had to 'discover' its agents, like Donald Maclean.

This report (dated 19 July 1939) was quoted from in the last chapter. It was also sent to London to the new resident. It gave the Centre's 'own' recommendations for Kim's future, which fully echoed the recommendations given by 'Man', already executed, and 'Pierre', who was soon to be.

Kim returned from London in late July 1939. He went to *The Times*. Afterwards, he gave his controller a report on his talk with the editor of the foreign desk and with his own thoughts on his future.

> After a lengthy discussion with my editor . . . it was decided that I would remain in Spain for a few more weeks or months, until the situation stabilises enough for me to leave.
>
> It was made clear that I would have a rather responsible and important post waiting for me . . . I could be sent to Berlin or perhaps to Moscow, if they set up a permanent bureau there.[2]
>
> The following conclusion can be drawn. From the point of view of attack,[3] Berlin would be ideal, since I would then be on enemy territory. In case of war in Europe,[4] that post would be liquidated instantly and mandatory drafting into the British Army could follow.
>
> From the defence point of view,[5] the ideal place would be Moscow for obvious reasons. There I would be in a very good spot for counter-espionage.

'Kap' reported on Kim Philby's talks with *The Times* to Moscow on 10 August 1939.

> 'Söhnchen' came here for negotiations with his newspaper. Staying on in Spain does not suit 'S', both from the point of view of our work and from that of a professional journalist

[2] A fine prospect: Kim Philby, OGPU agent, goes as the *Times* correspondent to Moscow, capital of the country he has never seen and with which he has tied his fate for the rest of his life.
[3] Philby means the possibility of the USSR's military attack against Germany.
[4] War against Germany with the participation of Britain.
[5] Attack on the USSR by Germany.

. . . In accordance with your instructions we recommended that he try to get a posting in Rome or Berlin. As for the proposal of 'Smolka'[6] for 'S' to become the nominal director of the Exchange Telegraph Agency, we write about it below, in a different section. 'S' is not inclined to accept that at the moment. 'S' informed me that in his time he had received instructions from 'Pierre' to become a deserter in case of war and to run to Paris and hide there until we get in touch with him through 'Mary' and get him another book.[7] He enquired if these instructions are still in force, and I promised to find out at home, which I am doing. I do not know the reason for these instructions, but it seems to me that if 'S' deserts it will narrow his capabilities for our work. A man with contacts and qualifications would be used for work in the rear, in headquarters institutions relating to the press, propaganda, and so on. Please give your instructions.

This was the first mention I found of the name Smolka. Kim had told me a lot about him. Even though this man may not have played a prominent role in his life, I am reproducing Kim's story about him, for other reasons. First of all, it is one more life story of the period; second, the story is curious and sheds more light on the relations between Kim and his Soviet colleagues; and third, I am recounting it because Kim found it necessary to tell me about this man, even though I had not asked Kim about Smolka or known of his existence.

Here is what Philby told me.

'In London there was a correspondent of the Austrian newspaper *Neue Freie Presse*, a man named Hans Smolka. I had met him back in Vienna. Whether he was a Communist or not, I do not know. He seemed to be, judging by his theoretical views – we had chatted more than once. But from the point of view of his own lifestyle, his love of comfort, I would not consider him a Communist. From his totally unambiguous words, I knew that he might have accepted the change in my political mood and my departure from my left-wing friends, but he had no intention of believing it completely. He often demonstrated that by various hints. We used to run into each other at

[6] Information on him below.
[7] Passport.

receptions and cocktail parties, and we had many friends in common. He often came to me with news items, and sometimes in the form of ordinary routine gossip he brought me very valuable information. And, you know, he would wink as he did it. He would tell me something truly important and wink – as if to say, You know what to do with this news. I got tired of that winking and I decided that we needed to rectify our equivocal relationship, otherwise it was in danger of going beyond the bounds of decency. He had become a naturalised citizen by then and held a rather significant position – head of the Russian section in the Ministry of Information.

'So one time, I said to him; "Listen, Hans, if in your present job you come across some information that in your opinion could help me in my work *for England* – and I winked at him – come over to me and offer me two cigarettes. I'll take one, you'll keep the other, and that will be a signal that you want to tell me something important."

'He agreed. I must say that I made that proposal to him independently, without asking permission from my Soviet colleague or informing him about it in our meetings, which, of course, was breaking the rules. Later it so happened that I had to leave London for a while on my official work, and I did not want to break my constant contact with Smolka for various reasons. So I introduced him to Guy Burgess. I told Guy all about my "winking" with Smolka, including that I was acting on my own initiative, without the permission of the Soviet colleague. And I warned him not to do anything vis-à-vis Smolka without consulting with me first. Guy, naturally, promised, but broke his promise. He told our controller all about it, and told it in such a complicated way (he later explained that he wanted to protect me, and I believed him) that he got everything all confused. His 'defence' was turned around against me. In other words, at the next meeting with my colleague I went through several extremely unpleasant hours. The colleague was stern. He said that I had no right to behave that way and moreover neatly read me the riot act from the Centre. I cannot remember any other such strong scolding from the Moscow. As a result, I dropped all relations with Smolka.'

Kim Philby did not tell me anything else about his work with Hans Smolka. He did say that as far as he knew Smolka went to Czechoslovakia after the war, was ill for a long time, and then was mixed up in the Rudolf Slansky affair, about which

Kim did not know very much. Later he ended up in Austria and according to Kim's information worked – just a few years before our conversations – as the chief economic advisor to Bruno Kreisky. Philby did not know what eventually happened to the 'maybe Communist, maybe not'.

I had the impression that Kim did not like Smolka very much. The stimulus for bringing up the memories of Smolka in our conversation was also insignificant and random – it could have reminded him of Smolka, it could have not.

At the end of his story about Smolka, Kim felt it necessary to stress one thing. Smolka knew a lot about him and about Burgess, and maybe he had known about the other members of the group. However, he had never told anyone about them, even though the business with Slansky took place in the late forties, while Kim continued to work for another thirteen years for the Soviets – in America, then in England, and then in the Near East.

In 1951 Guy Burgess and Donald Maclean defected to Moscow from London. Philby's name was mentioned in the press and in Parliament; there were reasons for suspecting that he was the 'third man'. Smolka had to have known about it, but he did not turn him in even then. Of course, Kim felt that even if Smolka had wanted to, he would not have been able to prove Kim's ties to the KGB. But his testimony would have given another link in the chain of indirect evidence against Philby; and the longer the chain, the heavier it is and the harder it is to escape.

Listening to Philby's musing, I had the impression that his story about Smolka was the continuation of a polemic he was engaged in with the authors of the rebukes sent by the Centre. He did not consider them just.

On 16 August 1939, two weeks before the start of the Second World War, Philby reported to Moscow:

The Times wants me to return to Madrid for a month, after which I am to go to St-Jean-de-Luz and report on the condition and opportunities of the press in Spain. I am afraid that this is not the time to insist on any other decision, since many of the people in charge are still on holiday. When I return to St-Jean-de-Luz I will repeat all the arguments I have given

before and I will ask them again to post me to London or
Central Europe.

While Kim was looking for the best way to arrange his future
work, the Lubyanka suddenly demanded, just a few days before the
start of the war, an explanation from the London resident on the
nature of the ties between Kim Philby and 'the British spy Talbott,
who was in the case of the enemies of the people Rozengolts and
others'.

I suppose the thinking at the Lubyanka was simple. What was the
relationship between the honoured agent 'Söhnchen' and the English
spy? There had been warning signs of this criminal relationship. No
wonder the former London resident Man, an enemy of the people,
had tried 'in his time' to sweep away all suspicions of Kim Philby
that had arisen among the more vigilant members of the service. Of
course, they were looking only at the surface: Talbott had contacts
with Germany, Philby kept a letter from the German Minister of
Propaganda in his desk. So they decided that Philby was a German
spy. But since the General Procurator of the Soviet Union, Comrade
Andrei Vyshinsky, a loyal Leninist, had established that Talbott was
a British spy, then they must return to the topic and look once more
into the relations between Talbott and Philby. Would it not be logical
to assume that 'Söhnchen' had not been working with the Germans
after all, but was tied to the same service as his dear friend Talbott
of the Intelligence Service?

Note the swift reorientation of the Centre: the decision to check
Kim for collaboration with the British, instead of the Germans,
came almost simultaneously with the signing of the Molotov-
Ribbentrop Pact.

In any case, just before the war, the Centre demanded an
explanatory note from the London residence – how and when
did 'Söhnchen' meet Talbott, and what was the character of their
relationship? However, the new staff of the London residence knew
nothing about that friendship. Naturally, they turned for help to
'Söhnchen' himself. Philby was surprised: the whole point of
his participation in the work of the Anglo-German Fellowship
and magazine that Talbott had published was developed with
the approval, and perhaps on the orders, of the Centre. Having
London tell Moscow what they already knew very well did not seem
logical. But his Soviet colleague insisted: no, no, there were new

circumstances and an explanation from 'Söhnchen' was extremely urgent. So Philby wrote a new explanation in the short time he was in London. The residence sent it to Moscow just five days before the war with a brief covering letter:

British spy Talbott was part of the trial of the enemies of the people Rozengolts et al. 'Söhnchen' knows Talbott well and according to him we knew about that friendship. We are sending you a new report by 'Söhnchen' about his last meeting with Talbott ('Söhnchen''s data).

These few lines are invaluable. The residence managed to absolve itself from all responsibility twice ('according to him' and '"Söhnchen"'s data') for the information sent to Moscow. The same letter informed then that 'Söhnchen' was 'headed back to Spain' on assignment from the newspaper. However, that trip did not take place – Hitler invaded Poland.

Before moving on to a new period in the life of the spy, I want to cite yet one more paragraph from that letter of 25 August 1939:

'Söhnchen' and 'Mary' ask us to review the decision refusing to pay them the money they now estimate at £45. Appendix N12 is a receipt for that debt. All those expenses were incurred during work for us by 'S' and with the sanction of our people. We personally feel that this debt ought to be paid.

I do not know if the accountants at the Lubyanka were very meticulous in their work on agents' accounts or whether the mails were slow, but the decision in red pencil on that paragraph – to pay the miserable £45 – did not appear until 20 September.

In those three and a half weeks that passed between the mailing of the letter and the appearance of the executive decision to pay, an entire era had passed: the world was at war for the second time in the century.

14

MOSCOW BREAKS OFF CONTACT

These were the first months of 'the phoney war'. Troops from the two sides would stand facing one another idly, as if admiring the landscape on opposite sides of the front. They organised sleigh rides and splendid Christmas parties.

However, behind these pastoral scenes, shown in newsreels on cinema screens all across Europe, full-scale preparations for the first strike were silently underway. Philby was one of those individuals who very keenly felt the full extent of the evil of what was happening. However, he told me almost nothing about his work for Soviet intelligence during the autumn and winter of 1939–1940. He evaded questions about what else he was doing during those months, besides representing *The Times* at its French headquarters, and about what he was passing on to Moscow. He was either being modest or he didn't remember or he didn't want to remember . . .

The editorial office at *The Times* had changed its initial plans to send Philby as their correspondent to Madrid as far back as the summer of 1939. After the victory of Franco's forces, Spain's capital gradually became a quiet backwater; the stormclouds had moved to the North and East, gathering over Danzig, over Poland, and over all of Europe. There was open talk in the paper about an approaching general European war, and the post of chief correspondent in this future European theatre of war operations was now being prepared for Kim Philby, who had proved himself brilliantly at the Spanish front.

Soon after the war broke out, the editorial office told him: 'Your press centre will be located in France at the headquarters of the British Expeditionary Force.'

He immediately informed the Soviet residency in London about this conversation. It was a matter of some importance: arrangements had to be worked out for meetings with Kim in France. At the beginning of October, Kap sent a proposal to the Centre for establishing contact with 'Söhnchen' in the French capital:

. . . 'Söhnchen' is leaving for the Western front [wrote Kap]. Where he'll be and for how long is still unknown . . . Terms of the meeting: 12 or 13 October from 12:00 to 12:15 p.m. at the Place de la Madeleine on the street near the entrance to the Thomas Cook tourist office, across from the Cathedral of the same name as the street. Identification signs: 'S' will carry the English newspaper, the *Daily Mail*. Our person should have the same paper. The password: our man has to ask 'S', 'Where is the Café Henri around here?' in English or French. The answer: 'It's near the Place de [*sic*] Republique.' The back-up meeting is on 1 or 2 November. Same time, terms, and place.

It's possible that he'll come to the meeting in an English military uniform if he doesn't have time to change clothes . . .

On the day of the meeting, 'Alim', an agent of the Parisian residency, came to the designated place at the appointed time carrying an English *Daily Mail*. He waited for a stranger at the Thomas Cook tourist office for fifteen minutes. But no one asked him for the address of the Café Henri. He stayed for another five minutes, adding his own time, but with no success. There wasn't a single passerby with a *Daily Mail* under his arm. Taking all the necessary precautions, 'Alim' returned to the Embassy and informed the resident that the agent had not come to the rendezvous. Philby didn't show up the next day either. The first contact with him didn't take place until two weeks later.

. . . The meeting with 'Söhnchen' took place on 1 November at the designated place. 'Söhnchen' is working at English Army Headquarters located in Abarque, near Arras. He explained that he missed the first meeting because it was impossible to get to Paris, and that he would be able to get to Paris only once a month. Arrangements for meetings with him were made. 'Söhnchen' brought material in English (see enclosed) . . . We bring to your attention the necessity for a rush translation of this material and request a response with your assessment . . .

The residency also notified Moscow about the second meeting with Philby in November. The material received from him was detailed and, according to the residency, just as valuable this time. 'Alim' offered him money. But 'Söhnchen' explained that he received an adequate salary, and that concealing extra resources or excessive expenditures from his neighbours in the officers' quarters where he lived would be, in his words, difficult. He refused the money.

> . . . 'S' is a bit nervous at meetings [the Parisian resident reported to Moscow on 7 November 1939] because he clearly understands the consequences of failure. I give careful instructions to 'Alim' before he goes to meet him. Until now 'S' appeared at meetings in military uniform, which is somewhat conspicuous, so we've now suggested to him that he wear civilian clothes . . .

Kim Philby appears differently in these reports from before. He misses assignations and, when he does show up, he is nervous: he stutters more than usual and is afraid of failure. What is wrong?

The first clue in our search for an answer may be found in one of the later reports containing an evaluation of 'Söhnchen''s work at the end of 1939.

> (From a report on the source 'Söhnchen' 1.4.41.)
> . . . In 1939 in conversations with 'Mary' he complained that as a result of working with 'Paul' ('Pierre' or Ozolin-Haskin) he is beginning to experience disillusionment with us. He never said this to us directly.
>
> The same report mentions that during his time on the Western Front Philby supplied the residency with valuable materials on the deployment of: the German army (according to English Military Intelligence data), the British Expeditionary Force in France in October and November of 1939 and its weapons, technical means etc., the French army's weapons and technical means until the middle of November, as well as 'some data on the Maginot line'.

Did Philby understand that the information on the deployment of the English and French armies and their weapons, and 'some data on the Maginot line', possessed hardly any vital importance for the Soviet Union, but was undoubtedly extremely valuable to Hitler?

I have no data showing that Stalin passed some of the materials that were received from Philby to German Intelligence. But this possibility cannot be ruled out. It is sufficient to recall the freight cars leaving the USSR loaded with bread and oil, bound for Germany after the world war broke out, and to realise that it was more than likely that Moscow supplied Berlin with the information Hitler needed about the English and French troops behind the Maginot line.

This was a difficult time for Kim. Perhaps he began to wonder whether the path he had chosen was the right one and whether the people in Moscow were worth his blind faith in them? Or had he just created them in his own imagination . . .?

The first stimulus prompting these kinds of thoughts were reports he read in the newspapers about repression on a mass scale in the 'promised land'. Of course, he received 'political instruction' and explanations about the 'intensification of the class war' from his Soviet colleagues. But he must have been surprised by the fact that practically all of the participants and creators of the Great October Socialist Revolution were declared traitors, conspirators and spies from various secret services. The commanders of the Red Army, who had created it in order to defend the Revolution from enemies, also proved to be spies who conspired with German generals to try to overthrow the Soviet state. There turned out to be a few too many conspirators and spies, almost more of them than the people against whom they hatched their plots.

Then came August 1939, when Moscow signed the pact with Hitler, an event which shocked not only Kim, but the entire world.

In the 'Report on the source "Söhnchen"' dated 1 April 1940 (there are many of these reports that repeat or supplement one another almost word for word – at times they contradict one other), the chief of the London residency would write:

. . . Contact with him has been very irregular, especially recently. Meetings with him were limited only to the passing of materials, and he was given no political instruction, to which he reacted overly sensitively. He even told source 'Stuart' about it . . .

'Söhnchen' is undoubtedly a very cultured and highly erudite individual, endowed with a broad outlook. He reads a lot of serious literature, particularly many scholarly works on the history of music. He has repeatedly emphasised that he has no other goal in life than working for the Revolution.

At the same time, according to 'Mary', to whom he complained in conversations, as a result of his contact with 'Paul' he was beginning to experience a certain disillusionment with us. He has never said this to us directly . . . A few times, he complained that the casual, irregular and unsystematic contact with us during his time in Spain often left him with one or another unresolved political and party questions. The signing of the Soviet–German Non-Aggression Pact caused 'S' to ask puzzled questions such as, 'Why was this necessary?', 'What will happen to the single-front struggle against fascism now?' However, after several talks on this subject, 'S' seemed to grasp the significance of the pact. 'S' greeted the liberation of the peoples of Western Ukraine and West Byelorussia by the Red Army with a burst of wild enthusiasm . . .

One can imagine the ambivalence and confusion that Kim Philby felt during those autumn months of 1939.

As regards the first 'disillusionment with us', does the writer of the report mean Kim's disillusionment with just those NKVD agents with whom he had to work recently, and whose human and professional qualities were lacking compared with those of his original mentors? Or is this a reference to the set of notions that comprised the country for which he was working? The disappearance of Theo and of Big Bill, the trials of Lenin's comrades-in-arms, the annihilation of the entire top leadership of the army, about which he had no doubt read, could hardly all fit together comfortably into this set of notions.

The Molotov–Ribbentrop Pact quite unexpectedly cast him, a Moscow agent, into Germany's and Hitler's camp. But one of the main reasons for his entering Soviet intelligence work was his conviction that only the Communists, only the Soviet Union, could provide real resistance to fascism! After all, the conversation with him on that bench in Regent's Park was about doing secret work in an international *anti-fascist* organisation! He had become involved with the Anglo-German Fellowship and an Anglo-German magazine, he had worked in Spain, first and foremost because of the struggle against fascism. Now he was Hitler's ally: and because of the pact signed by Communist Moscow and fascist Berlin, a real ally, not a phoney one. Rumours were also going around that all his former friends in the British Communist Party had received instructions from Moscow to cease anti-fascist campaigns and all anti-German activities.

To be sure, he had been raised in an unusual family, in which the head of the household did not conceal his disapproval of England's foreign policy which he considered imperialistic. This circumstance probably mollified Kim's suffering. He shared the elder Philby's contempt for Britain's imperial aspirations, but he could not join his father in approving of Hitlerite fascism.

Many of Philby's biographers assume that Kim inherited a rebellious, uncompromising and wilful character from his father and attribute his alienation from English society directly to his father's influence.

In the report already quoted, there's a paragraph that reads:

. . . Refers to his parents, who are well-to-do bourgeois, and his entire social milieu with unfeigned contempt and hatred. He never brings the subject up on his own in conversation, but when called upon to discuss it, he speaks without posing and bravado. . .

Kim's mercilessly critical, even scornful, attitude towards his father when he was young has been noted by many other NKVD agents who worked with him. This seems to confirm the assumptions of his biographers. But it seems to me that Kim Philby's father passed on to his son not only his wilfulness, but fostered in him a trait that is sometimes called the 'submissiveness coefficient'. In my opinion, Kim possessed this 'coefficient' to an excessive degree. His father forced his will upon him and overpowered him, despotically. He instilled contempt in Kim for the English establishment, and at the same time aroused hatred towards himself. Naturally, the son dreamt of liberating himself from his father's despotism. Finally, he did it. He got out from under his parents' 'cocoon' – he left it, and went into Marxism.

However, the 'submissiveness coefficient' stayed with him. Kim needed a finger to point the way, a leader to whom he could submit. Philby was a strong individual with a powerful will, a highly developed sense of self-discipline, and an active sense of initiative. Because of these qualities he needed leadership (from people or ideas) in which he could unquestioningly believe.

'Stefan', the London resident's assistant with whom Kim had that memorable meeting on the bench in Regent's Park and about whom Kim always spoke with genuine admiration and warmth, wrote about 'Sonny' in this way:

> . . . Profound, very serious in acquiring knowledge. Broadly educated. A real armchair scholar . . . Somewhat indecisive and, at the same time, extremely disciplined . . . Stutters a bit and is ashamed of this inadequacy. Sentimental . . . His wife was his first lover in his life . . . When difficulties arose in their relationship, they would confide in me and both followed my advice . . .

We can only speculate about how Philby experienced the contradiction that had appeared in his life. On the one hand, he had found the promised land and he trusted the people who came from there. On the other hand, he couldn't have avoided knowing that events were happening in the world that did not match what he understood to be the ideals.

Naturally, he learned to convince himself about the things that his Soviet mentors said (the 'burst of enthusiasm' when Western Ukraine and Byelorussia united with the USSR), but as it turned out, he fell far short of giving himself every single order, and carrying them out each and every time. In any case, he couldn't manage it without pangs of conscience or lightheartedly, which that clear gaze in his blue eyes many remembered expressed so well.

Perhaps this is why Kim's meetings with Soviet contacts during that period were irregular. Perhaps this is why he looked upset and nervous when he came to them. To the many doubts and disillusionments, yet another serious circumstance – one I've already mentioned – was added which radically changed his sense of himself.

England had joined the war against Germany. Here he was, working for an ally of Germany and, possibly, England's direct enemy *during the war*. The thought that Moscow was possibly passing on to Berlin part of the information he was providing to his Soviet colleagues about the British Expeditionary Force in France must have crossed his mind. The fact that not only was he passing on information to Moscow about the English and French armed forces, but at times about the German forces as well, didn't so much justify his actions as make his position even more difficult – because in this way he was supplying Moscow (and, via Moscow, we can't rule out Berlin) with the information that English intelligence had on German troops. Philby had long considered the Socialist Revolution 'has no national boundaries'. For a long time he had called his fellow countrymen 'the English' and the Soviet people 'our people' – all the Soviet colleagues who worked with him had noted this in their reports 'About the source "Söhnchen"'. However, after England had declared war on Germany, he couldn't help realising that he was working not only against 'English imperialism' – with which he, to put it mildly, did not sympathise, and considered it his right not to – but *against the English people.*

Communication between 'Söhnchen' and his Soviet contact from the Paris residency in the autumn of 1939 was difficult, irregular and with certain 'extra-curricular' difficulties. At the beginning of 1940 it broke off altogether, in an unusual manner.

On 20 February 1940 the London NKVD resident Kap informed Moscow that the source 'Söhnchen' had lost touch with 'Karp', the Paris residency agent, and couldn't reestablish it. As we know, these 'breaks' in contact had occurred earlier in Philby's work. Something else made this situation unusual. Three days after receiving this communication, Moscow issued Karp the directive to break off all contact with 'Söhnchen'.

We can only speculate on the reasons and considerations that were involved. We could, for example, suppose that Moscow took the complexity of its agent's psychological state and the change in his 'spy status' into consideration, since the USSR had allied itself with Germany which was at war with England. But that is too naive and magnanimous an assumption to make about the ruthless business of intelligence.

There's another variation that should not be ruled out: it was Kim's own idea to break off contact. But the Centre had reacted to it far too swiftly, too 'readily'. Why such haste? Was it the Centre's recent dissatisfaction with Philby's work? Or was it a matter of certain suspicions about him? It's unlikely that the signals about his 'dissillusionment with us' could have remained without consequences. The further unfolding of events will provide, if not a direct answer to these questions, then at least a serious basis for these assumptions.

Kim, as I've said before, said very little in general about that period in his work. He let fall only one fleeting sentence about the break in contact in 1940:

'It somehow happened that I lost touch with my contact in France . . .'

According to the documents, the attempt to reestablish contact refers only to the beginning of June 1940. And what's noteworthy is that it was Philby who took the initiative, and not the Centre. As for Moscow, it seems to have completely forgotten about its source 'Söhnchen' and written him off. Had the Centre wished to renew contact with him, it could have used a reliable route – through Litzi. However, judging from the documents, the Lubyanka was not undertaking anything, for reasons known only to itself.

Of course, the times were turbulent. The nine-month-long 'phoney war' and the idleness of the Allies on the Western Front allowed Hitler to complete preparations for a decisive blow. He swiftly occupied Denmark and Norway in April and May of 1940; on 10 May he invaded Belgium (which capitulated on 28 May), the Netherlands (which capitulated on 14 May), Luxembourg and – through them – France. According to the calculations of all the military specialists, it was supposed to withstand the onslaught of Hitler's troops for a minimum of two years. But the great European power capitulated on 22 June.

The British Expeditionary Force was swiftly evacuated. Discouraged English journalists, including *Times* correspondent Kim Philby, left France along with it.

All of these events were unexpected not only for Kim, but for his Soviet colleagues, for the Paris and London NKVD residencies and maybe for the Lubyanka itself. This factor of confusion also should be kept in mind in our attempts to portray the NKVD's relations with its agent 'Söhnchen' during the short months when Europe's political map was rapidly reshaped.

Three weeks before France's capitulation, the residency there ('Karp') notified the Centre that 'Stuart' (Donald Maclean) had received a letter from 'Söhnchen'. The latter wrote that he had successfully been evacuated from Flanders to London together with the Allied forces, and that he had in his possession extraordinarily valuable materials he had gathered and felt he had to pass 'to the appropriate hands'. 'Söhnchen' suggested two methods for establishing contact with him – sending him a letter either to the editorial office of *The Times* or to his club. The resident requested instructions from the Centre on to how to proceed.

'Söhnchen''s offer to reestablish contact, and also the promise of receiving 'extraordinarily valuable' materials from him, elicited divergent responses at the Centre. Agents at the executive level (section chief of the main directorate of state security at the NKVD, Senior Lieutenant Gukasov, and the authorised executive of this section, Lieutenant Kreshin) promptly submitted a report on 3 June 1940 to the deputy chief of the 5th department of the main directorate, P. Sudoplatov, with a recommendation to reestablish contact with Philby immediately. On 4 June, the latter replied that the 'People's Commissariat cannot send anyone to meet "Söhnchen".'

Not satisfied with a negative reply, Gukasov sent another report to the command that same day:

> In connection with 'Karp''s communication about 'Stuart''s receipt of 'Söhnchen''s letter, in which the latter insists on an immediate and obligatory meeting with him in view of his possession of extraordinarily important and valuable materials, I believe it necessary to arrange a meeting immediately with 'Söhnchen', who is in London, for the following reasons:
>
> 1. 'Söhnchen' has been working with us since 1934. From September to December of 1939 'Söhnchen' gave us valuable materials of a military-intelligence nature which were given a positive evaluation by the 5th directorate of the RKKA [Red Army].
>
> 2. Since 'Söhnchen' is working at the English Ministry of War, he may supply us with valuable information.

Gusakov further suggested that 'comrade Kap, who has a diplomatic passport with a permanent visa valid in wartime', be sent to London for this meeting. The same day a resolution appeared on Gusakov's report:

> The People's Commissar does not consider it possible to send a person to make contact with Söhnchen, given present conditions.

4.6.40. Sudoplatov.

The Centre did not wish to reestablish contact with 'Söhnchen'. Judging by Gusakov's reasoning, the leadership could have been motivated by several considerations: 'Söhnchen''s sincerity was doubtful; in his present position 'Söhnchen' was of no value to the intelligence service; the Centre was occupied with more important matters, making it impossible to send anyone to meet such an agent; reestablishing contact at the agent's initiative was fraught with provocation.

All these considerations could have served as the basis for the position that the state security leadership adopted, especially the last one – that 'Söhnchen' initiated the contact as a provocation. This is confirmed by another of the Centre's decisions. In it they suggested to the London residency that it pass instructions to 'Stuart' and that if he wished to avert disaster, he should cease all correspondence and all contact with Kim Philby.

Why was the Centre dropping one of its most valuable agents? Why should Donald Maclean ('Stuart') have to stop corresponding (to say nothing of having personal meetings) with his old friend Kim Philby? Why did the Lubyanka assume that their correspondence could in fact, lead to 'Stuart''s demise? If the Lubyanka was demonstrating its usual caution, then why didn't it mention that their correspondence could in equal measure lead to 'Söhnchen''s downfall? Perhaps 'Stuart' was considered a more important and promising source at that time. Perhaps the decisive role here was played by all that 'disillusionment with us' expressed by Kim. Maybe the agent's momentary sincerity had turned the Lubyanka against him, resulting in a lack of confidence in his loyalty and dedication.

Here's what Philby said to me in 1987.

'It turned out somehow that I lost my contact in France, and when I returned to England after the fall of Flanders, I found myself without a master, so to speak. What could I do? I had one alternative – to call Donald Maclean. I rang him, we met, and I said to him: "I don't know what you're doing now, but I've come back to England and have lost all my contacts. Help me . . ."'

'This was probably breaking the rules. But what was I to do? I had brought very interesting material, very valuable material, from France. It was absolutely necessary to pass it on. I trusted Maclean as I trusted myself. Of course, in the complex world of intelligence work, you probably can't trust anyone as you trust yourself, especially if you haven't seen a person for a long period of time, and one that can turn everything upside down at that. But I trusted Maclean. I didn't for a second doubt that even if something had radically changed in his life, he would never betray me and that I could speak with him frankly. In short, I asked him to help me repair the broken liaison. About a week passed and he called me. We met in a café and he told me everything I needed for a rendez- vous – the time, place, and password.'

It's possible that everything Kim told me was true. But it wasn't the whole truth. He didn't mention his first attempt to reestablish contact – his letter to Maclean – or that this attempt was rejected by the Centre. He didn't say anything about how long he had been without contact. From his story one gets the impression that he got in touch with Maclean when he returned to London and that contact was reestablished immediately. But actually after his first attempt (his letter to Maclean), *almost a year* went by before the liaison was reestablished. I don't know whether it was reestablished with Maclean's help, whether their meeting took place at all, or whether it was solely the letter (the one Philby didn't want to tell me about) that elicited the aforementioned reaction from the Centre. What is clear is that Philby did not wish to elaborate on how and by whom contact with him was broken and/or how the Centre rejected his attempt to reestablish it. He didn't know or didn't want to talk about the fact that his friend Maclean was denied permission to write to him. Now, it seems that in talking about a period that could turn everything 'upside down', what he had in mind was not a change in Maclean's opinion about the KGB, but the KGB's sudden about-face in its attitude toward him, 'the source Söhnchen'.

And so contact was reestablished. In the documents notification about it occupies only a few sentences. 'Vadim' for No. 6 on 24 December 1940 reports that he made contact with 'Söhnchen'.

Söhnchen works as a political instructor in the British Intelligence Service training centre for preparing sabotage agents to be fielded in Europe. Provides materials on the Intelligence Service.

One has to assume that this was the reason for suddenly reestablishing contact with the cast-off agent. It turns out that

what made the difference was that he had penetrated the Intelligence
Service! Now the People's Commissar could report 'Söhnchen''s
success to the appropriate place – the success of the same one who
unfortunately had been unable to carry out the special assignment in
Spain under the past leadership. But now, with the advent of the new
leadership at the GPU, he had penetrated the threshold of the *sanctum
sanctorum* of the British special services. A year earlier, the leadership
had given instructions not to distract the agent with urgent tasks and
even to break off contact with him for a time, so as as not to disturb
or accidentally compromise him. This turned out to be right. It seems
also that 'Söhnchen''s work at the training centre of the British secret
service was a total surprise to the Lubyanka chiefs – and they had
no idea how he got there. It isn't superfluous to cite Kim Philby's
own story about how he penetrated the SIS. He described his path
in sufficient detail in his book, *My Silent War*, but at the dacha near
Moscow he thought it necessary to return to this topic once again
to add some details that he omitted from his book.

15

ON THE BENEFITS OF
CHAMPAGNE WITH LUNCH

In September 1939 Philby informed his Soviet colleague that *The Times* would be assigning him as its chief correspondent attached to the British Expeditionary Force in France.

His colleague's response was entirely favourable.

'Excellent,' he told Kim. 'That's exactly what we need right now. But that's right now. Don't forget that your main objective is to enter the British Intelligence Service.'

The future had come up more than once in earlier conversations with Otto, Theo and Big Bill; they had often thought together about the kind of work, given the Centre's interests, that 'Sonny' should look for. The top choice was always work in the secret service. They considered journalism, even big-time journalism, merely a step towards the main objective. Philby had attained this step. He was on the staff of the most famous, perhaps the most influential, newspaper in the world. He had made his name.

As a war correspondent attached to the Expeditionary Force in France, he would always bring up the subject in conversation at any meetings he had with influential Englishmen. It was a simple plan. It was awkward for him to remain a journalist now. It was one thing to write about the Spanish Civil War, a war that was waged by foreign governments, but quite another to write about a war being waged on one's own country. He wanted to find a job in which he might serve his country better than working as a reporter.

'What kind of work do you have in mind?' his influential interlocutors would often ask him.

His answer sounded convincing enough: he knew German and Spanish well, and some French. As a student he had travelled a great deal around France and traversed all of Spain. He had visited Austria, Czechoslovakia, Poland and made his way to Greece. He had been studying international issues his entire conscious life. It was his main passion. As a *Times* correspondent he had learned to approach world events analytically, without prejudice, and without expressing his own personal political biases. He really didn't have any – he wasn't caught up in any of the political movements. Therefore, he would most likely be able objectively and competently to analyse and assess any information, facts or events that he encountered. But at the present time, impartiality had no place in a newspaper. In times of war, a newspaper had to be propaganda. There had to be censorship – and he knew what military censorship was from his experience in Spain. No wonder they say that truth is the first casualty of war.

These were the cards that he laid on the table as he added the innocent question: 'And what do you think about this?' – and looked at his interlocutor with his clear blue eyes.

'Of all the people you spoke to, who was it that finally got you into the secret service?' I once asked Philby.

Raising his grey eyebrows, the former 'Söhnchen' smiled and recounted an entire novella.

It's difficult to believe this, but I still don't know exactly who it was that gave me such a recommendation, whose word was the final one. My conversations with influential Englishmen probably prompted many to think that it would be most expedient to use a *Times* correspondent in the Intelligence Service. This kind of transfer would not have been seen as something unusual – many English journalists had worked with secret service branches. Then there were my contacts with the British Embassy in France and when I was in Spain – wasn't this using a *Times* correspondent to gather secret information? Many of my interlocutors agreed with me, and some said directly, that of course in times like these the place for a man with your knowledge is not with a newspaper, but in intelligence. Most likely, I wasn't the only one to whom they said this: that's what we were counting on. Incidentally, a few individuals brought up the subject on their own in conversation, without my help.

I have to say that once my ubiquitous and vociferous friend Guy Burgess, who was already working at one of the organisations linked to the secret service at the time, learned that they were toying with me and talking to me about the subject, he naturally began helping things along as much as he could. But he wasn't 'guilty' of getting me into the Intelligence Service.

If we're speaking about the external picture of the events, as I imagine them to be then, then the story has to begin with the following incident.

At the beginning of the war a journalist named Esther Marsdon-Smedley worked as a correspondent for the *Daily Express* in Belgium. When Hitler's forces invaded, she escaped to France and attached herself to the corps of foreign journalists there. After the fall of France she was included in the group under Philby's charge when they were evacuated to England. She was with them on the ship that crossed the Channel and she was on the train that delivered the journalists from Plymouth to London.

She once said to Kim during lunch: 'I can't imagine France under the Nazi boot. Let's drown our sorrows in a bottle of champagne!'

The waiter brought a bottle. She picked it up and began lamenting: 'Oh God, French champagne! And the bottle's French! What's going to happen to all of this now?'

They drank a glass. Having calmed down a bit, she asked: 'What are you planning to do?'

'I'll probably be called up. How can I avoid it?'

'The army? A person like you has to be a fool to join the army. You're capable of doing a lot more to defeat Hitler!'

Kim realised that the conversation was turning to his advantage and said: 'I don't know what to do, I don't have any contacts.'

She looked at him patronisingly, the way women of any age usually look at relatively young men.

'Never mind. We'll figure something out. I hope that you'll get a more serious offer, a more interesting one, one worthy of you . . .'

'I remember this conversation with the bottle of French champagne,' Philby told me. 'Soon after, we all wound up in England, in London, except for those who remained to rest in French soil forever.'

Officially I was still on the staff of *The Times*, but they didn't really know what to do with me at the newspaper. Approximately two weeks after my return to London, the foreign editor suddenly summoned me to his office.

'There was a call for you from the Ministry of War. A certain Captain Sheridan would like to see you,' he said and handed me the telephone number.

I telephoned the captain. He asked me to drop in for a talk which, as he put it, might interest me. And he added that he wanted to speak to me about certain special war work.

Naturally I agreed. I went to see him at the appointed time. We didn't have much of a conversation. He simply asked me to go to such and such a hotel, to such and such a room to meet a Miss Maxse.

I was familiar with her name. Marjorie Maxse was popular in journalist circles. Her brother was the chief editor at some publication, and she herself was quite a good journalist.

I went to that hotel, found the right room and introduced myself to Miss Maxse. She began with questions about what I had seen in Spain, what languages I knew, what interesting people I had met and so on in this vein. I answered in some detail as I sensed that this conversation was serious.

She then began to discuss with me the possibilities for conducting underground work in Europe: black propaganda, securing important information. She was soon carrying on an entirely professional conversation, not concealing her interest in my participation in this work. In response I reflected on the prospects of using labour unions in Austria, Hungary and Germany for this purpose. In short, we had a fruitful talk about what could be done and whom to recruit. I don't rule out that this conversation, which lasted for almost two hours, served to some extent as the embryo, the germ, of the organisation that later ran special operations against the Germans in Europe.

'Well then, we're prepared to do business with you,' she said in parting, 'and prepared to meet you again.'

At the appointed time, I opened the door of the same room that served as her office and much to my surprise, I saw Guy Burgess there. We greeted one another like old friends, without hiding, of course, that we knew one another from Cambridge, although understandably, we didn't say anything to her about our meeting in Gibraltar.

Miss Maxse began the conversation with me in the same vein as the one we had had last time. And Guy tried his utmost to present me in the most favourable light.

If I proposed something or advanced a certain idea Guy would immediately clap his hands and enthusiastically declare:

'A splendid idea! Right, Miss Maxse? Of course, you'll elaborate on it and it will become simply outstanding!'

In a word, when the second interview ended, a bit sooner than the first one, Miss Maxse asked me how soon I might be able to leave my post at the newspaper.

I answered in a way that would block all paths for her retreat: 'I'm actually already free today. Nobody seems to need me after my return from France. I can come here.'

'What about Monday?' she suggested, and asked me to come to Caxton House between the Broadway Buildings and the hotel where we were speaking. 'That's where you'll be working. You will ask the security guard to summon a man named Guy Burgess. He'll fill you in on the details . . .'

On Monday I came to the designated address. I requested a meeting with Mr Guy Burgess and my work in intelligence began from that moment on. The security guard told me that Mr Burgess was in such and such a room, and I obediently went there. Guy greeted me in an entirely official manner and led me to another room, the one that was to be my office. It was quite small. There was a table and a chair in it, and a typewriter on the table. And absolutely nothing else.

Guy looked around and said with satisfaction: 'A lovely little room. There's a chair and a table, and a typewriter as well.' Then he opened his eyes wide and and exclaimed with indignation: 'Wait a minute, they haven't given you any paper! How are you going to work!?

Having said this, he left and returned with a sheaf of foolscap. Very pleased with himself, he put it on the table next to the typewriter.

'There,' he said, 'now work.'

'Fine, so now I'll put some paper into the typewriter. And what am I going to type?'

'Why, I suppose you're right,' my friend agreed with me and immediately found a solution. 'Listen, let's go to somebody's office and discuss this matter . . .'

In short, it was a very funny morning. We went around to all sorts of people in all sorts of offices, large and small, and we joked, laughed, and at odd moments exchanged ideas about how to organise sabotage on German railway lines. And even though I knew that people who joke a lot sometimes

work very well, that morning I didn't get the impression
that the employees in this office were gathered there to do
serious work.

In any case, I came away from our morning rounds of the
secret establishment with almost nothing, and I never really
fully understood what it was that I would be doing. I sat down
at the table in my little room, picked up a sheet of paper, placed
it in the typewriter carriage and began to reflect.

At this time the door opened and, all of a sudden, Esther
Marsdon-Smedley's head appeared like a mirage and pro-
nounced with satisfaction: 'Oh, you really are here! What did
I tell you?'

And just as suddenly, her head disappeared.

From that moment on, I absolutely sincerely and honestly
believed that it was she, Esther Marsdon-Smedley, who was
the real moving force behind my entering SIS, she who could
not permit the country that produced splendid champagne in
beautiful bottles with beautiful labels to be under the German
boot. I believed that she and she alone was the one who had
accomplished it all. There had been too many coincidences –
including the sudden appearance of her head in the door – to
doubt my conclusion.

I thought when I met him at Miss Maxse's that Burgess was
the one who'd done it all, until he told me, ready to swear on
just about anything, that he wound up there completely by
accident, that he had just dropped by her office on business, and
had only at that point found out from her that I was supposed
to come and see her. And he then asked her permission to stay
during the conversation, since Kim Philby was his good old
friend and, it goes without saying, a completely remarkable
individual. He swore to me that he was not directly involved
in recruiting me into the secret service.

Much later, at the interrogation that Dick White conducted,
when Burgess and Maclean were on their way to Moscow, and
I was suspected of being one of their accomplices, White asked
me: 'Who recruited you into SIS?'

I replied absolutely frankly: 'As far as I know, Esther
Marsdon-Smedley.'

'Oh, yes,' he said, 'she was also a very well-known journalist . . .'

It wasn't very difficult to talk with White. But then, shortly after, came the time of the more difficult interrogations led by Milmo.[1] He also asked: 'Who recruited you into SIS?'

'As far as I can tell, it was Esther Marsdon-Smedley,' I said once again, and added that I had already given Dick White exactly the same answer.

Milmo coldly retorted: 'Perhaps you would be interested to learn that we met Esther Marsdon-Smedley, and the dear lady categorically denies that she got you into SIS. Burgess recruited you!' And he repeated three more times: 'Burgess, Burgess, Burgess!'

Although his words were a surprise to me, I didn't have to fabricate anything because I was genuinely, completely sure that Marsdon-Smedley had played the decisive role in SIS inviting me to work for them. And so I immediately replied: 'Listen, Milmo, if Burgess had recruited me and I tried to cover it up, why would I have named a woman whom you can ask at any time to corroborate my words? Why, all you have to do to meet her is go around the corner of this building. I named her only because I genuinely believe that she was the one who recommended me to SIS.'

Speaking to me on the terrace of a dacha on the outskirts of Moscow in the summer of 1987, Philby repeated: 'To this day I really don't know who it was that actually recommended me to SIS. Incidentally, I wrote quite a lot about this in my book'.[2]

It's really difficult to believe that Philby did not ultimately find out who 'arranged' his entering SIS, just as it's hard to imagine that the somewhat exalted lady with the complicated last name who had promised him work in SIS at lunch on the train was the

[1] *Helenus Milmo, later a King's Counsel and a judge. He had worked for M15 during the war as an interrogator. His bluff, forceful manner had won him the nickname 'Buster'. (PK)*
[2] As I've already mentioned, Kim Philby described joining SIS in his book, *My Silent War*. But I can't simply refer the reader to that book because the very significant incident with the woman who loved champagne wouldn't make any sense – there's nothing about it in the book. I hope the reader will forgive me for making certain infrequent parallels with Philby's book. I include them only when it's difficult to break the continuity of Philby's oral narrative, or when his manner of telling his story is no less (and perhaps even more!) important in understanding his character than what he's talking about.

'arranger'. Considering Kim's usual sense of discipline and caution, his constant adherence to the rule 'If you can keep your mouth shut, do it', it was conceivable that he wasn't telling me the whole truth either. But – amazingly enough – I found a document confirming his words.

It was written by Kim himself on 15 June 1942. As usual, Moscow did not trust its agent. Concerned that he wound up in SIS far too 'easily' and virtually without the Centre's knowledge, it demanded that 'Söhnchen' present a written explanation about how, in effect, it all happened. That is, Moscow was interested in the same question that the English investigator Milmo would later ask, and that Nicholas Elliott would ask him in Beirut further down the line. Each of them, however, was asking with a different objective in mind. Milmo asked in order to prove that the Soviet spy Guy Burgess had recruited Kim Philby into the British Intelligence Service; Elliott asked in order to convince Kim that SIS knew everything; and the Lubyanka asked in order to confirm or reject its suspicions that Philby was associated with the Intelligence Service even before he began working with the Soviet secret service.

I quote, in a somewhat abridged form, Kim Philby's written explanation submitted to the Centre in the summer of 1942.

('Söhnchen''s Report About Himself on 15 June 1942)
MY ENTRY INTO SIS[3]

In the beginning of June 1940, I was returning to England from Brest with one of the last units of the British Imperial Force that were pulling out of France. In addition to the troops on board the ship, there was a group of journalists, who were all correspondents attached to the British forces. There was also a woman, who was not part of the journalist group, who claimed to be a correspondent for the *Daily Express* in Belgium and Luxembourg. Her name was Hester Marsdem Smidley.[4] When we arrived, we all boarded the train in Plymouth. The train was overcrowded, and it turned out that Hester Marsdem Smidley knew the King's courier personally. He had a carriage in first class that had been reserved for him and invited us to it. Along the way we went off to the dining car

---

[3] The document is quoted from its June 1942 translation into Russian.
[4] The transliteration used in the translation is retained.

to have lunch. I believe that France had signed a truce the day before, and Hester, who professed a great love for France, was very depressed. In the course of our discussion of long-range political and military prospects, I expressed the opinion that England's position had become extremely dangerous. She asked me: 'What do you plan to do in this regard?' I answered: 'I suppose I'll be called up at any moment.' After this she deliberately changed the subject. I can only speculate about what happened later.

My guesses turned out to be nearly all true. Hester Marsdem Smidley was a correspondent in the Netherlands, simultaneously working for Section D of SIS, the section that organised sabotage. She was engaged in spreading propaganda, demoralising the enemy rear lines and increasing general contact in the work of the Allies. When Hester returned to London, she told Miss Marjorie Maxse, who was doing political work at the time in Section D, about me. One of Maxse's chief assistants was a friend of mine and when she asked for his advice, he spoke about me favourably. As a result, Maxse asked him to arrange a meeting for her with me. In the middle of June I met Maxse and her assistant at St Ermin's Hotel in Caxton Street near Victoria station. During the conversation Maxse stated that since my main proclivity was in politics, I ought to work for Section D and take part in organising a school for training propagandist saboteurs. I accepted the offer. Since my draft card was dated 24 June 1940, I had to join Section D between 15 and 20 June 1940. The school had opened at Station 17 near Hertford by that time.

Further on in his report, Kim wrote about the history of the school, and how he was put in charge of the Spanish section of SIS (he also talked further about this in *My Silent War*). I will quote a few lines from a note that Philby made at the very end of his report:

Note: when I was in Caxton Street on the day I began working for Section D, Hester Smidley dropped in and said to me: 'I'm very glad that you're here. I hope that you will accept this offer.' It was then that I understood that she recommended me for the job.

Back to 'Söhnchen''s Report about Himself:

. . . before joining SIS, and Section 5 as well, every prospective employee is checked out in SIS and MI5 records. As far as I can recall, these are the facts in the registry materials about me: that I was a member of the Cambridge University Socialist Society, that I subscribed to the *Worker's Monthly*, that my wife was of an anti-fascist persuasion and my father a man of extremist views. Apparently, none of these facts was held against me. My past was never subjected to careful scrutiny. A stamp [signifying] a superficial check of my documents in the two registries was all there was.

The document is curious in many respects. It confirms that Philby had been honest with Milmo, because even in 1942 he genuinely thought that he was recommended to SIS by the woman who had passed herself off as a *Daily Express* correspondent in Belgium and Luxembourg. Philby naturally did not mention the bottle of champagne; however, everything else that he wrote in the report, and said to investigator Milmo and to Nicholas Elliott, and laughingly told the author of this book in 1987, fits together.

What I don't know is when Kim had to be more careful with his answers, his choice of words, his explanations and reasoning: when he had cunningly and guardedly to avoid the traps set by Milmo, proving that he was not the 'third man', that he did not work for Soviet intelligence and was not a traitor, and the like; or when he tried to prove to his bosses at the Lubyanka that he was not playing a double game, not betraying Moscow's interests, and was not a 'plant' placed by the gentlemen of the British Secret Intelligence Service against them.

I also don't know in which instance he experienced greater difficulty. I can't say when the anxiety, or perhaps even the despair, that overwhelmed him was more bitter and painful.

Philby devotes a great many pages in *My Silent War* to his work for the British SIS during the war. There was no need to elaborate on this topic in our conversations. However, I heard a great many details from Kim that he didn't include in the book, as well as interesting thoughts about intelligence in general, and the British Intelligence Service in particular.

We left Philby in his little room into which Esther Marsdon-Smedley poked her head and disappeared, leaving the new SIS employee with the firm conviction that she was precisely the reason why he found himself sitting in front of a typewriter with a blank piece of paper, reflecting on what it was he might type on it.

At the end of the day, Guy Burgess came in and stated rather proudly: 'Here's a memorandum that I wrote. The chief has already signed it.' He put the piece of paper on the table in front of Kim.

The chief was Colonel Rendon, the head of the department in which Guy worked, and in which Kim was going to be working on a job of whose nature and content he had not the slightest understanding. Kim read the memorandum. It was a proposal to establish a training school for underground activities. Kim was surprised.

'Do you mean to say that there's no training school in your establishment?'

'No, there isn't,' answered Burgess.

This was the honest truth, a fact that was completely incongruous with the great glory of the British Secret Intelligence Service. That is why it nonplussed not only him, but later on his Soviet colleagues, both in London (as can be ascertained from the documents) and at the Centre.

In any case when he arrived in Moscow in 1963, and once again (for the nth time!) recounted the history of his work in SIS to his superiors, even then they couldn't believe that the famous SIS that had taught the most cunning and legendary agents did not have its own training school. They asked him the same question many times under different guises: 'What methods of training were used in SIS in this area . . .?' Each time, Kim had to tell his bosses again and again, even feeling somewhat embarrassed for the vaunted Intelligence Service, that it simply had no training school of any sort, before the war at any rate, and, therefore, no training methods. But even in the 1960s, when it seemed that this fact had been long established, checked and rechecked, the Cheka bosses did not believe him and shook their heads in disbelief.

'Of course, we've got to establish such a school,' Kim replied to Burgess and began to question the man whose idea had already been approved: where was the school to be located, when would it start up, how many instructors and how many trainees would there be?

Guy answered with his typical charming self-importance: 'My job is to come up with ideas. I came up with one and the chiefs immediately gave it their approval. As for turning it into a reality, that's what you'll have to think about. You're a lot better at details than I am.'

The typewriter on the table and the sheaf of foolscap that Guy had brought came in quite handy for executing this work. Soon after consulting several specialists, Kim wrote a paper outlining the issues and principles involved in creating the school: from the requirements for a building suitable for a school, a description of the desirable political orientation of instructors and students to a list of disciplines for theoretical study and practical lessons; for the organisation of sabotage, underground and wireless communications, and much more. Within a few days Kim submitted about twenty papers on the subject.

The school was finally set up. This was exactly the point at which contact between the Lubyanka and Philby was reestablished. It's logical to assume that Guy Burgess informed his former Soviet colleagues about all of Kim's movements within the corridors of the secret service, though I saw no evidence of this either in Kim's account or in the documents. It cannot be ruled out that according to the strict rule of conspiracy, introduced after the execution of all the previous residents and after Kim's attempt to reestablish contact by means of the letter that Maclean had passed on, the Lubyanka and the new director of the residency, 'Vadim', absolutely prohibited any form of 'cross' conversation with one agent about another agent or other agents. It was considered that 'agents on probation' didn't know anything and weren't supposed to know anything about one another's work in Soviet intelligence. How was it that the Lubyanka nonetheless gave permission to 'Vadim' to meet Kim, and why? Why was Maclean given permission (if we are to believe his account) to supply the time, place, password and other terms for the rendezvous? These questions must go unanswered here.

In any case, the report from 'Vadim', the KGB resident in London, that 'Söhnchen', with whom there had been no contact for almost a year, 'was working as a political instructor at the training centre of the British Intelligence Service preparing sabotage agents to be sent to Europe', caused jubilation at the Lubyanka. The Centre immediately demanded more detailed information about 'Söhnchen''s new job. What were his duties? Was he or could he be involved in deploying British saboteurs to the nations of Continental Europe? And the main thing: what could he report about the training of agents to be sent to the USSR?

The resident replied (at the beginning of January 1941) that 'Söhnchen' was working as a political instructor at the SO-2 training centre (the so-called 'Station 17'), that part of his duties included the political instruction of agents destined to be deployed to the Continent, in Holland, Belgium, France and, in particular, Germany. Regarding the USSR, the resident reported:

> . . . According to 'Söhnchen''s data, SO-2 has not sent its agents to the USSR yet and isn't even training them yet. The USSR is tenth on the list of countries to which agents are to be sent.

The leadership at the Lubyanka underlined this entire paragraph twice in red and placed two large question marks next to it. They could not believe that the training school of the British secret service was not preparing agents to be sent to the USSR. They reasoned like a Chekhov hero: 'This can't be so, because it can never be.' The euphoria about 'Söhnchen''s new position was again replaced by suspicion and doubt. A report was requested on the materials coming from 'Söhnchen'.

It was clear from a report submitted in March 1941 that from December 1940 to March 1941 'Söhnchen' reported, among other things, about the organisation of diversionary work by the British, the structure of 'Station 17', the management staff of the IS, and the staff employed at 'Station 17'. He also reported the names of agents who were deployed by the British to enemy territory, about Czech and Polish intelligence work against the Germans. But there wasn't a single piece of information from Kim Philby on the training of agents to be sent to the USSR or on the work with the agents already operating within it.

Nonetheless, the writers of the report concluded: '. . . "Söhnchen" is an interesting and promising agent; in this connection, work with him should be resumed.'

The recommendation to resume work with Kim did not mean that doubts about his value and even his sincerity had disappeared at the Centre. Was it worth working with an agent who did not consider the Soviet Union the main objective of the diversionary work of British intelligence? Was it worth reestablishing the liaison that the Centre had ordered to be broken off twice? Shouldn't it be broken off permanently?

This was the state of the Kim Philby affair at the Lubyanka in the spring of 1941.

Philby as a young man, just down from Cambridge.

Philby the intelligence officer, in Washington in 1949.

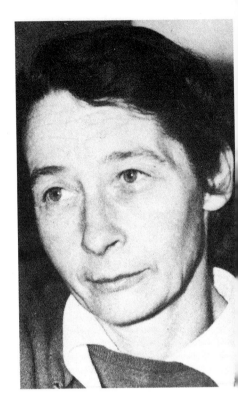

Philby's first wife, Litzi Friedmann.

Aileen, Philby's second wife.

St John Philby with Eleanor, Philby's third wife, and Harry, Philby's
youngest son, in Beirut.

Guy Burgess in Moscow.
(© Camera Press)

Donald and Melinda Maclean,
at Burgess's funeral.
(Associated Press)

Anthony Blunt. *(Observer)*

John Cairncross.
(Hemon-Tschaen/Sipa)

Arnold Deutsch. *(© KGB Archives)*

Teodor Maly. *(© KGB Archives)*

Alexander Orlov. *(© KGB Archives)*

Yuri Modin. *(Channel Four)*

Robert Bruce Lockhart.
(Hulton-Deutsch Collection)

Philby (extreme left) on the podium in the conference hall at KGB headquarters, July, 1977, after lecturing a gathering of high-ranking KGB officers. *(Phillip Knightley)*

Front, left to right: Genrikh Borovik, Philby, Rufina Philby and Graham Greene at a party in Borovik's Moscow apartment in 1987. *(V. Krokhin)*

Philby in his Moscow study in early 1988. *(Phillip Knightley)*

Philby's funeral. *(Associated Press)*

16

ON THE HARMFULNESS OF MYTHS

Did Philby know about the doubts which were circulating about him in the Centre? It seems to me that he did. Or he guessed about them. You can tell, if only from his overall discussion about the secret service, the value of information, and the myths about agents that agents sometimes create about themselves.

'Of course, that whole business with the training school that I wrote about in detail in my book distracted me from the main objectives of my work at SIS – I mean those objectives my Soviet colleagues set before me – but afterwards I managed to get back on the right course. And I also can't say that the task of establishing the school and working in it were entirely without benefit for me. It gave me the opportunity to meet countless SIS specialists who advised me about the school and, as a result of these meetings and conversations, I grasped the structure and orientation of SIS's work quite quickly,' Kim told me.

This is the point at which his ideas about SIS, in all likelihood, seriously contradicted the image of SIS that had taken shape in the NKVD. The fact is that the image of the omnipotence and absolute professionalism of the British Intelligence Service was nothing but a myth, and something of a literary one. To be sure, the English who went abroad in the eighteenth and especially the nineteenth centuries gathered an enormous amount of information. They were the leaders of the Industrial Revolution; the empire they had established afforded them the opportunity to travel practically everywhere in the world. Who took advantage of this opportunity, who travelled around the globe? Missionaries, botanists, geographers, geologists, merchants and, of course, military people. It was they who possessed all that information gathered in different countries. But this had nothing whatever to do with SIS, Kim continued.

The Secret Intelligence Service came into existence shortly before the First World War. At that time its reputation was not especially good, unless you exclude the art of deciphering, an area in which

SIS had achieved some success. In the period between the world wars, SIS was a small and extremely weak organization as well. Of course, there were some talented people who worked in it, but on the whole, it was a rather low-grade establishment.

Nonetheless, a river of information flowed into England. It was gathered by the people I mentioned. They came back from trips, went to their clubs, societies and scientific institutions which were linked up with one another, and exchanged the new data which they had acquired. It all flowed together like a river, although no one gathered it in an organised way.

If you trace the roots of the myth about the Intelligence Service's omnipotence and the great skill of its agents you will find them largely in English literature – in authors such as Rudyard Kipling and John Buchan. They were already beginning at that time to create the 'image' of 'early James Bonds'.

The French also played a not-insignificant role in creating the myth of the British secret service. England was more successful than France in the period of imperialist expansion and partition of the world. One had to justify one's failures: in France everything was blamed on the cunning British secret service.

This myth was created in Russian literature as well, particularly in Russian propaganda. In Russia the British secret service was considered the most skilled, the most treacherous and the most dangerous of all. Perhaps the fact that the English worked most effectively with white emigration had a role in creating this impression. But this work had no direct relationship to SIS; it was conducted through the Foreign Office and, primarily, through the army.

Among Philby's acquaintances in England was the English journalist Robert Bruce Lockhart. After he began working for the GPU, when he informed them that he knew this man personally, they were astonished, excited, inspired and confused all at once. They explained that his acquaintance was one of the most highly valued SIS agents, and the most cunning and treacherous spy of our time; they asked Kim to find out everything possible about his activities. Kim did all he could, but he never did find any evidence that Lockhart worked for SIS. Then later on, he found out for certain that Lockhart had never really been an SIS agent.

They objected: 'Why, he's even written the book, *Memoirs of an English Agent!*' That was true. But in England there are an innumerable kinds of agents. An agent is a person who works for someone: a writer has a literary agent; every company has sales agents, purchase agents etc. Take even the word 'agency'. It's used in the titles of various establishments – information, railway, airline. Are these establishments in any way related to the secret service?

Agent doesn't necessarily mean spy. When Lockhart was in Russia, in the Soviet Union, he was by no means an SIS agent. He served in the Ministry of Foreign Affairs of England, that is, he was an 'agent' of the Foreign Office. Naturally, it made no difference to the Soviet Union who was working against it – the British army, the Foreign Office or the secret service – but professionals really should know the difference.

When the Central Asian policy of the Russian tsars was being formulated and Russian aspirations towards India were being defined, these tendencies were opposed primarily by the British army, by its military intelligence. What was the life of an English officer in India like in those days? A bit of polo, a bit of cricket, a bit of a parade for which the officer drilled his soldiers; and for the common man in England the life of a colonial officer seemed, firstly, completely secure, and secondly, swathed in romanticism. That's why everyone was interested in finding out about it. It was a wide open field for detective and love stories. Moreover, there really were good agents in the army. All the well-known names in British intelligence were army people, not SIS agents. It was military intelligence that was involved in Afghanistan, Bukhara and Samarkand. Its people travelled there, met rulers and emirs, and returned with a bottomless pit of information. This also contributed to the myth of SIS's power.

Speaking about present times, at the end of the twentieth century, you certainly can't ignore the sophisticated level of technical means the British service possesses. But 'human' intelligence was not its strongest side by any means. The reason? A most banal one – money. The creation of a high-grade human secret service requires a great deal of time, patience and money. And SIS, like all other governmental institutions in England, experiences constant financial problems.

To be sure, insufficient funds are a constant problem and an international one. It exists to a certain extent even in the CIA. Many, many thousands of people work there. There are of course first-class minds, perhaps even outstanding ones, among them. However, even the CIA cannot avoid the trap that many secret services fall into: they believe what they want to believe. In part this is so because for many years they trained the kinds of agents who knew very precisely the kind of information the Centre expected from them and who sent in exactly that. Remember Graham Greene's *Our Man in Havana*; it has farce and hyperbole, but it captures these tendencies with absolute precision.

These same tendencies exist in the CIA. It was the CIA that gave the world the classic example of 'expected' information – such as the operation in the Bay of Pigs. The CIA used information from Cuban émigrés at that time. On the one hand, they wanted to intervene in Cuba very much, and on the other, they knew that there were ardent supporters of a solution to the Cuban problem by force within the CIA. So the information that came to it suited both sides. It was precisely this information that they put on President Kennedy's desk. The result was a fiasco and Allen Dulles's downfall.

There's another reason for the mistakes that occur frequently in intelligence services, Kim told me. After long indecision, a given country's intelligence service initiates some dubious operation. It takes the first step in the hope that if that step turns out to be unsuccessful, things can be turned back. Not on your life! After you take the first step, you fall hostage to yourself. You now have to take the second step, the third one and so on. The operation now takes on an independent existence, outside the control of the service. Money that was allocated for it has already been partially spent, people have been recruited and continue to be recruited, equipment is being supplied. When someone suddenly realises – colleagues, we're moving toward an abyss! – it's too late; the time has slipped away forever. His colleagues shrug their shoulders: so much money has been spent, so many resources have been allocated, so much effort has been put in. You can't turn back the clock – it would mean a colossal scandal.

In this way the operation itself begins to control its own creators and not vice versa. This happens frequently with people from the CIA. Vietnam is only one of these examples. They ran this business quite savagely. Recall if only the operation with the 'Meh' tribes. It was a perfect comedy. They collected money from the CIA, did nothing, and ran away.

It must be said to the CIA's credit that there were people in it who worked in Vietnam for a while, then raised doubts over the entire Vietnam operation. They wrote reports to their superiors about it.

But General Westmoreland didn't give them a fair hearing. He was the head of the entire military operation and would never have agreed to admit that anything he did in Vietnam had damaged America. The Vietnam War, aside from everything else, gave many people in the army and the CIA the opportunity to rise in rank, gain prominence in the public eye and advance in their careers – through murder.

'Admittedly, it's a complex affair for the CIA to work in such a nexus of bureaucratic ties and strands as Washington,' Philby ended. 'The most contradictory interests of diverse political and departmental groups intersect and clash. They don't let the CIA work for the truth, even those in it who genuinely have the desire to do so.'

Knowing Kim Philby's loyalty to the KGB, I didn't ask him questions either about the quality of 'human' espionage there, or about this institution's mistakes and crimes, or the role it played, let's say, in engaging Soviet troops in Afghanistan, as if in mirror-like imitation of the CIA's actions in the Bay of Pigs and Vietnam. I didn't want to spoil his mood.

Interesting as everything that Philby said was, scattering his life and thoughts as if on a canvas of reminiscences known only to him, we'd strayed too far in our conversation from that difficult time which for Europe was already war, but still prewar for the USSR. I tried to return our conversation to that time when, as Philby had told me, his contact with the residence in London was reestablished with Maclean's help.

'And so you met your new contact. This was already the fourth or fifth Soviet colleague who worked with you?'

'The fifth.'

'How does an agent feel when the Centre replaces his operative control, sends a new one?'

'This question can be answered, so to speak, strictly professionally. It can also be answered on the basis of personal experience. My relations with the colleagues from the Centre were based, of course, on a common ideology. In any case, I worked on the basis of conviction, believing in our common ideals. But as far as personal relations go, they can work out in different ways.

'At first, in the early years of my work in the service, I was absolutely convinced that if Moscow entrusted these people to do such sensitive and important work, it meant that they were impeccable from both professional and personal standpoints. All I had to do was follow their instructions and everything would be fine; their words and deeds were well thought-out, they couldn't let me down.

'This was the romantic period of my work. A bit later my attitude towards my Soviet colleagues became more sober; I gained not a little experience, and could judge what was correct and what wasn't entirely correct in their actions.

'I always say that I've been lucky in my life – Lucky Kim – and of course, there's no denying that I was very lucky with my first four contacts: Otto, Theo, Big Bill, and one another who worked with me in Paris after the war broke out. The first two were, in general, remarkable people. I've already spoken to you about them. One of them was a Czech, the other a Hungarian, and I had just come from Austria and become accustomed, so to speak, to the Central European surroundings. Perhaps that's why we understood one another very well.

'I was young, and they seemed elderly to me, which also helped their authority. But both of them were intelligent and experienced professionals, as well as genuinely very good people. Just to talk with each of them meant a lot to me and was a joy. At that time the rules of security were patriarchal; British counter-intelligence was virtually nil, and sometimes one of them might spend an entire evening in a café with me, talking about anything from literature and music to the latest political events.

'But the person about whom you're asking, whom I met in London after returning from France, was different. You might even say that this time I was unlucky with my contact. From the formal, professional standpoint, he was smooth as silk: precise, efficient, conscientious, knowledgeable about his work. But for example, if he had to convey instructions from the Centre to me, he'd get the paper out of his pocket and begin to read. Clearly, slowly, word for word, even though the picture was sometimes obvious from the first sentence. In cases like this, I'd sometimes say to him: I understand, it's clear. But he'd raise his eyes from the paper, look at me reproachfully and continue reading to the very end, to the very last full stop.'

His worst fault, or rather what bothered Kim most, was his total lack of a sense of humour. In short, their was no personal chemistry. Their relationship was strictly business. Each meeting was the fulfillment of a professional obligation, no more; and Kim did not hide the fact that those meetings would sometimes irritate him.

Only once did he seem different to Kim. It was in the autumn of 1941. Things on the front were going badly for Russia; Smolensk had capitulated, and the Germans were advancing on Moscow. They had had another routine meeting, discussing business, when he suddenly said to Kim:

'You know, I never thought it would get this far . . . The Germans are on the outskirts of Moscow.'

At that point for the first time, Kim thought, maybe he was being unfair to him. Perhaps there was a real live person with passions, joys and fears hidden somewhere deep inside him.

But that was the only time he showed his human side. At all the other meetings he was official, invincible, buttoned-up. When talk about business was over, it was obvious that they had nothing more to talk about: no chance of a soulful talk about music at a little café table; just to get away as soon as possible.

'Believe me, it's very important for an agent,' Kim explained to me, 'surrounded by danger and people in front of whom he has constantly to play a role, to know that he can unburden himself, speak his mind from time to time, and get not only professional advice but advice on the many problems which arise only because he lives the double or even triple life of a spy. Working without the possibility of this is a difficult, even risky, proposition.'

After he became more experienced in British intelligence work, and later during his contact with CIA agents, he could evaluate his Soviet colleagues with more objectivity. He told me completely frankly that all of those whom he met abroad in his work were professionals, and also good people with whom it was a pleasure to work – except for that failure in London in 1941, the only failure.

Certainly, he allowed that this man simply couldn't show his human qualities to Kim personally, and that his judgment was subjective. But Donald Maclean had exactly the same opinion of him. The fact is that he was both Philby's and Maclean's control in England at the same time. Then, in 1943 or 1944, this person was sent to America and he controlled Maclean again. Incidentally, Philby saw his name in an FBI dossier together with his photograph after he had departed from the United States. So he worked with Maclean for a certain period in Washington, and then they met again in Moscow, when Maclean and Burgess had left London. Maclean knew him well. Their opinions of him were identical.

Kim then told me a rather amusing story about an incident involving them in the USSR: it characterises the fourth contact.

When Maclean and Burgess appeared in Moscow in the early 1950s, no one knew what to do with them. Maclean, for instance, wanted to work very much. He was not yet forty, and full of energy; he was full of knowledge about all sorts of things, but no one knew what to involve him in or how. At first they were both put up in a dacha; the sweet life, so to speak. But out of idleness they began to get on one another's nerves and have disagreements. Maclean constantly asked for work. The KGB had misgivings about giving them work in Moscow, concerned about possible terrorist acts against them – that's why they sent them to Kuibyshev and placed them in separate apartments.

They gave Maclean work as an English teacher. For a man of his brilliance, intellect and knowledge, teaching English to students was simply absurd. So he suffered. His contact in Kuibyshev was that same person Kim had spoken of, Maclean's control in England and then in the States. Of course, he was informed all about Maclean's experiences. Maclean complained to him very often, trying to persuade him that he could be of much greater use to the country, that he had a great deal of knowledge, energy, youth. His control would listen carefully, write things down, promising to 'report' – and he probably did 'report' – but months went by (Maclean and Burgess spent a year or two in Kuibyshev) and nothing changed.

Someone once advised Maclean to write a letter directly to Molotov. Maclean wavered – could he dare disturb Molotov with such a personal matter? But time was passing, there was nothing else he could do, so he made up his mind.

On the very day that he decided to write, a call suddenly came in from Moscow. It was the 'mutual friend'.

'I'm flying into Kuibyshev tomorrow,' he reported. 'I have a very pleasant surprise for you!'

'Well,' Maclean thought with relief, 'I'll finally get work!'

He could hardly wait for his benefactor's arrival. The latter arrived the next day, just as he promised. He rang Maclean up and came over. He took off his coat slowly, walked across the room, solemly sat down at the table and began to question Maclean. 'Well, how are things, how are your spirits, what's new at work . . .?' and the like.

Maclean couldn't restrain himself and exploded. 'You promised me a pleasant surprise. Don't stall, tell me!'

'Here it is, it's in my briefcase,' his guest replied proudly.

He took a cardboard box out of his briefcase and handed it to Donald with satisfaction. Donald uncomprehendingly opened the box and saw: an electric toaster.

'You once complained that you didn't have a toaster. So we got you one,' his guest explained.

Maclean told Philby that he nearly broke our friend's neck. Kim related all this with characteristic humour, laughing, but the expression in his eyes was such that I had no doubt that he very much regretted that Maclean did not execute his plans regarding their mutual operative control's neck.

'How did the job search end?' I asked. 'Did Maclean write his letter to Molotov after all?'

'Yes, he did,' replied Philby. 'And he realised that he should have done it much earlier, because he was immediately summoned to Moscow and offered a position as a senior researcher in the Institute of World Economy and Foreign Relations, which was headed by the late Nikolai Inozemtsev. Incidentally, they became friends and Maclean worked well there for a long time.'

So that's the person whom the Centre assigned to reestablish contact with the agent 'Söhnchen' in England after it had lapsed for a year, virtually cut off twice by orders of the Centre.

In the same conversation Philby told me about two of his other Soviet colleagues. One of them worked with him in England after the war, 'a splendid professional and wonderful person'. They were good friends. 'Söhnchen' knew him by the name of 'Max'. He was a jovial, kindly man, who reminded Kim of his first two controls. He was easy to socialise with and to work with. It was during his residency that the well-known incident occurred involving Konstantin Volkov, the Soviet Vice-Consul in Istanbul, which Philby described in his book. Volkov asked for political asylum at the British Embassy and promised to give British intelligence important secret information for a certain specified sum. As an 'advance', he stated that he knew the names of three Soviet agents, two of whom worked in the British Foreign Office, while the third was head of counter-intelligence in London. As usual, Kim was lucky – SIS assigned him to work on the 'Volkov incident'. But he experienced several anxious weeks. To maintain his perseverance and calm, he relied to a great extent on 'Max''s support.

'Don't worry, old man,' Max would say when they met, 'we've seen a lot worse. The score will be in our favour.' (He was an avid soccer fan). These phrases were enough for Kim to get charged up with the faith that they would find a way out of this seemingly hopeless situation as well.

After working in Turkey Kim returned for a time to London, and there, to his joy, met Max again, with his simple but very effective manner of working. In 1957, Kim was told that Max died from a heart attack. He was only a bit older than Kim. The score of years had not come out in his favour.

In Istanbul Kim was 'controlled' by a Soviet colleague who was approximately his own age. The rules of conspiracy were observed very strictly there and each meeting lasted for a minute – only enough time for an agent to turn over his material and pick up a response. Kim actually never got to know his Soviet colleague in Istanbul. He could only recall that he spoke splendid English, but was somewhat nervous.

I listened to Kim's stories about his colleagues and thought how careful and tactful, how good-natured he was in his judgments, perhaps too good-natured. After all, they included all kinds of people, who differed in their characters and levels of culture, who had differing ideas about humour and decency, who dealt with an agent recruited abroad in very different ways. Some of them (we'll certainly see this later in the documents), mindful of their predecessors' tragic experience, considered that the best way to protect themselves against trouble was always to suspect the agent of disloyalty, of 'being double', of being everything else a foreigner with whom one had neither drank vodka nor broken bread could be suspected of being – and constantly and without fail to inform the bosses of your suspicions. Let the bosses sort it out. Why, there are so many enemies around! Comrade Stalin teaches us to recognise them and, if they don't surrender, destroy them – or rather, destroy even those that do surrender.

Fortunately, much to the credit of Kim's colleagues, those same documents attest to the fact that there weren't very many like that. Most colleagues who worked with him at different times rated both his work and his personal qualities very highly. When the time came to protect him from slander and suspicions, there were quite a few among them who did so with honour and courage, without giving a thought to the possible consequences to themselves.

Kim returned more than once to his account about his contacts, treating them undeviatingly with great respect. He almost never confused either their names or pseudonyms, or even the times he'd worked with them, although much water had flowed under the bridge since those days. This distinguished his accounts to great advantage from some of the archival documents (especially the reports 'On the source "Söhnchen", "Stanley", "Tom"', etc) whose authors often contradicted each another, confused nicknames, real names, the times when contact was cut off and reestablished.

But let's not be too nitpicking; after all, names aren't that important to us, and you can't always figure out which name was assigned to which person. Each one had several names. Should the person wake up in the night, I'm not sure that he would immediately be able to remember his real name. A spy's identity is truly multifaceted and complex.

Let's be compassionate towards those in the Lubyanka who tried in those turbulent times to keep all the names, nicknames and numbers of their co-workers and agents straight in their memories or on paper. There were no computers then and turning over the pages of a personal, working, operative – and Lord knows whatever kind of – file, the agents mercilessly mixed up all that spy fakery. In so doing they rendered it so secret that those whose work it was to do so could hardly figure out quickly who was who.

I came across errors and inaccuracies, even in lines about carrying out the sentence of VMS (the highest order of punishment). In one document the executed individual is described as a Polish spy, in another document, an English one.

That's how things were . . .

17

STALIN, HITLER AND IGOR MOISEYEV

The spring of 1941 was a difficult one for Stalin. He didn't show it, but he knew that those nearest him noticed his heavy, vacant stare, his fatigue and the frequent trembling of his left arm. His nearest and dearest: who would vouch that they were close to him? He had an entourage, but close to him? Someone, probably some Foreign Ministry type, had made up the terms 'near neighbours' and 'distant neighbours'. An idiotic conspiracy. Any fool could see that the 'near' ones were the NKGB, because it was next to the Foreign Ministry, facing it, across the square where that squirming clown Vorovsky stood. Army intelligence, the GRU, was more distant because they had situated themselves far from the Ministry of Foreign Affairs.

But there were spies and dissemblers in both places, as there were at Stalin's place – surrounded from far and near, but *surrounded* all the same, by spies, fools, hypocrites, toadies, liars, grey, incompetent people, and every one would gladly plunge a knife into him. Only he wouldn't give them this satisfaction. The Russian language is remarkably precise – a person's 'surroundings'. It was almost a military term. Each person is 'surrounded' his entire life, under siege. Only very strong people can break out, free themselves from the bindings of influence, think and make decisions independently.

Stalin spent a long time breaking out of the hostile encirclement, the 'near surroundings' of Trotskyites, Zinovievites, old-fart Bolsheviks who thought that they had pulled off a revolution, the riff-raff generals who had agreed to a pact with the enemy . . . Even if they hadn't agreed, even if it was all a mistake, it was all right, it was a useful mistake: it would teach them a lesson – others wouldn't agree . . . And that enemy was no longer an enemy . . . That is to say, not a total enemy.

Stalin had broken through this encirclement: the distant surround, the foreign one. He ruined all their plans with a stroke of his pen. Yet how cleverly everything had been planned: Anglo-Franco-Soviet negotiations. England and France, of course proposed a united front against Hitler . . . But the conditions of this 'united' front would be a front of isolated, poorly armed Russia against the enormous German war machine, aided by England and France. But it turned out that Stalin was not as simple as certain geopoliticians in the West thought he was. He turned everything about-face. The front formed up in the West, not the East. All of Western Europe, including 'great' France, had capitulated in a matter of some two to three weeks. The acclaimed Maginot line was no help. You can bypass any line; that's what Stalin did.

At the end of 1940, the beginning of 1941, Germany had already occupied France and Hitler's airplanes were bombing London. The mood in Moscow was very difficult. People felt that the war was approaching the borders of the Soviet Union. A dejected Ilya Ehrenberg returned from France, telling his friends about the terrible tragedy of the fall of Paris. He planned to write a novel about it. People listened to him carefully, trying to hold back their personal opinions. No one knew anything for sure and no one understood anything clearly: the August 1939 turnabout was too drastic; being an ally of German fascism felt too unfamiliar, but no one dared doubt the rightness of what had been done. It was easy for Ehrenberg – he had spent all those frightful years in France and some time in Spain; he didn't know Soviet reality.

Around January 1941, a routine reception for some event had been organised in the Kremlin. St George's Hall was lit with crystal chandeliers. The cream of the Party, state, military leadership and intelligentsia sat at round tables for ten to twelve people which had been set up all around the enormous, beautiful hall. At the end of the hall was a long table where the rulers sat. Stalin was there.

Moiseyev, still very young but already surrounded by the halo of glory and in good favour with rulers, had been invited. He was sitting at one of the round tables. Since his neighbour's name also turned out to be Igor, jokes began going round the table – people were deciding on the wishes they were going to make. When you find yourself among namesakes, you just have to think of a wish and it will come true.

Suddenly, at the height of the merriment, Moiseyev's neighbours quietened down and started at his back. He turned round. Stalin was unhurriedly walking towards the table. As always, he was wearing his military jacket, his trousers were tucked in his boots, and he was holding his pipe.

He came over, looked around carefully, searchingly.

'A jolly table,' he said in a not very friendly way. 'What are you laughing about? Or at whom?'

Moiseyev replied that there turned out to be two Igors at this table and that everyone was deciding on what wish to make.

'What kind of wishes do you have?' Stalin asked, melting slightly and stopping those who were getting up in the presence of the leader with a gentle gesture of his hand. Embarrassed, they began to state their wishes. Stalin listened, nodded with approval, then said with a crafty smile: 'I also have a wish. A secret one, so to speak. Will you take it upon yourselves to grant it?'

'Any wish, Comrade Stalin,' the guests responded joyously.

'Only I'm afraid that it's beyond your powers.' The leader shook his head.

'What is your wish, Comrade Stalin, what is it? Tell us! Any wish of Comrade Stalin's will be granted!' The emboldened table grew noisy, flattered by his imperial favour.

Stalin grew serious. 'There's a war going on in Europe. I have only one wish: that Germany defeat England as quickly as possible.'

The table fell silent. The words were too unexpected. Stalin grinned and walked away.

For the rest of the evening, guests approached the table that fortune had visited, asking what the conversation with Iosif Vissarionovich had been about. They received a word-for-word account.

That's exactly what Stalin wanted. He was relying on the story about his 'secret wish' ultimately reaching the German Ambassador in Moscow, and on the latter informing Berlin about it, when he had the chance. It was not excessive to demonstrate to Hitler one more time the loyalty of the Soviet leadership, its devotion to the duties which it had taken up. Nor was it excessive to remind simultaneously the intelligentsia of Moscow, which was alarmed by the fall of Paris, of his position; Stalin's position remained firm, and that's why the intelligentsia should keep their mouths shut. Their stupid, irresponsible and sometimes even provocative gossip could harm relations between the USSR and Germany. Stalin knew that there was no need to imprison tongue-waggers in order to stop the undesirable gossip in the capital during the winter of 1940–41. So many had been imprisoned and shot by that time that it was sufficient for him to utter a single sentence at a reception. The yapping dog would fall silent, curl its tail under and obediently return to its place.

Only the narrowest circle of individuals at that time knew about a memorandum which Sir Stafford Cripps, British Ambassador to Moscow, had handed to the People's Commissar for Foreign Affairs of the USSR, Andrei Vyshinsky, on 19 April 1941, and which Stalin was contemplating. In it, Cripps warned the Soviet government, with undisguised insolence: if the war between England and Germany lasted long, Great Britain would be tempted to conclude an agreement to end the war. The conditions of such an agreement, the Ambassador wrote, had recently been discussed in influential German circles: Western Europe would return to its pre-war situation, while Germany could thrust all its military forces unimpeded to the East to secure living space there.

Three weeks later, it seems Cripps's fears received confirmation. A German aeroplane landed in Scotland on 10 May, with no less than Rudolf Hess, one of those closest to the *Führer*, on board. The news shook the world. Everywhere people jabbered on about this being one of Hitler's tricks, of course, to sound out the possibility of peace-making with England.

Four days after Hess's appearance in Scotland, Stalin was given a report the Lyubyanka had prepared, based on material received from Kim Philby.

TOP SECRET
Report

Vadim[1] reported from London that:

1) according to 'Söhnchen''s data, Hess, after arriving in England, announced that he planned first of all to speak with Hamilton, a friend of Hess's from their participation in an aviation competition together in 1934. Hamilton belongs to

---

[1] Ivan Chichayev, the London resident.

the so-called Cleveland [*sic*][2] clique. Hess made his landing near Hamilton's estate.

2) Hess stated to the first official that recognised him, Kirkpatrick,[3] 'Nook',[4] that he brought along peace proposals. We still don't know the nature of the peace proposals.
(From Washington)

. . . Hess came to Britain with Hitler's full consent with the objective of initiating negotiations, since Hitler couldn't openly make peace proposals without damaging German prestige. That's why he chose Hess as his secret emissary.
(From Berlin)

. . . The chief of the American department in the Ministry of Foreign Propaganda Eitsendorf announced that Hess is in the best of health and has flown to Britain on a specific mission with proposals from the German government.

. . . Hess's actions do not constitute a defection, but were undertaken with Hitler's knowledge with the objective of proposing peace to Britain.

. . . The reliable Berlin source considers that Hess has realised the Nazi leadership's secret conspiracy of concluding peace with Britain before war with the Soviet Union is begun.

Four months after his first report, 'Söhnchen' sent in new data about Hess (Report N 338 dated 18 May 1941):

. . .1. Hess did not give the English any type of complete information before the evening of 14 May.
2. During talks with British military intelligence, Hess maintained that he had come to England to conclude a compromise peace, which should put a stop to the growing exhaustion of both warring nations and to prevent the final annihilation of the British empire as a stabilising force.
3. Hess stated that he continues to remain loyal to Hitler.
4. Beaverbrook and Eden came to see Hess, but this was denied in official reports.

[2] *The Cliveden set, a loose group of prominent British people, regular guests at the Thameside home of the Astor family, and known for its pre-war appeasement politics. (PK)*
[3] Lyman Kirkpatrick, former advisor to the British Embassy in Berlin.
[4] Signifies the Foreign Office.

5. In a conversation with Kirkpatrick, Hess stated that war between two northern peoples is a crime.

. . . 'Söhnchen' considers that now is not the time for peace negotiations, but that as the war develops, Hess may possibly become the focal point of intrigues and compromise peace conclusions and that he will be useful to the peace party in England and to Hitler.

Within a year and a half Lavrenti Beria will convey a special message to Stalin in which he will report that, according to reliable reports received by the same London NKVD residency, Hess was enticed into England by the British Intelligence Service. Knowing his Anglophile ideas, SIS kept all of his contacts under control and urged him to make the flight, calculating on causing confusion in the Nazi camp.

We're not examining the true underlying motives of Hess's flight here. However, with his two telegrams, Philby unwittingly was included with those people whom Stalin could consider provocateurs of a conflict with Germany. In any case, this opinion about him could have lasted until dawn of 22 June 1941, when Hitler attacked the USSR, and Stalin could be certain that not only Soviet agents, but even the politicians of Northern Albion, didn't necessarily lie all the time.

18

WITH SORGE

Naturally, I asked Philby the question 'What did he think was the most valuable information that he passed on at one time or another to Moscow?' more than once during our conversations. At least two traits of his character – his innate modesty and of course, his inner discipline – seemed to prevent him from answering fully. The question penetrated to the very core of a spy's work – what he reported to his Centre, what he was essentially working for, to what end he took on the severest of trials and *voluntarily* assumed such a burden.

Nevertheless, he did say a few things about the period when the USSR and Germany were at war.

'One of the most serious reports that I think genuinely helped Moscow was the information about several of Otto (the German Ambassador in Japan)'s telegrams, the same one who was a good friend of Sorge's. The Ambassador was directing these telegrams to Berlin, but the English deciphered the code and were reading almost all his dispatches. I remember one telegram particularly well; it was received, it seems to me, at the end of November or the beginning of December 1941. In it Otto informed Berlin that the Japanese would soon initiate major military operations to the south – against Singapore and other regions of Southeast Asia. This meant that military operations against the USSR were being cancelled or postponed. It was clear from the text and tone of the telegram that the Ambassador's information was absolutely definitive, not hypothetical. I immediately reported it to my Soviet colleague. This information played a not insignificant role: the Siberian divisions could now be moved from the Far East and sent to the West to support Moscow.'

'Didn't Sorge also report this?'

'That's the whole point! Stalin, as we know, didn't trust the intelligence service very much. But here's where luck was with me, or rather, with all of us. First of all, he wanted very much to *believe* that the Japanese would not start a war against the USSR, that the lessons of Hasan and Halhingol, where they had been defeated by the Red Army, had not been lost on them. Secondly, fortunately for us, my report was actually confirmed completely independently by Sorge's report from Japan. We not only didn't know one another, we didn't even know about one another's existence – but the information was identical. And this was a great success not only for both Sorge and me, but more importantly, for the country. The fact that these reports, sent independently, concurred could finally convince Stalin that the Siberian divisions could be sent to the vicinity of Moscow.'

'Did you send your information at the same time as Sorge?'

'It seems to me that it was at the end of November. Yes, yes, it was exactly the end of November. I remember clearly that I reported on Otto's telegram ten days before the Japanese attack on Pearl Harbor.'

'Which means that you warned Moscow about that, too?'

'No. There wasn't a word about Pearl Harbor in Otto's telegram. Only about the imminent Japanese strike to the south.'

'Otto didn't know about Pearl Harbor?'

'I suppose that the Japanese did not tell him about the imminent attack on the USA in order not to alarm Hitler. Hitler knew that if the Japanese attacked the United States, they wouldn't move against the USSR. Moreover, in this case, war between America and Germany was inevitable. But it was too dangerous for him. That's why the information about Pearl Harbor before the attack itself could have caused Hitler to respond negatively. Of course, this is my conjecture, I wouldn't guarantee completely that the Japanese based their actions on exactly this reasoning.'

'But it was Hitler himself, you know, who declared war on the United States.'

'After Pearl Harbor he had no other choice. It would not have been wise to wait until the USA declared war on him. I've often noticed that very few people remember that it *was* Hitler who declared war on the United States and not vice versa. The same was true of Italy: Mussolini declared war on the USA.'

'Not everyone, by any means, in the USA wanted to go to war against Hitler.'

'That's right. Besides, after the Japanese attack on Pearl Harbor, highly influential circles either of a pro-German or isolationist persuasion had good cause to cite the fact that the United States now had its own own difficult war in the Pacific Ocean. Why did it need another war? Why intrude in European affairs?

'In the seventies a report appeared in the press in America stating that Roosevelt knew about the attack being prepared on Pearl Harbor, but that he ostensibly did not undertake anything in order to convince the American people that they had to join the war in Europe. I don't think that's true. As a man brought up in the West, Roosevelt, in my opinion, could hardly have agreed to such sacrifices out of political considerations. Besides, even if he had succeeded in preparing the American navy for war alert, the Japanese wouldn't have called off the attack in any event. The whole issue of the USA joining the war against the Berlin-Rome-Tokyo Axis was extremely important. Sometimes I'd ask myself, "What if Hitler had not declared war on America?" Can the possibility really be ruled out 100 per cent that America might have refrained from declaring war on Germany in that case? No, it can't. In that case the history of the twentieth century could have turned out entirely different.'

'Do you regret that you never had your ten-day "vacation" trip to Japan in 1938? If you had begun working with Sorge, you would have more than likely shared his fate . . .'

'As far the trip goes, I can't say anything. But I can say that I regret very much not meeting him. And frankly, I even envy you the fact that you met Max Klausen, Sorge's wireless operator. It seems to me that it was in Berlin; I read about it in one of your books. As for collaboration, well, as you see, we did collaborate and we did so highly successfully in the case of Otto's telegram. I first found out about Sorge in the mid-sixties here in Moscow. I admired him then and still do. He worked in the most difficult conditions. You see, it's one thing when an agent works in his own country, in a familiar environment, and quite another when he has to operate in an unfamiliar country, and besides in a country like Japan, where a European doesn't have a chance to *get lost* in a crowd, he can't conceal himself, can't even get a check-up inconspicuously as I did in London. His actions – walking into a cinema, leaving before the film ends, getting in the Underground and dashing out of the door before the train leaves, transferring from one taxi to another and other such customary techniques – would have attracted the attention of dozens or hundreds of people. Someone would have immediately informed the police – this long-nosed European is behaving strangely. I was surrounded by friends whom I had known for a long time, I could get their advice, finally unburden myself. I was almost always in contact with my Soviet colleague. But Sorge worked in total isolation. The Centre recommended his assistants to him; he didn't know them beforehand. And in this whole unbelievably complex situation he operated impeccably. His failure was not his own fault; it was purely accidental. A woman, who was simply being questioned, merely mentioned a name completely by chance and it led to Sorge's trial.'

'You, too, had to work in unfamiliar countries, in Turkey and Lebanon . . .'

'Yes, but that's still not Japan. In the Middle East, generally speaking, I had pretty strong roots – Father was very well known there. Of course, what happened to Sorge could have happened to me. It could have happened in the country where I grew up. But all the same, I'll tell you frankly that I wouldn't have wanted to end up in his place.'

As Philby uttered this sentence he gave a shudder. He fell silent and without looking at me, grew thoughtful. Either he was contemplating the person whom we were talking about, his colleague who was executed on 7 November 1944, in Tokyo, or he was looking at himself, Kim Philby, whom the entire world called 'legendary', and 'fearless', and who uttered words on the terrace of the suburban Moscow dacha which perhaps surprised even him.

I kept silent. After a minute's pause Kim repeated: 'No, I wouldn't have wanted to end up in his place . . .' And he thought it necessary to explain: 'You know, I'm not at all an "impeccable" or "fearless" agent. I had many weaknesses. Now they no longer have any importance, but I was always aware of them. Here's an example. In the mid-thirties, as you know, I often travelled to Berlin, staying and working there for long periods both as an active member of the Anglo-German Fellowship and writer for the Anglo-German magazine, and as a Moscow agent. Once when I was in Berlin, I think it was in 1936, Hitler had just issued a decree that the only sentence for cases involving foreign spies in Germany would be execution by axe. I remember this decree almost put me into a state of shock. I was young, kept myself well-groomed, always tried to keep in shape and I regarded my intelligence work with a high degree of romance. I knew that it was dangerous, that it could end tragically for me. But this only added to the romance.

Long ago, back in Vienna and later, when I was already working for Moscow, I began to prepare myself for the thought that the threat of failure is always present in intelligence work, and so, therefore, is the death sentence. But for some reason I had imagined execution only by firing squad and had taught myself not to fear it. Now, all of a sudden, here was the executioner's block, the axe, the blood spurting from the neck. In short, I got frightened. Frightened in the most ordinary sense. I can also admit something else to you.' He looked at me seriously, without his usual friendly smile. 'I wouldn't vouch for myself should I be subjected to torture. True, I don't think anyone can.'

And Philby raised his hands slightly, palms up, which in the language of his gestures meant to say: you can think what you like about me, but that's exactly how it is, and no different.

He continued his thoughts.

'I was always lucky in life, I've already told you this. In many cases, had events turned out just slightly otherwise, I could have ended up in a entirely different situation, and you and I would not be conversing on this terrace. When associating with our agents after I came to Moscow, I always wanted to convey to them an important truth which I had learned through my own experience. Here's what it is. Of course, a man who's involved in the difficult, exhausting and by no means romantic work of espionage has no right to rely on luck or good fortune. He has no control over them. His circumstances can turn out to be so unfortunate that he won't be able to overcome them. And it's both absurd and immoral to criticise an agent in such a case. But if success does come, an agent has the obligation to take full advantage of it, even better, to take double advantage of it. To avail himself of all the opportunities that success brings, he has to examine them himself or at least intuitively guess what they are. I even wanted to entitle my book *Lucky Kim*, by analogy with Conrad's *Lucky Jim*. But then we decided that this title probably wasn't serious enough.'

'And so you came up with another one, *My Silent War*?'

'No, the French publishers came up with it. They were the first to publish the book. We couldn't print it in England; it would have been stopped immediately. That's why we began with France, America, Germany, Spain. The conclusion was reached that we were counting on: if the book had appeared in so many countries, why didn't the English public have the right to read it? Since the KGB certainly knew everything Philby wrote about, pleading issues of Great Britain's secrecy and security was completely absurd. So then it was published in England, too.'

I didn't consider by any means that my conversation with Philby about the information he passed on to Moscow during the Second World War was complete. So I kept returning him to that subject. As I've already said, he answered these questions with great reluctance, but – out of politeness – he did answer them.

'The most significant information which I passed on to Moscow while I worked in SIS? Well, to begin with, the general overview of SIS: its structure, the areas it was working in, directors, addresses, its most outstanding agents and that sort of thing. All the information that SIS possessed about the German *Abwehr*, Himmler's secret-service SD. What else?' A slight shrug of the shoulders and a lift of the eyebrows. 'At about this time the SIS began getting serious information about the state of affairs in the OSS as well, the American military-intelligence service from which the Central Intelligence Agency was subsequently created after the war. I also passed on this information, when possible, to the Centre, although it seems to me that they weren't terribly interested in it at that time. In 1941 I passed information on to Moscow about my conversation with one of the senior SOE officers. From this conversation I understood that a secret project to create the uranium bomb – that's what he called it then – was being developed. I don't think that he knew any details about it, but he said that this project was being developed with great speed. The Americans, according to him, knew that the Germans were also working on it, but were sure that they'd complete it before the German scientists did. He told me that in Washington they were already discussing how most effectively to use the new weapon. Against Germany or Japan? Or maybe keep it in reserve against the Soviet Union?

'Our conversation took place soon after the Allies landed in Normandy. It was clear that Hitler would soon be defeated, and the SIS officer said that they were certain in Washington that the bomb would not be dropped on Germany. At that stage of the war they no longer considered it a military card, but rather, from the post-war perspective, as a political one. Then he told me in so many words: "We want to raise the bomb and *suspend* it over Moscow. Just in case." I immediately informed the Centre about all of this and then, later, I kept close track of the Potsdam Conference, where Truman first told Stalin that America had atomic weapons. All my reservations regarding Stalin notwithstanding, I must say that both in Potsdam and all through the years when the bomb, as my interlocutor has put it, was "suspended" over Moscow, and the Soviet Union was doing everything to create its own bomb, Stalin conducted himself very skilfully, not showing the slightest hint of fear or even interest. He was in a very difficult situation: if anything had come up, he had nothing with which to retaliate.

'We can't rule out that he understood that "if-anything-came-up" would not come up. Having defeated fascism together, America hardly would have dared to cut the rope from which the bomb over Moscow was suspended. And did it really need to?'

Philby remained silent, and summing up his thoughts, said: 'That's the subject of another long conversation.'

Unfortunately, we didn't have it.

'I can imagine the impatience with which they waited in Moscow for your reports about the opening of the second front,' I once said to Philby. 'Did you have any luck passing any of it on?'

'Both Churchill and Roosevelt personally wrote Stalin a great deal about the plans to open a second front,' replied Philby. 'But as we can now state with certainty, it was almost always lies. They promised to open the second front in early 1942, then in 1943, but it wasn't until 1944 that they did so. And it wasn't until June, not at the start of the year, as they had promised. I, of course, reported the continuously issued new decisions to postpone the landing. At that time this was considered the most critical information and, understandably, it came in not only from Roosevelt and Churchill, and not only from me. My reports were rechecked – this is always important in intelligence service.'

I asked Philby: 'What did you know about the Soviet secret service obtaining American atomic secrets and were you involved in it?'

Kim nodded in the affirmative and answered immediately, as if he had anticipated this question and had thought of an answer to it ahead of time.

'I know *everything* about this affair. But I will never, ever tell anyone anything about it. This I'll take with me,' he said, emphasising every word, and putting both palms on the table, as if placing two seals over the words he had spoken, certifying the finality of his decision.

This most skilled and most disciplined agent wasn't to know that less than three years would pass before the 'eternal' secrets of atomic espionage came into the possession of any not very lazy historian or journalist.

Philby particularly emphasised one subject in the reports that he sent during the London period of his SIS work. He thought it necessary to speak about it.

'Since you've already asked about the information I was sending, I wanted to speak to you about this separately. Some of my reports which included secret information, plans, events, possibly had great significance. But in my opinion, sometimes information about what was *not* happening has no less and possibly even more significance. I call this kind of information "minus information". But it is very important!'

I intuited a polemical note in Philby's words and in the tone in which he had spoken them. He probably guessed from the expression of my face that I needed an explanation.

'The fact of the matter is,' he continued, 'that Moscow was very interested in what subversive and espionage work SIS was engaged in against the USSR at that time. As soon as I began to work there, my Soviet colleagues began to demand information about it from me. But I constantly reported that SIS was not engaged in any subversive and espionage work against the Soviet Union. Of course, we're speaking about that time. SIS was not permitted to engage in it then: the USSR was Great Britain's ally. But Moscow didn't believe it, didn't believe it for a long time' – he laughed – 'perhaps it still doesn't believe my "minus" reports from that time. And it kept demanding and demanding reports about it.'

Later, when I familiarised myself with the archival documents, the reason for Philby's polemical tone and the particular meaning which he attributed to that 'minus information' in our conversation became evident to me. Although its value is obvious (I compared it – and Philby agreed – with 'dead-end' trends in science), the documents nonetheless revealed to me an entire battle which the Centre had fought against Philby that nearly ended in a complete break with the source 'Söhnchen'.

19

So Who is the Real Enemy?

When you fly to Moscow today, from any city or country of the 'distant abroad,'[1] let's say London or New York, your plane will land at Sheremetyevo Airport. The Leningrad Highway connects the airport to the centre of Moscow. About fifteen kilometres before you reach the Kremlin, you'll see enormous 'porcupines' on the sides of the road – anti-tank barriers enlarged dozens of times which memorialise the area where Soviet defences held out through the autumn and winter of 1941 – the place where the smaller real 'porcupines' were located.

It makes your skin crawl to remember that Hitler's troops reached this very place. Today's symbolic 'porcupines' look as though they're stretching their iron arms up to the heavens, in supplication of aid for Moscow. From here German generals peered through binoculars at the outskirts of the Russian capital and sent telegrams to Berlin with assurances that in good weather, with a good pair of binoculars, they could see the Kremlin itself.

---

[1] That's what we in Russia today (I'm writing in the spring of 1993) call the countries which were not part of the territory of the former USSR, in contrast to the countries which were part of it as republics until December 1991; now they either are or are not members of the CIS – the Commonwealth of Independent States, which we now call 'the near abroad'. Evidently the words 'near' and 'distant' are fated to play a certain mystical role in our nation's history. It was precisely these words – as the reader already knows – that demarcated and still demarcate the boundary between the Foreign Intelligence Directorate of the State Security Committee (KGB) and the Army's Chief Intelligence Directorate (GRU) ('near neighbours,' and 'distant neighbours'). These exact words referred to Stalin's two dachas on the outskirts of Moscow: one located very close to the Mozhaiskoye Highway where he stayed quite often, worked in his last years and where he died (the 'near dacha'); the other located about eighteen miles from the Kremlin upon which he did not bestow his attention, but which was alway kept fully ready to receive both its master and any number of guests, whom he could invite there at any given moment (the 'distant dacha'). 'Near neighbours' from the KGB, 'distant ones' from the GRU, the 'near' and the 'distant' dachas, played, as we know, a large and often tragic part in the nation's history.

The generals were lying, because the Kremlin is impossible to see from there either in fine or bad weather, through poor or the finest Ziess binoculars. But it was true that the German troops were actually encamped some twenty kilometres from the Kremlin. At the very limits of its energy, the Red Army held them back; it held them back until it had gathered its strength and could begin its first major counter-offensive. Reinforced by the Siberian divisions which Stalin had risked moving from the Far East on the basis of reports, including Philby's, it beat the Germans back several hundred kilometres, winning its first major victory since the beginning of the war. British tanks – the first aid that Stalin received from the Allied anti-Nazi coalition – also took part in that battle near Moscow.

At long last Soviet newspapers could print photographs of hundreds of captured German soldiers. They looked sad and confused. They were wearing 'Goebbels boots', woven like ancient Russian *lapti* and worn by German soldiers over their shoes. The photographs aroused a great deal of interest. No less popular were photographs of smashed-up German technology.

The *Izvestia* photojournalist, Dmitri Baltermants, brought an excellent photograph to his editorial office: several smashed, still-burning tanks which he had assumed were German. A blow-up of the striking photograph appeared on the front page with the accompanying caption: 'acclaimed German technology which burns like a haystack'. All that first day the newspaper came out, Baltermants walked around on top of the world, but by evening he was fired from its staff and sent to a penal battalion. The fact was thus the indignant Ambassador of Great Britain had sent a note of protest to the USSR Ministry of Foreign Affairs because he had recognised the burning 'German' tanks as the British tanks which had just recently been sent as military aid to the Red Army.

Many years later my friend Baltermants, by that time a world-renowned photographer, told me about this. He was freed from the penal battalion after his 'first blood' (receiving his first wound) and considered himself lucky – this punishment was by no means the severest one that a journalist could have received in those days for 'acts of provocation undertaken with the intent of undermining friendly relations with the British ally' (that's precisely how they could have characterised his mistake had they so desired).

I'm recounting this to give the reader at least some small idea about how difficult the situation at the front was, in spite of the fact that the direct threat to Moscow had been eliminated, and about how uncertain the country's future was. Hitler's armies occupied Byelorussia and the Ukraine in just a few weeks. The partisan movement was just beginning to develop. Leningrad was under siege. War industries had been destroyed in the European part of the country, while the plants that they managed to evacuate had not yet begun production in the Urals. The government and the diplomatic corps were relocated to Kuibyshev. The possibility of a new offensive on Moscow by the Germans was absolutely real. The military concord with Britain and the USA which was to play such a large part in defeating Hitler was just being set up. The difficult hot summer of 1942 lay ahead, with the German breakthrough in the south, the capture of Sevastopol, the hoisting of the swastika-emblazoned banner on Mount Elbrus, the highest peak in the Caucasus Range, and the battle of Stalingrad.

What should the foreign intelligence service of a government that has come to mortal danger do during months and years like these? What should have been of greatest interest to the KGB at that time? I'm sure that any well-reasoning person would reply: information about the enemy's armed forces and war plans against both the USSR and its allies, and information about German espionage and subversive activities at the rear of the USSR and its allies.

In this respect Kim Philby, who had the opportunity at his new job (by that time he had been transferred to London and was working in Section 5 of SIS, under Major Felix Cowgill), to become familiar with decoded German telegrams, was an invaluable asset to Moscow.

But in the spring of 1942 the NKVD undertook an analysis of the material that had been received from Kim Philby from September to December 1941 and came to this conclusion:

> . . . Despite the fact that 'Söhnchen' has been systemati-
> cally sending a lot of interesting material recently, however,
> the materials *on the main issue of SIS work against the USSR
> and about its agent network on our soil* [author's italics] are
> extremely insignificant, while the information that was
> reported, such as the fact that SIS had not had and still
> does not have an agent network in the USSR, is highly
> dubious.

If 'The Hotel'[2] has a hundred agents, recruited in Europe over the past few years, mainly from countries occupied by the Germans, there can be no doubt that our country gets no less attention. Counter-intelligence work on Soviet territory shows that the British send their most skilled agents here . . . Is it possible to imagine that British intelligence is not at present undertaking or preparing several major practical initiatives ensuing from England's general policy at this stage of the war . . .?
5 April 1942.

So the *main issue* that interested Soviet intelligence in the spring of 1942 after the battle on the outskirts of Moscow in the interlude before the Nazi attack on Stalingrad and the northern Caucasus in the summer was information about the work of SIS agents against the USSR . . . That's what it had already been in the autumn of 1941, when the Germans were outside Moscow. You can see it in the text – it's the information received from Kim Philby for the period September to December of 1941 that is being analysed! He was being asked this main question, and his 'minus' answers that 'SIS had not had and does not have a network of agents' caused not satisfaction but, the opposite, irritation and dissatisfaction, in Moscow.

It was as if England, not Germany, had attacked the USSR on 22 June 1941, as if Churchill, not Hitler, had encircled Leningrad, and as if the British Prime Minister were advancing on Moscow and preparing for an offensive on Stalingrad, not the German *Führer*!

You can imagine with what redoubled energy and persistence that 'tiresome bore' in the London residence continued to get Kim Philby to answer the question which the letter from the Centre in Moscow identified as the main issue, the most important. In Moscow they expected a simple answer which would confirm someone's suspicions, someone's certainty that the British SIS was deploying a network of agents against the USSR, fielding their most experienced agents here, and preparing hostile acts against its ally in the anti-Nazi coalition.

What goal were those who were trying to get such an answer from Kim Philby pursuing? Whom would this have served? Were

[2] SIS.

they trying simply to toss Stalin extra evidence of his 'brilliant perspicacity' regarding the deceit of the British, his long-time conviction that the British secret service (second to the former Polish one, of course!) was the most treacherous, 'most anti-Soviet' one? Perhaps Stalin needed these facts in order to show to his Politburo colleagues that he, Stalin, was right, or in any case, that he had every reason not to trust the British when they warned him about Hitler's impending attack on the USSR.

Can one fully rule out the scenario that somewhere in the highest ranks of the KGB there was a man who, in the interests of Germany, deliberately wanted to drive a wedge between the Allies – Britain and the USSR?

About three months went by; the new German offensive had already begun, not, however, where Stalin had expected it and not where his army was preparing to repulse it. The offensive did not begin against Moscow or Leningrad; it rolled like a ball along the dusty roads of the Azov Sea deprive region toward the steppes of the Don, the Kuban region, Grozny, Baku and Stalingrad in order to deprive the centre of Russia, Moscow and the Ural region of oil.

That the situation that Soviet troops would face at the end of the summer of 1942 would be desperate was clear to any well-informed person in Moscow. The highest-echelon officers of Soviet intelligence were, naturally, part of just such a circle of well-informed persons. But they kept on demanding an answer to the same question from Kim Philby with remarkable stubbornness: the network of agents and the subversive work of the British against the USSR.

In July 1942 the London residence put Kim Philby under the control of a new operative, whom the Centre called 'Bob'. 'Bob' replaced the man with whom Kim, as he put it, 'was unlucky'. 'Bob' was the person who had to endure at first-hand the Centre's ever-increasing interest in the 'main issue'.

'Bob' reported on his first meeting with 'Söhnchen' on 25 July 1942, in a separate letter which was composed in careful phrases.

. . . I met 'Söhnchen' for the first time. 'Vadim' introduced me to him and also to 'Tony'.[3] After 'Vadim' left I discussed the following questions with 'Söhnchen': What is his specific

[3] Anthony Blunt.

work in 'The Hotel' as the head of the counter-intelligence section on Spain, Portugal, and their possessions? Are there other similar counter-intelligence sections for other countries such as the USA, USSR, and others?

'Söhnchen' said that his section deals with the struggle against the infiltration of hostile agents into their intelligence organisations in Spain and Portugal, as well as with the penetration of hostile agents on the 'Island'.[4] . . . Similar counter-intelligence sections, but which are not important, handle other countries. He says, for example, that there's only one person each assigned to the USA and the USSR and that these people work in one section which handles several countries . . . Then I asked him if he had any acquaintances or good friends who work in the Russian section. He replied that he didn't. Perhaps he has access to materials in the Russian section. He said probably not to those in verbal form, but during his duty work he might be able to get access to them, although very infrequently. Then I asked him about the content of these telegrams. He replied that it was nothing important. To my question about whether the British network in the USSR communicated by telegraph or whether the names are sent by post he replied that it is not required that the names be sent by post. Then I asked him if there where any names of British agents here in the USSR that were mentioned in the correspondence for this time period. He said that he gave two of these names to 'Vadim' . . . I asked what he knew in general about the work of the British against us. He answered that the only thing that he could conclude from their telegrams was that they complain about the difficulties of working there and the impossibility of obtaining good information. I asked him whether they are apparently working against us. He replied that they undoubtedly are, he doesn't know how, but he thinks that the British are carrying on their work against us through the Poles and Czechs who turn over information to them *in situ*. But he doesn't think that they turn over all of it, because part of the most interesting information they send by post or telegraph. And the information received here by the Czechs and Poles very rarely gets to them (SIS). It might get

[4] Great Britain.

there, but only to the highest ranking chiefs. I asked: 'Does their establishment read the Polish telegrams?' 'Söhnchen' replied that it doesn't, that the Poles have their own code that the British haven't deciphered yet. I asked him why. He replied: 'Because they're concentrating all their efforts on the German codes.'

They read the Polish diplomatic bag quite often, but not all the time. Further on, I asked him if the sources were indicated on the materials sent in by the Poles and received by them in the USSR. 'Söhnchen' replied that no, the Poles do not give their sources to the British. I told him that the work of the British, the Poles, the Czechs and anyone else who was against us was the most important matter that could interest us.

. . . Our conversation dragged on too long, and 'Söhnchen' had to catch the bus that takes him to work and to his home. That's why we ended at that point. 'Söhnchen' was nervous during our talk and stuttered more than he had previously. Perhaps this can be explained by the fact that he is in contact with a new liaison person: 'Bob'.

The Centre was not satisfied. It was not satisfied with 'Söhnchen''s or 'Tony''s answers. Nor was it satisfied with 'Bob'. It was the Centre's view that 'Bob' was working very poorly with them. He treated '"Söhnchen"'s and "Tony"'s *suspicious* [author's italics] underestimation of the work of the British secret service against the USSR with insufficient attention and vigilance'. He 'doesn't respond appropriately to the fact that "S(öhnchen)", "T(ony)" and "M(ädchen)" are in touch with one another about their Moscow work' and 'declares that cutting off "S," "T," and "M" from one other is impossible.' The Centre demanded that 'this be investigated immediately' and to this end proposed the following: 'to talk with each of these agents carefully and skilfully about the others, clarifying with each of them separately what their particular relations are, then comparing the received information, and to attempt to establish at whose initiative these meetings and conversations about contact with us take place and precisely what each of them has said about it . . .'

The Centre directed the residence's attention to 'the new signals from "Söhnchen" and "Tony"' to which much attention should be paid: 'the new statement by "Söhnchen" in his talk with "Bob" about

"The Hotel"'s weak work against the USSR and "Tony"'s statement about the absence of the "Hut"'s work against us on the territory of the "The Island". The suspicious nature of these statements is also aggravated,' the Centre emphasised, 'by the fact that neither "Söhnchen" and "Tony" even attempted to plead ignorance in this matter, but staunchly tried to justify this obvious absurdity, doing so obviously entirely deliberately.'

This was, I suppose, the first time the Centre directly accused its agent Kim Philby, and Tony Blunt along with him, of the deliberate distortion of information.

But the residence did not plan to admit its mistakes so readily, nor did it plan to 'surrender' Kim Philby. In early October 1942, when the Germans were stationed near Stalingrad, when their defeat in the fiercest battle of the Second World War was still a very long time ahead, when Red Army soldiers clung to every mound of land and every destroyed building to keep the Germans from the Volga (only some several hundred metres away), the London resident was, its seems, also expending his last efforts to defend his position and the reputation of his agent.

In his letter of response to the Centre, he reported that 'Söhnchen' was a very disciplined agent and conscientiously carried out the Centre's instructions. Of course, he was a 'more independent agent than "T", "M', and others,' the resident wrote. 'Why? This can be explained by the fact that "S" considers himself a sort of originator of this policy and prides himself on this to some extent.' The resident affirmed that 'S' clearly understood that 'We are primarily interested in "The Hotel"'s work against the USSR. But unfortunately, dealing with this main issue lies quite outside the specific work in which he is engaged, even though he works at "The Hotel". Therefore, it is imperative to set up other objectives for him which he can pursue while searching for opportunities to work on the main issue.'

The resident openly called the Centre's accusations against 'Söhnchen' 'incorrect and non-objective'. And he brought to his defence facts such as these:

At your instructions [he wrote], 'Söhnchen' brought 'The Hotel"'s agents' file of its work on gathering political information in our country from 1940–1942. There are several sources in these materials who provided 'The Hotel' with information on the aforementioned question. Of course, this agents' file is not an indicator of 'The Hotel''s work, as there is practically *nothing serious* in it. But we put before 'Söhnchen' the main objective of passing on to us the same type of files not only for this period, but for the previous five to seven years as well. 'S' said that he would try to do this, but that it would require a great deal of time, because he can't review files which are not directly related [to his work] without some sort of appropriate reason. We told him that he must use whatever plausible and reasonable pretexts in order to get these files. If he can't get them to us so that they can be photographed, then let him copy excerpts from the files where 'The Hotel''s network of agents and its sources of information here are mentioned. We are expecting this file presently and we remind 'S' about it each time. Our wish to obtain everything that interests us is unquestionable. But human capabilities also have to be taken into consideration. Wishes alone are still not opportunities.

What was this 'extreme necessity' that forced the London residence of the NKVD at the time of the battle of Stalingrad to assign its most valuable agent to search SIS for information about the political situation in the USSR that had been gathered by British intelligence five to seven years earlier, in 1935, thereby risking his life and, incidentally, Allied relations as well?

The last sentence in the resident's letter about the difference between wishes and opportunities was, frankly, extremely brave for that time. The entire tone of the response in general – in defence of Kim – was absolutely not in line with the abusive tone of the instructions received from the Centre.

The resident also added to this that 'after talks with "S" about the need to attract new people to work with us, "S" suggested a close friend of his who works in his establishment and who has a fairly good future . . .' Along with his letter to the Centre the resident sent a character reference of 'Söhnchen''s friend and reported that 'Söhnchen' was given the assigment to 'study him in more detail and keep us constantly informed about him'.

The Centre also expressed concern about Kim Philby's relationship with his father. The resident tried to placate the Lubyanka about this issue as well. '"Söhnchen"'s father lives very far from him,' the resident wrote. "S" has no contact with him. The latter still continues his pro-Nazi politics and associates with pro-German elements. "S" has nothing to do with him and doesn't want anything to do with him. Generally speaking, "S" considers his father not completely well in the head.'

However, apparently understanding that it was not safe only to praise 'Söhnchen' (which could bring more of the Centre's wrath upon him), the resident felt it necessary to underscore his faults as well: '. . . I have formed the opinion,' he wrote, 'that "S" is a great alarmist. One day several weeks ago, when the situation near Stalingrad was very difficult, he was in a very bad mood and he said that everything was lost: the Germans had broken through to Stalingrad, they were not far from Grozny, and he said that we should expect the capitulation of both these places and, possibly, of Baku. We asked him where he got this informaton. He replied that people were nattering about it at work. We had to calm him down, telling him that he had no reason to be worried, that while the situation was pretty serious, our commanders had been in tough situations many times before and had always found a favourable solution which brought the fruits of victory – this would undoubtedly be the outcome of this German offensive. Our people are fully confident of the rightness of their cause and of their victory, so there was no need and no reason for him personally to panic. This calmed him also, but the fact that he suffers from faint twinges of panic can in no way be denied and as we proceed in our work with him, we'll have gradually to eliminate this . . .'

The resident was sufficiently careful in corresponding with his superiors, but his arguments, which were expressed in the most careful form, still unequivocally underscored the Centre's lack of decency in persistently trying to obtain from Kim Philby only that information which suited the Lubyanka. Reading this correspondence you come to the conclusion that the main threat to Soviet agents in the most perilous work that they were engaged in abroad came not from the counter-intelligence of the country they were working in, but from their own Centre, from 'their own people'. Nonetheless, even in this most difficult situation of dual danger, in the most suffocating of times, there were people of honour amongst the agents who, at their own risk, came to the defence of the fates and reputations of people, whom they generally did not know, from the Centre's lethal attacks. There were people who had enough nobility and courage to demand justice and truth from the Lubyanka, even when it was clear that justice and truth did not please the omnipotent centre deliberately.

'The Hotel's Agent File' which Philby obtained aroused great interest in Moscow, of course, but as the resident warned, it did not fulfil its expectations. On 20 January 1943, in their letter to London, the bosses made a new attempt to bring both the residence and Kim Philby to their senses, proposing an acceptable solution to the problem.

> . . . For nearly a year now we have put before you (with 'Söhnchen''s help) the goal of an in-depth examination of 'The Hotel''s work against us. In our letters we have indicated in detail what was of primary interest to us . . . At first 'Söhnchen' turned over quite a good deal of material, but unfortunately it does not by any means reflect 'The Hotel''s actual work on our territory. Discuss the content of this material in depth with 'Söhnchen'. Ascertain from him whether, in his opinion, the material he turned over is *exhaustive* or only *a portion* of the material that he could obtain . . .

If you translate the half-transparent hints of the Centre into simple and clear language, the meaning of this letter is as follows. Why, in the end, should we fight over this? You know we're only talking about a few reports in which it would be so easy to write that SIS is conducting a huge campaign against the USSR, moreover not from case to case, but constantly. All the previous extremely puny material received from the source 'Söhnchen' would be useful to confirm this provided one condition is met – that he writes in his next report that 'the information that he passed about the SIS work against the USSR is in no way exhaustive, but represents only a tiny part of what he succeeded in procuring, since access to this material is very problematic – the treacherous SIS guards them especially carefully'. If 'Söhnchen' did not have the direct facts, that, essentially, was all that was necessary. The Centre also demanded in its letter that 'the source "S" be studied constantly, and tested and re-tested', because his constant statements that the SIS 'is not engaged in a broad campaign against the USSR are far too suspicious'.

In short, not only was a plan of action outlined in the brief letter to the London residence but prompting in the form of words ànd entire sentences that the Centre wanted to read in the next report from the source 'Söhnchen' about the work of SIS against the USSR. This simple method of espionage, when an agent could turn over the blueprint of an ordinary vacuum cleaner as a secret atomic reactor, was described at the end of the thirties by Graham Greene, a former co-worker of Kim Philby's, in the novel *Our Man in Havana*. But as we see, a similar idea was expressed by the Lubyanka back in Janaury 1943. It is so similar that, were I not convinced that neither Philby nor Greene saw these documents, I would have thought it was plagiarism by a well-known writer from the GRU.

To all appearances, the path hinted at by the Centre did not inspire the London residence. The material that the Center needed was not turned over to Moscow. Understanding full well what a continuation of the conflict with his superiors could lead to, the London resident wrote his next letter to the Centre on 10 March 1943, in a tone of both obedience and meekness without, however, losing a sense of dignity or humour, laced with the occasional whiff of mockery.

> 1. We've been concentrating all our work with 'S' on issues of 'The Hotel''s work against us. But the results, as you know, are not what we would like. It's possible that to a certain extent *this depends on us, too, that is, our weak leadership of 'S'*, [author's italics] . . . With regard to the nature of his work and his position, 'Söhnchen' states that he has nothing to do with the operational sections of 'The Hotel' not only in his countries (which are taken care of in terms of counter-intelligence), but the sections which are engaged in work against us as well. He states that this is why we haven't received and are not [now] receiving the information that we need about 'The Hotel''s work against us . . .
>
> 2. He's evidently fairly well regarded at work. In January 1943, when the pay scale was reviewed, he received a rise from £600 to £750. 'Vivian', the director of the section in which 'S' works, once said in conversation with 'M' ('Footman' was present) that 'S' is the only man in 'The Hotel' without any enemies. Based on this, as well as what 'S' says, he's on good terms at 'The Hotel'.
>
> 3. He's married and has a child. His wife doesn't work. She's

been constantly ill since giving birth, spending months at a time in hospital. In relation to his wife's illness we offered him financial assistance a few times. He has always refused it and said that he doesn't need it now, but that he'll ask for it when he needs it. Along the same lines, he has always answered that the country needs this money more, and it would be put to better use for defence, while he can get along without our help. He handed in a report on his wife along with his material.

4. Meetings with 'S' take place in London once every ten to twelve days, in the customary way, as with other agents. Sometimes, when the opportunity arises, he brings separate files to photograph (only when we ask him). In these instances we meet him in the morning and return the material in the evening. This, of course, is inconvenient and incorrect according to operational procedures, but it's the only way to get the documentary files that 'S' can't copy, because they're too large. Earlier, as far as we know, he used to have a 'Minox' but his photographs weren't very good, and at your instruction we took the camera from him . . .

5. We've recently raised the issue with 'S' about his submitting a summarising, complete and detailed autobiography with notes on all his contacts, all his work with us, in English institutions, and the like. 'S' says that unfortunately he doesn't have the time, that in his opinion *now is the time that attention should be paid primarily to getting information, and not to writing various autobiographies* [author's italics]. We pointed out the error of his conclusions to 'S', told him that his life and welfare were of no less interest to us than his information, that he'd still have to illuminate his life in more detail so that we would be fully informed about his life, everyday affairs, contacts and the like. He promised to write his autobiography as soon as he gets a bit freer and his wife feels better. We think we'll receive it in the near future . . .

This half-resigned letter apparently convinced the Centre that although London had changed its tone, they still didn't understand the true meaning of the problem that had arisen and apparently didn't plan to follow the Centre's advice.

Kim undoubtedly felt the tension of the situation in which he was involved. The pain, not that he ever talked to me about it, also persisted for a long time. I judge this by how persistently he defended the value of 'minus' information; by the amount of detail he used in describing the sources of the genesis of the myth of the British 'secret service''s omnipotence; by the fact that he did not consider it necessary to speak about the letter which he sent to the London residence through Maclean; and by the fact that Maclean was forbidden to associate with him. He also didn't tell me that he had to write innumerable autobiographies, explanatory notes and reports about himself, his wife, his children, his father, his friends and neighbours, while they kept asking and asking questions, studying and rechecking. How did he manage to join SIS? (I've already cited his own written report about this.) What was his new wife like? How did he spend his free time? Who were his closest friends? What did he talk about with other members of the group of agents that he knew? What did they talk to him about? What were his relations with his father? All his verbal answers were immediately reported on; all the written ones were sent to the insatiable Centre.

'. . . I spoke with "S" about his family, father, sisters etc,' Philby's operative control reported to Moscow after a routine meeting with him.

It turns out that one of 'S''s sisters got a job at his recommendation more than half a year ago in the counter-intelligence section of 'The Hotel'. She works as a filing clerk; part of her duties is to keep track of all the people who are mentioned in the telegrammes intercepted by the 'The Resort''s military intelligence. 'S''s sister's name is Elena; she is eighteen years old.

About one every two to three weeks 'S' meets his father. According to 'S''s information, his father continues to lament the fact that the British will obviously win the war . . .

Among the documents there is a report written by Philby in 1943 about Aileen Amanda Furse, who had recently become his wife (the marriage was not legally registered because Kim was still officially married to Litzi Friedmann).

. . . Below I report the details about my wife which you requested. (I had hoped to question her in more detail about her past, but unfortunately, she fell ill again before I was able to do so.) She was born 'Aileen Amanda Furse'. Her father was an army officer who was killed in the last war. She was born on 24 August 1911. When she completed her studies in 1933, she went to work as a supervisor in Marks & Spencer (this is a shop). Flora Solomon,[5] who supervised her, spoke with her. She worked for nearly four years in the Marks & Spencer shops in the provinces as an office manager (Oxford, Slough, Reading, Leeds, Glasgow etc). In 1933 she was appointed the administrative supervisor in London, a position she retained until 1940.

In 1933, through a friend of hers, the lawyer Basil Herbert, she met Frank Birch ('Birch'), with whom she became good friends. At that time he was mainly interested in yachts and the theatre. They met regularly. When the war began, 'Birch' was appointed head of the Naval Section in Bletchley (GC and CS) and she went there with him infrequently, that is, on agent assignments. Her role in these instances was as a cover (that is, when they were together, it looked completely normal and did not arouse suspicion). I never succeeded in finding out why 'Birch' was interested in things of this nature, since his work was entirely different (he was involved with cryptography, and not the affairs of others). I also did not question her about this activity for understandable reasons: because I completely respect the secrecy of 'Birch's' work and because I want her to respect the secrecy of my work. In any case she has not met 'Birch' since the autumn of 1940.

Her political views are socialistic, but like the majority of the wealthy middle class, she has an almost ineradicable tendency towards a definite form of philistinism (petite bourgeoisie), namely: she believes in upbringing, the British navy, personal freedom, democracy, the constitutional system, honour etc. She cannot, for example, understand that personal freedom to a considerable degree is incompatible with contemporary democracy; she sees this incompatibility as an abuse of democracy which can be eliminated by democracy itself. I am certain

---

[5] *Flora Solomon, daughter of a multi-millionaire Russian banker, was a family friend of the Philbys. She introduced Kim to his second wife, Aileen. In the early 1960s, by then a strong supporter of Israel, she decided that Philby was too pro-Arab in his writings. She reported to MI5 that he was a Communist and had tried to recruit her for secret work in 1937. This helped build the case that Philby was a KGB agent.(PK)*

that I can cure her of these confusions, although of course I haven't yet attempted to do so; I hope that the revolutionary situation will give her the necessary shake-up and cause a correct revolutionary response. Incidentally, she is an atheist.

Translated from English by Garanin. 15 May 1943.

20

PHILBY – DOUBLE AGENT

The Centre's persistent demands to supply it at any cost with information about 'SIS's broad campaign against the USSR' did not abate. To all appearances, the Kremlin's secret agent did everything to satisfy the somewhat masochistic tendencies of his masters. For example, he found a way to look through the correspondence of SIS with its agent in the USSR from time to time. The SIS station head, known in his 'firm' by the number '95,000', was in Kuibyshev, along with the Embassy of Great Britain, after being evacuated from Moscow. But Kim Philby's study of this correspondence added nothing new to the 'main issue'. The file stated as follows: '95,000' had no Soviet citizens whatsoever who worked as secret agents either in Moscow, Kuibyshev, or anywhere else on Soviet territory.

But the Centre could not believe this. If the London KGB resident had at his disposal a significant number of secret agents in England, how was it possible that his counterpart in the USSR had none? At every meeting Kim's operative control tried to make him understand and scolded him for negligence, as if he, 'Söhnchen', were responsible for SIS's failure to have a network of secret agents in the USSR.

It would seem that the Centre should be jubilant: SIS was not engaged in anti-Soviet work on Soviet soil; all the energy of counter-intelligence and espionage could be transferred to more pressing problems. But the KGB's logic during Stalin's times was a special kind of logic. Every *oblast*, municipal and regional administrative unit or section of the KGB in those difficult days of repression had a quantitative plan for exposing and arresting 'enemies of the people' within their jurisdictions. If there weren't 'enough' of these enemies, they were fabricated, because 'not fulfilling' the plan was considered proof of poor work or even sabotage on the part of the secret service.

Thus the KGB residence in London bore 'responsibility' in a certain sense for SIS's insufficient anti-Soviet activities. However paradoxical this seems, it could suffer because of the passivity of its English colleagues.

Kim tried to help his anxious Soviet colleagues (and himself as well) in whatever way he could. He, of course, did not stoop to fabricating SIS agents, but supplied his mentors with reasons which could, at least temporarily, moderate Moscow's appetites. At one meeting with his Soviet contact, Kim told him that the '95,000''s lack of a network was most likely due to the relocation of the bureau to Kuibyshev and the chaotic evacuation of the Soviet population. SIS had simply lost contact with its network of agents in the USSR. This being the case, then '95,000' and his co-workers were now intensively involved in searching for lost agents and finding new ones.

This was convenient and even convincing reasoning, and could be developed further. Given '95,000''s supposed interest in recruiting Soviet persons, Philby suggested taking advantage of this and planting a smart agent on him. 'Despite the fact that "95,000" will be very cautious, a very well-trained and prepared agent could be and should be planted on him,' the London resident, 'Vadim' (Ivan Chichayev), wrote to Moscow, reporting on 'Söhnchen''s suggestion . . . 'Such a person can gain authority and will be extraordinarily useful at the present time, and particularly in the postwar period.'

I don't know if the Centre took advantage of Philby's suggestion, and if it did, whether it had any success with it. Heaven knows what tricks they played. All secret services in the world play these games. But it should be remembered that while the Centre was discussing proposals about this 'game', the Germans were storming Stalingrad, approaching Vladikavkaz, had hoisted their banner with its swastika on Mount Elbrus, and had held Leningrad in the grip of siege for a year already.

Neither the critical situation at the front nor Philby's reasons and proposals placated the Lubyanka when it came to the search for the British agent network. The Centre's persistence grew, as did its dissatisfaction with the reports by Philby, Blunt and others on the 'main issue'; so did irritation with them and, stimultaneously, suspicions about them.

I came across this sentence in one of the Centre's letters to the London residence: '"S(öhnchen)"'s and "T(ony)"'s reports that SIS is ostensibly not conducting active agent work on Soviet territory contradicts our counter-intelligence data, which shows that such work is being engaged in on a broad scale and actively; moreover, very qualified agents have been sent into action.'

Perhaps one of the keys to understanding the reason for the Centre's persistence lies hidden in this sentence: counter-intelligence had come out ahead in developing an area that someone needed; intelligence had to catch up on it. Why did Moscow need the subject of British treachery at all? We've already made an attempt to answer this question. I'll add just one more thing to those reasons. If the thought of concluding the 'second Brest-Litov peace' was drifting around in Stalin's head at that critical time, then information about the two-faced, deceitful policy of the Allies would have proved useful in justifying such a move.

Suspicions about the 'interns' also could have furnished a good 'spare version'. The reason why they were not turning over the required material was that they were SIS agents planted in the Soviet network. Most importantly, if they were SIS agents, this fact alone proved the thesis of the English ally's treachery, which was what *had* to be proved.

The person in the NKVD who was most zealously working on the 'spare version' was a certain blue-eyed blonde, inclined to plumpness and the exposure of conspiracies. She worked in the Information Service of the Intelligence Directorate of the GUGB from 1942 to 1944. The blonde's name was Elena Modrzhinskaya.

Her job was to evaluate agent information, determine its level of reliability and significance, and propose the addresses to which this or that information should be sent. Granted, she was only one of many workers whose duties were exactly the same. But she stood apart from the others by her level of education, her intelligent command of the Russian language, her knowledge of two foreign languages – English and French – and also by her conviction of her own rightness and the inexhaustible energy with which she searched for enemies everywhere.

It was precisely the extraordinary wealth of information received from Philby, Blunt, Cairncross and Burgess that gave her the opportunity to express her suspicion of its authenticity. She reasoned logically enough. Could the British *enemy* really be considered such a fool? Was it possible that SIS still hadn't detected the leak of such precious information? Was it really possible that the people who worked there were so irresponsible and unprofessional that they failed to notice that Soviet agents were carrying out documents from SIS by the suitcase? Was it possible they didn't check an individual's past thoroughly before accepting him for secret work? And if they did run a check on him, how could they have given access to top-secret documents to Kim Philby with his Communist views, his participation in the Vienna events, his Austrian Communist wife? No, this was all too incredible.

This was how she persuaded her superiors. Since suspicion, euphemistically called 'vigilance', was never considered a sin in my country (in contrast to trustfulness, which Stalin called 'the sickness of idiots' and which was an unforgivable sin), people were afraid of disagreeing with this energetic lady, although by no means everyone agreed with her.

Intuitive disagreement is one thing; Modrzhinskaya's logically constructed arguments, backed by documentation, was another. She actually did have many questions on the interpretation of this or that information received from the agents in London to which those who believed in Philby's loyalty could not immediately find answers. She contended that the information coming from him was false, advantageous to the British and did not address the main issue – the work of British agents against the USSR.

Even the leadership had difficulty arguing with her, not only because she was energetic and her arguments often sounded convincing, but also because such disagreement could lead to considerable risk. What if it suddenly turned out that Modrzhinskaya was right? Who would be sent to the executioner's block then? First of all those who did not believe the vigilant lady; and the number of completely innocent people sent to the executioner's block was so high (in the internal NKVD jail, where executions were carried out in the basements) from all the floors of the Lubyanka building beginning in 1934 that the big chiefs hardly wanted to stake their lives on this card for the sake of defending 'interns' whom no one, in general, knew personally (except for a handful of controls).

'Blue-eyed Gretchen' and her supporters (there were not many, however, according to the accounts of contemporaries) used every opportunity to prove that they were right.

At the end of the summer of 1943, as a gesture demonstrating solidarity between the Allies, the anti-Nazi coalition officially presented the USSR government with material on the activities of German intelligence in Bulgaria and Romania. This material, received by the Chief Intelligence Directorate of the Red Army (GRU), was then sent to the NKVD for assessment. The NKVD's Information Service came to the conclusion that the British had by no means turned over all that they knew in this area. This opinion, expressed in written form, was officially sent through the GRU to Cecil Barclay (the official representative of SIS in the USSR), and the latter sent it to London. Kim found out about the message that Barclay had sent to SIS and passed on notes from it to his Soviet colleague, explaining that he hadn't seen Barclay's actual dispatch, but took the notes from the verbal account of an SIS co-worker, O'Brien. The Soviet residence sent Kim's report to Moscow, and the loop was closed.

A few days later an irate epistle from the NKVD flew to the London residence:

> . . . We bring to your attention the fact that the two texts were totally identical was discovered when the text of the evalution which we sent to 'our military neighbours' and the text of 'S''s report on it were compared. Your supplementary report that 'S' did not see Barclay's telegram himself, but found out about its content from O'Brien's account proves that 'S' is lying to us in the most insolent manner, when he tells us that he hasn't seen Barclay's telegram. Bear in mind that our evaluation was sent to the English in Russian, then it had to be translated into English and sent by telegraph to London. It is difficult to believe that O'Brien could have repeated this telegram to 'S' by heart, and the latter in turn could have written it down from memory. We have no doubt that 'S' had Barclay's telegram right in front of him . . .

Modrzhinskaya's logic, her decisive grasp and correct understanding of the chiefs' psychology, is evident in the telegram.

Here's another example.

Philby passed on to the KGB residence in London the text of the telegraph message sent on 4 October 1943 by the Japanese Ambassador in Berlin to the Japanese Ministry of Foreign Affairs in Tokyo about his conversation with Hitler and Ribbentrop which SIS cryptographers had decoded. This same telegram was received in Moscow from another source. In comparing the two texts, the KGB Information Service discovered that an important concluding paragraph concerning Hitler's intentions vis-à-vis the USSR was missing from the text that Philby had passed on. Here's the paragraph:

> . . . Hitler is still planning to assume the offensive next year (1944) on the eastern front. But judging from his explanation, you can conclude that this offensive will differ from previous ones in its scale. The future of German–Soviet relations is a serious problem which will depend in large degree on Hitler's decisiveness. Therefore, since there have been no changes in Hitler's intentions, it is premature to speak of a change in Germany's course. However, it is clear that Hitler is speaking differently from before, and it is possible that depending on the behaviour of the Soviet side, he will try to use political means to regulate the problem of German–Soviet relations.

This is truly an important point. The discussion was of possible attempts by Hitler to use political means to get out of the war with the USSR, which could be understood as the intention to conclude a separate peace treaty with the USSR. Such a prospect could hardly please the British. If Philby deliberately did not pass on the last paragraph of the telegram, it was indisputable evidence against him.

Of course, the text of the telegram deciphered by the British and passed on by Philby was accompanied by a footnote which said that the last part of the telegram received by the British cryptographers from the radio interception service was unintelligible and therefore could not be decoded. However, the Chief of the First (Intelligence) Directorate of the NKGB of the USSR, Commissar for State Security of the 3rd Rank, Fitin, rejected this explanation. In a report to the People's Commissar for State Security, Merkulov, he stated that a comparison of the text of the London telegram with a similar document which the NKGB had in its possession showed that the passages 'not decoded' and 'left out' by the English turned out to be precisely those parts of the Japanese telegram that they were not interested in passing on to Moscow. 'We do not accept that the given document was not fully decoded by the British,' Fitin reported to the People's Commissar, 'therefore, we consider that the detected discrepancy confirms our suspicions that the source "S" is serving as a channel to supply us with specially selected and doctored documents from which everything the British consider it unnecessary to inform us about is excised under the guise of gaps and distortions.'

The telegram of the Japanese Ambassador became the last straw that forced the NKGB to reach a final decision.

A new letter dispatched from the Centre to the London residence appeared on 25 October 1943 (a different person was in charge there, whom Moscow called 'Igor'). The letter discussed the fact that after careful analysis of the group of sources 'S', 'M', 'T', 'L' and 'S' (that is, Kim Philby, Guy Burgess, Anthony Blunt, John Cairncross and Donald Maclean) the Centre had come to the conclusion that they were evidently working on the instructions of and with the knowledge of British intelligence and counter-intelligence. What's more, the first three had more than likely been planted by the 'The Hut' into the left-leaning student body at Cambridge even before their first contacts with the GRU. 'There is no other way of explaining,' wrote the Centre, 'how "The Hotel" and "The Hut" could entrust such critical work in such responsible areas to individuals who were involved in Communist and leftist activities in the past.'

Other reasons were added to the logical reasons with which we are already familiar.

For example, 'during the entire period that "S" and "T" worked for the British special services, they did not help expose a single valuable 'ISLANDERS' agent either in the USSR or in the Soviet Embassy on the "Island"'.[1] The Centre considered that 'M' and 'T', in proposing more than once that they act as gunlayers and recruiters, had attempted to plant experienced 'enemy' agents into the GRU network. As an example of these attempts it mentioned Smolka, 'whom "S", "M" and "T" were foisting on the residence with the aim of planting an individual whom the "Island" wanted into our network'.[2]

But that wasn't the primary evidence.

The primary evidence consisted, in the Centre's opinion, of the

---

[1] The thought that there might not have been an SIS agent among the employees of the Soviet Embassy in London doesn't even occur to the writers of the letter.

[2] This is the hidden reason why Kim Philby unexpectedly told me Smolka's story, emphasising more than once that although Smolka was not a Communist and was subjected to persecution in connection with the Slansky affair, he did not, however, betray any of the Philby group.

fact that "'S'"'s and "T'"'s material about "The Hotel"'s work against the USSR as obvious disinformation', since these sources stated 'that at the present time the "The Hotel" is allegedly not engaged in active work against the Soviet Union'. The Centre stated further that after analysing carefully these circumstances, it had come to the conclusion that Kim Philby, Guy Burgess, Tony Blunt and John Cairncross[3] were agents of the British intelligence service who had been planted into the NKGB agent network. With regard to Donald Maclean, the NKGB allowed the possibility that 'The Hotel' was using him 'blind' – that is, it was simply keeping him under its control through 'S', 'M', 'T' and 'L'. The letter which Philby sent to the residence through Maclean was mentioned as an example. 'Using this simple method,' the Centre stated, 'Philby was checking to see whether or not Maclean was in contact with Soviet intelligence.'

To tell the truth, this decision by the Centre astounded me.

'How could they have come to these conclusions?' I asked myself, judging, of course, from the vantage point of a person who knew Philby's entire future in contrast to those who wrote the letter in October 1943. How could they have come to such an arbitrary interpretation of the circumstances? There was no direct evidence of betrayal. There were merely mental deductions, constructed on shaky suppositions (not even on indirect clues which didn't exist), that SIS could not accept into its ranks people who were 'tarnished' in their time by leftist inclinations, that Kim Philby had passed a letter to the London residence through Maclean (mentioned above) not in order to turn over the valuable material that he had gathered but to check 'Stuart''s connection with it and so on. What if all the Centre's assumptions turned out to be false? Surely the writers of the letter who had branded the group of interns as 'double' had to comprehend that this possibility was more than likely. They then would be the ones held accountable for the destruction of a group

---

[3] The letter was dated October 1943; Cairncross had turned over to Moscow the priceless information on the direction of the planned summer offensive by the Germans (Kursk-Orel-Belgorod) nine months earlier. He was the one who informed the Soviet command about the most strictly guarded secret information – the thickness of the armour on the new German tanks. The letter said the following about this information: 'The valuable documentary material about the work of the Germans against the USSR, passed on to us by these sources, doesn't prove anything, since these materials did not cause any harm whatsoever to the interests of the "Islanders".'

of the most valuable agents who passed on first-class information to Moscow, 'if only' on German war plans. How could they have decided to make this move?

But I underestimated the writers of the letter. Following all that I've recounted were sentences which delighted me with their simplicity. Further on the document stated that 'in spite of the fact that the residence is undoubtedly dealing with double agents, the Centre is nevertheless interested in maintaining contact with them. Because, as stated in the letter, 1. In the case that contact is broken, the Islanders will intensify the search for our other[4] "interns" in connection with which difficulties will arise for creating our new independent network on the "The Island". 2. Given the unquestionable attempts made to disinform us, this group of "interns" nevertheless turns over valuable material about the Germans and other matters. 3. Not all the questions about this group of "interns" have been completely cleared up . . .'

Making such a 'dual' decision, the Centre was ordering the residence to limit the sphere of the 'interns" assignments to information about the Germans, and not to allow the content of the new assignments to in any way reveal to 'The Hotel' and 'The Hut' the issues which *actually* interested Soviet intelligence. At the same time, the Centre demanded that 'all the work with this group of "interns" be conducted in such a manner as to reinforce their conviction that we trust them completely'.

This was a smart move. On the one hand they stated that Philby and his friends were 'doubles' (here's the long-sought-after example of SIS work against the USSR!), and on the other, they admitted that 'not all the questions about this group of "interns" have been completely cleared up' and suggested that contact with the group be maintained. In this way the Centre had the opportunity to satisfy someone's maniacal desire to get evidence of the work of British intelligence against Moscow, to deal with those people from the residence and the Lubyanka apparat who overzealously defended agents, and simultaneously to deflect possible accusations about the liquidation of the most valuable agent network, if it turned out that the network consisted of people who were loyally working

---

[4] Besides 'this group', comprising Philby, Blunt, Maclean, Burgess and Cairncross, there were 'other "interns"' active on 'The Island', that is, other agent groups, united under a general name.

for Soviet intelligence. In that case, its activities could be explained very simply: in the end, the direct obligation of any secret service to check constantly its agents for 'doubleness'.

In our conversations I asked Philby more than once about the professional suspicion, if one could express it this way, that exists in secret services. For obvious reasons my queries had nothing to do with the tragedy played out between 'Söhnchen' and the Centre from 1942 to 1944. Philby did not dwell on this topic, aside from those instances when he engaged in a hidden polemic about 'minus' information or mentioned the fact that Hans Smolka turned out to be a trustworthy individual.

The young employee of the Russian Foreign Intelligence Service, who was posted in the room where I leafed through the documents in the archival dossier of Kim Philby, filled in this blank. After learning about the topic at hand, he gave me a small lecture which I will retell here in abbreviated form.

'The difficulty of the already none-too-easy life of an agent,' he said, 'consists also of the fact that he knows that there is a special service in the Centre for which he works, which checks and rechecks all its agents and all its sources of information, not out of maliciousness or capriciousness, but because that is its official duty. In doing so, it is obliged always to assume the worst. A civilian will exclaim: "Why, it's a tragedy for a person to have to bear the weight of constant distrust day and night!" Yes, for a civilian, it's a tragedy. But for an agent, it's a given with which he deals from the very moment he begins this work. He knows that this service exists. He knows that its function is to suspect him professionally of disloyalty. Professional suspicion does not, by any means, mean distrusting an agent. It's simply one of the methods of constantly checking people who work in this sensitive and ruthless field of human endeavour. This notion must become habitual for the agent – he lives and works with it. It's true that it doesn't make life more pleasant. In the process of such examination the most diverse scenarios are considered. In receiving any information from a source, the specialists accepting it always ask themselves several questions: Whom does this information profit? Did the source have access to it? How can this information influence the relations between countries? Will it cause harm to our country? Finally, what harm can it cause the intelligence service, various high organs or the interests of the country where the agent is working? This last question is one of the most effective testing criteria. If the harm brought to the agent's own country is discernible, then doubts about the source's loyalty are brought down to a minimum.'

This is how a nice, tall, young Russian agent instructed me. It was tough, but logical. One could agree with this logic in principle, if one didn't know – in the particular case of Kim Philby – the main reason why the source 'Söhnchen' had been denied trust. This had nothing to do with professional suspicion; it was related to the conscious desire to extract, at any cost, information out of the agent about SIS's work against the USSR, not because it corresponded to reality but because, for some reason, the Centre sorely needed it in the most difficult period of war with the Nazis.

21

'Henceforth "Söhnchen" Shall Be Called "Stanley"'

Declared a double agent, 'Söhnchen' continued to work. The London NKGB residence continued to receive material from him and send it to Moscow. As we know, there was no order to break off contact with him.

He had no luck photographing documents. Photography was not the most outstanding of Kim Philby's many talents. He made use of the old and dangerous but tried and true method – he would take secret papers from his office in his briefcase when he left work, give them to his Soviet contact, retrieve and put them back in place the next morning. Of course, anything could have happened. But – 'Lucky Kim!' – there never was any danger.

As Kim said, today it's even difficult to imagine the degree of carelessness with which secret documents were guarded in SIS at that time. No one ever once asked him, as a matter of fact, why he took them out of the building. Apparently, other SIS employees were also guilty of the same sin and took secret documents home to work on; otherwise Philby would inevitably have attracted attention to himself. It's doubtful whether anyone can tell today who of these employees took documents to work on, and who took them to be copied by heaven knows which agents.

For a short period at the end of 1943 Philby passed on to his Soviet control political and war information about the Soviet Union that had been received by SIS, data about its residences, the work of the counter-intelligence section, radio intelligence and counter-intelligence activities, documents related to the Allies' strategic war plans, the correspondence between the British Military Mission in the USSR (Mission No. 30) and the British War Ministry, material on SIS work in the USA, the correspondence between SIS and '95,000', data on SIS counter-intelligence network on the Iberian Peninsula, a diagram of the organisation of the American Intelligence service, the telegraphic correspondence between the Foreign Office and the British Embassy in Spain . . .

Philby worked so actively, it was as if he wished to convince his enemies in the NKGB to the bitter end that a 'normal' secret agent (not a plant) could not possibly possess such an amount of information of the highest quality and carry it out of a secret establishment with impunity in such absurd quantities.

Conscientiousness and 'luck' inevitably elicit suspicion as well as praise. The better an agent works and the luckier he is, the more he'll arouse his Centre's suspicions about him. That's only one of the paradoxes of this profession. Kim Philby must be given his due – he did a great deal to furnish the Centre with these kinds of reasons against himself.

Here's another example.

'Igor' reported from London that 'S' turned over to the residence SIS 'supervisory file' from which the residence found out that 'K', one of the prominent people in Tito's inner circle, was regularly supplying an SIS representative with whom he was in touch with information. 'Igor' was immediately asked to what degree this material could be believed, and he was made to understand that since 'K' held a responsible position, the accusation against him was not a simple matter. If everything was confirmed, there would be rewards; if not, heads would roll.

At the same time a letter recounting the information received from Philby was forwarded to Dimitrov. His response came very quickly. It expressed gratitude for the signal, but also doubts as to its reliability. Moreover, it expressed the opinion that this 'was either a very clever game played by enemies of our unity and success or the informers' wish to distinguish themselves by employing any means, without considering the consequences of such information . . .'

Several instructions jotted down on this letter make up a brief but expressive play on the subject of how the chiefs wash their hands of such matters:

FITIN (raising his eyebrows with surprise): 'Comrade Korotkov, from whom did you receive such information about "K"?'

KOROTKOV (eyebrows raised to the same level of surprise): 'Comrade Shustov, I request that you report on this.'

In the end, the chiefs' 'washed fingers' would point to 'Igor', the resident in London. The proposal was made to him that he urgently report on the quality of the file on which the signal was based, as well as 'to report your personal opinion about the suspicions which you expresssed'. 'Igor' was asked to send, with the next outgoing mail, a microfilm of the entire SIS agent supervisory file which in itself should certainly have been extremely valuable to the KGB.

One can guess at the Centre's ambivalence towards it. On the one hand, a thorough thrashing from influential people who knew 'K' threatened considerable trouble and confirmed suspicions that 'Söhnchen' was continuing his dirty game. On the other, the KGB would finally receive the evidence which it so sorely needed of active work by SIS against the USSR and its Communist allies. From this standpoint, Philby was a fine fellow who once in a blue moon turned over the information that the Centre needed and demanded.

As the multi-experienced Yuri Ivanovich Molodin, the brilliant Soviet agent who worked in London with Blunt, Burgess and Cairncross after the war, once put it to me: 'My dear fellow, if you so desire, you can deduce completely opposite conclusions from any information! And it was done often. If it was very necessary.'

Among Philby's reports from early 1944, there are more than a few valuable reports on which the course of history depended. These include, for example, material about the possible separate contacts the British and Americans had with German emissaries (initially in the Pyrenees – territory that came under Kim's jurisdiction).

In early April 1944 'Igor' sent to Moscow Phiby's data information on the time of inception, place and scale of the operation 'Overlord' that had been told to 'S' by an agent of SIS counter-intelligence involved in training special counter-intelligence invasion army detachments. Of course, Stalin had received information about it from Churchill and Roosevelt, but the details and clarifications received from its agent 'in the theatre' were not superfluous.

However, in addition to his work for the KGB, as the reader suspects, Kim continued working for SIS.

'Kim Philby worked very well in SIS' is not Philby's or my evaluation of his work. These words belong to Kim's colleague in the secret service, the excellent political scientist, historian and journalist, Hugh Trevor-Roper. Philby himself spoke to me about his work in SIS with innate modesty. However, one could also be persuaded from his account that Philby's colleague in SIS was not exaggerating.

At first, when he lived in the suburbs, his work did not satisfy him very much: he was hampered by having to keep up relations with his secret service friends and to meet his Soviet colleague. According to Philby this really was a contradictory and chaotic period in general and his information, as he supposed, disappointed Moscow.

'Even if I had had the opportunity to meet Churchill or Gaitskell,' he said, 'the information received from them at that point would have been contradictory: that's how confused everything was at that time.'

But then – as always in his life (he repeatedly insisted on this and, it seems, convinced me of it) – a bit of good luck fell into his lap. Several subsections urgently needed specialists on Spain, because it was quickly becoming an important target of fascist Germany's activities both from the standpoint of military operations against the British navy and as a transshipping point through which Germany sent its agents to England, Portugal, Latin America, the USA and Canada.

As always, one of Kim's numerous friends (to all appearances, he really had no personal enemies in SIS), Tommy Harris, who worked in MI5, mentioned Philby, whose articles from the Franco camp during the Civil War in Spain were still fresh in the memories of many. He was immediately considered suitable. The head of MI6 summoned him, talked with him, and asked him a simple question: Would he agree to transfer and work with them?

'When do I start, sir?' Philby replied.

That's how he landed in the very heart of the secret service of Great Britain. Of course, the volume of documentarily confirmed information that was turned over to Moscow immediately increased many times over. But it would be incorrect to understand Trevor-Roper's words to mean that 'Kim Philby worked very well in SIS . . . for Moscow'.

He worked for SIS productively as well. It was impossible to work in any other way, if he wanted to make his contribution to the struggle against Nazi Germany and simultaneously climb the career ladder, that is, aim for the goal which his Soviet colleagues had set him.

Philby devised an efficient and inexpensive way to expose Nazi agents in Spain. As we're aware, British cryptographers had deciphered German codes and were reading practically all the encoded German telegrams transmitted by radio. These included telegrams exchanged between the German residence in Spain and its Centre in Berlin. They mentioned the codenames of German agents in Spain – 'Sommer', 'Margo', 'Federico' etc. Judging by these telegrams, the agents did not stay in one place, but travelled all round Spain. Philby's method consisted of the following: his people established good contacts with Spanish airline companies and purchased passenger lists from them. From then on everything was done very simply. Let's say that there were three passengers with German last names in the airline passenger lists of planes flying the Barcelona-Madrid route. One could assume, from the encoded telegram, that one of the three was 'Margo'. The next time, according to another telegram, 'Margo' was flying on a given day from Madrid to Seville. All German passengers on flights that day were established using the same technique. If one of the three who flew from Barcelona to Madrid previously was listed among them, one could assume with considerable certainty that he (or she) was the agent nicknamed 'Margo'.

Of course, not all German telegrams lent themselves to being deciphered. Some were encrypted in a double code. For example, the result of a deciphering might be the sentence 'A large consignment of beer has been sold', but it was impossible to understand its secret meaning.

Around the time I was having talks with Philby, information appeared in the press that Churchill knew about the impending German air attack on Coventry because of the German telegrams then being deciphered. But he didn't undertake anything to defend the city, out of fear that the Germans would realise that their telegrams were being read in London. I asked Kim if this was possible. Philby answered in the negative and told me this story.

After the German air attack on Coventry, expert cryptographers returned to studying telegrams which might have had anything to do with the air attack. They came to the conclusion that they could have cracked the second code in which the time and targets of the aerial raid lay.

In the telegrams the operation was called 'The Moonlight Sonata'. The cryptographers thought that they should have guessed this: it had to do with an air attack at midnight. Three places where the operation would be carried out were named in code in the telegrams: 'Reganschwern' [*sic*] (umbrella), 'Einheitpreise', and 'Korn'.

With hindsight the cryptographers castigated themselves for their lack of imagination. 'Umbrella' was of course Birmingham, where Chamberlain had strolled around with his famous umbrella. 'Einheitpreise' means an inexpensive shop; and the most famous company in the world that runs inexpensive shops is 'Woolworth'. What was meant was the city of the same name. (Philby was probably mistaken here.) The word 'Korn' was a bit more complicated, but the cryptographers declared that it, too, could be deciphered: Coventry was the only large city in England that contains the letters 'K', 'O', 'R' and 'N' in the German transliteration.

That's the kind of possible decoding they were talking about. But everyone knew it could only be done with hindsight. Even geniuses could not guarantee breaking the second code in the German telegrams before the attack.

Nevertheless, according to Philby, the British and Americans knew a great deal about the movements of the German navy, air force and the *Abwehr* ground troops. They knew about the movements on the Eastern front. But they certainly did not inform the Soviet command about all of them.

Yuri Modin explained the secretiveness of the English to me. They were certain at the time that Moscow was inundated with German spies who had penetrated both the KGB and the General Staff. If German agents had found out that the British were passing on decoded German telegrams to Moscow, Berlin would immediately have changed its codes.

Modin himself felt that there were no Nazi spies in these institutions. If there had been, something surely would have surfaced this many years after the war. But he never heard about anything like this.

But secrets always surface. I became convinced of this many years later, when Philby and his former colleague, Graham Greene, met in my house in Moscow for a 'literary' supper (that's what I call it – besides Greene and Philby, my friends the poet Andrei Voznesensky and his wife, the prose writer Zoya Boguslavskaya, the writer Vladimir Karpov, and my children, who are also all journalists and writers, were enjoying their presence). The two Englishmen began to reminisce about the past when they had worked together.

It was during this very conversation at the dinner table in 1987 that I heard Kim casually let fall a sentence – that one of his agents (SIS, not KGB!) was Peter Ustinov's father.

I saw my son Artyom's eyes grow round with amazement. I asked: 'Do you mean that same Peter Ustinov, with whom only today Mr Greene and I participated in the Moscow International Forum of the Intelligentsia? The one who got to speak with Gorbachev?'

'Of course,' replied Philby. 'His father was one of our extremely valuable agents.'

And they continued their conversation as if nothing had happened.

I wasn't able, unfortunately, to ask Kim about Ivan Ustinov's work in SIS. Bits of information flickered through the Western press later about the elder Ustinov's involvement in intelligence work. But I found a document, which confirms the words he let drop at the dinner table, in Philby's archival files of that period.

I'm mentioning it not so much because we're speaking about the father of a famous writer and actor, but because Ivan Ustinov was assigned a mission of great significance and sensitivity in which Moscow was very interested in at the time.

The issue of the possible conclusion of a separate peace treaty with Hitler occupied, in general, a large role in Kim Philby's work for both secret services. SIS wanted everything to happen in this area from the USSR's side, and the KGB followed the possible moves taken by the British and Americans in this area extremely carefully.

The document below illustrates this.

TOP SECRET N15 (incoming N158/148 7.01.44). 'Igor' sent in from London the following observation from 'S'. At the end of November 1943 counter-intelligence suggested to SIS that a major secret service agent be sent to Portugal – Ustinov, Ivan Platonovich (nickname U-35) – to establish contact with those German opposition circles which wanted to join the Allied side.

SIS chose Ustinov not only because he worked as a press attaché in the German Embassy in London, but also because he came well recommended as an agent. Thus, for example, Ustinov had recruited the German diplomat Von Putlitza in the Ministry of Information to work temporarily in the printing section of the British Embassy. The SIS agreed with the SS's proposal.

On 6 December 1943 the head of the Spanish-Portuguese [Sub-]Section of counter-intelligence of the IS directorate, Philby, spoke on behalf of the IS with Locksley (A. Cadogan's secretary) about this. Because Eden was not in London at that time, Locksley said that the resolution of this matter would have to be postponed until Eden returned. According to Philby, Locksley said that it was impossible to know in what frame of mind Eden would return from the Teheran Conference. Personally Locksley did not think that Ustinov's trip could cause any harm, if he were to be given the strictest instructions not to become involved in politics, and to engage only in intelligence work.

However, Eden could find sending such a person a great risk. In Locksley's opinion, Eden might possibly want to avoid any type of activity that could serve as the basis for circulating rumours about peace negotiations between the Germans and the English.

At the end of December 1943 the Ministry of Foreign Affairs informed the IS that it agreed to Ustinov's trip to Lisbon under the following conditions:

1. Ustinov must refrain from discussing any sort of peace proposals, no matter from whom they issued, and engage only in intelligence work.

2. While in Portugal, he had to be under the control and direction of the IS counter-intelligence resident, Charles de Salis.

3. Charles de Salis had to report on Ustinov's activities in detail to the English envoy Hopkinson. Ustinov had to carry out all the political directives to the letter that Hopkinson gave him.

The instructions that the London residence had been given regarding work with the 'interns' had taken effect. Following all the necessary precautions, they were met on assigned days and talked to, and they were relieved of the enormous amount of material they brought in; no one showed them that the Centre considered them double agents or that they were not trusted.

True, the London residence did stubbornly report to the Centre that those bits of 'Söhnchen''s material that it could check using its own resources – comparing it, for example, with similar material received from 'L' (John Cairncross) – were found to be identical. But the Centre did not respond to these reports: Cairncross was also considered a double.

One can only speculate about whether Kim Philby felt a cooling-off towards him at that time. On the contrary, perhaps he noticed the unexpected appearance of a special, strained 'friendliness' which could only arouse worry and alarm in a sensitive person. But this conjecture is too late. I couldn't ask him this question. And I wouldn't have. Perhaps the disciplined Philby wouldn't have answered, or launched into reasoning about how he wasn't 'sup-posed to know'. In these cases – as with 'minus information' or with Smolka – he carried on the polemic indirectly.

Not all of us have the desire to learn about the history of our illness and its diagnosis, or whether or not it is correct or wrong. But when it comes to one's dossier, if it has been kept by the secret service, whether the KGB or the FBI, everyone would probably look at it willingly. I'm certain that Kim Philby would have responded to the opportunity of leafing through the volumes of his KGB dossier with very deep and serious interest, and, I'm sure, with excitement.

The KGB chiefs' evaluation of his work meant a great deal to him, perhaps even too much, including when he was getting on in years. Simple bureaucratic inattention aroused suspicion in him that he was not being trusted. He would be tormented by injustice, retreat into himself, seek salvation in alcohol, think of suicide. He would have found a great many things to be distressed about, especially in the war years up until 1944, when he had done so much for Moscow, in the documents which I got permission to examine only after his death.

But there was trust in him, and the noble courage of his defenders as well. I've already discussed this, and there will be more about this further on.

A person of great charm, he compelled everyone with whom he had a chance to associate personally to believe in his loyalty. He did not always succeed in winning this trust through his enormous work, through the documents he turned over to the faraway Centre in Moscow. His incredible capacity for work delighted both intelligence services – both SIS and the KGB; however, as we've seen, it also elicited the opposite reaction in the latter.

By some inexplicable means, the spy managed to create and maintain – even posthumously – a certain aura of nobility around

himself in this dirty business of the oldest profession which he so
brilliantly represented and in which he worked in such a highly
professional manner.

Whether this aura is deserved or not – that is another question.

The proposed collaboration between SIS and the KGB which was
to have been established after Hitler changed from a 'unilateral'
British enemy to a bilateral, and then a trilateral British-Soviet-
American one, never bore fruit. If there had been a child, it would
have been a 'test-tube' baby, an artifical one which did not please
the 'parents.' The British were unhappy with the fact that Soviet
intelligence and counter intelligence were not supplying London
with serious materials. The KGB and GRU saw only anti-Soviet
conspiracy in all the activities of the British intelligence services,
while the material the latter turned over, say about the German
secret service, Moscow saw, first and foremost, as an attempt to
foist disinformation on it.

Since the times of the Entente nations' intervention in young
Soviet Russia, Stalin had long considered Churchill (and perhaps
not without good reason) 'the most vicious enemy of the Soviet
state'. Churchill, waging war with Hitler, was possibly trying to
prove that in the name of defeating a common enemy, he was ready
to revise his views of the Russian ally, ready effectively to collaborate
with Moscow; shielding himself from Moscow's eternally exposing
squint, it seems that he finally agreed with the characterisation that
'Uncle Joe' had given him.

It became obvious in the first half of 1943 that the Germans would
lose the war. As Philby told me, people in SIS, who were
thinking about the future, began to figure out what the primary
target of their activities would be after the defeat of the Axis
powers. They came to the conclusion that the 'firm' would have
to deal with the secret service of the USSR and the intelligence
services associated with Communist Parties in other countries –
in short, with international Communism, whose authority, of
course, had increased a great deal due to the imminent victory
over fascism.

I think that at the Lubyanka they experienced some satisfication
when Kim Philby passed to them a copy of a note by one of the
deputies of the SIS chief which said:

. . . The contradictions between Great Britain and the Soviet Union are as great as those between Britain and Nazi Germany . . . Soviet Russia is our friend only while it can obtain benefit from this friendship. It does not trust us and will exert all efforts in espionage activities against us even in years of friendship. When it will obtain everything it can from a friendship, it will inexorably activate all the secret forces against the ideals for which Britain struggles . . . In this way our most dangerous enemy after the war can turn out to be the secret aggression of Soviet Russia . . . But we must not permit this error – we cannot trust the Russians in the same way we can trust, say, the Czechs and Americans or give them information which might betray an important or sensitive source or allow officers of local Soviet intelligence to study our organisation anywhere . . .

At the beginning of summer 1943, SIS had enough work against the Germans, the Japanese and the Italians. But looking ahead, the leadership decided to establish a small section in SIS in advance which was to be given the mission of collecting material primarily related to the struggle against international Communism, to begin the work which, in time, would require great attention. The new section was headed by Curry, an employee of MI5, an experienced career officer close to retirement age.

Two to three weeks after Philby handed his Soviet colleague a written report about SIS's plans, the latter said at a routine meeting: 'Your report created a big impression in Moscow. A sensitive but very important mission is being set before you. When this section is finally properly established and begins broadening the scope of its work, it will be extremely important for you to become its chief.'

If what Kim told me was the truth, and it's difficult to doubt it, then a contradiction, even an unnatural situation, had developed in the Centre in relation to Philby. On the one hand, he had been officially declared 'a double agent', and on the other, he was being given the assignment of becoming the chief of the future anti-Soviet section of SIS.

At the end of 1943 the NKGB agent in London sent a letter to the Centre which also demonstrates that the attitude towards the 'interns' in the Centre remained unresolved and ambivalent.

In answer to 'S''s report about Vivian regarding 'S''s recommendation to hire 'Mädchen' as Curry's assistant, Vivian stated verbally that 'M' belongs to Bohemian circles and because of this, will not be suitable for this kind of work.

Judging by this record, there were two forces battling in the KGB. One was a group of influential employees (Modrzhinskaya and others), which the chiefs supported, who proceeded from the assumption that the 'interns' were provocateurs who were planted into the British intelligence network on the instructions of SIS. Another group (which the chiefs possibly also supported) continued to work with the 'interns' as before, trying to use them to obtain valuable information and, to this end, even attempted to plant them in important positions in SIS.

This muddle could not continue for long. Who was this H.A.R. Philby after all? An SIS plant? A 'double agent' or a 'loyal spy', who was working for the KGB not out of fear, but out of conscience? Who were his friends? Who were they, this whole group of 'interns?'

A definitive decision was finally made at the end of June 1944.

TOP SECRET. REPORT

Passed to John[1] about work with 'S'. 'The Hotel''s agent supervisory file No. 95670, which you sent with mailing No. 10, is of great interest to us. We were able to obtain documentation by way of other channels which corroborates to a great extent the material which you sent on the file. This is a serious confirmation of 'S''s honesty in his work with us, which obliges us to review our attitude towards him and his entire group. Further contact with them should be based on the consideration of their great value to us, and any possibility of failure must be excluded from work with them.

On our behalf express much gratitude to 'S' for his work, especially for passing to us the aforementioned file. If you find it convenient and possible, offer 'S' in the most extremely tactful way a bonus of £100 or give him a gift of equal value. 29.06.44.

---

[1] The code name of the new KGB resident in London.

So Kim's official rehabilitation was helped by the new documents which he could carry out of SIS for a short period of time, long enough, however, for the Soviet residence to photograph them.

But one cannot exclude another reason that might have guided bosses who had just declared Philby a 'double' and a 'traitor'. This reason might have been something like: if Kim Philby has prospects of becoming the chief of the anti-Soviet section of SIS, why consider him a 'double'? Wouldn't it be better to take credit for all his outstanding success? To declare 'Under our supervision our agent has attained a success unprecedented in the history of Soviet espionage'?

A joyous day arrived for the residence. They realised that the letter rehabilitated not only Kim Philby and his friends, but the residence itself, whose directors, to their credit, courageously defended their 'charges'. In those years (as well as in many others) this was a dangerous and often led to the death of the bold spirit.

Knowing Kim's character, they did not venture to offer him £100. They decided it was appropriate to give him a gift.

On 18 August 1944, Kim wrote a note of thanks by hand to the KGB chiefs and, that same day, gave it to his Soviet colleague during their meeting.

Knowing the customary elegant style with which Kim Philby wrote everything in his tiny but legible handwriting (usually without a single error), I fear that the Russian translation quickly done at the KGB does not give a true impression of the letter. But I had no opportunity to see the original.

> I am deeply grateful for your communication and the gift which was passed to me by Max.
>
> This communication inspires and excites me deeply. And binds me more closely than ever to those whom I always considered real comrades and friends, although I never saw them. More than ten years have passed since our collaboration began. And during this decade of work I have never been so deeply touched as now with your gift and no less deeply excited by your communication.
>
> Both the communication and the gift permit me to be absolutely sure that I have made a certain contribution to the greatest achievements of the Soviet people.
>
> Accept my heartfelt thanks.

As if symbolic of Kim's rebirth, two days before Philby handed his thank-you letter to his Soviet colleaguge, the Centre issued the instruction: 'the source "Söhnchen" is to be called "Stanley" from now on'.

Kim Philby was not to be told this.

Yuri Ivanovich Modin told me that Yelena Modrzhinskaya advanced to the rank of colonel in the service and left the KGB the same year, 1944, that Kim Philby and the other 'interns' were 'rehabilitated' (they were also rechristened 'athletes'). Later on she was head of a sector of the Institute of Philosophy of the USSR Academy of Sciences. The department staff called her nothing less than 'our private-colonel' behind her back. Later, in the late forties and early fifties, the blue-eyed bundle of unmasking energy became one of the pillars of the struggle against 'cosmopolitanism' and 'Zionism'. The blonde, who was putting on weight, found the opportunity on the one hand to slake her personal thirst for exposing 'conspiracies' and, on the other, to advance fairly well up the career ladder.

22

Shouldn't a Double Agent Have Two Decorations?

In *My Silent War*, Philby recounts at length and with great interest how he worked to be appointed chief of Section 9, how he won friends and shouldered aside possible rivals, but most importantly, how diligently he worked to get to the position.

One document shows, according to Kim, the restraint and wisdom with which the London residence informed the Centre of the opportunity facing him.

Memo on the Meeting with 'Stanley', 29 August 1944.

During this meeting 'S' informed me that there is a discussion [afterwards] at 'The Hotel' about sending him to Berlin . . . as the chief of counter-intelligence for 'The Hotel'. This will require about two years. His mandate will include working on all the illegal organisations of the Nazi Party.

On the other hand, Vivian made his suggestion to appoint 'S' instead of Curry, that is, as chief of 'The Hotel''s anti-Communist and anti-Soviet work beyond the cordon. This means that 'S' will have full information on the work on the fraternal[1] intelligence and ours from 'F' – the 'Hut' directorate.

'S' feels that work on anti-Soviet activity has greater potential, even though it is rather an equivocal situation.

'S' also reports that according to Cowgill there are fifteen people working at the 'Resort' on our ciphers. Menzies proposes to add many more people at the 'Resort' to work on deciphering. 'S' tells me that this should be avoided, since the 'Resort' has a lot of experience in deciphering.

This was sensational news: Kim was being proposed as head of

[1] The Communist Party.

the anti-Soviet, anti-Communist section of the SIS, which would run all the work of the British special services against the USSR and all the Communist Parties of the world. What could be more important? Where else in the world would a Soviet agent hold a comparable post?

But in the memo the news is placed between two other bits of information: the possibility of work in Berlin and a warning about an increase in the work of SIS cryptologists on Soviet ciphers. I suspect this was no accident. They wanted to show Moscow that Kim was not trying to take over Section 9; he was allowing the more experienced comrades at the Centre to make this decision. Of course, being chief of Section 9 was full of prospects, but it was for the Centre to decide. If anyone ever suspected that a plant had made this amazing rise up the corporate ladder, there was an answer: it wasn't Philby who made the choice, it was the Centre.

Naturally, in just two or three days, Kim was called for a special rendezvous and told that the Centre was *extremely interested* in his taking over instead of Curry. Bob reported to the Centre that very day: 'Stanley was pleased by this decision.'

In October 1944 the appointment of Kim Philby as head of Section 9 was announced.

This was the Centre's reaction:

> The new appointment is hard to overestimate. First of all, it is important to see the significance the British attach to working against the fraternal intelligence services all over the world and our service. The creation of Section 9 and the numerous resolutions on its work, which we saw in the last mail, speak for themselves. After the war the significance of this sector, apparently, will grow even more. As head of Section 9, 'S' will have access not only to documents of Section 5, but also of the F department.
>
> To all appearances, 'S' is moving up in his institution, he is respected and valued. He must retain this position and work so that his reputation continues to grow.

The Centre was very pleased, and not only because a NKGB agent was made chief of Section 9; it was also because such a section was created: a section to do anti-Soviet and anti-Communist work. At last the Lubyanka saw what it had been seeking in the bowels of the SIS. At last everything Comrade Stalin had taught them had come to pass. That same year the Centre thanked Kim once again and ordered the residence to give him another valuable gift. Kim wrote yet another elegant thank-you note, ruined as usual by the bureaucratic intelligence translation into Russian before it was filed (and now can appear only in a second translation back to English):

> I must thank you once again for the marvellous gift, which I accept with enormous enthusiasm and satisfaction. I hope that the help that I managed to give you in the past will be improved in the future, and that the trust accorded me in the past will be justified in the future.
>
> The prospects that have opened before me in connection with my recent change at work inspire me to optimistic thoughts, and all that remains is to realise them in concrete form. Once again, thank you for your encouragement. 11 December 1944.

Philby describes his work as head of Section 9 in *My Silent War*. I will deal only with those aspects that he did not cover there but did tell me in our conversations in Moscow.

The position in which he found himself as head of Section 9 was equivocal and even, as he put it, 'idiotic'. The section very quickly became one of the preeminent departments of the SIS, changing the intelligence priorities of that organisation to counter-intelligence directed against Soviet espionage and the Communist movement in Europe, and particularly in the Balkans, Italy and France. Sensing that, the best officers of SIS transferred to Philby's section, offering their services. These were people primarily of the same age as Kim, still young and energetic, who had joined the SIS during the war. The chief of Section 9 had the opportunity to create a brilliant organisation, gathering the most talented people to work with him.

This was the paradox.

'It was an idiotic situation!' he repeated. 'If all my operations against the Soviet Union and the Communist movement failed every time, I would soon be fired. If I achieved success every time, I could do significant damage to the Soviet Union. There was no single way out of the situation. In every case I had to make a decision.'

Sometimes he had enough time before an operation to discuss it with his Soviet contact, who could discuss it with Moscow. In such cases, there was even time for orders to come back from the Centre. They treated his problems attentively there, realising the complexity of his situation, and so they sometimes demanded that he do everything possible to 'block' or ruin a coming action and sometimes advised him not to interfere.

An example of 'blocking' is the well-known incident with Konstantin Volkov, which Kim Philby details in his book. This is the oral version.

In August 1945 the vice-consul of the Soviet General Consulate in Istanbul, Konstantin Volkov, appealed to the British acting consul, Chantry Page, with a request for political asylum for his wife and himself in England. In exchange Volkov promised to give the British secret information, including data on three Soviet agents holding responsible posts in England: two at the Foreign Office, and one in the administration of the British counter-intelligence service.

He was talking about Kim Philby and two of his friends – Maclean and Burgess. Volkov promised to give their names the moment he received guarantees of defecting and the sum of money he requested in pounds sterling. In accordance with Volkov's request, the British Consulate in Istanbul was supposed to send Volkov's offer to London by diplomatic pouch and not by cipher telegram, since he was afraid of deciphering.

To Kim Philby's great luck, the head of the SIS, receiving such an unusual and promising offer from Istanbul, decided to give this delicate matter to one of its most talented administrators: Kim Philby.

It goes without saying that the news of Volkov's threat became known to Moscow instantly. By the time Kim Philby arrived in Istanbul in September to deal with the situation, neither Volkov nor his wife was in Turkey. They were both taken away on a Soviet plane to Moscow.

That is how the Volkov affair was 'blocked'.

But when a twenty-five-year-old cipher clerk at the Soviet Embassy in Ottawa, Igor Guzenko, who had been working there from 1943, asked for asylum in Canada in September 1945, Philby could do nothing.

Guzenko turned in many Soviet agents in the West, whose names or codenames he knew from his work in Moscow and in Ottawa.

Among them was the British scientist, codename 'Alik', who, Guzenko knew, had worked on the atom-bomb project at Chalk River, Ontario. 'Alik', according to Guzenko, had given Moscow information on his work. Guzenko did not know the scientist's real name, but counter-intelligence quickly figured it out: the Soviet agent was the well-known scientist Dr Allan Nunn May. But even then, Philby did not simply sit back and watch.

According to the documents, it is quite possible that the list of Soviet agents Guzenko had revealed was first sent to Moscow in September 1945 by Philby.

> TOP SECRET . . . Stanley reports that he managed to learn details of the information turned over to Canada by the traitor Guzenko. Stanley also copied excerpts from a letter by the director of the 'Hut', Petrie, addressed to Menzies in the Mayor case.[2] Stanley says that there is a certain confusion in connection with the affairs at 'The Hut' and at 'The Hotel'. As a result of these affairs the British intelligence and counter-intelligence organs are undoubtedly going to take effective measures soon against illegal activity by fraternal and Soviet intelligence. Stanley was a bit agitated himself. I tried to calm him down. Stanley said that in connection with this he may have information of extreme urgency to pass to us. Therefore Stanley asks for another meeting in a few days. I refused a meeting, but I did allow him to pass urgent and important material through Hicks.[3]

In the next missive from London to Moscow, Stanley analysed the evidence they had against May. He concluded that they did not have enough yet to arrest or try him. In order to get direct evidence 'The Hut' could try provocations, Stanley warned. They were already discussing the idea of sending their own man pretending to be from the KGB to meet May and break him. They were planning to send Ivan Ustinov, according to Philby.

But even though the analysis of the situation and Philby's advice were invaluable to Soviet intelligence, they did not manage to save May for the KGB. He was arrested in 1946 (without,

[2] Klugman.
[3] Guy Burgess.

as far as I know, the 'provocation' Philby had been concerned about).

Among the information obtained from Guzenko was some that directly involved Philby. Guzenko said that the NKGB had an agent in the SIS who held an important post. Together with the signal from Volkov, Guzenko's information could have been a serious threat for Philby. However, the situation in the SIS remained not only calm but predisposed to promotion.

These two dangerous bits of information did not have a resonance until several years later.

From time to time the chief of Section 9 visited the European capitals, to familiarise himself with the activity of local Communist Parties, part of his job. He informed his Soviet colleague of the results of these inspection tours.

Here are a few reports passed along by the London residence to the Centre in 1945. They give an idea of Kim's work for Soviet intelligence in that period and of the character of his relations with the Lubyanka.

January 1945

Stanley had another baby, now he has three children. Bob.

Stanley reports that 'Hotel' and 'Hut' at present are studying the information again that was passed along by Krivitsky on the activities of Soviet intelligence and its agents.

After the baby's birth, Stanley brought a lot of interesting agent information as well as copies from some 'Nook' documents. I am sending all his materials to you. Stanley's mood at this meeting was bad, since his newborn was at death's door. I tried to console him, and our meeting was very brief, because he was in a hurry to get home.

February 1945

Menzies sent a directive to his '92,000' and '89,000' regarding the development of active work by 'The Hotel' against Soviet institutions on territory taken by the Red Army . . . Stanley's mood is good, the child is on the mend.

March 1945

In late February S flew to Paris to consult with 'Hotel' people on doing anti-Communist work and on preparing plans for 'The Hotel''s work in Germany.

Stanley informed me that in Paris he spoke with the chief of 'Hotel' counter-intelligence on the prospects and possibilities of developing anti-Communist work there as well as work against Soviet intelligence. For the moment, according to Stanley, there is nothing being done along that line, since the counter-intelligence group has a very small staff, which, basically, is working on German diversionary organisations.

Stanley flew to Rome to check out possibilities of organising work against local fraternal organisations and to find in Rome suitable people among 'The Hotel''s bureau to do such work. According to Stanley, the administration of 'The Hotel' has decided to keep Section 9 from any degree of contact with local counter-intelligence service – French, Italian and so on – since they fear that those services could be infiltrated by Soviet agents.

May 1945

Stanley reported that the counter-intelligence section of the OSS in Italy has set up a microphone in the building where Togliatti works, thanks to which they can monitor all conversations in that building.

In accordance with the order of Comrade Petrov I informed Stanley that from now on we will meet only once a month. S. asked for the reasons and I told him that we value him highly and therefore do not want to subject him to excessive risk through frequent meetings.

(From a letter to London from the Centre)

Desiring to mark the many years of very valuable help to us from interns Stanley, Hicks, Johnson, Eduard and 'Harry', in order to encourage them for future successful work with us, we intend to thank them for their work either with a lifetime pension or some other form. At your usual meetings find out their opinions and wishes. Inform us of your ideas and opinions on this matter, find out what size pension would suit them, if they express the desire to receive one, and how the payments should be made and what the cover story will be to explain the presence of the money.

S informed me of a plan to bug simultaneously all the telephone conversations of all staff in Soviet institutions in England. S presumes that this will be undertaken by Section N of 'The Hotel'. During three months afterwards, depending on the results, they will decide whether this should be continued or dropped.

David Boyle asked all 'The Hotel' bureaus to inform him of what they know about the technology of the organisation of the Soviet diplomatic courier service and also asked them to report if there is a possibility of organising the removal of documents from the Soviet diplomatic pouch. Stanley said that Boyle has set as his goal to obtain the removal of at least one document from Soviet diplomatic mail.

All interns refused a pension with the excuse that they will not be able to explain extra money for savings, since they live in England and their lives must be modest and their savings cannot exceed their income. Eduard and Hicks also refused any pension, but expressed the desire to receive regularly £25–35 sterling for operative needs. Others do not feel that discussing this issue is proper. Bob.

June 1945

Stanley returned to London from his trip. Stanley said that he was in Athens and stopped in Rome on the way back. From Rome on Menzies's orders he flew to Frankfurt for a conversation with General Long, chief of Allied military intelligence on the Continent. The aim of this conversation was how to organise gathering of military and political information about the Red Army and about the situation on the territory of Germany occupied by the Red Army. S reports on his conversation with Long and other members of intelligence in Frankfurt with his material.

July 1945

Stanley reported that the reorganisation of 'The Hotel' should be completed by October–November. Stanley noted that the whole committee regards questions of the reorganisation of 'The Hotel' in the light of how the future structure of 'The Hotel' can best do espionage work against the USSR. Committee members express the thought that the priority in work against the USSR should be given to the issue of studying the achievements of the Soviet Union in its work on new secret weapons, particularly uranium bombs and so on.

August 1945

(Bob from London, answering the question as to what people call S, writes.) Harold Adrian Russell is known as Kim in his circle of friends. He is known as Kim at his office, too. He got this name, taken from the Kipling story *Mowlgli* [the Russian translation of *The Jungle Book*], as a child.

Recommendation: It took an awfully long time to establish S's name. Too bad that Bob did not know this name before we asked. Could the story be read so as to get an idea of Kim's character?

(Mysterious are the ways of spies: Kim Philby, without suspecting it, developed his Moscow bosses' taste in English literature, at least for Kipling.)

(From a letter to London from the Centre)
Our source Johnson passed to us the testimony of Krivitsky, the traitor to the Homeland, former resident of the intelligence administration of the Red Army in England, which he gave to British counter-intelligence. In his statement Krivitsky announced that Maly sent a British journalist from a good family who sympathised with the Soviet Union and who was recruited on ideological grounds to Spain to assassinate Franco.

This example must be kept in mind when working with valuable agents. In his work Krivitsky had no connection to Stanley, but apparently using the loose lips of our former staff at the residence in England, he received top secret information on Stanley.

Stanley is an exceptionally valuable source, who works with us for ideological reasons. His eleven years of flawless work with us is irrefutable proof of his sincerity.

Bearing in mind the eleven years of work with us and the position Stanley now holds at the Intelligence Service, we can be sure that he will be able to be of incalculable help in the future. Our goal is to protect him from discovery.

We cannot rule out the possibility that Kim learned about the leak from Krivitsky only in 1945. This was another piece of upsetting news. (It was also in 1945, on a trip to Paris, that Philby learned that the address to which he mailed all his letters from Spain to 'Mlle Dupont' was none other than the Soviet Embassy. I do not think that this discovery added confidence in his KGB colleagues and their concern for his safety.)

But the days in Spain were long ago and he did not see any signs of suspicion toward him. On the contrary he was advancing at work. So there was no basis for great anxiety on his part or that of his Soviet contact, even though this was not the best news.

By then, did Kim Philby also know about another defector, 'Big Bill', Alexander Orlov? Moscow, as far as I know, never did warn him about any danger that could come from him. Kim learned that Orlov was in the USA quite by accident, as he told me, not from the KGB but from SIS papers.

I do not know whether he tried to discuss this far from joyous bit of news with the Soviet colleagues or whether he maintained a disciplined silence. But I am almost certain that of the two possibilities, the latter is more likely. It may have been more than ordinary discipline. It may also been the simple thought that would have come to the experienced agent: why not assume that Alexander Orlov's defection was not a ploy by the Centre? If the Centre did not deem it necessary to warn Kim Philby about Orlov's defection and the possible danger, then there was nothing to fear from 'Big Bill'.

Could Kim Philby have explained in any other way Orlov's silence about the 'interns' (the lack of suspicion toward them confirmed this silence) and the silence of Moscow about Orlov? He could not have known that Orlov had written a letter to Yezhov, promising not to reveal any GPU agents in Western Europe, but on one condition: the

GPU would not touch Orlov's relatives still in the USSR (only his wife and daughter left with him.) Stalin realised that he was dealing with a serious man and he did not touch any of the relatives.

That was the anxious state of things on the one hand. But there was another side that inspired Kim; and it was more than the recognition of his work by his friends in the KGB. Philby was getting very high marks from SIS as well.

According to Philby, the main method at Section 9 for collecting information about the underground Communist movement was by intercepting radio communications between Moscow and Communist groups in Europe. They had started intercepting during the war and continued after VE-Day. This alone gave them an idea of the basic parameters of the Communist movement in Eastern Europe.

Churchill's goal was to hinder their communications. But unsuccessfully: the Red Army was on the territory of these countries. Churchill and the Allies were unwilling to take military measures: in retaliation Stalin could direct his troops in a southern direction – to Greece. They would easily reach Athens; nothing would have stopped them. So Churchill's task existed apart, on its own, and life went on in its usual course.

Section 9 began its work by gathering information that could be used to discredit individuals in Soviet embassies and Communist activities in other countries, to create provocations against them, to force or encourage them to defect to the West. Philby, trying to slow down this area of work, insisted that it was not effective enough.

But he paid a lot of attention to interrogating former Soviet POWs and other displaced Soviet persons. According to Philby, they did not know very much about the Soviet Union, but to compensate for that, they were very eager to tell whatever they thought British intelligence officers wanted to hear. Archival documents show that some material about their interrogations was passed by Philby to the KGB residence. It's unlikely that they made life any easier for the people who came back to the Soviet Union after the war.

At the end of the war the British got their hands on almost the entire files of General Gehlen, chief of Hitler's counter-intelligence. They used it to get a maximum of information on the Soviet army.

Philby had the opportunity to study the Gehlen reports and notes. They were of interest to him both as chief of Section 9 and as KGB agent (Moscow had to know what Gehlen knew about the Soviet army). However, the material did not impress him. Usually, it was made up of a preponderance of hedging phrases like 'the possibility cannot be ruled out that events will develop in the opposite direction'. Often, the predictions ended that way. In 1942, for instance, Gehlen had predicted that by winter the Russians would undertake the main counterstrike in the direction away from Moscow. But the glorious Soviet attack began near Stalingrad.

So the Gehlen material contained many errors, which the British could have seen for themselves long ago, during the war, when they read almost all of Gehlen's information, which they intercepted and deciphered.

The British wasted about a year and half on Gehlen, and then dropped him, not because they were disillusioned in him, but because the contents of his office required enormous funds. The British, who felt the money was beyond their means, made a clever move – they handed Gehlen over to the Americans as 'a friendly gesture'. The Americans latched onto him.

The use of the German secret service against the Soviet Union did not begin, according to Philby, until after the war. It is quite possible, he thought, that they had considered it earlier, but had taken no actions so as not strengthen Stalin's suspicions that the Allies could undertake a separate peace with Hitler. Since the British and the Americans on their side were afraid of such a peace between Germany and the USSR, questions of any sort of contact with Germany were considered highly sensitive.

In explaining this, Philby said: 'It was done not because the British and Americans liked *us*, but because it was in their interests. In the end, it was *our* blood that flowed most heavily at the front. And they were interested in extending *our* struggle against Hitler.'

At first I thought that he had misspoken, or that I had misheard. But no, Philby meant exactly what he had said: 'our blood', that is, the blood of Soviet people. 'They' referred to everyone else. Philby used 'us' for Soviets in talking with his Soviet colleagues from the KGB. They were all very impressed by that. Many noted it in their reports on meetings with Kim.

Kim was a great psychologist. I told him about my talk with the Nazi saboteur Otto Skorceny in Heidelberg not long before his death and how Skorceny, who had nothing to lose, recounted how he had 'escaped' from the Darmstadt camp for German POWs awaiting trial for denazification. In the Western press the escape of a famous Nazi from the Darmstadt camp was described as 'the most mysterious and daring operation' of all the notorious Hitlerites had ever undertaken. Skorceny, laughing, told me that there had been no operation. The American commandant of the camp had readily allowed the war criminal to leave and had even given him his Cadillac and driver so that Skorceny would not miss his train.

Philby was not inclined to explain the story of Skorceny's 'escape' with political or military considerations. He felt it was the chaos and muddle reigning in Europe after the war, as well as the kindliness and political naivety of many American officers. Most of them wanted to forget about the war and that the Germans had been their enemies as quickly as possible. Even though soon after the war, the Americans recruited many Nazis.

Kim said that he did not know whether there had been consultations between Britain and the USA on coordinating anti-Communist work in the future. Moreover, as chief of Section 9 he was ordered not to inform the American services about his work.

It was quite possible, Philby continued, that this decision was made to keep the Soviet Union from suspecting the existence of some anti-Soviet front among its allies. However, he was certain that the Americans had their own subsection like his Section 9. Hoover, for instance, whose main concern during the war was the infiltration of German and Japanese agents in the United States, nevertheless actively worked against Communists, and not only in the United States but in Latin America (South America in those days was officially within the sphere of the FBI).

Philby considered another possibility: both sides, Britain and the USA, had made an agreement in deep secret to coordinate anti-Soviet and anti-Communist work by their counter-intelligence services, since Stalin had no reason during the war to suspect his allies of a secret conspiracy against the USSR.

As chief of Section 9, Philby was also a member of the Joint Intelligence Committee (JIC), consisting of representatives from the SIS, M15, the Foreign Office, the army and navy.

The people from M15 and the Foreign Office, according to Kim, were reasonable, informed, and understanding. But the army and navy men were absolutely crazy.

One such crazy man was Ian Fleming, later celebrated for his James Bond novels. According to Philby, he was 'a calm, balanced

man, who behaved with dignity, but who was seething with
wild passions'. No one would have thought, Philby said, that he
would become an author of such popular novels. He attributed the
metamorphosis to Fleming's 'inner wildness', which stimulated his
fantasies of 'supermen'. Fleming was popular with women, but his
imagination in that area too far exceeded reality. He found an outlet
for his passions, putting all his fantasies of supermen, pistols, women
and cars onto the shoulders of Bond.

Philby had not seen any of the Bond movies, but he had read
a few of the books. His general impression was that 'he had
achieved the rare combination of exciting plot with dull heroes
and overwhelming boredom'. These ruthless words were spoken,
naturally, with a measure of humour. Kim tried to protect his nerves
and not get upset over trifles.

He managed to find humour in his own dangerous work. He told
me with pleasure about a postwar visit to Leningrad by a British cruiser.
This was the first official friendly visit in the history of Anglo-Soviet
relations by a British military ship to the USSR. Even though the visit
was a friendly one, it was thoroughly prepared by the JIC, and the
representatives of the army and navy behaved in a bizarre way.

On the cruiser's deck they had built a booth from special blueprints
that did not look any different from any other construction on deck.
It held secret cameras for panoramic pictures of anything important
that came along the ship's path. Even though MI6 and the Foreign
Office were not thrilled – what if the Russians notice? It would create
a scandal! – the 'wildmen' prevailed. The work was top secret and
took a long time. An elite group was charged with building the
room and placing the cameras.

So the British cruiser, flags of love and friendship unfurled and
fitted with powerful espionage cameras, entered the Gulf of Finland
with an innocent air. The secret cameras clicked at all the Soviet
military ships and other objects of interest. The first object their
tiny super-secret cameras captured was an enormous Soviet camera,
openly placed on a huge tripod in the middle of the deck of a friendly
Soviet military ship, clicking away at the friendly British cruiser and
the friendly British ships accompanying it: another example of spy
humour.

In an official report on Philby, written before his appointment
as head of Section 9, there was the following: 'A substantial minus
in Harold Adrian Russell Philby is the lack of experience with the

Communist world. However, this can be rectified by active work in that area.'

Much has been written about Kim Philby and the SIS during the war, including by him in *My Silent War*. But very few books (his is among them) mention that for his work in the SIS during the war, for his contribution to the victory of Britain and its allies over fascism, Philby was decorated with the Order of the British Empire, the third highest in England. He was the only person in SIS who joined during the war to receive this high honour.

It was awarded to him in late 1945.

A bit earlier, in August, for the same achievements – a great contribution to the victory over fascism – another high honour was bestowed upon him.

TOP SECRET. TO CHAIRMAN OF THE NKGB USSR COMRADE MERKULOV. 7 August 1945.

In accordance with the value of the materials obtained by 'Stanley' and passed to us during the Great Patriotic War and his conscientious work for over ten years with our organs, we appeal for awarding him the government decoration, the Order of the Red Banner. (Signed by the chief of the Main Intelligence Directorate of the NKGB USSR.)

The regulations on decorations state that the Order of the Red Banner is given for combat and should be worn on the left side immediately after the Order of Lenin, the highest decoration in the USSR.

Shouldn't a double agent have two decorations?

23

To a KGB Agent from
the CIA with Love

Soon the heads of SIS realised that Philby had managed to gather
highly valuable information on the activities of Communist Parties
in the shortest possible time, once again demonstrating diligence and
initiative. That meant he could continue moving up the ladder.

They were preparing the highest rungs for him. They saw him
as a future leader of SIS and perhaps even head of the whole
organisation. Menzies once told someone that he would be happy
to vacate his chair as director of SIS for someone like Philby. That
is why they felt it necessary for Kim to work in an SIS station. The
absence of work in the Communist sphere had been taken care of
and now he needed battlefield experience.

They chose Turkey, a nation friendly to England that shared a
border with the USSR. Kim would head SIS bureau there
under cover of First Secretary of the British Consulate in Istanbul.
Philby was not, however, a career intelligence officer who had gone
through all the steps. He came to the secret service during the war,
from journalism.

Kim was moving from success to success.

He planned to move to Istanbul with his family. By then he had
been married for several years to his second wife, Aileen, even
though their marriage was still not registered officially. Litzi knew
about it, just as she had known about his affair with Frances Doble in
Spain. She considered herself free and after that shared her life with
the famous German Communist, Georg Honigmann. They lived in
East Berlin. But legally, the marriage had not been dissolved.

In order to marry the woman with whom he had children, Kim
had to divorce Litzi. For that, he had to see her. Of course, there was
no way he could keep a divorce secret from SIS. Of all the possible
ways to act, Kim chose the only correct and bold step. He went to
his direct superior at SIS, Vivian, and told him the truth: not the
whole truth, but only the truth.

He said that he had met a young woman in Vienna in 1933, a Jewess who was carried away by Communist ideas. In order to save her from the Nazis, he married her and brought her to England. They separated soon after. Now he needed a divorce and for that he had to see her, even though she lived in East Berlin. Philby's story did not arouse any suspicions from Vivian, and he was granted permission readily.

They met in Vienna and agreed that she would sue for divorce on the grounds of his infidelity. In September 1946 the decree was granted and a week later Philby married thirty-five-year-old Aileen, who was expecting their fourth child at the time. A few months later, in February 1947, after a brief training course at a special intelligence school, Philby was off to Turkey, as First Secretary at the British Consulate.

The two and half years in Turkey were not a waste of time either for the SIS chief or the KGB agent. In his first identity, he acquired a lot of experience in the field, and in his main work, accomplished many things. Not only did he gather information on diversionary groups sent into the USSR, which he occasionally passed on to his Soviet contact; more importantly, he could compromise the very idea and the plans for sending these groups into the USSR with the Turkish government.

The initiative for these plans, which were regarded with high hopes by SIS in London, came primarily from Philby himself. His superiors were convinced that if several groups of people were sent into Georgia or Armenia, and informed locals that they were from the outside world and gave them some gold, the locals would start weaving a spy network for SIS and prepare a rebel movement against the authorities.

To make sure that the hopes he himself raised would be seriously undermined or even better completely buried in the minds of the SIS leadership was a major achievement for Philby. He selected the perfect tactics for it: he remained an energetic enthusiast of the diversionary plans in the hope that life itself would bury them. He had every basis for that hope.

His plan, which was approved by SIS, was to start by sending five or six groups of five or six people in for several weeks. But it became clear quite quickly that it would not be easy to find volunteers for these missions. Through the old man Dzhordania, Prime Minister of Georgia in 1918 and now head of the Georgian Mensheviks in Paris, they attracted just two young men.

They were energetic lads who had just turned twenty (one was called Rukhadze). Their parents had left Georgia after the Revolution. They were both born in Paris and knew of Georgia only by hearsay. But they spoke Georgian. From Paris they were sent to London for training in elementary diversionary techniques and six weeks later brought to Istanbul.

Kim accompanied both to Erzurum. There he handed them gold coins and provisions and handed them over to Turkish intelligence. The Turks took them to the Turko-Soviet border. Upon their return, they said that soon after the young men had stepped onto USSR territory, they heard shots. One of the young men fell. The other the Turks saw running through the forest.

Many years later Philby was a guest in Tbilisi, and the chairman of the KGB of Georgia asked him: 'I heard that you were in Turkey in 1948. Did you ever meet a young man named Rukhadze?'

'I did,' Philby replied, waiting for the next question.

But the next question did not come. The KGB chairman changed the subject.

I asked Kim what he felt about sending young men to a certain death.

Philby replied softly, as if to himself.

'It was an unpleasant story, of course. The boys weren't bad. Not at all. I knew very well that they would be caught and that a tragic fate awaited them. But on the other hand, it was the only way of driving a stake through the plans of future operations.'

After it was shown that diversionary operations on land were impossible, Philby suggested doing it by sea. The idea was to send patrol-cutters from Riza, say, to the Soviet side somewhere between Batum and Sochi. London agreed, but asked that there be Turkish support, for without it the expedition would fail.

Philby went to Ankara to see the head of the secret service. The latter was full of enthusiasm about the plan and said: 'Don't worry, it's as simple as can be. You give us the cutter, we fill it with our agents, and then we give you the information we gather.'

It was clear that the head of the secret service wanted a new cutter. Kim explained to the Turk that they needed a special boat equipped with special technology, and the British preferred selecting the crew themselves. The chief's enthusiasm dimmed visibly, he offered more coffee, and changed the subject. Philby did not know whether any attempts to try his idea were made after he left Istanbul as SIS chief, but as of summer of 1949 it had not been attempted. He hoped that it, too, was dead and buried.

In Istanbul Philby lived on the Asian shore of the Bosphorus, in one of the loveliest houses on the coast. He described the house with pleasure. He had spent some of his best years there, which remained forever in his memory. One of his Bulgarian friends, who visited the house not long before I spoke with Kim, had told him that the house had been turned into a tourist attraction: a café, a garden, a marvellous view of the Bosphorus, and a memorial plaque on the wall that read: 'The greatest spy of the twentieth century, Kim Philby, lived here, 1947–1949.'

Philby laughed as he told me this, but it was clear that the Bulgarian's news had given him pleasure.

He remembered another place in Turkey more than the rest. In May 1949, somewhere between the villages of Igdyr and Tuzludzhu, Philby walked right up to the border of the country he served. The border passed along the crest of a hill and was marked by a striped border post. Agitatedly he approached the post, touched it, and even put his foot on Soviet territory, for the first time in his life. A second later, he pulled it back. But one of his companions photographed him.

I told Philby about an American movie in which the plot hung on a photograph that must have been taken in that area. The agent for the Soviet Union had been photographed many times with Mount Ararat in background, on the Turkish side. But in one picture he is photographed with the mountain seen from the Soviet side. This photograph was used as proof that he had been in the USSR.

'That happened to me!' Philby exclaimed.

He picked up a sheet of paper and started sketching. 'It's quite simple. Look, here's Mount Ararat. Here's the border, and here's the Turkish village called Aralik. The border is the Araks River. I was photographed against Ararat from the Soviet side, but I was not on USSR territory, I was on Turkish soil. And the photographer was also on Turkish soil, because there's quite a bit of land, about five kilometres, between Ararat and the border. There's nothing mysterious about it. Just people trying to prove something that had not happened.'

Despite the fact that SIS chief in Turkey managed to ruin

almost all the operations he was supposed to be running against the USSR, he must have been useful in other ways to his 'firm'. That would explain the ever-increasing evaluation of his work by SIS.

In August 1949 Philby unexpectedly received a telegram from London suggesting that he return to a new post. If he was willing to accept it, he would be chief officer in charge of liaison between the SIS and United States intelligence agencies, and he would be posted to Washington.

During his stay in Turkey, Kim had been pulled out four times, three times for consultations in London, Cairo and Baghdad, and once to London to take a course in military training. The six-week course was considered mandatory for all officers in 'field' conditions. They were taught to use hand weapons and explosives: how to place the explosive, set the fuse, and then leave unhurriedly, without attracting attention. Officers were given lectures on partisan fighting, trained to deal with secret papers, and taught everything else necessary to work underground in enemy territory. It was done so that the officers who sent diversionaries into the USSR and other countries would know what they would be doing there, and so that their agents would be sure that the officers understood what they were expecting them to do.

Despite the fact that all four trips from Turkey were routine and explained in the telegrams, Kim felt anxiety each time: were they really calling him back for consultations and training? Or was it an excuse to bring him out and arrest him? Someone could betray him, someone could let something slip, someone could be recruited, some enemy agent could be working in the KGB. Kim was lucky: he was not called to Baghdad, Cairo or London under any hidden agenda. Even when he was recalled in 1951 from Washington to London for an investigation, he had been informed of what was awaiting him at home. This time Kim felt no anxiety. He realised that this was a very important offer. On accepting it, he would become the key figure in relations between SIS, the FBI, the CIA and the National Security Agency of the USA. In other words, he would be at the heart of Anglo-American secret cooperation. There was a gentlemen's agreement that neither SIS nor its American partners would ever do anything major without checking with each other or at least informing the other of proposed actions. From now on these agreements and information would pass through him as chief liaison officer. That meant that the new position would keep him fully informed of all the most important affairs of both SIS and the American services.

The telegram also informed him that in taking the post, Philby would automatically become chief of SIS bureau in Washington and that the position would be upgraded just for him. This had to mean that SIS was more than happy with his work and continued to see him as a promising figure in the British Intelligence Service. This new post was only two or three steps away from the directorship of SIS.

Philby told his Soviet contact about the offer and without waiting for Moscow's agreement began packing his things in preparation for the move. He was sure that the Centre would not have a problem with his new post.

In August 1949, Philby was only thirty-seven years old.

'The people around me in Istanbul,' Kim told me, 'were rather saddened by my departure. I was a good boss, easy to get along with, and I did not push them too hard . . . The only man who expressed dissatisfaction with my coming departure,' he continued, 'was the British Ambassador in Turkey. He felt that there were only two people he could depend on, who could work well in Turkish conditions: the press attaché and me. The press attaché had been recalled to London three months before me. And now I was leaving. When I brought him the news, he cried: "Who am I supposed to work with now?"'

(I can remember no other occasion when Kim so openly recreated praise for himself. But his memories of work in Istanbul were set apart from the rest; he truly loved that period of his life and work.)

His Turkish colleagues saw him off with honours and not without a surprise. One of the heads of the Turkish secret service, a certain Colonel Peredzh, gave Kim a farewell banquet. Kim knew that the colonel used to work for the royal Yugoslav intelligence and then became a secret agent for SIS, earning $1,500 a month from Philby. He constantly complained about a lack of funds because his own Turkish agency paid so little.

But when it was time for Philby to leave Turkey, the impoverished Turkish colonel threw a lavish party for his British patron. All the senior officers of the Turkish secret service, all the senior staff of the British bureau and of the consulate, were invited. The tables groaned under the abundance of food and drink.

At the end of the evening the colonel brought out a leather box with a dozen Dunhill pipes and gave it to Philby as a farewell gift. The gift was worth a fortune – Dunhill pipes were very expensive.

'I cannot accept this treasure!' Philby started to protest.

'Nonsense!' the colonel said casually. 'Just a souvenir.'

Philby thought: 'You get fifteen hundred dollars a month from SIS, a quarter of that again from your own service. Who else is paying you, if you can give such parties and such gifts?' He accepted the 'souvenir' and decided that SIS did not know its secret agents well. The colonel obviously was being paid by the Americans as well. He wondered if the CIA knew that its agent was also working for SIS.

He could have asked himself an even more interesting question: what would the CIA do if it learned that its secret agent, officially working for Turkish security, was also making money at SIS and giving very expensive gifts, paid for by the Americans, to a KGB agent?

The reception, given by people from the Turkish, British and American services, was the last one before Philby's departure for London. Even though there were many other invitations and he was leaving Turkey with some regret, the new post was so tempting and opened up such opportunities that he did not want to stay an extra day in Istanbul.

Kim Philby left for London without getting Moscow's permission. The Centre never reproached him for that.

24

Manuscripts don't Burn, and Neither Do Ciphers

On his very first day back in London, Philby dropped off his things and called the office.

Since the telegram offering him the new post had been signed by Easton, Philby went to see him, his present boss in charge of relations between the British and American intelligence services.

Philby respected Easton. He was a subtle intelligence agent. You could report on the most complicated situation to him, and he would quickly see the system in it, a certain order. Out of the chaos he would create a picture that could be understood. Philby did not imagine, as he sat in Easton's office, that a few years later his boss would be involved in investigating his case, that he would regard Kim with curiosity and disbelief when they met. A systematic, wise and rational man, he would be tormented by the questions: Why did Harold Adrian Russell Philby, who had a brilliant future, most likely director of British intelligence and consequently in line for a title, need to work for the KGB?

Easton was not that presentable. He was short and plump, with a round face, fat cheeks, and heavy lips, a face you would not notice in a crowd. But his intelligence was manifest as soon as he started speaking. Kim knew that he was not silky smart, but dangerously smart. He never raised his voice, but could kill with a word filled with irony and sarcasm.

Kim was extremely careful talking to him.

Easton explained: his main goal would be cooling down the ties between SIS and the FBI, and activating them with the CIA, but to do it in a way that would keep J. Edger Hoover, head of the FBI, from realising it and taking offence.

SIS had worked with the FBI for many years. The American representative had come to London, and Philby knew him well. He also knew several others from the FBI who had been in London during the war. The counter-intelligence groups in the USA and England had a regular exchange of information.

During the war SIS had very close contacts with the American Office of Strategic Services (OSS). But Truman disbanded the OSS after the war and left only a small and not influential part of it – the Central Intelligence Group. As the Cold War developed, Truman realised that it had been a mistake to drop the OSS and that the United States needed a large active intelligence organisation of an offensive, rather than defensive nature. Thus the CIA developed.

The CIA had a lot of money, a large staff, and people of high rank. While the agency had in the past begged for information from others, the CIA started banging its fist on the table and demanding information on the spot. It was with this new, influential organisation that Philby had to increase contacts as the SIS representative.

The work would be delicate, since Hoover did not like the CIA, seeing the new organisation as a rival in both influence and budget allocations. As, for the third organisation, the National Security Agency, Philby would have to deal with it, too, since British experts were working there with Americans on deciphering Soviet secret telegrams.

Easton filled Philby in on all this and set a schedule for preparation for the move to Washington – one month.

After Easton, Philby went to see Menzies. Menzies was known for his personal wealth and good personal contacts with Churchill. Philby felt that a good cavalry saddle suited Menzies much better than the chair of director of the SIS (Menzies had been a cavalry officer in the First World War). Perhaps Menzies shared Philby's opinion and understood his limits, because he never became too deeply involved in the SIS's problems. Whenever anyone tried to involve him, he made a joke and changed the subject. The half-hour meeting with Menzies was full of amusing memories of Menzies's trips to America and his dealings with the OSS boss, Donovan, and Hoover. Philby couldn't remember a single story.

After his meetings, Philby was in a marvellous mood, and went off to see the chief of counter-intelligence, Maurice Oldfield.

Oldfield gave him some news that instantly changed his mood. The counter-intelligence chief told him that British cryptographers in London had deciphered around 200 Soviet ciphered telegrams sent in late 1944 and early 1945 from New York to Moscow and from Moscow to New York. Only ten per cent of the telegrams were completely deciphered and of the rest there were fragments and separate words. This was enough to be absolutely certain that in 1944–1945 the Soviet special services were receiving valuable secret information from a source in the British Embassy in Washington and from another source in Los Alamos, where they were working on the atom bomb. The Soviet agent at the British Embassy had the codename 'Homer', and they did not know his real name. Counter-intelligence was working on finding this 'Homer' and discovering the source in Los Alamos. But these institutions were huge. At the Embassy, for instance, there were over 900 British staff members plus clerical and technical personnel, mostly Americans.

The fact of information leaking from the British Embassy in Washington was not news to Philby. Back in Istanbul his Soviet colleague had asked him if he had heard anything about British counter-intelligence or the FBI acting on a possible leak from the British Embassy in Washington at the end of the war. Philby did not know anything about it and the question had been put in a general form, without specifics. Now it was clear that he had been talking about this.

Of course the Americans were particularly interested in the leak at Los Alamos. But Oldfield did not know if the two sources, at Los Alamos and the Embassy, were connected. He told Kim that they had managed to decipher some of the telegrams from late 1944 and early 1945 only very recently – in 1949. Oldfield also told Kim how it was possible to decipher them at all.

After Germany's invasion of the USSR in 1941, the Soviet Embassy in Helsinki burned their secret papers before evacuating, but they were sloppy. The Finns found a codebook in the mound of ashes that had not been fully burned. The key to several dozen words could be figured out. The Finns gave the codebook to the Germans. They tried to use the book for deciphering Soviet telegrams but apparently unsuccessfully – the Soviets used a double code: to every figure that stood for a word yet another figure was added in the final enciphering, a figure that was not known to the Germans and without which you could not learn the original number that stood for a certain word. Since the additional number was used only once, it was impossible to determine even with the most diligent work. But the Americans had a stroke of luck.

FBI agents illegally searched the premises of a purchasing commission from the USSR in New York and photographed as yet uncoded telegrams. The work went more easily after that. The cryptographers reasoned simply: the telegrams of the purchasing commission had to mention lists of materials to be shipped from the USA to the USSR. Therefore the longest cipher-telegrams sent in those days from New York were most likely to be from the purchasing commission. The cryptographers studied all the agreements and contracts of the Soviet-American negotiations on delivery of material. Knowing the lists in the material, they could find groups of numbers standing for individual words but also understand the principle of double coding – adding a specific number to all number groups standing for words.

To their surprise and joy, they discovered that one of the lists of secondary coding was used twice by mistake. Deciphering the telegrams from the Soviet Embassy in Washington to Moscow, intercepted long ago and stored at the FBI, suddenly became simpler. By 1949 the Americans had deciphered almost 200 Soviet telegrams completely or in part.

This was very troubling news. The first thing that Philby did after speaking with Oldfield was to go to the SIS library and request several reference books, including a list of Foreign Office staff by year.

During Philby's preparations for his move to the USA he was given a small office in the building, and he could leaf through the reference work without interruption. In the list of people who worked at the British Embassy in Washington in 1944–45 he naturally found the name of the man he thought of immediately when he heard Oldfield's story. He did not need the reference work any more. The agent 'Homer' was the same man Kim had recommended fifteen years earlier, in 1934, for recruitment as a KGB agent and whom he had himself recruited. Donald Maclean had worked at the British Embassy in Washington in 1944 and 1945.

(When Kim Philby arrived from Istanbul in London to prepare for his move to the USA, Donald Maclean was at the British Embassy in Cairo as attaché and head of Chancery. His career at the Foreign Office was brilliant. But in Cairo, he was known among the Embassy staff and his numerous friends not only for his talents and for being the youngest attaché in the Foreign Office, but also for something new. Donald Maclean began having crises of nerves in Cairo, often accompanied by drinking. A double life cannot be an easy trial for anyone, even the most brilliant people such as KGB agent 'Homer'.)

Philby had to inform his Soviet contact immediately. In September 1949, his contact in the KGB residence in London was a man 'Stanley' knew as 'Max'. Kim had worked with him for a year and half in Turkey. They had an excellent relationship.

Their first meeting had had an amusing side to it. It was 1946. Kim set off for his first rendezvous with his new Soviet colleague, following all the regulations for action, checking carefully, and performing all the necessary balancing acts. He planned on doing the last check for a tail – going into a movie theatre, sitting in the last row, and leaving before the film was over – not far from the café where they were to meet.

He came in during the newsreel before the feature. The newsreel was about the arrival of Dynamo, the Soviet soccer team, in London. Kim peered into the faces of the Soviet soccer players on their first trip to London. They were going to play Chelsea and Arsenal. There was a lot of publicity about the coming games and Kim thought then that seeing this particular newsreel right before meeting his new Soviet contact was a good sign. There was a crowd at London airport, including people from the Soviet Embassy. An energetic man, with an Asiatic cast to his features, led the ceremony and told people where to stand, to whom to give which flowers, when to start the speeches and so on. After waiting an appropriate amount of time, Kim left the theatre, made sure no one followed him, took a taxi, went a few blocks, got out, took another taxi for another few blocks, then walked several hundred metres to the café where they were to rendezvous.

He looked around the small room: not many people. The new contact was supposed to be at a table to the right of the entrance. There was a man, with a book, the author's name in large letters: Mark Twain. He was the one. Kim looked at his face and recognised the Embassy man in charge of welcoming the soccer team at the airport. Kim chuckled.

He went over to the table, put down his newspaper (as prearranged), said the password, heard the response, asked for permission to join him, got it, and after sitting down, said cheerily: 'I know you very well.'

The man with the book turned pale, but replied calmly: 'You must be mistaken. I've never seen you before.'

The new contact was obviously expecting a provocation. Kim hastened to reassure him. 'I just saw you in a newsreel. You were meeting Dynamo at the airport,' he said and smiled.

Kim's new Soviet colleague smiled back in relief. 'I thought this was a trap!' he admitted.

'Max' turned out to be a man with a pleasant personality and excellent professional characteristics. They quickly developed a good personal relationship, which agents need as much as oxygen.

Kim told his Soviet contact about his talk with Maurice Oldfield and what he had found in the reference books. Max's face grew haggard. He was an open man, emotional and temperamental, and he probably had one serious flaw as a spy: his eyes were the window to his soul and he never could control them.

Max immediately reported to Moscow on Kim's conversation with Oldfield. But neither Moscow, nor the KGB residence in London, nor Kim Philby could do anything in this situation for the time being. They could only wait and behave with extreme care and caution.

Kim Philby got ready for his trip to the United States. He tried to meet as many Americans as possible, particularly people from the former OSS in London who now worked at the CIA. Many of them were pleased by Kim's assignment to Washington, because they had known him from work and they all had friendly relations with him.

He met with Max at least once a week. The month of preparation for work in Washington flew by. There was nothing new on the worrying problem of leaks. But the search by British counter-intelligence and the FBI continued intensively.

The last time Kim met Max was three or four days before his departure. He told him everything that had happened over the week – nothing substantial, no important news. It would have been an ordinary, routine meeting if not for his imminent departure. After all, they had grown close.

In a very few years Max would be gone. He died young, at the height of his powers, at the age of forty-five. He died unexpectedly from a heart attack. Philby learned the news with great sorrow.

25

FIRST THING IN AMERICA

The SIS liaison officer with the US secret services travelled to New York on the luxurious *Coronia*, a Cunard Line ship like the celebrated ocean liners *Queen Mary* and *Queen Elizabeth*.

A pleasant group formed around Kim on board, including Osbert Lancaster, a famous English theatre critic (also a critic of architecture and design and a marvellous caricaturist), and Douglas Bask, from the Foreign Office, who was going to Washington to inspect the living conditions of the embassy staff.

Bask was supposed to report to London about the material conditions of his shipmate, too. It goes without saying that Kim used all his charm to ensure that the inspector did not overlook his financial needs. Philby was supposed to have an allowance in Washington on the level of a brigadier general (even though he did not have the rank), which was not bad at all. But after studying the situation in Washington, the inspector added an extra £100 a year to Philby's salary.

He went to America with his family, Aileen and the children. His relationship with his family, Philby told me, is a problem for a spy. He has to compartmentalise himself very strictly, his thinking and his feelings. One side is open to family and friends and everyone around them. The other belongs only to himself and his secret work. Did he betray his loved ones by always wearing a mask?

His family problems were complicated by Aileen's mental instability. For most of the time, there were no signs, and she was cheerful, gregarious, took care of her husband, and devoted a lot of time to her children and house. But when one of her spells came on, she would behave in the most unpredictable and inexplicable ways, sometimes doing monstrous things: setting their house on fire, wounding herself with scissors. Kim took her to the best doctors. The sickness would go away for a time and then resurface. Her nerves acted up this way no more than once or twice a year, but it would be very difficult for Kim and the children. He felt that it went back to the stress of the war. But when they had been married for about eight years, her mother told him that Aileen's nervous crises had begun when she was fifteen.

There were no excesses on board ship. Aileen, the children, and Kim all felt fine.

The FBI agent who met the *Coronia* in a launch was sent to help the highly placed SIS representative – as the USA considered Philby, not without foundation. The FBI man took the guest through customs and emigration very quickly, simplified by Philby's diplomatic passport, and half an hour later moved them into their hotel room on the twenty-fifth floor of a hotel overlooking Central Park.

Kim looked out of the window, seeing the street from such a height for the first time, and felt sick – his hands were in a sweat and a cold emptiness formed in his belly. He had a fear of heights. He had no problem in an aeroplane but it was hard to look down from a cliff or balcony. It began when his father took him for a trip to Spain during a school holiday when he was eleven. In Cordoba, he took his son to the cathedral. They went up the bell tower. Just as Kim looked down onto the square, the bell rang out, and the tower swayed. Kim saw that even his valorous father had turned white, and the boy panicked. Ever since then, he had had a fear of heights.

Fortunately, they spent only one night on the twenty-fifth floor in New York. In the morning the FBI agent brought them tickets for the train to Washington, and Kim and his family went to Penn Station to take a train for the capital. A few hours later they were met at Union Station by Peter Dwyer of the SIS whom Kim was replacing. He took them to a hotel with suites at normal heights.

Washington won the Soviet agent's heart. And not surprisingly. Kim had arrived on 1 November, when the city was ablaze with autumn's red and gold. The capital of the United States, as Philby recalled, did not have slums then, and there were beautiful buildings, lawns and parks without fences.

Telling me about it, Philby added with a smile: 'I realised one thing then. If you are rich, if you have a lot of money, you can organise your life in a rather pleasant way.'

The first official to whom Dwyer introduced his successor was Sir Oliver Franks, later Lord Franks, the British Ambassador to the USA.

At their very first meeting he informed Philby that he would not be interested in the details of his coming work. But he asked Kim to bear one thing in mind: he should not have conflicts with either the FBI, the CIA, or the National Security Agency. All conflicts with these organisations could lead to a deterioration of international relations; and the Ambassador would either have to argue with the State Department or punish the guilty one. To tell the truth, of the two alternatives, the Ambassador preferred the second, because it was not good for the British Ambassador to argue with the Sate Department.

Philby appreciated the humour and directness of the advice, and promised to do everything not to create such problems. He did not know then that in just two years he would be the reason for an international scandal.

Dwyer was one of the people charged with finding the source of information for Moscow on the top-secret 'Manhattan Project' at Los Alamos. He had been working on it before Philby arrived. Once Kim arrived he hoped to get away to Canada. But instead of a quick departure, and quite unexpectedly, I gathered from Kim's story, they were both involved in a problem that was worrying the secret services of at least three countries – England, the USA and the USSR.

As Philby told me, there were references in the deciphered telegrams to the movements of KGB agents from Los Alamos to Washington and back again. They compared this information with data on the travel of scientists at Los Alamos.

I recalled Philby's experience in Spain when the SIS 'effectively and cheaply' found German agents by comparing flight lists with deciphered German telegrams on the movements of German agents. I don't know if Dwyer was familiar with this experience. He might have heard of it and was actually doing it before Philby got to Washington. But since Philby was working on finding the Soviet leak at Los Alamos, Philby had to suggest the method he had used in the Pyrenees. He could not remain passive if he wanted to avoid suspicion. When objective data led them to the conclusion that it had to be Klaus Fuchs,[1] Philby naturally could not deny the obvious or try to focus the investigation on a false path.

[1] Klaus Fuchs was a German scientist who emigrated to England after Hitler came to power. In England he took part in British nuclear research. In 1942 he was sent to Los Alamos with a group of British nuclear physicists.

In any case, it was only after Philby had moved to Washington that Dwyer settled on Klaus Fuchs as a suspect. All the other suspects were rejected. This happened just a few days before Dwyer's departure for Canada. (The last alternative 'candidate' for the leak was the famous British scientist Professor R. Peierls, who had brought Fuchs in 1940 to work on the atom bomb and later worked very closely with him. But they determined that on the dates that the 'leak' from Los Alamos was meeting his KGB contact in the USA, Peierls had been in London. That freed him from suspicion.)

It is possible that Philby's arrival in Washington and his participation in the search for the leak of secret information from Los Alamos hastened the discovery of Klaus Fuchs. Kim did not clarify the situation during our conversations. Of course, the very fact that he thought he could talk about his work with Dwyer on comparing the KGB telegram and the dates of travel by scientists from Los Alamos shows that, in this case, Kim was rather frank.

Philby also told me about an episode in his life that allowed him to suspect that long before the events he was describing, he might have had something to do with Klaus Fuchs without knowing it.

During the Civil War in Spain, when he was the *Times* correspondent in the Franco camp, he travelled to England twice in 1938. Litzi, his first wife, asked Kim to set up a meeting for her with his Soviet contact. She had met a man whose friend was working on problems of developing new forms of energy. She wanted to tell the people in Moscow about this friend.

'I don't know what it is,' Litzi had explained, 'but as I understood it, he's talking about using the energy of one lump of coal used in stoking a steam engine to travel from Moscow to Vladivostok and back again.'

This was the first Philby had heard about atomic energy. He did not have any contact with his Soviet colleagues in England at the time. His rendezvous all took place in Spain and France. But realising that this was important, even if he did not quite understand it, Kim spoke to Burgess, whose contacts in London were in place.

According to a strictly obeyed, unwritten law about not exchanging information that is not absolutely necessary (which, according to Philby, truly simplifies an agent's life), Kim never spoke to his wife about this and she never brought it up. But he sometimes wondered if Fuchs had not been the friend of Litzi's friend who had wanted to tell Moscow about his work in atomic energy.

Fuchs was arrested in England. He was interrogated by William Skardon, a brilliant master in his work, who had learned to question suspects with the police. Skardon understood Fuchs, a noble man who had given himself totally to science and who hated fascism. Philby felt Skardon used Fuchs's nobility. He began persuading the scientist that he owed an unpayable debt to England which had given him refuge, excellent work, and moreover, complete trust as a man and as a scientist. Even though Klaus Fuchs was, of course, faithful to Communist ideas, did not bourgeois England deserve his gratitude? Fuchs had done a lot for Communists by giving them atomic secrets and naturally had hurt the British, who had not counted on such ingratitude from a man they had saved. So why not restore the equilibrium? Why not heal the wounds he made in people who had come to his aid in hard times?

I do not know if these were the words Skardon used. But this is how Kim Philby created a scenario for the interrogation and explained that such arguments could have affected an honest and decent man. Fuchs confessed to Skardon that he had contact in America with someone from the KGB.

The trial took place on 1 March 1950, in the famous London courthouse the Old Bailey. The entire examination of the case took ninety minutes. Fuchs had expected the death sentence, but he was given fourteen years in prison. This was explained by the fact that the USSR had just recently been an ally in the war. Seven days later in Moscow the newspapers carried a statement from TASS:

> Reuters news agency reported on a recent trial in London of the British atomic scientist Fuchs, who was sentenced to fourteen years in prison for revealing state secrets. The General Prosecutor of Great Britain Shawcross, who led for the prosecution in this trial, announced that Fuchs allegedly had passed atomic secrets to 'agents of the Soviet government'. TASS is empowered to report that this statement is a crude invention, since Fuchs is not known to the Soviet government and no 'agents' of the Soviet government had anything to do with Fuchs.

Klaus Fuchs died in February 1988, a few months before Kim

Philby's death. He was buried with great honours in Dresden, where he had lived. His numerous medals and decorations, which he had received from the German Democratic Republic, lay on satin pillows behind his coffin. But there was not a single decoration from the USSR, the country for which he had done so much, sacrificing his name and his life. Moreover, there wasn't a single representative of the USSR among those who saw Fuchs on his final journey – and there were many people at the cemetery.

Apparently the TASS statement of 8 March 1950 applied throughout 1988.

Fate had it that the news that stunned the world – that an atom bomb had been set off in the Soviet Union – became known at approximately the same time as Dwyer and Philby were 'unearthing' Klaus Fuchs.

Kim learned about it from Wilfred Mann, the scientific attaché at the British Embassy in the USA. One morning Mann ran into Kim's office and said: 'Just listen to what's happening! This telegram from London says that Moscow exploded an atom bomb!'

Mann stared at Philby. Kim felt he had to play dumb. 'Is that very important?'

'Important?' exclaimed Mann. 'It's damn all from the military point of view!'

'I understand the military point of view,' Kim replied quite calmly. 'But what about the scientific point of view?'

'It means that they've obtained plutonium!' Mann continued heatedly. 'We never suspected that they could have plutonium.'

'Is this a major achievement for them?' Kim went on with his game.

There was nothing in the newspaper that day, and Mann's announcement was based on a service telegram from London. Kim immediately went to the CIA to find out their reaction to the astonishing news. The headquarters hummed like a struck bell.

Kim heard all sorts of things there, heated words about dropping the bomb on the Soviet Union as fast as possible, before it had an arsenal of its own. There were more cautious judgments about the possibility of underground factories in Siberia where they could make new ones all over again. There were even sober questions:

where was the guarantee that Moscow would not retaliate to an American bomb with its own bomb on Washington? And if Moscow today could not make a responsive strike, who would stop Stalin from moving his armies into Western Europe and occupying it in the course of a month?

Kim regretted that he could not tell his Soviet colleague about the arguments. But he did not yet have a contact in Washington. Either something had happened, or there was a problem, or, perhaps, the KGB did not want to disturb him in the first months of his time in the USA in such a high position.

The KGB reestablished contact with him only nine or ten months later. The first meeting took place in New York. The others were set somewhere between Washington and New York – Baltimore or Philadelphia. To Kim's great joy, his friend Max, his former contact in London, worked with him for a while. They never had personal or professional misunderstandings.

But the day the 'Russian bomb' went off was still a long time before he would be back in contact with the KGB, and Kim acted alone, saving up information for future meetings.

26

WARNING MACLEAN

The detonation of the Soviet bomb vastly increased the tension in Soviet–American relations.

The basis of the fear of the Soviet Union in America, as Philby saw it, was what had occurred in Czechoslovakia in February 1948. That fear grew after the USSR atom bomb exploded.

'No one in America ever considered the possibility that there could have been objective reasons for the February events,' he said. 'Everyone was convinced that Stalin had annexed Czechoslovakia.'

The main topic of professional conversations in Kim's milieu was the Soviet Union, Eastern Europe, and the threat of Communism in Western Europe. Of course, the CIA had its own interests in the Near East, and the India–Burma problems and Iran were troubling, too. But it all took a back seat to the question of relations with Moscow.

According to Kim, ninety per cent of his work with the American secret services was concentrated on operations against the Soviet Union, against Communist regimes in neighbouring countries, and against Communist movements in Western Europe.

Philby told me that during his entire stay in America, he had no more than two or three business discussions on the problems of the Near East. Their content did not even remain in his memory, it was all so secondary and unimportant compared to the great worry on everyone's mind: the growing influence of the Soviet Union.

Of course, the Korean War preoccupied many people. But MacArthur was dictating his conditions there. He was in charge of intelligence and counter-intelligence, and he did not allow anyone to interfere in his affairs.

I did not learn whether or not Philby had anything to do with that war and if he passed any information about it to Moscow. He did not bring it up, limiting his comments to the one about MacArthur, and I saw no documents in his file relating to the Korean War.

But when the British and American secret services were operating to overthrow the Communist regime in Albania, Philby was right in the thick of things. His connection with the KGB had been reestablished by then and naturally it did not help the success of the Anglo-American undertaking. In our conversations, however, he stressed that even without his reports to Moscow the action was doomed, because its creators had underestimated the real and effective control of the Albanian authorities. Philby did not sink to repeating the assertions in the Communist press of that period that 'the entire Albanian people supports its government'. He spoke more cautiously.

'I do not intend to say that the people were happy under that regime, but the CIA did underestimate the degree of the control the authorities had over the country,' he told me.

Philby writes in detail about the Albanian operation in his book, *My Silent War*, as he does about the work of the CIA in sending units of Ukrainian nationalists into Western Ukraine. Not one of these diversionary groups achieved success. Even though Kim Philby did not ascribe the failure of diversionary operations as a whole to his own activity as a Soviet agent, his role was significant.

The growing CIA played an active part in diversionary affairs, something that Allen Dulles gave much of his efforts to even before becoming head of the agency. And it was Dulles, whom Kim liked personally, that Kim blamed for many of the CIA's failures.

Once, in talking about him – and such conversations could last for hours – Kim suggested I read a large book about the head of American intelligence. He directed my attention to a quotation from Ilya Ehrenburg, who wrote in the fifties that Allen Dulles was 'the most dangerous man in the world'. Ehrenburg continued: 'If Dulles got into heaven by mistake, he would start organising coups and shooting at angels.' Dulles, when he heard what Ehrenburg had written in a Soviet newspaper, was overjoyed and asked for that newspaper page. Whenever he gave a speech he would cheerfully show the newspaper and quote the Soviet writer to great applause.

Kim also considered Dulles a dangerous man. The source of that danger was his inclination towards 'espionage romanticism'. If someone proposed a plan of operation that resembled a detective thriller, you could bet that Dulles would approve it. This weakness for cloak-and-dagger stuff was a real danger – not only for those against whom the operation was directed, but for his own country. Thus many of the actions approved by Dulles simply because they were bold were doomed to failure. The Albanian operation was one, as was the planned action against Bulgaria. This was also the case with the Bay of Pigs, which was the end of the career of the legendary chief of the CIA.

Menzies, the head of the SIS, was also a romantic to some degree. It is thought that Graham Greene used Menzies as his model for his intelligence chief in *Our Man in Havana*. However, Menzies was a more limited man than Dulles and therefore more grounded and realistic. For instance, he realised that the SIS was controlled by the British government in general and the Foreign Office in particular. Dulles, however, regarded the CIA almost as an alternative to the government and the Department of State. He believed that the CIA could handle the country's foreign policy. He felt that everything that the government, State Department and armed forces, hampered by American and international laws and controlled by Congress, could not do the CIA could do. He lived by this postulate.

'I read somewhere,' Philby said, 'that Dulles had doubts about the Bay of Pigs operation just before its start. But it was too late, things had gone too far. Too many people were involved, including the President of the USA, the military, business circles in the South, and so on. And he could not find the strength to go to the President and say: the operation has to be cancelled, it is doomed to failure . . . I don't know if that's true,' Philby concluded, 'but it certainly resembles the truth.'

In the autumn of 1949, when Kim arrived in Washington, the Bay of Pigs was a long way off. Much closer was the search for the leak at the British Embassy. The services turned to it once Fuchs had been found. Since the espionage was taking place on the territory of the United States, this was within the competency of MI5 and the FBI.

British counter-intelligence felt that the spy at the British Embassy should be sought only among the clerical and technical staff, since 'an English diplomat could never betray the English crown'. The FBI also first looked at the support staff at the Embassy, but for a different reason. The Embassy hired mostly Americans for those jobs. Since almost every American has relatives abroad – Italian, Jewish, Baltic and so on – the loyalties of these people are divided between America and their historic homeland. The FBI was not interested in Anglo-Saxons, Swedes or Germans – they could not be suspected of double loyalties. But the FBI did not trust people from other countries, particularly those with roots in Russia.

The FBI made a list of every American on the staff at the British Embassy and began gathering information on each of them methodically. Their neighbours and friends were questioned about their relatives, habits and quirks. This gave no results, but it distracted the FBI from the right direction. If they discovered, for instance, that a staff member had a Latvian mother, they began scrupulously gathering information on her: where she lived, who her friends were, how often she saw her child, what those meetings were like – an endless net of questions that the FBI hoped would catch their fish.

This required many FBI agents, unlimited time and incalculable money. It yielded nothing. Kim knew what the FBI was doing, supported by the British and, naturally, did not do anything to straighten them out. But he did not express particular delight, either – he was cautious. Two or three times a week he telephoned his friend Mickey Ladd at the FBI and asked for news, if they had found anyone with a Russian uncle or a Ukrainian aunt. Ladd usually replied succinctly. 'A big zero.'

Kim derived pleasure from the thought of how much time the FBI was wasting on useless work and had created so much paperwork that it would cost a fortune just to destroy. But he could not feel at ease. The contents of the deciphered telegrams from the Soviet residence based on information from their source at the British Embassy revealed the high position of that source. For example: the leaks took place just when the British and Americans were particularly interested in the situation in the Balkans and Eastern Europe, and the telegrams were filled with names like Subacic and Mikolaicik, and those of anti-Soviet leaders in Romania, Hungary and Bulgaria. Any normal person would eventually realise that the source of such information was no chauffeur or cleaning woman. Kim knew that sooner or later the FBI and MI5 would start on the diplomatic staff.

Some of the telegrams that Philby had seen showed, to his horror, the dates of meetings of the source with the KGB contact: 'Homer will be in New York on such-and-such a date,' the telegrams would read. 'I will give him the instructions accordingly.'

These two circumstances – the high political level of the information passed to Moscow and the dates of the meetings with 'Homer' in New York – led to a uncomfortable conclusion: eventually the noose would tighten around Maclean and they could be getting very close very soon.

Philby was supposed to remain in Washington until the autumn of 1951. Once he was back in London, he could be sent almost anywhere and he would not be able to help his friend. He had to act before he left Washington.

The situation was complicated by the fact that Maclean did not know about the latest developments. He had returned from Cairo to London, but the rumours about his scandalous behaviour in Cairo had reached the capital before he did. He was having breakdowns and drinking heavily. He should have been fired from the Foreign Office. But his service record was so good and his abilities so outstanding that they decided to keep him on, but only on condition that he get treatment: he was suffering from nervous exhaustion.

Maclean's spiritual crisis was so profound that he asked the Soviets to end all contact with him. Philby told me that he thought this was a tragic mistake on both sides – for Maclean, who asked for it, and for the KGB, who agreed to it. In those difficult times, Maclean needed their support. But instead, 'Homer' had not had any contact for over two years with the people who could have warned him of the coming danger.

Kim and his controller understood that the FBI would get to Donald Maclean and the entire group would be in danger then. Kim did not fear for his personal fate, because he felt that even if Maclean were arrested, they would not have, could not have, any direct proof linking Philby to Soviet intelligence. He was sure the same held for Maclean himself. But the scandal, the suspicions and interrogations – even if they did not lead to a trial – would ruin their careers, both Maclean's and Philby's. The many years of meticulous work in setting up friendly relations and contacts, in winning trust, in moving up the ladder at the British Intelligence Service, all the far-seeing strategic planning at the Lubyanka for Philby – it would collapse in one hour. Philby's brilliant future with British intelligence had not been doubted by anyone. How could he risk a career that could bring the unprecedented opportunity for a KGB agent to become chief of SIS?

He had to find a way, he had to take measures that would protect him from any suspicion no matter what happened. I can assume that at least three people were thinking about this constantly: Kim Philby, his Soviet colleague, and Guy Burgess, whom fate and his superiors to the Foreign Office had appointed as First Secretary of the British Embassy in Washington in the summer of 1950, and who now lived with the Philby family.

Burgess's appearance in Washington has a direct bearing on the rest of the narrative.

When Kim received a letter in the summer of 1950 from Guy, announcing his new post and asking for permission to stay with Philby for a few days until he found his own apartment, Kim, taken aback by the unexpected request, agreed. But 'the few days' dragged out into over a year.

From the point of view of intelligence practice, this was madness. It was inconvenient personally, too. The fifth Philby child, named Harry, had just been born. He suffered from convulsions and Aileen spent all her time with him. She wrote sad letters to her friends: 'Who do you think has come? Guy Burgess! I know him all too well. He'll never move.'

She wasn't exaggerating.

Perhaps Philby, knowing his friend's flamboyance, his fondness for drink and his explosive nature, hoped to keep him under his eye as long as they had to work together in Washington: it would be easier to control Burgess and to influence him for the better. That may have been the reasoning of Kim's controller. There may be another explanation: Kim felt that he could make such decisions independently.

But Kim's hopes for moderating Burgess's behaviour did not come to pass. Guy created several scenes in Washington, even at diplomatic receptions, and his aggressiveness did not diminish, and there were no periods of calm between squalls of temper. Kim was a true friend and did not abandon Guy in difficult situations. On the contrary, by his presence he tried to show that Guy's behaviour was not typical of him, and that essentially he was a marvellous, charming and kind fellow.

After consulting with his Soviet colleague in the winter of 1950–51, Kim sent a memorandum to London maintaining that in his opinion it did not make sense to look for the person who gave such high-class political information among the support staff of the British Embassy, but among high-ranking diplomats. He also reminded his superiors about the evidence of Walter Krivitsky and the hints of Konstantin Volkov that there was a Soviet agent from a respectable English family in the Foreign

Office, recruited by the Soviets in the mid-thirties, when he was a young man.

His calculations were simple. This memorandum would not hurt Maclean, first because the FBI and the British counter-intelligence would sooner or later find him anyway. Secondly, the bureaucratic machine that was working in one direction now would turn very slowly to start looking for a leak among the diplomats. But whichever way events turned out, Philby would always be able to use his memo in order to distance himself from Maclean and to get rid of any suspicions.

Vivian's reply came quickly. The chief assured Kim that the idea in his memo had been under consideration for quite a while. However, as Philby wrote in his book, there was no evidence that anything was being done in that direction. Kim's preventative move, as history has shown, was fine except for one thing: whether Kim's idea was new to SIS or 'already under consideration', as Vivian had written, events unfolded with a rapidity that stunned Philby.

By the winter of 1950–51 counter-intelligence was focused completely on the diplomatic corps of the British Embassy. By spring, the list of diplomats under suspicion was down to ten people. The top spot belonged to Donald Maclean (as it had once on the list of candidates for recruitment that Kim had brought from Cambridge to the KGB in London).

It should be pointed out that MI5 had begun looking at Maclean before the list was compiled. The nervous exhaustion with which he returned to London from Cairo was not a common illness among diplomats in general and certainly not among people from the Foreign Office. MI5 had no proof, of course. However unusual such illness may be, it is not evidence of working for a foreign power. But the very fact that it could be caused by an inner doubling of the personality was confirmed by doctors.

And certainly, very quickly, as Philby had expected, someone from MI5 working in Washington decided to use Philby's method from long ago in Spain, and used quite recently for finding Klaus Fuchs, that is, comparing the dates of meetings mentioned in the deciphered telegram with the dates of travel of the diplomatic staff out of the capital. It was not a difficult task. Senior diplomats did not buy their own tickets, but gave request forms to the staff member in charge of travel. The travel officer had his files. The very first search revealed that almost every time a telegram was sent from New York to Moscow with information from the British Embassy, Donald Maclean had been out of Washington a few days before that, travelling in the direction of the city of skyscrapers.

His trips were not direct evidence of collaboration with Moscow, but they allowed the agents to pick one name out of the list of ten and to concentrate on it. There was no time to lose. Maclean, living in London and suspecting nothing, could be called in for questioning at any moment.

Philby had not seen Maclean since 1940. He knew that he had had a nervous breakdown and that he had broken off contact with the Soviets two years earlier. Kim was not sure whether or not Maclean intended to remain loyal to the Soviet cause. He worried that he would not have the strength to withstand interrogation.

The only certain way to warn Maclean was to send Burgess to London. He agreed. As soon as Burgess got to London he would make a very natural visit to the chief of the American section of the Foreign Office, that is, Maclean, and during their conversation he would put a sheet of paper on his desk with the date, time and place for a rendezvous. Burgess would not say anything about it, because they assumed that Maclean's office was bugged.

Burgess was also supposed to tell 'Peter', his controller in London, about everything that was happening in Washington. Together they would make a plan taking into account the recommendation of Kim, Burgess and the Soviet resident in Washington: Maclean had to defect to the USSR.

27

BETRAYAL IN LONDON

In London, Guy Burgess followed the procedure developed in Washington. He visited Maclean at his office. They then met at a restaurant, and he told him everything. Of course, he got into contact with his controller, 'Peter', filled him in, and coordinated his actions with him.

'Peter''s real name is Yuri Ivanovich Modin.

Modin was just over seventy years old in April 1993, although he looks younger. He met me near the building in Kalyaevskaya Street in the middle of Moscow which houses the Association of Veterans of Foreign Intelligence of Russia, recently created by the former PGU (First Main Intelligence Directorate of the KGB). He wore light raincoat, a beret that could belong to a Basque peasant or a Montmartre artist jauntily angled on his grey hair, with a smiling, rosy-cheeked, tanned face, and a grey beard: Porthos in his senior years, or maybe Peter Ustinov. During our conversation he managed to resemble both.

That day Yuri Ivanovich was duty officer at the Association, which had, as I understood it, several modestly furnished but clean rooms in the building that belonged to the Foreign Intelligence Service of the Russian Federation.

Modin had had dealings with Burgess, Blunt and Cairncross when he was with the Soviet residence in London. He never worked with Philby. He never even saw him abroad. They met only when Philby moved to Moscow, though they had naturally heard of one another. Modin's pseudonyms with the agents he controlled were 'Peter' or 'George' – some called him one name, some the other.

Modin's Story(1)

When they were discussing in Washington the best way to let Maclean and the residence know of the danger threatening him,

Kim demanded that Burgess insist in London that Maclean leave hurriedly for Moscow.

'He cannot remain in London,' Philby told Burgess. 'He'll crack under questioning.'

Burgess came to London, met Maclean, and told him everything that had happened in Washington, that he was under surveillance, and that it was likely that he would soon be interrogated. Then he asked the question that worried all of us. 'Will you be able to withstand interrogation?'

Maclean thought and admitted honestly: 'No, I won't. I'll tell them everything about myself.'

Guy Burgess let me know about this at our very next meeting.

We discussed the question and came to the conclusion that we had to arrange Maclean's defection as soon as possible. Burgess was instructed to meet him again and suggest that he leave. Burgess followed the instructions, but Maclean refused categorically.

'Why?' Burgess asked.

Maclean replied: 'I cannot do it if only because Melinda is going to have a baby in three weeks. What kind of a man, what kind of a husband would I be if I left her at a time like that?'

This was a complicated and risky situation. So we decided to appeal to Melinda and tell her everything.

Melinda knew about her husband's work for Soviet intelligence. They had met before the war in Paris, where Maclean was an attaché and later third secretary at the British Embassy. They were part of a bohemian crowd of young diplomats, French artists, wealthy Americans. It was there that Donald met Melinda, fell in love and proposed. But she did not accept right away. Maclean had to work at it.

I think the deciding factor for her was Maclean's decency. He was an absolutely honest man. Everyone who met him came to the same conclusion – Maclean would never deceive you under any circumstances.

When the marriage was pending, he admitted honestly: since I love you, before you take the final step, I must tell you that I am working for a secret Communist organisation tied to Moscow. I am its agent.

She listened, thought about it, and said that she wanted to

marry him anyway. I think his confession did not scare her off but, on the contrary, convinced her of his nobility and honesty. By the way, he had not checked with his controller about this confession. But the residence learned of it. And not from him. At first he had no idea that we knew.

In 1943, when our residence was developing new ways of contacting Maclean, less dangerous for him, someone suggested using Melinda as the go-between. She agreed. For some reason the plans were not realised, but she certainly knew of her husband's secret work.

So, when it came to Maclean's departure, we decided to appeal to her openly. Without hesitation, she said: 'He has to go. Don't let him worry about me. Everything will be all right.'

Philby told me he thought it was a mistake then to insist on Maclean's departure. If he had remained in London after their warning, he would have been interrogated by an investigator from MI5. But the investigator would not have had any direct evidence against him, only oblique indications. His illness? That was no proof of anything. The coincidence in the dates of when the Soviet cipher-telegrams were sent and Maclean's trips to New York? Why should he know why the Soviet residence sent its telegrams to Moscow on certain days and not others? Without a doubt he could have decisively rejected all the charges, and then quit the Foreign Office in protest. Then in a year or two, when things had quietened down, he could as a free man have taken a vacation in Switzerland and stopped for a weekend in Vienna, where he would call at the Soviet Embassy, give his name and ask for help.

His departure for the Soviet Union could have been easily explained: on the one hand, a revival of his Communist leanings from his youth and, on the other, the unforgivable insult from the people who dared to subject him to questioning and to suspect him of espionage for Moscow. Burgess and Philby would have avoided becoming part of the whole story.

'I don't know about Burgess,' said Philby, 'but I would have been able to continue working actively for our intelligence service for another ten years or so. Until the next crisis.'

The way was open for Maclean to go to Moscow. Melinda had no objections. They did learn, however, that Maclean was under surveillance, but that was hardly an insurmountable problem. 'Peter' knew how British tails worked, all their strong and weak points. He had learned long ago from Anthony Blunt, who knew British intelligence's system of visual surveillance inside out. They left all the arrangements to Burgess, who was not being followed, naturally. Moreover, whenever Maclean was with Burgess, the tails felt more relaxed. No one expected Maclean to do something rash while in the company of a responsible person from the Foreign Office.

In Washington, Philby worried. He was the first to learn of the surveillance of Maclean – he had handed the information he received from SIS over to the FBI personally (and we can be sure that his Soviet colleague learned about it instantly, too). Disaster could come at any moment and then, forget Maclean's defection. The last signal that the dénouement was about to break came to London from Philby himself. He used the fact that Burgess had left his car in the embassy garage and that the transport director had asked Philby several times what to do with Burgess's Lincoln to formulate an urgent dispatch to Burgess. 'Urgent measures must be taken on the Lincoln, otherwise it will be too late and the car will be sent to the dump.'

He waited for events to unfold in London.

On Friday 25 May 1951, Burgess reserved twin berths on the Calais ferry, leaving Southampton for France at midnight. He also rented a car, packed his suitcase and said goodbye to his roommate, Jack Hewit, went out of town to see Maclean (he told another friend, Bernard Miller, that same day: 'My young friend from the Foreign Office is in trouble. I'm the only one who can help him'), dined with the Macleans and then drove his friend to Southampton. They arrived fifteen minutes before the ferry was due to sail. They abandoned the unlocked car on the pier and hurried aboard. A sailor shouted something about the car – what should be done with it? Burgess shouted back. 'Leave it. I'll be back on Monday.'

Neither ever returned.

In his book, Phillip Knightley quotes Kim Philby on something he told him in 1988:

The unplanned part was that Burgess went too. We knew that

Burgess's going put us at risk but Blunt[1] and I decided to stay and stick it out. The whole thing was a mess, an intelligence nightmare, and it was all due to that bloody man Burgess. The KGB *never forgave him* [author's italics]. They kept us apart in Moscow to avoid recriminations over what had happened. I could understand that but I was sorry about it when I heard that he had died. He'd been a good friend.

Philby told me about this episode a little differently,

At least there was some logic in Maclean's departure in 1951. But what remains a mystery for me to this day is the departure of Guy Burgess with him. What for? The only explanation I can think of is that perhaps my Soviet colleagues in London saw that Guy Burgess was upset and on the verge of a nervous breakdown himself. He was going downhill. Most likely, after all the scandals in Washington, he was going to be fired from the Foreign Office. He must have understood that in that case he would not be of great value to Soviet intelligence, either . . . It was very difficult for Guy Burgess, perhaps more difficult than for Maclean or myself, because he was an explosive, emotional man, whose energy needed an outlet. To keep himself in check, to say nothing about his second life, required enormous effort. And he had another difficulty. At Cambridge he was considered one of the most brilliant students of the year, perhaps the most brilliant. Everyone acknowledged that. Whatever he took up, he did brilliantly. However, he never did anything seriously for any length of time, he merely showed great promise. That is tolerable in a man of twenty, twenty-five, even thirty. But when a man is thirty-five, people start asking; 'Really, when will that promise bear fruit?' He was still young, but his career was going downhill. There were many more scandals and scenes in his record of achievements.

---

[1] Modin told me that after the defection of Maclean and Burgess, he got orders from Moscow to meet Blunt and persuade him also to go to the USSR. Modin did this, but Blunt refused categorically. 'I know what living conditions are like there,' he admitted. 'I am not accustomed to them. As for the suspicions against me, there will be suspicions, certainly. But I have thought about what they could accuse me of and I have decided that they have no direct evidence. I will withstand it.' And he did.

And perhaps *our people* at the London residence had decided: if he moves to Moscow he will be safer there than in London. This is how I explain Burgess's defection to myself now. But then, in 1951, I had no explanations at all. I simply knew that I had landed in the soup. That was I knew.

In this version Kim Philby does not mention Burgess's 'betrayal.' The key phrase here is 'perhaps our people at the London residence had decided'. Even though Philby does not make clear whether the residence initiated this or whether it was responding to Burgess's request, he does not say that the KGB allegedly 'never forgave Burgess'.

I think Philby was more honest in his conversation with me, because in fact things in London went rather differently.

After Melinda gave her husband her blessing to go to Moscow, the way was open. But a new obstacle appeared. Maclean suddenly told Burgess that he would not go to Moscow without visiting Paris. He had to say goodbye to the city of his youth – too many memories.

Burgess reported to 'Peter'. All right, spend a few days in Paris, the controller said. But Maclean expressed his fear that in Paris he would not be able to control himself, that the flood of memories and feelings would start him drinking. And if he started drinking, he would be caught. In other words, Maclean needed supervision. Anything could happen. The residence decided that the best candidate to supervise him was Guy Burgess. Burgess objected: his departure together with Maclean would mean the end for Kim Philby, first of all, and secondly, the end of his own career as a diplomat and, therefore, as a spy.

'Peter' reported Burgess's position to his bosses. They told him to calm Burgess down: he would bring Maclean to Moscow and go straight back. No one in London would ever know where he had been.

It was 'Peter', aka Yuri Modin, who told me this.

'Wasn't there any other way? Couldn't they find anyone else to go with him to Paris? Couldn't you have gone with him to Moscow, Yuri Ivanovich?' I asked.

'Of course there were other possibilities,' my interlocutor replied. 'I offered to go. I could not be seen with Maclean during the trip, but I would know exactly what he was doing in Paris. I could have protected him. But they did not accept my proposal: you never know what could happen, and it would be better to have a friend with him, to have Burgess. He could keep him in hand. But in that case, Burgess should have been told honestly, if you go, you won't come back. That's what I felt then and that's what I suggested should be done.'

'But he wasn't told?'

'No. He went off with Maclean in the complete certainty that he would soon be back in London. And he arranged everything to create the impression that he had left on urgent business and would be right back.'

'He believed them?'

'I don't know. Maybe he did, maybe he simply pretended to. But he obeyed. And when he arrived in Moscow, they did not let him leave.'

'You mean, he was tricked. And they didn't care a fig for his fate or that of Kim Philby!' He shrugged and smiled. The tragedy of those people took place so long ago that it did not seem to worry the old spy now. 'So, the KGB did not care about the personal fate of Philby and Burgess. But they had betrayed the interests of the cause! In betraying Philby, they ruined the career of their own agent, who could have become chief of SIS! Why did they do that?'

Modin shrugged and smiled again. 'It just happened,' he said.

He told me one more story.

'When Kim came to the Soviet Union in 1963, Burgess was in the KGB hospital in Pekhotnaya Street. Fatally ill, his days were numbered. He was told that his friend was in Moscow. Burgess asked them to tell Kim to come visit him before his death, to say goodbye. But Kim did not come.'

Modin, recalling this, laughed without kindness and said: 'That says a lot about a person, doesn't it?'

'So Philby never saw Burgess in Moscow?'

'Never.'

'Not once?'

'Not once.'

'Even when he was dying?'

'No.'

'What' – I sought the right word – 'will-power it must have taken to refuse to see an old friend on his deathbed.'

Modin replied softly: 'Yes, he was a special man.'

The uniqueness of Kim's character was seen also in the fact that he did not want to blame his superiors for anything, or perhaps did not want to be torn by doubts over the competence of the KGB, the organisation he served and wanted to believe in. So he turned his anger against Guy Burgess, whose fault in the matter was much less than that of the KGB.

There could have been a more complex psychological game here, too. Unwilling to express his anger directly to the KGB, Philby demonstratively rejected his friend – so demonstratively, that the KGB *had* to comprehend the enormity of their betrayal of Philby.

Or perhaps the truth was simpler. The KGB never did tell him why and how Burgess left with Maclean. They may have even lied to him, blaming Burgess. In which case the KGB had betrayed Philby and Burgess twice over.

I do not know how things actually happened. Nor do I know if the KGB understood the desperate signal from their exposed agent. I suspect that they did not accept the signal, or pretended not to understand it.

28

FRIENDLY FIRE

The disappearance of Maclean and Burgess from London that Friday night was not noticed until the following Wednesday or Thursday – Kim did not remember exactly. But he did remember that it was early in the morning when Geoffrey Patterson, the MI5 representative in Washington, called him and said that an urgent telegram, 'For your eyes only', had come and there was no one to decipher it, since his secretary had the day off. When a telegram with that heading came, only the personal secretary of the addressee was permitted to decipher it. The assumption was that the secretaries were thoroughly vetted people. ('Just as checked as we, their bosses,' Philby said with a touch of irony.) Masses of secret material went through them. Patterson asked Philby to send him his own secretary for deciphering. Kim agreed. But he did not like the early call, even though he did not know the contents of the telegram. He even planned to get to the Embassy early, but stopped himself: he had to act as if nothing were wrong.

He arrived at the usual time. After a wait, he went to Patterson's office. The telegram had been deciphered, and Patterson stared at Kim wildly.

'Kim, something horrible has happened!' Patterson said.

'What?'

'The bird has flown.'

'You mean Maclean?'

'Worse! Burgess went with him.'

'Burgess?' Philby cried. 'But this is madness. What does Burgess have to do with it?'

Kim realised that Patterson was right – something horrible *had* happened: Kim had not expected Guy Burgess to flee.

They discussed the situation and came to the conclusion that things were much worse than they had seemed at first. Philby noted that Patterson said nothing about the fact that Burgess had lived in

Philby's house, even though there was no obvious connection with Burgess's defection.

Philby went back to his office. He had things to consider. Everything was happening much more swiftly than he had supposed and there was a completely inexplicable factor, a terrible factor – Burgess had left without any warning.

Philby had things at home that had to be disposed of immediately – a camera for copying documents, flashbulbs, lenses. He could not banish the thought that the telegram Patterson had read to him was not the only one that London had sent to the Embassy in connection with this defection. Who could be certain that his name had not been mentioned? Philby also assumed that the FBI in London had informed Washington about the disappearance of Maclean and Burgess. What would the FBI do now?

In order to get an answer to that question and to clarify his suspicions, Philby suggested that Patterson accompany him to see Mickey Ladd, to find out what the FBI was going to do. The FBI had every reason to act now: the leak at the British Embassy had occurred on US territory, Soviet intelligence had been working on US territory, and one of the missing British diplomats had spent the last year of his life on US territory.

Patterson agreed and called Ladd to tell him that he and Philby had to see him urgently.

Philby's brain registered every detail. The fact that Patterson decided to see Ladd with Philby could mean that Patterson and Ladd had a plan and were going to grab Philby together. On the other hand, Patterson was not such an actor to carry off a role. Most likely, Patterson still considered Philby his ally.

When they entered Ladd's office, he met them with a calm gaze and a calm phrase: 'Well, what's happening there, boys?'

Patterson put a copy of the telegram on his desk. Ladd read it, without hurrying, his cigar clamped in his mouth, and then inhaled and regarded his visitors with a smile. 'Well, you've made a mess, boys.'

He was clearly friendly and spoke to both of them, not isolating Philby in any way.

Ladd also knew that Burgess had lived in Kim Philby's house. He must have remembered that it was Philby who introduced him to Burgess. But Ladd must have also remembered that he had liked

Burgess and that they met frequently, often publicly, and were always friendly and happy to see each other.

'Ladd had reasons to hush this up,' Kim thought. 'Many people were witnesses to his good relations with Burgess.'

This was a supposition, naturally, rather a wish, not a fact. But Philby was convinced of one thing during their meeting with Ladd: he had not received any telegrams from their man in London. The text that Patterson put on his desk had been a surprise.

Ladd, like Patterson, did not mention that Burgess had lived at Philby's house and did not say anything about having met Burgess through Philby. Philby noted that, too.

Patterson and Philby went back to the Embassy. Philby waited for what seemed a proper time and then went to see Patterson. 'I think I'll go home and have a drink.'

Patterson agreed that this was probably the best course.

At home, Kim went to the garage, got a shovel, and put it in the boot of his car. Then he picked up his copying camera, the accessories and the film. It was all in a single bundle – just in case – and ready to go. The bag was in a locked suitcase, which no one ever opened. Philby did his photocopying at night, when the household slept: dangerous, but he had never been caught.

A few minutes later he was driving away from the house. He went over the Arlington Bridge and along the left bank of the Potomac, past the Pentagon. About ten kilometres later he entered a woodland covered with thick brush. Kim stopped the car and looked around. He had not been followed. He went up a hill, dug a hole, put the bag with his camera in it, covered it up, and walked about two hundred metres through the woods parallel to the road, and only then came out onto the road. He had left the shovel in the woods.

He had picked the spot a long time ago. The whole trip took under forty minutes.

'I wouldn't be surprised if the camera were still there,' Kim said with a smile.

But he didn't feel like smiling then. This was the most difficult period of his stay in Washington. He had to pretend that nothing had happened, he had to continue his work, maintaining contacts with the FBI and CIA – carrying on as usual.

Except for one thing. He had to call off his meeting with his Soviet colleague. That was too risky, especially since his contact at that period was not a member of the embassy staff but an illegal who did not have diplomatic immunity. Kim did not want to set the FBI on him.

Philby did not see any signs that the CIA or FBI had any suspicions of him. In any case, no one suggested it. Superficially, nothing seemed to have changed in the routine of his work. But thousands of big and small cogs were whirring in his brain. Kim was calculating all the possible situations that could come up, all the possible actions that could be taken against him and his own responses or preemptive moves.

A few days later the SIS sent him a cipher-telegram. His superiors wrote that since Kim Philby knew Guy Burgess well personally, they were asking him to comment on the latter's departure with Donald Maclean and also to inform them if Philby had any ideas on the motive of Burgess for taking this step.

Kim replied in a ciphered telegram about a page in length. He told them that Burgess had been his friend for many years, and that it was impossible to imagine that he could lead a secret life. His departure with Maclean was a total surprise to Philby and the reasons for it a total mystery. Philby was not lying: Burgess's move had been just that for him.

There was nothing strange about the telegram from London. Everyone knew of his friendship with Burgess and that he had lived in his house in Washington for a year and that they had appeared at most of the dinner parties in that year together. Moreover, Philby had always emphasised his friendship with Burgess, trying to smooth over the displeasure and irritation that Burgess's irrational and unpredictable behaviour created in diplomatic society.

Philby remained a loyal friend even when that friendship damaged his reputation. So Burgess's treacherous departure, as he considered it, was all the more an unexpected blow.

The telegram from London, innocent in content, was nevertheless the first harbinger of a coming avalanche of questions which he would have to answer soon – either in London or perhaps even in Washington. Philby went through the points he would most likely have to answer.

Regarding his friendship with Maclean, he expected no danger. He had not seen him since 1940. Moreover, in late 1950, he had sent a memorandum to London that could have been the key that

led the services to Maclean. So there could be no problems for him
there. He had a solid alibi.

What about Guy Burgess? Philby prepared an answer that could
turn a highly dangerous circumstance – Burgess's residence in his
house – into an almost incontrovertible win. Assume that a SIS
officer or even an investigator asked him: 'Doesn't it seem strange
to you that a man who was apparently an agent of a foreign power
lived in your house in Washington for over a year?' His answer
would be: 'Do you really think that if I had the slightest suspicion
that Guy Burgess was working for a foreign power I would have
allowed him to live in our house?'

He had a second answer prepared. 'If I had been told that a foreign
power was looking for a secret agent among the British Embassy
staff, I would consider Guy Burgess to be the very last person the
foreign power should approach.' (Which, by the way, was exactly
the situation back in 1934 when Philby made a list of his Cambridge
friends and placed Guy Burgess last.)

And then: who would imagine that Philby would allow Burgess
to live in his house the better to work on the same criminal activity
for a third power? Only a very naive person who knew nothing
about the rules governing communication between agents of the
same service and who had probably not read a single spy thriller.

Another question for which he prepared was: 'Who warned
Maclean and Burgess that the first interrogation of Maclean was
to begin on 28 May 1951? Was it you, Mr Philby?'

This is what led up to that situation.

On the morning of Friday, the very Friday when Burgess drove
Maclean to Southampton for the midnight ferry to France, the minister of the Home Office signed permission for MI5 to interrogate
Maclean. MI5 hoped to catch Maclean unawares and that he would
confess everything. But just the reverse happened: Maclean and
Burgess caught MI5 and the Foreign Office unawares on Monday
morning, when there was no answer at Maclean's office.

Suspicions arose instantly: someone had warned Maclean, otherwise why had they left on Friday night?

Kim was ready for that question and told me about his preparations. His answer would have boiled down to this: the people hunting Maclean made two unforgivable mistakes. They started surveillance on him and stopped giving him part of the secret documents he
used to receive. They themselves warned Maclean of the danger.

How could a man who allegedly had worked for a foreign intelligence service for seventeen years not notice that he was being watched and that his access to certain documents had been stopped?

The questions and answers appeared in Philby's brain like subtitles on a screen and were put away neatly in the shelves of his orderly mind.

The complexity of existing in Washington in those days was not so much in finding convincing answers to the questions he expected but in the fact that this occupied his brain every second, and kept his nerves strung tight day and night. This was when he was supposed to appear *more* normal than ever.

Soon came news that suprised him very much. An officer unknown to him who was in Washington on army business unconnected to Philby rang his office and asked to call to give him a letter from London. In the sealed envelope Philby found a sheet of paper covered with Easton's handwriting. Among other things, he told Kim: 'Very soon you will receive a telegram which will ask you to come back to London. I feel it important that you follow these orders without delay.' After that came a few meaningless phrases.

The letter surprised Kim. Why send a letter warning of a telegram to recall him to London? He had never seen this in his work, he had never even heard of anything like it. If he had received the telegram without the warning letter, he would have gone to London anyway. Easton was either warning Philby not to expect cloudless days in England (which he expected without the warning) – or was he suggesting that he follow Maclean and Burgess?

In Kim's arsenal, defection was one possibility. The plan was the same as the one developed in London, but the geography was different. He had settled with the Soviet colleagues in the USA that in the case of extreme danger, Philby would fly to Mexico or any other country in the Caribbean basin with a Soviet embassy. At the embassy he would ask to see the First Secretary – and everything would be fine. Since he was cut off from his controller, the decision to defect would be his.

But he was not prepared to use this extreme method. His spinning cogs led him to the conclusion that his enemies could not have direct evidence against him. Oblique evidence was not enough for a court. He would save himself from prison, at least.

He remained in Washington to await the promised telegram. It came. He was told to go to London 'for consultation'.

As Easton had suggested, Kim followed the instructions quickly.

A Soviet shell had blown up next to Philby in Spain once. Now it had happened again – except, this time, the shell was of much greater force.

In Spain the shell had been fired in his direction by accident, probably by a Spanish artilleryman, but here the gun was being aimed at him – consciously or stupidly – by Moscow. Once again, Moscow artillery was 'friendly' fire, shooting its own people. After all, it was the Lubyanka that had decided that Burgess would defect with Maclean, even though there was no great need for it. And they had not even deigned to warn Philby that he was in danger.

Moscow in general was not particularly concerned about individuals. 'Worry about the masses, not individuals', was the unofficial slogan and certainly the principle of the Party. So total lack of concern about one man's fate is not surprising. What is surprising is that Moscow was calmly allowing the destruction of one of its most valuable and promising agents. Maybe the KGB thought they could be mass produced?

Philby realised that the shock wave from the defections was going to knock him down. To his credit he remained clear-thinking and controlled; he did not lose hope of success and, as we shall see, got out of a difficult situation brilliantly when others would have given up.

Once, as we talked about this episode in his life, I quoted a verse from the famous poem by the Soviet poet Alexander Mezhirov, who had spent the entire Second World War at the front.

We stand under Kolpino.
The artillery is firing on its own.
It must be our scouts
That gave the wrong info.
Firing. Hitting. Firing.
The artillery is firing on its own.

Kim listened, smiled, nodded and said that he knew the poem. But he did not say another word. I do not remember a single occasion when Kim criticised his bosses in the KGB. Donald Maclean, apparently, was a different sort. When he arrived in Moscow in 1951 he wrote a furious letter to the KGB accusing them of betraying Kim Philby, of tossing this agent to the lions. I do not know what response Maclean got. I wouldn't be surprised if there were none.

29

'God, I Told Him So Many Lies!'

Philby left the Washington he had come to love – forever, as it turned out – and arrived in London.

It was not in vain that every cell of his brain was working furiously, not in vain that he strained every nerve in search of the best way of behaving under questioning, the best answers to the questions of the interrogators.

The interrogations began almost as soon as he arrived, even though his arrival seemed to have disturbed his superiors at SIS. Easton, in particular, had feared or hoped that Kim Philby would follow the example of his friends and would vanish en route from Washington to London.

But Philby did not vanish. He was firmly convinced that he could take the pressure, avoid the traps prepared for him. The only thing that worried him was what always worried any agent – had there appeared somewhere in the world, from some defector, some archive keeper, or some cryptographer working on Soviet telegrams, new information against him that he knew nothing about? But here he had to depend on his usual luck.

The first session of questioning was done by Dick White with Easton present.

White behaved in a friendly way, trying not to make Philby anxious, and asked for his help in working out 'this horrible business with Maclean and Burgess', since everyone knew of his long-standing friendship with the latter.

Kim expressed his readiness to help and to understand for himself, since the defection had been a shock for him, too. He would do everything he could to establish the truth. He had tried once to prevent a mistake, when he sent a telegram from Washington warning the SIS that it would be very unwise to set up surveillance of Maclean or deprive him of certain secret documents, because that would warn him and he would respond. So it had happened. The fact that Burgess went with him showed, first of all, that Burgess himself was mixed up in something dirty, and secondly, that having learned that Maclean was being watched, he assumed that MI5 would find out about him, too – and that precipitated his escape.

In this manner Philby started off by reminding them about his telegram and of the fact that the direct cause of Maclean and Burgess's defection was the crude mistake made by SIS.[1]

At the end of the conversation Dick White asked Philby to go home and write down everything they had discussed. The request was fully logical and polite.

Kim felt that the conversation had gone very well for him and he diligently fulfilled the request. However, in the written version he made a mistake that he had avoided in conversation. The mistake was not terrible, but a shame, and evidence of how White's friendly tone had softened up Kim.

Kim's strategy in describing his relations with Maclean and Burgess was very simple. Yes, he had been friends with Burgess for many years, and they saw each other frequently. As for Maclean, Kim might have seen him in their student days in Cambridge, but he had not seen him since and did not even remember what he looked like. They were practically strangers.

So, in his written explanation, he always called Burgess by name, Guy, keeping in mind their long-standing relationship. He called the other defector only by his surname, Maclean, to show his distance. But in writing down one of his conversations with Dick White he called Maclean 'Donald', with no surname. The next investigator, Milmo, latched onto this. Milmo was not very quick, but he was persistent. During his meeting with Philby, he said: 'You maintain that you do not know Maclean at all. Yet in your written statement you call him by name, Donald, as if he were an old chum. Can you explain this slight discrepancy?'

Kim had an interesting sidelight: in ordinary life he was perhaps too nervous, at least he thought so. But in dangerous situations he became very calm, with complete control over his nerves and his thought processes. In this seemingly trifling situation, which was actually complex and unexpected – how could he have made such a

---

[1] Much later Kim became convinced that the people who had made the decision to have Maclean followed were even more at fault than he had supposed. Many year later, in Moscow, Maclean told him that he had discovered the surveillance very quickly. There was even an instance when the car following him hit the bumper of Maclean's taxi.

mistake? – which required a convincing explanation, Kim handled himself well.

'When I worked in Washington,' he said, 'I had a secretary who knew Maclean well from a previous assignment. She called him Donald. And so, if he came up in conversations, we sometimes called him Maclean and sometimes Donald. I suppose that is why I made that strange error in my report.'

'The amazing thing,' Kim told me, 'is that the story about the secretary was absolutely true. She really did call him Donald sometimes when she talked about Maclean. But how I remembered that and how I got the idea to use it as an explanation for my lapse – honestly, I don't know.'

If there were a way to move the lever marked 'Be Careful!' a notch higher in Kim's nervous system, he would have done so after this carelessness with Maclean's name. But there was no higher position.

Dick White was not a professional investigator, he was a professional intelligence officer. So his interrogations seemed simple. But by the end of the third session Kim sensed that White was growing convinced that Philby was the 'third man' in the Maclean-Burgess case. All of Philby's explanations, all his answers, no matter how convincing they sounded, irritated White. He did not shout or insult Philby, of course, but Kim could see his face redden and his collar tighten.

At the end of their third conversation, White said goodbye drily, but did not shake Kim's hand. He never returned to question him further.

But the interrogations did not end.

After the sessions with White, a letter came from Bedell Smith, chief of the CIA, addressed to Menzies, chief of the SIS. The American told the Englishman that the CIA did not consider it possible for Mr Philby to continue as the liaison officer between the two services.

The letter was not unexpected by Kim. The logic of events inexorably led to this development. But that did not make the situation any less painful. Kim Philby was called in by Menzies, and he expected to be asked to resign.

This also followed logically from Burgess's defection. Kim had been prepared for it for a long time, so prepared that when he saw Menzies, he beat him to it, saying that he understood the ambivalence of his position and was therefore tendering his resignation, which he asked be accepted. The chief replied that this was the very thing he was going to propose to Kim, with great sadness, and he was glad that Kim understood.

Kim was told that instead of a pension he would receive £4,000, half immediately, and the rest in £500-payments every six months. A wife, several children, £2,000 and no job – this was not the best situation to find oneself in Philby's circle in England in the early fifties.

Add to that the nervous tension. It was made up partly of the need to prepare for further interrogations and of the surveillance that had been established on him. They did not watch him constantly, but from time to time. Once every week or two weeks a policeman would appear near his small house in the country, which stood apart from the others, and made his rounds for several hours, to make sure that the 'bird was in the cage'. The aim of this obvious surveillance, Philby thought, was not only to see whether the bird was in the cage, but also to warn him: behave, because the state does not sleep. He also assumed that there was covert surveillance, too, but he was not sure. He doubted that MI5 had the means to arrange for constant covert surveillance of him. But they must have done some spot checking, to know how often he took trains, where he went, what he did. He was absolutely sure that his telephone was bugged, even though he had no evidence.

Of course, the SIS worried that he would leave the country. But they did not have the right to stop him, because they would have to charge him first, and there was insufficient evidence for that.

One fine November morning, when trees blazed red and gold on both sides of the road to London (Kim remembered them well), he was interrogated by a professional investigator: Milmo.

Philby knew the man, and when he came into the room, Kim said: 'Hello, Buster', using his nickname.

The investigator gave him a hard look in return, to show that the friendly tone was not welcome, and when Philby reached for a cigarette, he said severely: 'This is a legally official investigation, Please do not smoke.'

Milmo was not the smartest of the British investigators. But he was definitely the most aggressive.

After that he began his interrogation, and it was harsh. He shouted and he banged his fist on the table. His assistant Martin, whom

Philby knew well too, wrote down in a little book every move that
Philby made, his reaction to every word the interrogator spoke.

The first interrogation lasted about four hours, and it was very
unpleasant for Philby. He was nagged by one thought: during the
war, Milmo was usually brought in at the stage when the suspect
had to be destroyed. Other interrogators softened them up and he
finished them off. In that sense he was an executioner. Kim could not
help thinking that this time, too, Milmo was sent in to make the final
blow, to finish him off, so that he would break. But since they did
not have enough evidence, they might have got new information.
Could he manage to explain whatever new evidence there was?
However, the conversation continued and none was forthcoming.

Once of the surprises Milmo did bring out was a question based
on Walter Krivitsky's testimony, that the OGPU had sent a young
British journalist to Spain in order to assassinate General Franco.
Milmo threw this accusation at Philby with a look of pure triumph
on his face.

'Who was that young journalist? Was it you?'

But Philby had prepared himself for that question a long time
ago. 'If the OGPU had wanted to kill General Franco, do you
really think that I would have been the best candidate for them?
There are hundreds of professional gentlemen for such work. I had
six interviews with Francisco Franco. I was as close to him as I am
to you. But, as far as I know, he is still alive.'

Milmo had to move on to another question. He continued the
attack, tossing noose after noose over Philby, bringing up new
charges. Most of them were expected and Kim had answers.

'You wrote a letter to the Foreign Office with a request to allow
your wife, née Litzi Freidmann, to move from Paris to London,'
began one of Milmo's broadsides. 'You knew very well that she
was a Communist. This was after the Molotov-Ribbentrop pact,
when the Communists had become allies of the Nazis. And you
brought a Communist to England! You damaged the interests of
your homeland.'

Philby replied calmly. 'She was my wife. However, we did not
really live with each other. We separated, but we separated as friends.
If the Germans had taken Paris, they would have thrown Litzi into a
concentration camp. Under those circumstances how could I refuse
my wife's request for help, how could I not help her move to
England?'

This was a losing proposition for Milmo. He simply added one charge after another. He wanted a long psychological assault on Philby, hoping that Philby's nerves would give out, that he would break, hands up. He did not succeed.

Kim had only one thing to worry about – not to lose patience under any circumstances, to stay in control. He had to remain calm and look confident in his rightness. Just as he had been lucky in all the other sticky situations in which he had found himself, he was lucky this time, too.

'If it had happened to Burgess,' Philby told me, 'I'm afraid he would not have behaved as he should. He always wanted to show how smart he was, and he would never have missed an opportunity to spread his tail. But the golden rule for being interrogated is to say as little as possible.'

Milmo got nothing. Ten people, including Menzies himself, who sat in the next room and followed the interrogation through a hidden window, were dissatisfied at the way Milmo was working. One lawyer later described it as 'the stupidest man in the world cross-examining the cleverest'.

But they did not retreat. Moreover, like Dick White, they were certain of his guilt (Philby thought). So Philby did not beat Milmo. In fact his passport was taken away. That meant that now he would be treated not as a witness but as a suspect. But they did change the interrogator.

He was the famous William Skardon, celebrated among other things for breaking Klaus Fuchs in January 1950. Skardon was first-class. A former police officer, he had joined MI5 during the war and remained with a reputation as one of the smartest investigators. He was around forty-two then, of average height, with a moustache, and known for his amazing calm and wonderful manners. He was not upper class but petit bourgeois, but his manners were impeccable. He was a gentleman, and a very dangerous one. Kim knew of his reputation and how brilliantly he had dealt with Klaus Fuchs.

Skardon began his first interrogation, which was at Kim's house, with these words:

'Listen, Philby.' Using his last name, Kim explained to me, was proper since they were not acquainted. 'Listen, Philby, we can have this conversation from two points of view, your choice. One is that you are guilty. The second is that you are not guilty. Which do you prefer?'

Philby calmly replied: 'Without a doubt, our conversation must be based on the objective truth, which is that I am completely innocent.'

After he told me about the beginning of the first interrogation, Kim suddenly burst out laughing, flung open his arms as if about to embrace someone, and still laughing, said: 'God, I told him so many lies then!' He even made the sign of the Cross over himself – the only time I ever saw him do that.

Skardon went back to early days, with questions about people that Philby should have met as a student, in his opinion. He was particularly interest in a man named James Klugman.

Klugman had been an active Communist at Cambridge. When the Second World War started, Klugman volunteered at an army officers' training camp. But MI5 interfered and threw him out. This had happened before Germany attacked the Soviet Union, when Communists were considered allies of Hitler. But he wanted to stay in the army, and enlisted as a soldier. He was sent to Egypt, where he performed well and was promoted to sergeant. Someone noticed his hard work and he was made an officer and taken into the SOE – Special Operations Executive – in charge of sabotage operations with resistance movements in Europe. Located in Egypt, he became head of the Yugoslav department of the organisation and worked there very well. As Philby told me, to a great degree thanks to Klugman's influence, the aid that the SOE gave to the Yugoslav resistance movement under Mihailovic was funnelled to Tito's partisans instead.

Klugman worked at the SOE for about a year and a half until MI5 discovered him again. But they also discovered to their horror that he was a lieutenant-colonel, even though he was not supposed to wear even a junior officer's stripes. MI5 made a report to the SOE, but they didn't care, because Klugman was not only one of their best officers, he was irreplaceable. While the struggle between SOE and MI5 went on, he continued working in that influential post.

After he told me this, Philby added that Klugman, as far as he knew, was not tied to Soviet ('our,' as Kim put it) intelligence. He simply worked honestly in accordance with his Communist and anti-fascist convictions. However, MI5 apparently won over the SOE, because he was demobilised before the end of the war and he returned to King Street in London, to the Communist Party headquarters. There, he naturally told them all about his work in

Egypt, including switching the support from Mihailovic to Tito. Since MI5 had been bugging the headquarters at King Street for at least three years, they learned everything he had to say. But they could do nothing with him, because what he had done was not only not sabotage but, on the contrary, an example of model service of a British officer giving his all to destroy fascism.

When Skardon questioned Philby, Klugman was still alive. The investigator was very interested in the ties between the English Communist leader and a member of the SIS. Kim thought that Skardon wanted to prove that his suspect had been under Klugman's influence ever since Cambridge and therefore had had close ties with the Communists over the years.

Skardon's technique in interrogation was to start the conversation on some unrelated theme – architecture in Washington or Chinese cooking – and then spring a trick question. Kim offered me this as an example.

During the questioning by Dick White, Philby was asked if he had ever known a woman named Edith Tudor-Hart. Kim naturally had met her. It was she who brought him to a bench in Regent's Park in June 1934 and introduced him to Arnold Deutsch – 'Stefan' aka 'Otto' – aide to the OGPU resident in London, Philby's first Soviet contact. It was that woman who helped form their entire group. Austrian by birth, she had emigrated to England and married an Englishman. Philby thought that Edith had started working with the OGPU either in England or in Austria.[2] Kim gave me the conversation with Dick White about Tudor-Hart in dialogue form.

White: Do you know a woman named Edith Tudor-Hart?

Philby (thinking): Edith Tudor-Hart? Was that the name? I don't recall . . .

White: In that case, perhaps you will be interested in learning a few things about her. She was a professional photographer and was a defendant in the Glading case on Communist espionage. Glading was arrested and imprisoned. (Pause.) I repeat, that woman was part of his trial.

[2] From the archives, it seems that Edith Tudor-Hart was recruited by Arnold Deutsch ('Stefan') in 1929. In 1934 she recruited Litzi Friedmann ('Mary') and recommended Kim Philby for recruitment.

Philby (stammering): Th–th–that's really interesting. B–b–but what d–d–d–does it have to do with me?

White (with a triumphant smile): Here's what. Since we suspected her ties with the Glading case, we tapped her telephone. And once this woman rang her husband at home and asked him to destroy immediately the negatives with your picture.

Philby: What c–c–can I do about that? I've been ph–ph–photographed by many people. But I d–do not recall being ph–photographed by a woman of that name.

They were talking about the famous photo of Kim Philby, printed in many books about him: young, charming, with a pipe in his mouth.

Edith Tudor-Hart had taken a brilliant photo; and when she found herself in danger, she destroyed the negative. But Kim had a print. However, neither White nor anyone else could prove that she had taken that photograph.

Therefore Skardon tried the following. During a general conversation, flipping through his notebook, he suddenly 'recalled' something.

'Yes, by the way, before I forget. I believe you told Dick White that you never met a woman named Elizabeth Tudor-Hart?'

Philby noticed right away that Skardon called her Elizabeth instead of Edith Tudor-Hart. Skardon was obviously expecting Kim to correct him: 'Not Elizabeth, Edith.' And then the investigator would have the psychological edge: 'It's amazing how well you remember the name of a woman you claim never to have met.' All this flashed through Philby's brain and he replied calmly: 'Elizabeth Tudor-Hart? Yes, I recall that White asked me about her. But I d–don't remember m–m–meeting anyone by that name.'

That was lucky. Kim thanked his stars for avoiding that trap. But then he thought: what if Skardon had sprinkled dozens of traps like that throughout, and he hadn't even noticed them?

Skardon's tricks demanded colossal attention, and were a strain on the nerves. They could force him to make a mistake. But not Kim.

Skardon always interrogated Kim at home. He made special trips to see him. During the questioning, Kim noted, he never was rude or insulting. He was always very polite and considerate. His goal was obvious – to make Philby like him in the way Fuchs had come to like him.

'Fuchs got too comfortable in Skardon's company and that's why he told him too much,' Kim told me.

Between sessions a week or more might pass. Then the telephone would ring and Skardon would ask politely if he could see Kim again. After receiving permission, he would come. Kim remembered five or six such visiting interrogations.

Then, around January 1952, without any warning, it all came to an end: the calls, the visits, the questions, the traps. Without any explanation. Nothing. Skardon disappeared. He had given up. The famous Skardon had given up!

'In my opinion,' Kim Philby told me, 'that was a mistake on his part. If he had taken a break for three months or so, and then returned and started repeating the questions that he had already asked, it would have been very hard for me. It's easy to remember the truth, but you can't always recreate precisely a lie that you were forced to tell three or four months earlier. And I told so many lies!'

So, the interrogations ceased. Whether that meant that he would be left alone, Kim did not know. He had to make his own estimation of the situation.

The only profession besides espionage that he knew was journalism. He decided to return to it. It was a perfect excuse to go to Spain, for instance. He made the choice for two reasons: first of all, he still had excellent contacts there, and secondly, Spain was at one end of Europe and the Soviet Union at the other.

Philby sent a letter to Skardon requesting the return of his passport, saying that he was planning to go to Spain to try his hand at journalism again. Would he return it? Three days later the postman handed Philby an envelope for which he had to sign. The envelope contained his passport.

Without any difficulty he obtained a Spanish visa and in May 1952 went to Madrid. But before he had even called half his old acquaintances, he got a letter from a friend in London who had worked with him during the war. The friend was offering Philby a job in London in an export-import company. This meant a solid salary, and Kim readily accepted.

Freelance journalism is nerve-racking. Here was a chance for a weekly salary, perhaps not very large, but definite and regular, which gives life a pleasant rhythm. Philby went back to England, deciding that the return of the passport, the unhampered trip to Spain and the job offer were all good signs.

Of course, from Madrid he could have easily gone to Vienna, say, dropped in at the Soviet Embassy, asked for the First Secretary, told him his name, and so on . . . But he did not know what the plans were for him in Moscow. Perhaps, not wishing to repeat the mistake of 1940, he decided to leave the question of resumption of contact up to the Soviet side, let them take the initiative when they wanted to.

'I worked a year and half for that firm,' Philby said. I hated every minute I spent there. To this day I do not understand the logic of that work. Why, sitting in England, you sell Libyan walnuts in Philadelphia, and from Philadelphia you send something else to a third country – still not England – in order to sell it there. These secrets of commerce were boring to me, and I wasn't good at figures, either. To my delight, the firm went bankrupt after eighteen months. But amazingly, it hadn't been my fault. Some transport section got things all mixed up in deliveries, and the firm foundered. I'm not surprised, trying to manage trade between Libya and Philadelphia from England!'

He was free again and life lost its rhythm.

30

LONELINESS

It was 1954. Philby had not had any contact with Soviet intelligence for over four years.

The first news from his Soviet colleagues came through Anthony Blunt, professor of art history at London University, an art historian with an international reputation, and experience with MI5, where he had worked during the war, and with the OGPU, whose secret agent he had been since 1937 (he had been recruited by Teodor Stepanovich Maly a few months before the latter was shot in the Lubyanka).

Blunt usually gave a public lecture every week on art history. After one lecture a sturdy, rather square-shaped man approached him. Blunt had met him several times about four years earlier. It was his Soviet contact.

'Professor Blunt, I have a painting that is unsigned, but I'm told that it is old and valuable. I would like to show it to you.'

He showed Blunt a reproduction of a painting the size of a postcard. On the white edging there was a written message: 'Angel, 17 June, 8 p.m.' The Angel was a pub where Blunt had met his Soviet colleagues a few times. He realised that the Centre was sending him a signal about re-establishing communications, which had been broken off soon after Maclean and Burgess left the country.

At the appointed hour he arrived for the rendezvous. They spoke about Blunt's affairs and then the Soviet colleague enquired how Philby was doing. Blunt replied that he was all right even though his life was complicated and he was financial difficulties.

The controller said that the Centre was looking very seriously into the re-establishment of communications with Philby and asked him to give Kim the date, time and place for the first meeting.

Blunt found Kim and told him everything.

Kim described in his book how thoroughly he checked for tails before going to that meeting with his Soviet contact. I will quote from it:

With the spotlight focused on me, I had cut two appointments with my Soviet friends. But when the date for a third came round, I decided that they probably needed information and that I certainly needed encouragement. It had to be an all-day job. I left Crowborough early and drove to Tonbridge where I parked the car and took a train to London. I was last to board from a deserted platform. At Vauxhall I descended and after a good look round took the Underground to Tottenham Court Road. There I bought a hat and coat, and wandered around for an hour or two. After a snack lunch at a bar, I did the cinema trick, taking a seat in the back row and slipping out in the middle of a performance. By then, I was virtually certain that I was clean, but still had a few hours to make sure. I wandered round districts which I had never seen before, on foot, by bus, and on foot again. It had been dark for an hour or two before I finally set course for my rendezvous. What passed there is no concern of the reader.

I leave on Kim's conscience his statement about the 'two appointments' he had cancelled in London. No one had made any appointments with him in those dangerous times. As for the third meeting, for which he made such long and complicated checks, and the content of which he did not reveal in his book, he was much more forthcoming with me.

'In the book I wrote in great detail how I spent the whole day before the meeting. And I finished it, if you recall, with the sentence: "What passed there is no concern of the reader." But today I can admit to you that there was nothing to tell about that meeting. Nothing at all happened. Because the meeting did not take place: the Soviet colleague did not show up. Apparently, out of considerations of safety, or for some other reason.'

His words seemed tinged with bitterness and perhaps offence: even after all that time.

Philby felt it necessary to smooth over the impression of reproach toward his Soviet friends and he added a polite explanation: 'Naturally, there *were* serious reasons for such caution. At the time I was in a very complex situation, and I could have been followed. If counter-intelligence had shown up and found me with a Soviet contact, I would have been destroyed in a minute.'

In that case, the residence should not have set up a meeting, I thought. After all, Kim was isolated, cut off from the only friends with whom he could be frank. That meeting would have meant so much to him! I can imagine how he felt when he came home.

There is yet another version of that meeting. It carries on from what Philby wrote in the book and what he told me.

I learned this third version from Yuri Ivanovich Modin, that 'square-shaped' man who approached Blunt after his lecture with a postcard, and was in charge of the operation on meeting him and Philby. It was more than Kim had described.

Modin's Story (2)

In 1954 we received information that Philby was in financial straits. SIS had given him a small one-time payment, which naturally was not enough. And then our leaders took a decision to help Kim Philby financially. I was charged with handing it over. But meeting with him was extremely dangerous, because if such a meeting were discovered, he could be tried and he would have no excuses. We thought for a long time how best to solve the problem and finally I suggested allowing me to meet Anthony Blunt. His position, after all, was not as complicated as Philby's.

I have told you that when Maclean and Burgess fled, I received orders from the Centre to meet Blunt and persuade him to do the same thing – defect to the Soviet Union. But he refused categorically. He announced that, on the one hand, he could not live in the Soviet Union, could not adjust to our life, and on the other hand was certain that he could stand up to questioning. And he did, even though he was interrogated for thirteen years – until 1963.

I had to wait three months in order to meet Blunt – such a meeting was dangerous for him, too. The problem was that there was no communication with him or with Kim Philby. When we parted in 1951 after his refusal to move to the Soviet Union, we agreed on the conditions for a possible re-establishment of contacts. But our plan did not work for some reason. And it is very difficult to re-establish lost communications. So in 1954 I was told to find the professor, go to exhibitions, museums, lectures on art history, 'Do what you need, but find Blunt.' And with maximum caution.

I must tell you that the three months I spent on that search improved my knowledge of art incredibly. But I couldn't manage a meeting with Blunt. Then I read an announcement of a protest meeting being held over the destruction of some arch in Italy, an architectural gem, and the meeting was being held at the institute where Blunt was the director. He would be the main speaker. Naturally, I hurried to the meeting. I got a seat in the front row so that he would see me and recognise me. I sat and waited. The meeting was a noisy one with people shouting and waving their arms about. The usual. But he paid no attention to me at all. As I later found out, he didn't see me. I had a plan all worked out. I knew that after the meeting he would be surrounded by people who wanted to talk to him. I decided that I would approach him, too, as one of the last, when the crowd was thinning out. I had brought along a postcard, a reproduction of an Italian Renaissance painting. As I recall, it was a Venetian family. The postcard had a white border. I wrote the place, date and time for our meeting in that border.

He was surrounded, as I had expected. The crowd seemed to have no intention of leaving. But he started making his way towards the exit. If he leaves, I thought, this will have been a total waste. So I went over to him with the postcard, said that I had heard that the painting had been moved to some other museum and I wanted to know where it was now. He took the postcard from me, looked at me closely, then at the card, and said: 'Yes, yes, I'll try to find out. I'll try.' He returned the card to me. I supposed he had understood the signal. He had clearly recognised me. But would he remember where and when?

As it turned out, he did. We met as agreed. He told me how things were going with him, how he was being questioned, what they asked. He told me about Philby's interrogation, too. It was from him that I first heard the names Milmo and Skardon.

I told him that I was supposed to get money to Kim because he was experiencing difficulties. But I did not know how best to do it.

Blunt said: 'The best way is to give it to him yourself, to meet him. He really needs that. Maybe more than the money.'

'I do not have permission to do that,' I replied.

'Ask.'

'I don't think they'll give me permission,' I said. 'Because if there's a failure, it will mean the end of Philby.'

He thought for a bit and made an offer. 'All right, I'll do it.'

We agreed on our next meeting, so that I could give him the money. We were talking about £5,000. In those days that was a lot of money. I was working at the Embassy as press attaché and First Secretary, and I got £100 a month, that is, £1,200 a year. That was a lot of money then. So £5,000 should have lasted him a long time.

The time came for our second meeting. I followed all precautions and arrived. Blunt arrived, too. We talked. Suddenly I noticed this shadow hanging around, some man. I told Blunt instantly. He looked embarrassed. I realised that he had been fooling me. He had not come alone.

'That's Philby,' he said. 'He came just in case. He hoped that you would get permission. Or decided to see him on your own. It would mean a lot to him.'

But I didn't have any sanction for that. I am a disciplined man, so we did not meet . . . I never met him abroad. Just that shadow I noticed flitting by.

That's your sixth sense working. With time, your intuition develops. Blunt had taught me a lot. He had started out in counter-intelligence at the beginning of the war and he was in charge of surveillance. He did it very conscientiously and introduced many proposals on how to improve their methods and so on. I might add that the British are good at surveillance. Americans come nowhere near. He knew it all thoroughly, and when we met I told him: teach me how you do it. He helped me cram in how the British work, what their weak sides are, what the strong sides are. So whenever we met, we could talk calmly. We knew that no one had followed us. Then, this time I noticed a man. I had never seen Philby, so I couldn't recognise him. But I sensed that there was someone superfluous wandering around. They had agreed that Philby would remain at a visual distance, so that if I wanted to talk to him, Blunt could call him over. But naturally, I would not do that. I gave Blunt the money, and we talked about our business. That's how the meeting ended.

That is how I interpret Philby's phrase that the Soviet contact 'did not come'.

In his book, *My Silent War*, Philby wrote:

> Several times in this period, I revived the idea of escape. The plan, originally designed for American conditions, required only minor modifications to adapt it to European circumstances. Indeed, in some ways it would be easier from London than from Washington. But each time I considered the project, the emergency appeared to be less than extreme. Finally, an event occurred which put it right out of my head. I received, through the most ingenious of routes, a message from my Soviet friends, encouraging me to be of good cheer and presaging an early resumption of relations. It changed drastically the whole complexion of the case. I was no longer alone.

I believe that Philby meant that failed meeting with Yuri Modin and the encouragement in the form of £5,000, which apparently meant a lot to him then (even though I can't imagine how he could have used it without drawing attention to himself). As for 'an early resumption of relations', he would have to wait several more years.

The sentence 'I was no longer alone' did not correspond to reality.

Philby's loneliness was aggravated by his family situation.

It was clear from Philby's book that Aileen was unbalanced, and the fact that he was out of work added to her nervous tension. There were other problems in their relationship. Around 1950, while in America, they separated. They maintained the façade of a marriage for the sake of the children. Philby later thought that it had been a mistake, that a clean break would have been better, but that is not what they did.

He had not noticed anything strange about her behaviour for the first eight years. She acted and seemed absolutely normal, until her crises would come on. Philby turned to a famous English psychiatrist. He had known Aileen before the marriage and told Philby that he might be able to cure her, but there were no guarantees. A cure could be attempted, but only if Aileen agreed. She exhibited suicidal tendencies. She wounded herself, often severely, in order to get attention. The psychiatrist assured Kim that the disease was not hereditary, but there was the danger that a child could imitate its mother's behaviour. He worried about this. But fortunately, the children were all right and none exhibited her symptoms.

In order to start the treatment, she had to admit that she had inflicted the wounds on herself. Kim was supposed to get that admission out of her. Telling her psychiatrist was not enough and for some reason would not be a legal basis for the treatment. In other words, Kim had to interrogate her. She was marvellously evasive and clever about not giving direct answers. It took about ten days of increasing pressure to get her to admit it.

After her voluntary consent, she was placed in an expensive psychiatric clinic. But she began to consider Kim the cause of her illness becoming public knowledge. She became hostile to him for forcing her admission, too. Finally, their relationship was completely destroyed.

That was the situation, complicated personally and professionally. In those difficult times, Philby could not count on any support from Aileen. Of course, she did not know about his ties with the KGB, but the reason for his dismissal was clear – because of the defection by Maclean and his friend Burgess. But she latched onto the fact and began dramatising it in a dangerous form for Philby. She insisted on talking about it with friends and asking questions like: 'What do you think, to whom should a wife's allegiance belong – her country or her husband?'

One of her friends came to Kim and said: 'You have to stop her, because what she says in public can be very damaging to you.'

But how could he stop her? How could he forbid her to say such things? It was unpleasant and dangerous. Then she did something unthinkable. She called their old friend, Nicholas Elliott, who worked at SIS, and told him that Kim had gone.

'Where?' Elliott asked warily.

'I think to Russia.'

'How do you know?'

'I got a telegram from Kim.'

'What does the telegram say?' Elliott was stunned.

'It says: "Farewell forever, love to the children. Angel."'

'Who's Angel? What does Angel have to do with it?'

'Simple. It's his initials.'

'Initials?'

'His initials are H.A.R.P. So he signed the telegram Angel, because angels play the harp.'

Nicholas later told Kim that this had been horrible news for him. He immediately called the duty officer at MI5. The officer informed the special section and they put a watch on all air and sea ports. Nicholas hurried to Kim's house to see the telegram for himself.

'I don't have a telegram, they read it to me on the phone, because they could tell it was urgent and important,' Aileen explained.

'In those cases they send a confirmation immediately.'

'It hasn't got here yet.'

Nicholas hurried to the post office, turned it upside down, but naturally did not find any telegrams. He went to the main post office in London, where he made an official inquiry. But they found nothing there, either. Then he realised she had made it up.

That evening he rang the Philby house and Kim picked up the phone. When he heard Kim's voice he said with great relief: 'Thank God, it's you at last.'

'Who were you expecting it to be?'

'I'm glad you're home.'

'Where else would I be at night?'

'The next time I see you I'll tell you where else you could have been tonight,' Elliott said.

As Kim told me, this episode, strangely enough, made his situation somewhat easier. Even though there were rumours that his own wife did not trust him, this let people know that Aileen was crazy and therefore her story was not to be trusted.

Kim Philby lived under constant pressure in those years. Suspicions hung over him like a black cloud and whenever an espionage sensation flashed in some remote corner of the world, attracting newspapers, Kim always worried that the scandal would somehow lead the reporters to him.

Finally, that was exactly what did happen.

31

VICTORY IN DEFEAT

In late 1954 yet another spy came in from the cold – the KGB defector Petrov, who had worked in Sydney. He brought with him the names of several secret agents and code tables. The news soon appeared in the English press. Journalists maintained that Petrov had revealed the Third Man who had warned Maclean and Burgess of imminent danger.

In the summer of 1955 Philby's name appeared in newspapers next to the words 'Third Man'. Of course, Philby's name had been on many people's lips without official revelations, even though it had not appeared in print. One famous woman journalist wrote: 'The name of the third man was known to enough people in Fleet Street to fill England's largest football stadium.' The newspapers could not openly call Philby the Third Man or a Soviet spy – the threat of a huge fine for libel is no joke.

When Kim talked to me about it, he joked: 'I was in two minds: hope that it would happen and I would get loads of money that would keep my family for years, and worry that Petrov had brought in something substantial that I did not know and which would make me lose my case. According to English law, you have to tell your barrister everything and he decides whether he should try for a not-guilty verdict or admit guilt and hope for a lesser sentence. But I could not tell a lawyer the whole truth or even part of it.'

What Philby had feared and anticipated came to pass. One evening in September or October of 1955 he saw a passenger in the Underground reading a newspaper with Philby's name in bold headlines.

The newspaper quoted an MP, Lipton, who had enquired in Parliament whether the government was planning to continue hiding the fact that the not-unknown Kim Philby was the Third Man who had warned Maclean and Burgess.

All England knew what happened next, and not only England. Everything to do with the KGB work of the two missing English diplomats, scions of respectable families, graduates of Cambridge, the holy of holies of the British establishment, was of great interest throughout the world. The disclosure of the Third Man's name by a Member of Parliament was the Number One Sensation.

But a lot of time has passed since 1955. People who were born that year are almost forty now. I do not think it will be amiss to remind them of what happened.

When he got home, Philby immediately called Nicholas Elliott at SIS. Elliott was a friend who did not believe Philby *was* a Soviet agent.

'My name is in the newspapers,' I told him. 'I have to do something.'

'I agree with you. Certainly. But let's think about it for a day, at least. Don't do anything for a day, all right? I'll call you tomorrow.'

Philby couldn't sue the newspaper where he saw the headline. It was the *Evening Standard*, and it merely quoted Lipton's statement in Parliament. According to British law, nothing said in Parliament is actionable.

The next day Elliott called back.

'We've decided that you naturally must respond. But it should be done only when the Parliamentary debates begin. Please bear up for two weeks.' And then he added: 'And we have another request. Please turn in your passport once again.'

'Of course,' he replied. 'It's a pure formality, isn't it?'

'Naturally.'

But the conversation did not end there. Elliott also asked Philby to come in so that they could carry out another interrogation. But he explained that the questioning would be done not by MI5, not by counter-intelligence, but by the SIS. He named two people, officers whom Philby knew well, who had worked under him in MI6 counter-intelligence.

'Of course I'll come,' Kim had responded. 'But I have a request for you. I'm hounded by reporters, but I am not making any statements. So if you want me to get to you alive, please send a car for me.'

A day or two later they sent a car with a driver who had taken special training for this sort of work. He took Philby to a safe-house apartment in London where they planned to question him. He was anxious, because it was possible that they had got new material against him through Petrov. On the other hand, he was counting on psychological superiority over people who had worked for him.

The interrogation was mild. They asked all the questions that had been asked before. They ran the whole thing once again from beginning to end. Philby had no problems with the answers. They were firm but polite and at the end asked him to come back in two days.

'Will you send the car?' he asked.

'Of course.'

Two days later, when they had probably completed transcribing the tapes of the interrogation, they met once again at the apartment. They asked two dozen questions, clarifying some points. He responded, wondering if there were a bombshell in reserve. But Philby thought that they had no new information on him. Otherwise, why play hide-and-seek for so long?

At last, they were done. One of them said: 'Mr Philby, we have been working on your case very thoroughly, we've looked through all your answers in previous interrogations, we've studied all the documents at our disposal, and you may be pleased to know that we have come to a unanimous decision about your innocence. We also must inform you that SIS has given the same recommendation to the Minister of Foreign Affairs to respond to Mr Lipton in Parliament.'

Kim was very happy to hear that, and told them so with absolute sincerity. Then he asked a question that had been bothering him.

'Tell me, please, why you have come to such a positive conclusion about me, while MI5, as far as I know, is just as adamantly certain of my guilt?'

They replied: 'There has been no change in the evidence against you. But we feel that if you were guilty, you would not have behaved the way you did these last four years.'

They must have meant that surveillance had not given them anything. For four years Philby had not met even once with his Soviet colleagues or any other contacts that could have been used against him. Naturally, he did no spying. There was nothing odd, suspicious, or prejudicial about his actions. He had made a second trip to Spain, a two-week holiday at the invitation of a friend. To leave the country twice and to return twice, without an attempt when abroad to make contact with anyone suspicious, without an attempt to escape – all that had the desired effect.

Kim learned something important – they had nothing new on him. He did not need to be told that SIS wanted to avoid a scandal of the Third Man as much as he did. Thus the decision to break contact with his Soviet friends and leave it up to them to re-establish contact had been the right one. His friends knew what was happening, and if they felt that he needed to leave the country, they would have arranged it, Philby felt.

There were ten days or so before the Parliamentary debates. The press was besieging him. He decided to hide at his mother's. He moved in, hid the telephone under pillows, and pulled out the front-door bell. It was the first time in many years that he and his mother were alone. The children were in the country. The only outsider was the cleaning woman who came every morning – she was their only contact with the outside world.

Kim's father was not in England at the time. His mother lived alone, her health wasn't bad and she felt well, but she had no friends and did not go out. She had absolute faith in Kim's innocence and naturally supported him wholeheartedly. They had never been close, even though they had a good relationship. He was always grateful for everything that she had done for him, and he enjoyed being in her house during those difficult days. They grew even closer, because they were under siege together from the press.

Naturally, reporters harassed anyone who could say something about Philby, including the cleaning woman. They tried to bribe her. But she was firm and did not say a word. Once the doorman of the building came to them late one evening and said: 'Sir, if you would like me to throw any of these gentlemen down the stairs, just let me know.' Philby was pleased. Shortly before, the gardener had made a similar offer that involved his pitchfork.

Kim told me that this was a common attitude towards journalists in those days in England. They were not particularly popular. They did not grow more respectable later. The business with the persecution of the Royal Family had made a bad impression on people. When someone was killed, reporters rushed to get the widow's reaction. It showed their ruthlessness and shamelessness. People came to see that the press often violated elementary decency, Philby said.

His name did not appear frequently in the newspapers then, but Lipton's quotation was repeated often. Once he got a letter from the *Sunday Express*. They offered to sponsor a debate between Philby and Lipton. They would pay Philby £100. He did not respond and went deeper underground.

He had never met Lipton, who had a reputation. He always asked questions in Parliament that did not bear directly on the main political line. Sometimes he was fed information to bring up a question in which someone had an interest. Philby did not know exactly how the information about him had reached Lipton, but he read somewhere that it came from a journalist named Jack Fishman, who wanted to publish it but could not until it was first raised in Parliament.

The Parliamentary debates began. Philby kept the radio on and finally heard what he had been hoping for. Harold Macmillan, the Foreign Secretary, responded to Lipton's query with a government statement to the effect that Philby had performed his duties conscientiously and well, and that there was no proof that he had betrayed the interests of the country.

Kim told me this was a very happy moment for him. He rang Elliott and asked: 'Well, and what do we do now?'

'Let's wait and see what Lipton does in response to Macmillan's statement.'

But Philby did not agree with this advice. He did not want to wait to see what Lipton would do. The man should be forced to apologise. Only the press could do that. So Kim decided to hold a press conference.

It was not difficult to arrange, because his phone began ringing right after Macmillan's speech. The first caller was from Reuters. Philby's mother answered the phone. She told everyone who called: 'Kim will be here tomorrow at eleven in the morning.'

That gave him about twenty-four hours. He worked on his tactics for the press conference. He decided to begin with a short statement, an apology that he would not be able to answers all their questions because his work involved state secrets. That would allow him to use that concern and his long ties with SIS to avoid any question that seemed awkward. He had to dominate the press conference; it had to be in his hands from the start. If Kim started being defensive, it would add confidence to Lipton's crusade. He could not allow that to happen.

He spent the night well, getting a full nine hours' sleep. By eleven the staircase was filled with a crowd of reporters. He had not expected so many people.

'My mother's place is not the Albert Hall,' he said opening the door, 'it's just an apartment, but do come in.'

He began this way: 'Gentlemen, I have invited you to my mother's apartment in order to make the following statement.'

He stressed the fact that they were in his mother's apartment, to remind them that they had to behave properly, as they would in the home of any respectable, elderly lady.

He went on to say that he had spent twelve days under the onus of an accusation made against him by Colonel Lipton in the House of Commons. If the colonel had any evidence to prove his words, he should officially present it to the appropriate authorities. Otherwise he must either retract his accusation or repeat it outside the walls of Parliament; and he knew what he could expect if he did that.

Kim's statement took ten minutes and he saw three or four reporters run off. That was a good sign: that meant the statement would appear in the evening papers. It added to Kim's confidence. He was ready to take questions.

'Have you ever been a member of the Communist Party?'

'No.'

'How long have you known Burgess?'

'Since Cambridge.'

'What is your political position?'

'Usually a bit left of centre. But I adhere to no dogmas. I am a pragmatist and an opportunist.'

The questions were very elementary. What could a reporter ask him that he had not already answered in the meat grinder of the interrogations of Milmo and Skardon?

A tough nut might be a question about the basis of his friendship with Burgess. Guy was an aesthete, Kim was not; Guy was homosexual, Kim was not. What did they have in common?

He would have been very careful in replying, bearing in mind Burgess's sexual preferences and the fact that the real basis of their friendship was a shared world view and political persuasion. He would have replied that Burgess was good company who made things interesting, fun and gay. But even he knew that wasn't a very convincing answer.

He was always on the look-out for that question. He had expected MI5 and MI6 to have asked, but it didn't occur to them to push it: an evident mistake. The reporters didn't think to ask, either. They were satisfied by his answers, the 'sensational' news he was giving them, the hospitality, which included beer and sherry on the table after the press conference.

At the end, two hours later, an American correspondent said: 'I see you understand the habits of the press very well.'

The reports in the evening papers were accurate. The morning ones were not only accurate but, Kim felt, positive towards him. No one distorted anything or made any serious attacks on him.

'Listen, you've had brilliant coverage today!' said a reporter who called him that morning.

The evening of the press conference, Philby listened to the BBC report on the Parliamentary debates. Lipton's name was not mentioned. The colonel had sat in silence that day. But when accounts of the press conference appeared in all the papers, Lipton asked the Speaker of the House for permission to make a personal statement. He was given the floor, and he said that he was rescinding his charges against Mr Philby and apologised to the House.

The MPs responded in total silence and apparently had no sympathy for him at all.

'That is how this episode in my life ended,' Philby told me in Moscow in 1987. 'There was no more unpleasantness in the press and the unpleasantness from MI5 ended, too. Life went back to its normal routine.'

Was this 'episode,' several years long, yet another example of Lucky Kim's incredible fortune, or the ruin of the long and patient work to create a life for the brilliant spy? From the point of view of the Lubyanka's far-reaching plans (Kim Philby as the future chief of SIS), this was a tremendous failure, caused primarily by the NKVD's mistake. But for Kim, this business could have ended much more tragically. From that point of view, he had been lucky. Kim felt that an agent could not be criticised if circumstances turned against him beyond his control. He could and should be criticised if he had an opportunity and he didn't use it.

In this episode all the circumstances were against him – and almost all were beyond his control (his own mistake, albeit not a decisive one, was allowing Burgess to live in his house in Washington). But Kim Philby used all the opportunities, even the tiniest ones, to defend himself, to get out of an extremely difficult situation with dignity, but also to preserve some possibility for agent 'Stanley' to work again.

Philby's life in its normal routine did not last long. The telephone rang and Lucky Kim's fate took another sharp turn.

32

A Spy Once More,
But for Only One Side

The unexpected telephone call came in the summer of 1956.

It was Kim's old friend, Nicholas Elliott. After some general chitchat, Elliott asked Kim to come down to the firm.

'Something unpleasant again?' Kim asked with a laugh.

'Maybe just the opposite,' Elliott promised.

The conversation was interesting and not unpleasant. Would Kim agree to go to the Middle East as an SIS agent? Elliott stressed that it would be as an agent, and not as an officer or a staff employee.

'Under what cover?' Philby asked.

'Journalism. You know the profession.'

'But who would send me there? What publication?'

'I hope to persuade David Astor, editor-in-chief of the *Observer*, to find work for you there. They do have a correspondent in Cairo, but we want you in Beirut. Astor will pay you his salary, SIS theirs.'

This did resemble a return to a 'normal' life, to what he had always done; journalism and espionage. There was nothing to think over, no one to confer with. He had not met his Soviet contact since the middle of 1951 in the USA, before Maclean and Burgess had defected.

He agreed on the spot.

It was arranged just as Elliott had proposed. Kim went to Beirut as the *Observer* correspondent. Through his own friends he also got commissions from the *Economist*. So he had three areas for his work in Beirut: two overt, as correspondent for the *Observer* and *Economist*, one covert, as a secret agent for SIS.

He did not know whether he would also be able to start up again what he considered his *main* work. But he hoped that after his very first publication in the English press, his Soviet friends would know his new address.

Philby ends *My Silent War*, published in 1968, with a description of the episode with Colonel Lipton, Macmillan's speech in Parliament, and the following words:

Despite these dramatic events, my work abroad had not yet ended at the time. From 1956 to 1963 I was in the Middle East. The Western press published much speculation about that period of my work, but for the time being I leave it on the consciences of the authors. Actually, the British and American special services can reconstruct pretty accurately my activities up to 1955, there is positive and negative evidence that they know nothing about my subsequent career in Soviet service. The time will come for another book in which I will tell of other events. At least Soviet intelligence was interested in knowing the subversive activities of the CIA and SIS in the Middle East.

The time to write another book never did come.

As far as I know, I had the fortune of being the only person to whom Kim talked about his work in the Middle East.

Where did the SIS get the idea to use a person for their needs who had been enmeshed in a web of suspicion and lies? What were the leaders of Her Majesty's secret service thinking?

Philby explained it this way: 'I couldn't know the real reasons. But this is why, I think. Despite the fact that there were many people at SIS who thought me guilty, there were those who were absolutely convinced that I had been accused unfairly. I told you before that it was not difficult for me to appear the typical bourgeois. Externally, I always was one. I just had to cut off my political views. The people who were acquainted with me simply could not imagine that their friend could be a Communist by conviction. They sincerely believed me and supported me. There was also a large group of people at SIS who doubted my guilt. They were basically sympathetic towards me. Even though they did not manifest it actively, they could be considered my allies to some degree. So in order to get a final result to the question of all the doubts and disagreements about me, they decided to send me to the Middle East in that position.

'They must have argued it this way: "Kim Philby is a professional spy, he knows our needs very well, he knows what we want. His father will help him establish excellent contacts in the Middle East.

If he is truly innocent, he can be of great use to us in that region. If he has ties with the Russians, we can wait patiently, until he makes a mistake in the Middle East that will allow us to establish his guilt more definitely and then talk to him accordingly. In four years in London he did not reveal himself to us. But he couldn't do it anyway. All ways were blocked to secret material, and the Russians could not have been very interested in him. But in Beirut, he will start working again for British intelligence and he will have valuable contacts. The Soviets will want him again, if in fact he has ties to them.'"

This is the picture Kim Philby painted for me (and must have painted for himself in 1956). As for the goodwill of people like Elliott, Kim felt that it was based primarily on a desire to spare SIS another spy scandal in London. If it were to happen in Beirut, they figured, it would have less publicity.

Philby felt that this was the error of their calculations. The offer of an SIS job in the Middle East involved many agencies that feared a scandal: the Foreign Office, MI5 and MI6. In each department there were various points of view on the issue. Any decision made in those circumstances could not be well thought through, because it inevitably involved compromise.

'We tend to look for a solid logical line in the various cleaner decisions of the intelligence services,' Philby said to me. 'But every such decision involved the human factor. And that means that you can never exclude the possibility of a mistake, simple stupidity, as in chess. By the way, that is the great lack in spy novels, where the authors write their plots, even complicated ones, very logically. The most complicated logical construction is predictable and expected. These writers exclude the human factor, that is, error, in their work. There is only one writer who writes about intelligence with the human factor always present. That, of course, is Graham Greene. There is always some completely illogical, unexpected thing in his books. That's why they are all so truthful and human.'

I recalled those words of Kim's when Yuri Modin replied to my question about why the Lubyanka made Burgess rather than Modin himself accompany Maclean from London to Moscow. He said simply, sipping his tea: 'It just happened.' And he may have been correct: the human factor was definitely at work here. When as a result Philby lost communication with his Soviet colleagues for several years, it was on the one hand a cruel trial for him; on the

other, Kim found one great advantage: he made decisions on his
own. As his duel with the all-powerful MI5 showed, he was not
so bad on his own. The compromise among many points of view
increases the probability of error.

As always, Philby made a point of avoiding the topic of the KGB's
mistakes in our conversations. Looking through my notes, I found
only two such mentions.

One referred to his amazing discovery that the postal address given
to him by his controllers for the letters he sent with such difficulty
from Spain to Paris was in fact the Soviet Embassy in France.

The second occasion came during his time in the Middle East.

Kim Philby was nervous as he prepared to move to Lebanon. He
was worried not only because he realised that this was a test, and
that there might even be provocations and traps. He was also nervous
because he did not know the Arab world at all – he had never been in
it before. Despite the fact that he was the son of a famous Arabist,
he could not imagine the reception he would get from foreign and
local diplomats and journalists. How would the Arabs treat him?
How much would the furore over the disappearance of his friends
and the recent accusations in Parliament against him affect his work?
This would determine whether he would be able to use this opportunity to restore the trust of the people in SIS who considered him
the Third Man with Maclean and Burgess. In that situation the only
correct way to behave was to work as conscientiously as possible
for SIS.

Despite the advantages of making independent decisions, he
would have given a lot for the chance to confer with one of his
Soviet friends, or simply to exchange a few words (that was the
'human factor' at work). But there was no contact. He had to bear
the entire burden of the stress alone during those years.

Of course, he could have said to hell with it and run off a long
time before. The possibility of 'taking off' in case of extreme danger
was always there. But Philby did not want to run, even in the most
difficult months of his struggle. His firm decision was not to leave
the battlefield, to stay on in England as long as he could, and to
salvage if not his career then his reputation. Only then would his
Soviet contacts be restored. He would continue working; not in the
same capacity as before, but he would still work for the Soviets.

The SIS proposal to work in the Middle East meant that he had made the right decision, it had yielded visible results: he was given the chance to rehabilitate himself. How he used it depended on him. But had he not always used every opportunity to the best of his ability?

Kim Philby arrived in Lebanon in August 1956.

He stayed with his father who lived in a mountain village twenty minutes from Beirut. He chose the Normandy Hotel for his office. I do not have the impression that he rented a room there. He used the lobby. He made arrangements with the hotel to receive his mail there, read the newspapers and write his articles. It was convenient. The mail came faster than to his father's village. There was a good bookshop nearby, where Kim bought his papers every day: Lebanese, British, French and German. The concierge, a kindly man, helped Kim and even got him a typewriter. So the lobby of the Normandy Hotel became the unofficial bureau of the correspondent of two authoritative British publications.

Talking about that time, Kim mentioned with satisfaction that for many years afterwards, taxi drivers passing the Normandy always pointed it out to their passengers: 'There's the hotel where the famous Kim Philby lived.'

The first three or four days in Beirut were given over to visits to the British Embassy. Kim met his old friend Paulsen there. He was chief of SIS for the Middle East with his headquarters in Beirut. It had been located in Cairo, but after some troubles there, it was moved to the capital of Lebanon. Kim received his instructions from Paulsen – the priorities in information-gathering.

Kim had been given general instructions in London, but Paulsen made them more concrete. The main interests were centred on the leaders of Arab nationalism. In that sphere, thanks to his father, Kim felt capable.

His father came to Beirut two or three times a week, and sometimes every day, and he always dropped in to see his son at the Normandy. Kim went into the mountains to spend the night with his father and cool off from the Beirut heat. Their relationship improved. St John Philby was happy that his son was back in shape and readily introduced him to all his Arab friends.

He knew personally almost all the Arab nationalist leaders. Kim started meeting them soon, too. The leaders were well-disposed to him because of Philby senior's profoundly pro-Arab position, which they expected Kim to share. Kim tried not to disillusion them in his articles. As a result, the first information that Kim passed on to Paulsen based on his conversations with the Arabs got high marks at SIS.

Once again, as he had in Spain, Philby successfully used his journalistic opportunities to ask questions without arousing suspicions about his work as a spy. Even though journalists ask questions in search of news and interesting events for the newspaper, which are not compatible with what a spy needs (usually rather boring details of economic and political life), a clever and careful combination of questions – as Kim told me – can yield important information without upsetting the person being interviewed.

Of course, as Kim pointed out with a smile, at that time the Arabs considered all British and American correspondents to be spies. They had good reason. Paulsen, for instance, was always surrounded by newspapermen. He knew many of them personally, and was happy to talk to them. They regularly dropped in, bringing piles of information. But the difference between their material and the material Kim brought was that Kim's was supposed to be secret information that his colleagues in journalism would not ordinarily be seeking. Therefore Paulsen paid Kim a regular salary, and made do with lunch invitations and bottles of whisky for the others.

Kim Philby started every day in Beirut by reading the newspapers and his mail at the Normandie. That took approximately an hour. Then he went to the British Embassy, to chat with the press officer and hear the latest embassy news. After that, Kim went to the US Embassy, to see the press officer and the other diplomats dealing with politics. He was met in a friendly way at both Embassies.

Kim felt that the Americans and the British had coordinated their attitude towards him. Even though he had no evidence, he sensed that the staff at both Embassies had been warned to be careful in their dealings with him. However, they were all terribly polite. As for the espionage scandal involving his name, they let him know that they considered him a victim of a misfortune that could strike anyone in political life. In all his time with the Americans in Beirut, Kim could remember only two or three times when, in an argument about the situation in the Middle East, his opponents were overly aggressive towards his point of view. The English never showed any hostility towards him. After the Embassies he usually went to visit one of the Arab leaders.

There were no suspicions at all about him among the Arabs. Of course, they had some idea of the spy scandal around him, but they were not very interested. What they cared about was whether the English journalist was pro-Arab or pro-Israeli. Naturally, he was pro-Arab. And, as he told me, he was 'totally sincere about it, since I knew that Moscow's position at the time was just that'. Once convinced that he was sincerely pro-Arab, his new friends stopped wondering whose spy he was: British, American or Russian. They were much more interested in how many times he had been married, divorced, and why. So the atmosphere for work in Beirut was much more simple and comfortable that he had expected.

He did a lot of travelling. At least twice a month he left Beirut, either for Amman or Damascus. Four or five times a year he went to Saudi Arabia. These trips were valued by the SIS. The British did not have diplomatic ties with Saudi Arabia then, and any information from there, especially such authoritative information from Philby, who met high-ranking officials, was awaited with impatience at SIS.

For Philby the problem was not the lack of information, but an overabundance of it and how to select it. In those days, kings, princes, shahs and advisors of every rank had no idea in the evening of what their actions would be the following morning. State plans changed quite frivolously overnight. The most valuable information obtained today was often useless tomorrow.

He travelled so much that any memory of Lebanon first brought back Beirut airport, of which he was sick and tired. He had been there so many times: leaving, returning, or hurrying there to interview some important politician, or picking up a friend, or seeing one off.

'What I hated most of all was the loudspeaker,' Kim told me and turned his hands upwards, as if calling on higher authorities as witness. 'To this day I can hear its roar in my ears. We were told it was for our own good: the announcer was telling us about arrivals and departures. He was using various languages: Arabic, English and French. But I could never tell which language that monster was rasping in.'

Then came major changes in his personal life.

In 1957 his mother, Dora, died in her sleep in England. Kim and his father were stunned. Neither had understood how much she had meant to him, particularly St John Philby. Perhaps that lack of understanding is what had led Dora to drink so much gin in her final years, drowning her sorrows.

Kim drank a lot himself. But there was no other way to hide from the thoughts that gnawed at him.

His only friends at first in Beirut were Sam Pope Brewer, the *New York Times* correspondent, and his wife, Eleanor. Kim had known Brewer in Spain, where he had been a correspondent during the Civil War. The Brewer family, especially Eleanor, helped Kim settle in Beirut and make good contacts. 'What touched me first about Kim was his loneliness,' Eleanor wrote in her book, *The Spy I Loved*.

> He knew no one in Beirut. A certain old-fashioned reserve set him apart from the easy familiarity of the other journalists. He was then forty-four, of medium height, very lean, with a handsome, heavily-lined face. His eyes were an intense blue. I thought that here was a man who had seen a lot of the world, who was experienced, and yet who seemed to have suffered . . . He had a gift for creating an atmosphere of such intimacy that I found myself talking freely to him. I was very impressed by his beautiful manners. We took him under our wing. On his visits to town he usually came to see us and soon became one of our closest friends.

Kim fell in love with Eleanor. And she was drawn to him. Her husband often travelled for the newspaper and his absence promoted their relationship. They found excuses for seeing each other several times a day. When they could not, he wrote her little notes, which were delivered by a boy. 'Deeper in love than ever, my darling. X X X from your Kim.' And that same day: 'Deeper and deeper, my darling. X X X from your Kim.'

The pleasant American woman was totally won over.

'Like his beautiful manners, Kim's skill in writing letters was a reminder of a civilised way of living, particularly appealing to an American. They drew me into his daily life by the little incidents he described so wittily and gracefully.'

What did sophisticated Kim see in the simple woman from Seattle, whom some of his friends in Beirut considered stupid and awkward? He gives the answer in a letter addressed to her.

You are one of the easiest, most soothing presences I have ever met . . . Now, darling, I know you have had a bitter experience . . . But do you also know what it is like to be chivvied? I have had it at least twice; and *that* is difficult. One of the most wonderful things about you is that you have accepted me as I am – except for *araq*, and quite rightly – and that you haven't tried the common female trick of trying to turn me into the sort of man you would have liked to think you loved.

How much of this is his personal fantasy and desire to invent her, and how much is real attraction to a simple, open woman 'without complexes' who loved him deeply and with whom he could forget his loneliness is hard to say. But he was deeply sincere in his feelings for her. During our conversations in Moscow, he always stopped talking about her as soon as Rufina, his last wife, entered the room or came on to the terrace where we were talking. He was not very forthcoming about the marriage, the way he was about Litzi and Frances and Aileen.

On 11 December 1957, Aileen died. She had been a sick and prematurely aged woman (she died at the age of forty-seven), working as a cook for a family.

In his book, *Philby, KGB Masterspy*, Phillip Knightley writes that most likely 'Aileen finally knew of Philby's treachery, the secret he had kept from her all their married life, and her drinking was one way of obliterating the knowledge.'

She died of congestive heart failure, myocardial degeneration, a respiratory infection and pulmonary tuberculosis.

Kim and Eleanor (who had gone to Mexico for a quick divorce) got married twice – once in Beirut in 1958, and a second time in London, in January 1959 (since the British Embassy in Lebanon could not recognise Eleanor's Mexican divorce). Her former husband, Sam Pope Brewer, who was the first person Kim told about his plans to wed Eleanor, said: 'That sounds like the best solution. What do you make of the situation in Iraq?'

33

'I'VE BEEN WAITING SO LONG'

Days, weeks and months passed; the work for SIS was going well. But the people for whose sake he had got mixed up in this business, for whose sake his former life had been disrupted, seemed to have no intention of re-establishing ties with him. Perhaps they did not even know where he was, even though his signed articles appeared both in the *Observer* and *Economist*. The articles were on topics of great interest to Moscow – the Middle East. On an analytical level, they were so high that they were read by serious politicians, economists and area specialists. That alone should have prompted the Lubyanka to see that their agent was not only alive and well in Beirut but had access to major sources of information.

Yet two years had gone by since his arrival in Beirut (and six years since communication was broken in 1951), and there was still nothing from the KGB. Philby would get furious sometimes: don't they read the papers? Or did they really no longer need him? Did that mean that everything he had done was now tossed into the dustbin?

But true to his rule of never blaming his Soviet colleagues, he would find excuses for their silence. They did not want to risk him. They did not want to endanger him. They knew better than he that SIS had sent him there not only to get valuable information but to catch him the moment he tripped up and made contact with Moscow.

He would not allow himself to think of trying to re-establish contact himself, and not because he was afraid of being followed. He would manage to get rid of a tail, especially, since he was sure that he was not being followed. At least, he had never noticed anything in the two years in Beirut. His intuition, which he trusted, told him that there was no surveillance – not by the British, not by the Americans, not by anyone like the Lebanese. Something else held him back. His initiative in re-establishing contact might be met with suspicion by the KGB. He had been mistrusted by the Lubyanka before. No one had said anything to him about it then, but he had sensed it. The most valuable information for Moscow was burning his hands at the beginning of the war, but there was that unexpected break in communication. He remembered trying to get through to Moscow with Maclean's help, sending a letter with him. He remembered how nothing came of it except getting his friend in trouble. Until they made their own decision at the Lubyanka to re-establish ties with an agent called Harold Adrian Russell (Kim) Philby, there would be no contact, even if he had the most valuable information in the world for them.

In late summer of 1958 Kim was in a chair in the lobby of the Normandy. As usual, he was going through his mail and newspapers. The lobby wasn't very crowded. However, he noticed a man of thirty-five or so, solidly built, who came in from the street, and talked softly with the concierge. Kim's heart started pounding: he was looking for Kim! He was a Russian!

The concierge pointed out Kim's chair. The visitor headed for it.

He came over, sat down and introduced himself: Petukhov from the Soviet trade mission in Lebanon. He asked if he could take a few minutes of the famous journalist's time. At the same time he took out his card and handed it to Kim. It read: 'Soviet Trade Mission'. And beneath that: 'Petukhov.'

Kim suppressed his agitation. Just because he was Russian didn't mean he was from the KGB. He was an ordinary trade representative, interested in the economic and political problems of Lebanon.

'Please go on, Mr Petukhov.'

'I read your articles in the *Observer* and in the *Economist*, Mr Philby. I find them very deep. I sought you out to ask you for the favour of your time for a conversation. I am particularly interested in the prospects for a Common Market of the Arab countries.'

Well then, so it was. The question was very topical, discussed in all the newspapers, and the request seemed natural. The visitor spoke fairly good English with a Russian accent.

'Whenever you like,' Kim replied.

'Thank you.' Petukhov gave him an interrogative look.

'You can come to my house. I will make you some good tea,' Kim said, surprising himself.

Eleanor was taking sculpture classes at the American University in Beirut. He knew she had a class the next day and would be gone almost all day.

His father had left for Saudi Arabia a long time ago, and Kim had an apartment in Beirut, where he lived with his new wife. It was small but comfortable. Kim thought his visitor was a bit surprised by the invitation to his house. But he agreed, thanked him, took Kim's card for the address, and left.

Kim's brain feverishly went through the possibilities.

One. The Russian did read the *Economist* and was interested in the problems of the Common Market for Arab states. That is what they would discuss tomorrow at Kim's house. Likely? Not very. An ordinary member of a USSR trade mission would hardly accept an invitation to visit the home of an unknown Englishman, the correspondent of a reactionary magazine, the *Economist*.

Two. A trap. The visitor would start talking as if he were from the KGB. But actually, he would be working for the SIS, on their orders. No. He could easily ring the Soviet mission and check whether they have a Mr Petukhov there.

Three . . .

The hell with one and two and three! Kim would not ring the Russian mission. It was enough that he had the opportunity. The Russian would not talk to him about the 'Common Market'. He would talk about business. He had been sent to re-establish communication.

Of course, after six years of interruption, setting the first meeting with a KGB agent in your own apartment was more than careless. No wonder Petukhov looked surprised. However, he did not offer another place, apparently considering the Normandy lobby inappropriate for the discussion of other addresses. He said, 'All right,' thanked him, and left. But Kim was certain that the meeting carelessly set for his apartment would go well.

Petukhov arrived the next day at three, right on the dot, as they had agreed. Kim led him out onto the veranda, which had a marvellous view of the city. After enjoying it, Petukhov said: 'You have a nice apartment. May I see it?'

'Don't worry,' Philby replied. 'We are alone here. My wife has classes at the university. And the servant has two incomparable attributes: he makes marvellous tea and does not speak English.'

Petukhov listened closely and nodded. But he checked the apartment anyway and met the servant.

Kim was enjoying this. He was absolutely certain that things would go the way he had hoped. He decided to have a little fun: he sat his guest down and with a serious face began talking about the complexities of a Common Arab Market. He named the economic causes, the political ones. He mentioned that the Arabs were divided and did not trust one another.

The guest did not listen for more than a few minutes to Kim's lecture. Then he rose, looked around once more, and said: 'To tell the truth, I haven't the slightest interest in the problems of a Common Arab Market, Comrade Philby.'

Kim extended his hand.

'I've been waiting so long for you.'

Petukhov told Kim that he was told to establish contact with him and that from now on he would be Kim's controller. They made a plan for arranging and scheduling meetings.

Kim's apartment in Hamara (Red) Street was not far from the Soviet Trade mission. Petukhov, who went to work there at the same time every day, passed Philby's balcony. He came back the same way. If Kim needed a regular meeting, he should go out on the balcony and lean on the railing with a newspaper in his hand. That would be a signal to Petukhov: the meeting would take place as planned, at the planned time and place – everything that had been arranged.

For an urgent meeting, there was another signal. Not far from Hamara Street was a fenced park. Kim would chalk a cross on the wrought-iron fence. It was placed near the ground, so Kim would bend over pretending to lace his shoe. (Later they decided to draw the cross higher up, so that Kim would not have to bend so low, and then they dropped the cross completely. If Kim needed to meet urgently, he would be out on the balcony, but with a book instead of his newspaper.)

In other words, they used the classic methods employed by spies in all the services since biblical times. Nothing new had been invented in the six years Kim had been out of the game.

Petukhov was interested in why Philby was so sure that he was not being watched. Kim explained that the conviction was not only the result of his observations or of his intuition. There were only fourteen people or so at the SIS branch in Beirut, including clerical workers. They simply did not have the forces to observe him regularly. It was not appropriate to ask for help from the Lebanese. Everyone knew that you if you told a Lebanese a great secret, all the Lebanese in the area would know it. Philby's contacts with the Arab leaders would have fallen apart, and SIS was extremely interested in his maintaining them.

Petukhov listened to his conclusions, but did not lose his vigilance and followed instructions. Therefore they never met again at Philby's house. There was one occasion when they met in a restaurant, disobeying all the rules, because they were friends and they were hungry.

After Kim told me this, he said: 'Please, if you write about me, do not depict me as a flawless spy who thinks about everything and knows everything ahead of time. I made lots and lots of mistakes. Can't be helped – the human factor. I always remained a man. And, perhaps, there's no great sin in that.'

They met after sunset and in the beginning Eleanor wondered where her husband was off to at dark. Kim would reply patiently: 'You know, dear, that I work for British intelligence.' (She knew that, he told her with SIS's permission.) 'And according to regulations, unfortunately, you cannot ask me questions in that area. If only because I can't answer them.'

Thus, he now had two covers. One as a journalist, which he used to cover his work for SIS; and work for the SIS helped him hide his KGB contacts from his wife. The meetings with Petukhov went on regularly, approximately every ten days, always in Beirut, never out of town.

They arranged for Kim to supply Petukhov with copies of all the material he gave to SIS on his meetings with the Arabs, condition that Moscow would use the material with extreme caution, so that SIS would not guess the source. But it became clear quite soon that his conversations with the Arab leaders were of little interest to Moscow. At the time the USSR's position in the Middle East was very strong, very influential, and the KGB had plenty of sources on the Arab leaders.

Moscow wanted to know something else: the plans and actions of the British and the Americans. Here Kim's opportunities were much weaker, almost nil. The goodwill and politeness of the English and American diplomats was combined with profound reticence in conversations with him.

On his almost daily visits to the British and American Embassies, Kim tried not to ask questions that would arouse suspicion. He preferred talking about topics from the newspapers. He hoped that in discussing what everyone knew for a quarter of an hour, he would catch a few glimmers of truly valuable information among the clichés. Those glimmers *have* to appear in the conversations of people in the know.

And they did. But they were few and far apart.

He discussed the problem with Petukhov. They tried to find a way out. But it was hard. A thick wall surrounded him. There was also the constant threat hanging over him that he could be fed misinformation and then caught when it was passed. So he never quoted his sources exactly and never put his eggs in one basket. There was another constant danger – the possibility of the Soviet codes being deciphered. If the British or Americans had it, sooner or later they would know the truth about him.

Of course, even in this situation he had successes. For instance, he got to know the American businessman, Miles Copeland, and his wife. In his youth, Copeland had worked in the CIA. Even though he most likely did not work for them in Beirut, he was in close contact and helped them under his business cover. Before the revolution in Egypt, he had worked in the American Embassy in Cairo. The CIA got each of its officers to maintain contact with two or three Egyptian revolutionary officers who seemed to have a future (Nagib, Nasser, Sadat and others). Copeland developed a relationship with Colonel Nasser. They became friends and he continued the relationship while working in Beirut at the same time as Philby.

The American was a friend of Paulsen; and so he knew very well that Philby worked for SIS. He also knew the situation with the espionage scandal involving Maclean and Burgess. Nevertheless, he readily helped Philby, introducing him as journalist to his many Egyptian friends. In his meetings with Copeland, Philby was always on the look-out for the glimmer of information that might appear.

I asked Philby if Nasser could have been an agent of Copeland's, that is, of the CIA. Kim responded confidently: 'Nasser was never his agent. That is absolutely clear.' He added after a pause: 'They were simply friends.'

There was another high-placed American who treated him well in Beirut – the CIA chief, Papelwhite. He liked to talk to Philby about Arab problems, even though Kim never initiated those conversations, fearing that Papelwhite was feeding him disinformation. But his fears were groundless. As for leading Arab intellectuals, especially the Palestinians, Philby never had to urge them to talk or pose questions. They seethed with boundless energy and wanted to talk so much that Philby's only problem was to remember everything.

In 1960 the new SIS chief in Beirut arrived, Kim's friend Nicholas Elliott. They began using Philby more actively, which made him happy. They decided that it would be stupid to hide their old friendship and their former work together. It could be misinterpreted. So they saw each other with their families, visiting each other's homes. But Kim could not break through the wall of Anglo-American caution. And Moscow was not very enthusiastic about his information.

Of course, he could have easily named all the SIS and CIA agents in Beirut, Amman and Damascus – everywhere that he travelled. He could interpret the oblique information he got during his conversations with his fellow Englishmen and with the Americans. He could put together replies, hints and opinions to get the general picture. Some questions were discussed quite openly in his presence, and Kim knew that these topics were not very significant. Others, they avoided. That gave him information, too: this was the important topic. Interestingly, SIS never asked him about Soviet activity in the Middle East, not once – he never heard a question on this highly important topic, which confirmed yet again that they still had suspicions about it.

Sometimes he told his SIS contact that he had met some Soviet journalist or other. The answer was always the same: he is a Soviet spy, avoid meeting him. No one from the SIS ever asked him to cultivate relations with a Soviet correspondent. Why not? Kim thought that SIS considered it too dangerous: it would make a very complex game. Good spies prefer simple moves. In a complex game that, 'human factor' can crop up with a simple error that will destroy a complex construction.

In one of our conversations Philby said: 'In summing up that period, I can say that I acted properly in agreeing to move to Beirut. My calculations were correct. I made good contacts. I showed myself well to SIS, which was important. But for my main work, Beirut is a sad page. I did not understand right away that it would be very difficult for me to be truly useful for Moscow. The British and Americans were cautious with me. And I had to be cautious with them, so as not to arouse any new suspicions . . . Working outside is very hard. Work inside, when you're under suspicion, is twice as hard. That's why my work in the Middle East did not give me great satisfaction. Nor to the Centre, I imagine.'

He had reasons for not being pleased with what the Centre demanded of him.

Once, Petukhov passed Moscow's request to develop and recruit a cipher clerk from the Pakistani Embassy. How could he explain an acquaintance from a totally different social stratum and educational level? What could a famous correspondent of two major British publications, a journalist who was on good terms with the ambassadors of England and the USA, have in common with a Pakistani cipher clerk? The only explanation that would come to mind was that Kim Philby was interested in the ciphers. Business like that should be given to a local resident, who could do it better and unnoticed. Politely, but firmly, Kim asked the Centre to rescind its order.

This was the second case that he mentioned in our conversations when he was upset and surprised by orders from the Centre. I would not rule out the possibility that there were more such surprises. But Kim never deviated from his rule not to criticise his superiors from the KGB. Even as he told me of that particularly ridiculous and dangerous assignment, Philby felt it necessary to soft-pedal. 'Of course,' he added, looking at me with his clear eyes, 'sometimes it was hard for the Centre to take into account the circumstances on the ground.'

Nevertheless, Philby still did do some recruiting of agents in the Middle East; more than once, perhaps. But he told me of only one case. It is worth many.

I have already mentioned that whenever we talked about the books written about him, Kim usually had a commentary about them: sometimes a serious comment, more frequently an amiable joke. Sometimes, handing me a book to read from his home 'Philbyiana', he would add a brief and elegantly written notation – what was worth reading in the book and what was total nonsense.

He said once:

'A lot of silly things have been written about me. Judgments. Damnations. Insults. Shameless tripe. One journalist enjoyed proving the amorality of my entire life. He showed evidence. I drank too much. And I had more wives than is proper for a decent man. And I was a hypocrite, and a slob, and a liar. He worked up a righteous wrath about me. He left out only one amoral act of mine: how I recruited him as an agent in Beirut in a matter of a few minutes without any great effort.'

Philby spoke and spread his arms in a show of wonder: how could anyone be so forgetful? There were several books on the table by various authors. I asked which one he had in mind. He smiled and as usual promised to tell me about it later, when the opportunity arose.

Here is the story that Kim first told me, using a letter, P, for the journalist. P was a British subject, a freelance journalist in the Middle East. He spoke French and German very well, and had good Arabic, which made it much easier for him to get good sources. Kim was very impressed by P's knowledge. He seemed a good man. He was anti-Communist, of course, but not a fanatic, and he had good contacts with Algerians, Lebanese, Syrians and Egyptians. One day Kim invited him for tea at home. A long and thorough discussion of the situation in the Middle East convinced Philby that P could become a pretty good agent for SIS if they wanted him.

Philby wrote a memo to Elliott: here is a man who could be useful to SIS. This is his background, this is his knowledge etc. Elliott replied that he was an interesting candidate, but he had to consult London, in case there were any compromising facts about him.

About two weeks later Elliott told Philby: 'London agrees. Are you sure he will?'

'I can't guarantee it, but I'll try.'

Kim invited P for another afternoon and told him: 'Knowing your wide knowledge and contacts, there are certain people who feel that you could be of great use to the English government, if you would agree to look for the answers to certain questions that could arise from time to time.'

P regarded Kim, thought, and asked a very reasonable question. 'What guarantees can you give me that my answers will be sent to the British?'

Kim noted that word on his espionage scandal had travelled far and replied: 'I can introduce you to someone else in the British Embassy, and you will deal only with him, and I will have nothing to do with it.'

'All right,' P responded. 'I am prepared to talk with him, if he likes.'

That was the entire recruitment. Philby introduced the journalist to Elliott. The next day Elliott thanked Kim and said that P had agreed to work for SIS, for money. P also thanked Kim for introducing him to Elliott. He did it in an embarrassed way. After all, agreeing to spy for money is not the most noble action. Kim told him that they should avoid meeting now. P nodded, happy to hear that.

But they did bump into each other once. About two months later Kim was in Cairo. He was having lunch at the Fontainebleau. His table was by the door, which opened and in walked P. He recoiled when he saw Kim.

Kim said: 'Don't worry. If we run into each other once or twice by accident, it's all right. But in general, you should be more careful. Sit down, we'll have lunch together.'

P sat down in confusion. He mumbled something. But he couldn't eat. He quickly said something about not feeling well and left.

'Maybe he was getting his revenge?' Kim said, laughing, as he finished the story, and added: 'Here's his book.'

He picked up a book that he had prepared for me and read the author's name aloud. It was a famous English journalist. 'That's his name.'

This story continues.

In 1963, when Philby had left Beirut for Moscow, P took his place at SIS. But he did not work for long in the Middle East; Kim later heard that P moved to England.

'I doubt that he worked at SIS for long,' Kim said. 'But undoubtedly, he remained a "friend" of the firm. The SIS usually uses such "friends" over and over.'

I put P's book in my briefcase, to read at home, and asked a question I had been planning for a long time.

'Did you ever recruit an agent for the KGB, pretending to recruit him for SIS?'

Kim laughed. 'You're a writer and you want interesting plots. But in intelligence we do not like complications. They're unreliable. And often dangerous. Recruiting an agent for the KGB while pretending to recruit for SIS doesn't work. A chance conversation, a chance meeting, the agent's desire to see someone else from SIS besides me – and it all falls apart.'

He thought for a while, smoothly waving away the smoke from

his cigarette, which he lit against his wife's wishes. Then he spoke softly, almost to himself.

'There's a simpler way that is possible. I recruit an agent for SIS. With its official approval. I become the only contact for the new agent. Everything that he brings me I naturally turn over to SIS. And at the same time, to Petukhov. That's possible.'

'Is the agent English? Or could you recruit an American?'

'It's harder with an American. Roosevelt and Churchill had signed an agreement not to do covert operations against each other.'

'Harder or impossible?' I pressed him.

'Harder,' Kim said after a while. 'But possible.' He got into the spirit of the game and began developing the plot. 'Imagine that I meet an old friend from the CIA in Beirut. I know that he is sick of his firm. Not because he does not like the American way of life, but because he is a live person. He considers himself honest. But the CIA, in his opinion – which holds for the whole world, by the way – has not only honest people who share his world view, but also scoundrels, and careerists, and outright fools. They're the ones who got America into the pointless Vietnam War, prepared the aborted Bay of Pigs, and so on. If I were to persuade him to start working for SIS, I would use these arguments: he would not be working against America, but in her interests – to get rid of the people at the CIA whom he hates – the careerists, liars, scoundrels, in effect, the enemies of his country. They can be thrown out only with truthful information which, thanks to him, SIS will get to the government circles of the USA. The truth will counteract the dishonest game the CIA clique is playing. The US government will wonder why those people are deceiving Congress and the President. That's an example of one argument I would use. There could be more. But suppose such a man agrees to work for SIS. Naturally, I would solemnly promise that his actions would never be known in America. Therefore he would have contact only with me, Kim Philby, and with no one else at SIS. I would show him the special stamp we use at SIS – "guarded". It meant that a document with that stamp could not be shown to the Americans at any price. I would tell him that this will be stamped on all the documents I get from him . . . I would even promise him that no one but me would know about him as a source in SIS. And I would tell no one at SIS about him. I would pay him myself. My salary would be enough for that.

'And at the same time, without knowing it, he would be working for the KGB.'

I listened to Kim and tried to guess: was he inventing this or had something like this happened in his life?

Kim went on. 'It would be very good if the American were of Arab origin. He would be outraged by the pro-Israeli position of the CIA and the USA. I would tell him that at SIS there was a strong public opinion that was more against Israel than against the Arabs. If he wanted to increase the pro-Arab stance at SIS, he had to give these people the appropriate information.

'And finally,' Kim concluded, 'this man should not work in the Middle East. He would work in the USA and come to Lebanon from time to time to visit his Arab relatives. That is how I would meet him, if we were to take seriously our purely fictional version of my recruiting an American CIA officer in the Middle East.'

The master spy regarded me with his smiling, innocent blue eyes.

34

FLIGHT

It was Kim's seventh year in Beirut. Many things had happened there. His marriage brought comfort. Eleanor loved him sincerely; he knew that and responded as much as his confused life as a correspondent of two publications, and as an agent for two intelligence services, allowed.

In 1960, his father died, outliving his wife by only two years. The death was very hard on Kim. They had become close in his last years. Maybe for the first time in his life, Kim began to love his father and to be proud of him. But fate decreed that even his father's death would be a symbol of their closeness. St John lived in Saudi Arabia and spent the summers in London, but that year he went to Moscow to a Congress of Orientalists and then, after some time in London, decided to visit his son in Beirut for a few days before returning to Saudi Arabia. Early in the morning of 30 September, St John fell ill, gasping for breath, and fainted. Kim took him to the hospital. They said it was his heart. A few hours later, his father regained consciousness for an instant, said, 'God, I'm bored', and died that evening, in the arms of his grief-stricken son.

If Kim were to write another report on his father for the KGB, I doubt that he would have used the cruel and scornful formulae he had in the past.

He anxiously watched every spy scandal (in case it turned against him) that flared up in the world, and usually they reflected badly on the intelligence services involved. In 1961 George Blake, an SIS officer who had been working for Soviet intelligence, was arrested in London. He had been living in Lebanon, like Philby, studying Arabic. He was tricked into returning to London and grabbed there. The court gave a frightening sentence: forty-two years. In late 1961 Anatoly Golitsyn, a Soviet agent, defected to the West in Finland. News like this was not pleasant for Philby.

His work did not give him any particular pleasure, or any great disappointments. He did not expect peaks or valleys. His relations with SIS seemed to have stabilised. Of course, he could not hope to resume a major career in it, but his name had probably been rehabilitated in society. His long and sinless (as far as people could tell) sojourn in Lebanon had to have a positive effect on the attitude towards him of the most cautious diplomats and journalists. This helped Kim to get more valuable information from them, without expending more effort, and which he immediately sent to Moscow. His communications with Moscow were working well and he was finally once again useful to the Centre.

Naturally, he had to be wary at all times. SIS probably had no intention of closing his file and still hoped to catch him by leaking him disinformation. He couldn't have known about this attitude, held and acted upon, as some researchers claim, in 1960 by Dick White and Kim's old friend, Nicholas Elliott, who came to Beirut as chief of the SIS station. They sharply increased Philby's work as an SIS agent, hoping that Moscow would want to take advantage of Kim's new opportunities and access.

The period when Elliott was in Beirut passed uneventfully for Kim. Elliott returned to London, and the new SIS chief was Peter Lan. Things went on as usual. Even the work of a master spy can become routine, especially when the spy got sick, like an ordinary mortal. He caught cold: flu and bronchitis at the same time. It was just then that things changed sharply in the fate of Harold Adrian Russell Philby.

On 10 January 1963, Nicholas Elliott returned unexpectedly for Kim to Beirut. The meeting that I described at the very beginning of our narrative took place. Elliott's trip was preceded by events that related to Kim Philby directly and obliquely.

A year earlier, in December 1961, Anatoly Golitsyn, a KGB officer, came to the CIA chief in Helsinki. He had prepared thoroughly for his role as defector, gathering the tiniest details that would help him give the Americans new information about Soviet agents abroad. Among that material, they say, was some new data unknown to SIS, shedding light on the work of 'Sonny'.

As Phillip Knightley writes, a few months later, Flora Solomon, whom Kim had considered a long and faithful friend of his family, told Victor Rothschild that Kim Philby was a Communist and that it was improper for the *Observer* to trust such a man's interpretations of events in the Middle East. She explained that her comments to Rothschild were prompted by her outrage over the one-sided, pro-Arab tone of his articles. Rothschild set up a meeting for her with MI5. She told them how Kim had tried to get her involved in some secret international activity during the Civil War in Spain, activity that she thought was connected with the international Communist movement, and with Moscow.

So Nicholas Elliott, Kim's old friend from SIS, was sent to Beirut in order to . . . Actually, no one seems to be able to define simply what Elliott's goal in Beirut was. Philby himself posited various thoughts that could have directed SIS to send Elliott to confront him. In any case, it happened the way Kim told me about it. Here's the rest of that meeting.

They were alone in his secretary's apartment. No one else was there. Philby did not know if the conversation was being recorded or not.

'So, you're planning to start it all over again?' Philby asked Elliott.

'Yes,' he replied. 'But it will be different this time. Now we know that you had worked for Soviet intelligence right up to 1949.'

'Who told you that?'

'It doesn't matter who told us. The important thing is that it was a man who knows all the circumstances of your case well.'

'But it has nothing to do with reality!' Kim replied, knowing that he was telling the truth as far as the ridiculous date, '1949', was concerned.

'Listen,' Elliott said, on the attack once more, but from a different angle. 'You stopped working for them in 1949, I'm absolutely certain of that. Now it's January 1963. Fourteen years have gone by. In that time your ideas and views have changed. They had to change. I can understand people who worked for the Soviet Union, say, before or during the war. But by 1949 a man of your intellect and your spirit had to see that all the rumours about Stalin's monstrous behaviour were not rumours, they were the truth. You decided to break with the USSR. Certainly, you wouldn't have worked for them after Khrushchev's secret speech. Therefore I can give you my word and the word of Dick White that you will get full immunity, you will be pardoned, but only if you tell it yourself. We need your collaboration, your help.'

'Thank you for the promise of immunity and all the rest, but

I've told everything that I know many times – to the SIS and
to MI5.'

'That's not enough. You have to tell what you had been keeping
silent about. Our promise of immunity and pardon depends wholly
on whether you give us all the information that you have. First of all
we need information on people who worked with Moscow. By the
way, we know them.'

He took out a sheet of paper and showed it Philby. It had half
a dozen names. Two of them were his English contacts. So it was
impossible even to think about agreeing to the proposal from White
and Elliott. Kim read the list, shrugged, and said that he did not
know the people or anything about their possible contacts with
Moscow.

They talked some more. Elliott insisted that everything he said
was true. Philby denied it. The conversation was polite and calm.

'I understand you,' Elliott said. 'I've been in love with two women
at the same time. I'm certain that you were in the same situation in
politics: you loved England and the Soviet Union at the same time.
But you've worked for the Soviet Union enough, you've helped it
enough. Now you must help us.'

He was trying to use the same method that Skardon had used
on Klaus Fuchs. They talked for about ninety minutes: always the
same thing, over and over. Elliott said his lines, Philby said his.
Essentially, Kim's entire life was a non-stop interrogation.

Perhaps it had been from that moment when he ran into an
old acquaintance in the library who would not shake his hand,
merely asking if Kim had worked for the secret police before
going to Vienna or had been recruited in Austria. Kim had not
known what to say and walked away. Or earlier, in Austria,
when he had had to prove his loyalty to his friends; or later,
when he'd been under suspicion at SIS and the questioning
began, unofficial and formal, friendly and professional: Dick White
– he was easy, no problems with him; then Milmo – much
harder; and Skardon – the great pro, it was hardest of all with
him . . . And now, this interrogation, ambivalent, vague, with
unclear, goals, from Elliott, who had always treated Kim well,
and, maybe because of that, the most dangerous. He asked all the
questions that the press had asked. Philby produced the answers
that he had prepared in his head just in case he ran into someone
where he *shouldn't* see anyone he knew, or be seen with someone

he *shouldn't* be seen with. Wasn't that a daily, round-the-clock, non-stop interrogation?

Then there was the KGB. Did not his friends, his Soviet colleagues, whom he idolised and considered people without flaws, professionals without blemishes, not subject him to an endless interrogation, checking and rechecking his information, comparing it constantly to other sources? Didn't they force him to write his biography over and over at a time when the country was in danger, when he should have been spending all his time getting information to help the war effort, yet instead they made him write about himself, his wife and his parents, explaining one part of his life and then another, repeating, repeating, repeating it over and over, in the hopes of catching him out in a contradiction?

That was the most popular form of interrogation. 'Tell us how you ended up in . . .'

'I've told you that already.'

'Never mind, tell it again. We like it, you're a good storyteller.'

Didn't he have to answer questions from the Centre, put to him endlessly by his Soviet colleagues in London during the war?

Kim got home about five. At six he was on the balcony. He was holding a book, not a newspaper. He needed an urgent meeting.

Petukhov passed the house at the appointed hour. He glanced at Kim. He did not react, but Kim knew that he had noticed the book. They would meet that night.

They met, after extreme precautions naturally. Kim had the feeling that Elliott would not start having him followed the day of their first meeting if only because neither he nor anyone else would think that Kim Philby would meet his Soviet contact, if he had one, right after talking with Elliott: that would be too dangerous, too challenging.

Kim told Petukhov what had transpired with Elliott. He listened attentively, nodding from time to time, as if to say, 'We were expecting this. It's nothing to worry about.'

When Kim finished, Petukhoy said: 'I think your time has come. They won't leave you alone now. You have to disappear. There's no other way. There's room for you in Moscow.'

Kim said, with relief: 'I had hoped that you would make the offer.'

'Arrangements will take some time. How long can you wait before answering?'

'I can gain a week. Maybe ten days. But no more. It would be hard to drag it out beyond that.'

'All right. I'll walk past your balcony every three hours every day. If you see me carrying a newspaper, that means I have to meet you for a consultation. If I'm carrying a book, that means everything is prepared for your departure, and you have to get moving.'

The next day Elliott called Philby and invited him to lunch. They had a pleasant meal – Kim and his wife, Nicholas and his secretary. There was no talk of business. At the very end, Elliott mentioned that he was returning to London the next day and that Peter Lan would be handling 'the question that interests us'. Lan was the Beirut SIS man, Elliott's replacement, the third intelligence chief while Philby was there after Paulsen and Elliott.

A day passed, two, then three. Lan showed no interest in Philby at all. But on the fourth day he rang. Lan asked after Philby's health and if there were anything he wanted to tell him.

'Nothing new yet,' Philby replied. 'I've told everything I know. If something else comes to me, I'll let you know right away.'

That day he had a consultation with Petukhov and told him about Lan's call.

'The noose is tightening,' he said. 'Elliott must have left strict instructions. They won't wait very long.'

'I'm ready,' Philby replied.

'I know you're ready,' he said. 'But I need more time, five or six days.'

Kim wondered where he would find the time. Then something happened that confirmed yet again that Kim's luck always held.

Peter Lan was an avid skier. Before the war he had been on the British ski team in the Olympics in Germany. There was a lot of snow in Lebanon that January. All the newspapers wrote about the ideal skiing conditions. So, as Philby dropped in at the Embassy on the following day, he heard from his friend that Lan was taking a four-day trip into the mountains.

'Four days!' thought Kim. 'Four whole days! Petukhov will be able to get everything ready by then. They won't do anything against me while the bureau chief is away.'

Petukhov sighed in relief when Philby told him the news.

Lan went into the mountains. Philby waited for the signals. He went out onto his balcony every three hours. But Petukhov did not appear. Philby started worrying – had something happened to him?

It was the fourth day of Lan's vacation. He was due back in the evening. Kim was very anxious. He came out on the balcony, three hours after the previous time, almost without any hope of seeing Petukhov. Suddenly the familiar figure appeared in the distance. Petukhov was approaching the balcony quickly, carrying something. Kim couldn't tell at first which it was, a book or a newspaper. When he got closer, Kim saw, to his disappointment – it was a newspaper. That meant there was no departure, just another consultation. They were running out of time.

Kim arrived at their meeting quite upset.

But Petukhov said: 'Everything's ready. Now!'

'What do you mean, "now"?'

'We have to go.'

'You mean for good?'

'Of course. Everything's ready. They're waiting for us.'

'But you didn't have a book in your hands.'

Petukhov looked at me in amazement. 'What an idiot I am! I forgot all about it! Well, never mind, there's no retreat. Let's go.'

'But I haven't shaved, I'm not dressed, I'm not ready to leave!'

'Don't worry about it, we'll take care of everything. You have to ring home and tell them you'll be late for dinner. That you have business and you'll get a bite in a restaurant.'

Kim phoned and said he'd be late. No one suspected anything strange at home. They checked for a tail. Everything seemed all right. A short time later they were in a car, Philby in the back, Petukhov in front with the driver. Next to Philby was a stranger. The stranger, Philby later learned, was either the Soviet resident or his deputy.

The car started. Petukhov handed him an ordinary business card, with the ordinary Russian name Ivanov. 'Not for keeps, Comrade Ivanov,' Petukhov said. 'You'll be giving it back to me later.'

The car headed for the harbour. They stopped at the control point: document check. But the driver said curtly, 'Soviet Embassy', and the guards saluted.

They came out on the pier. To the left was an American destroyer, to the right a Soviet ship called the *Dolmatova*. The car, not surprisingly, turned away from the destroyer. Philby tried not to look back, nor towards the American ship.

The man sitting in the back with Philby was tense, but twice he spoke encouragingly: everything is fine, everything is going the way it should. Philby was not calm. In his heart he knew that they were not being watched, but intuition is one thing; this was dangerous and could end in tragedy. He could not rule out the possibility of surveillance and arrest. He thought about all the mistakes he had made in his life. None had ever led to tragedy. Maybe he would be lucky this time too.

There were only a few yards left to the gangway. The car stopped. They quickly went aboard. The captain led Philby to his cabin. They poured out Cognac. There were five men. The captain said a few words of welcome, he spoke a little English. Philby could see that he was agitated too.

Petukhov took away the Ivanov business card and gave Philby another. Now his name was Villi Maris. Petukhov told him he was from Riga. Philby had nothing against that – why not Riga?

They finished the bottle in ten minutes. Everyone left. In another fifteen minutes, Philby heard the engines start. A short while later, Philby knew they were out at sea: there was a terrible storm. He told me it was, nonetheless, a wonderful night.

In the morning he took a look at his cabin. Everything he needed was there, including warm underwear and clothes: everything for his future life in the Russian winter. They even remembered shaving things.

He tried to imagine what was happening in Beirut. If Eleanor did not raise the alarm, then certainly Lan would ring in the morning, back from his ski trip, to find out if Kim had anything new to tell him. She would tell Lan that her husband was missing. What would they do? What could the *Dolmatova* expect *en route* to Odessa?

Kim had the satisfaction of leaving right under their noses. That meant that they knew nothing about his ties with Petukhov. That meant the work had been done clean. He wondered if Lan would get into trouble for his ski trip.

Various thoughts crowded his mind. It was a long way to Odessa.

★   ★   ★

That is the external picture of the events that took place in Beirut in January 1963. Beyond it lie hidden causes, calculations, intrigues, clashes of interest in the cruel world of politics and intelligence. What was *Philby's* explanation of what happened in those thirteen days between Elliott's arrival in Beirut on 10 January and the departure of the *Dolmatova* out of Beirut on 23 January with a passenger named Villi Matis on board?

Philby told me that he found Elliott's arrival illogical and strange. Let's say that on the basis of information against Philby from the defector Golitsyn they decided to arrest and try him. In Lebanon, under local law, they could not do that. But they had many ways of overcoming that obstacle.

One: they could invite him to London for a consultation with the *Observer*, say. In England he would be in their hands.

Two: They could arrest him in the British Embassy, drug him, and bring him out of the country by plane or boat. He wouldn't have been able to resist.

Three: in late 1962 Philby had written a letter to the *Observer* requesting permission to take leave in London in July 1963, in order to see his children. They could have waited a few months. They could not have been expecting Philby to defect because, as it turned out, they knew nothing of his contacts with Petukhov and believed, moreover, that he had broken off with Moscow in 1949.

Kim never could understand where they got that idea from. The only explanation he could find was that something *had* happened to his Soviet contact in the USA in 1949 and he did not meet him for a long time, almost a year. Perhaps the man who gave them the information truly believed that he had stopped working then. When Philby's communications were re-established, that man was no longer around or did not know about it.

Maybe they had other plans for Philby. They may have wanted to begin without an arrest – that would have caused too much scandal, and another espionage scandal would have been bad for SIS. Maybe they wanted to get Philby to cooperate, to play a double game. But they made a fatal mistake, in that case. They promised him immunity on condition that he tell them everything. They wanted information on specific people. That meant that they did not understand his character or his principles. They were forcing him to defect.

There is a point of view, Kim told me, that SIS was trying to get him to leave, in order to avoid a scandal. But he didn't believe it. The scandal his defection caused, with the Soviet newspapers playing it up, created a much greater scandal than his forced return to London or even his arrest would have done. Many people realised that, including Hugh Trevor-Roper.

It seems predictable, now. But the decision to send Elliott to talk to Philby was not made in circumstances conducive to peaceful analysis and consideration. Philby thought it was taken after a meeting of the committee, where everyone gave an opinion, these opinions were combined, and a compromise was reached. They were proud of their compromise. But the results – well, we know what they were.

The committee consisted of representatives from SIS, MI5, the Foreign Office, the Army, the Navy, and the Air Force. Each department naturally gave its own point of view and proposed its own plan of action. Philby described a possible version of the meeting. MI5 demanded urgent measures and would not wait until July. SIS asked, not without irony, what urgent measures MI5 was proposing: killing Kim Philby or bringing him to the Embassy and keeping him there under arrest? And SIS would offer its own plan – since Kim Philby had not had contact with the Russians for fourteen years, if we approach him calmly and politely, we might be able to get him to play a double game. That must have been the basis of Elliott's trip.

Kim understood the logic of their decision. Elliott had been a friend. He had always defended Philby. He did not believe in his second life. But he saw new documents, incontrovertible proof (they must have been transcripts of Golitsyn's interrogation), which convinced him that Kim Philby had worked for the KGB until 1949. He came to Beirut to get his friend out of trouble. The only way to avoid deserved punishment was for Philby to accept his offer to cooperate and be a double agent.

But that logic overlooked certain important circumstances, Philby pointed out to me.

One, they thought that Philby had no contacts with the KGB in Beirut. If they had had any doubts, they would have acted differently. But the absence of contacts with the KGB for fourteen years, since 1949, meant that the information they had hoped to get about the work of the KGB would be very limited. 'My knowledge of how things worked at the Centre was basically nothing. As for concrete information about people with whom I had been in contact, they had to understand that I would never agree to name them,' Kim said.

Two: in order for Philby to become a double agent, he had at least to re-establish contact with Moscow. But any attempt by an agent to do that after fourteen years could mean only one thing to Moscow – suspicion of a double game.

These seem like elementary considerations. But they had been overlooked. That often happens when the people making a decision try to include all the interests of everyone taking part in the decision and compromise, hoping to please everyone.

Philby's strategy in his talks with Elliott was simple. He had developed it long ago. First of all, he had to learn what new material they had. As soon as he heard the date, 1949, he knew that they were unlikely to have anything worthwhile. So he did not change his strategy: he demonstrated total indifference to the tiresome question of his possible KGB ties. He knew that he was innocent. No 'proof' – direct or oblique, no papers – worried him. Therefore he naturally denied everything, claiming that any witnesses against him were false, fabricated only to trap him. 'I don't know what Elliott was feeling when he left Beirut. I do not rule out the possibility that he was certain that he had planted doubts in me and made me think about the arguments he had used. My goal was to win time, if only a few days, and to do nothing that could push them into decisive action.'

Philby did not think that SIS was one hundred percent sure that they would win in court. It was quite possible that they found Golitsyn to be a weak witness. Philby doubted that they had enough proof for a trial; and if Philby were acquitted, SIS would have looked very bad.

Kim later read that Golitsyn's evidence was filled with blatantly stupid statements. For instance, he spoke of thousands of Soviet agents in England and millions in the United States. He maintained that the worsening relations between the USSR and China was just an act invented by the KGB in order to fool the West and lull it into a false sense of security.

'What was the role of the Americans in the Beirut story?' I asked.

'The Americans do not participate in the committee I told you about. It deals with British affairs, British law, and in these cases the British are very careful about intervention by foreigners. They do not invite anyone who does not have a direct bearing on the situation. Of course, the Americans were informed about the case, but they were informed unofficially. So the members of the committee – unofficially, too – were informed of the US position. I am certain of that.'

'What position could the USA have had on you?'

'Since we are talking about the CIA, the "cousins", as the British intelligence services called them then, and since they were doing rather extreme things then, I can imagine that they could have proposed a more "radical solution". An "accident", you know, a car crash, murder by an "unknown terrorist", "accidental poisoning", anything like that, including "suicide", or a slow death that takes six months but requires only a grain of a special drug in a glass of whisky. By the way, that would have been the simplest way to avoid a widespread scandal. No person, no problem.'

'Graham Greene describes the slow, certain death in *The Human Factor*.'

'Yes. When I read the book, I wrote him a letter, expressing my doubts that the English would do something like that. After all, it was more typical of the "cousins" than SIS. And he agreed with me. In the British intelligence services at the time, people often said, "Our cousins recommend . . ." or "suggest". Sometimes it was said with excessive seriousness, hiding irony. The English never liked the advice of "our cousins". Allen Dulles knew that and he tried to avoid official recommendations to the British. He knew that simply out of protest, national pride and stubbornness they might reject a recommendation or do just the opposite. But privately, such recommendations could be made.'

'Could the Americans have done it independently, without letting the British know?'

'They could, even though that was riskier. By the way, I heard that after I vanished from Beirut, a "cousin" came, who was independently looking for Kim Philby. I don't know from which service – but both the FBI and the CIA were interested in my case. It's quite possible that Hoover hoped there would be a scandal that could be blamed entirely on SIS and the CIA. Dulles did not want a scandal. My work for Moscow when I was in the USA should have been work for the FBI. But I was under the CIA when I was in America. So the scandal would damage them. Hoover would have come out of it with less damage, especially since the FBI had nothing to do with me when I worked abroad. In Beirut, for instance, there were no FBI people. Only the CIA.

'When I left Lebanon, it was the failure of SIS, primarily. Even though the CIA and the FBI had their share of stock in me, it was SIS that went bankrupt. MI5, British counter-intelligence, which was always at war with SIS, took advantage of it. The main argument was that we always told you that Philby could not be trusted, and instead of getting rid of him, you entrusted him with work in Beirut! SIS, of course, blamed them, MI5.'

'Who paid for this failure?'

'Many people were asked to leave SIS – first of all, Nicholas Elliott and a few of my close friends. They were not sacked with dishonour, but nevertheless, they were asked to leave.'

'What happened to Peter Lan after his ski trip?'

'A good question,' Philby said with a smile. 'I thought of him when I considered the possible consequence of my defection on the people at SIS. After all, he left to go skiing at the most serious moment, doing nothing to prevent any action on my part. He returned the evening that I was sailing out of Beirut on the *Dolmatova*. The next morning he rang my house. Eleanor answered and said that I was not in. He asked her to tell me, "as soon as Kim gets back", that I should ring him. It was urgent.

"But I have no idea where he is! He's been gone all night," Eleanor told him, hoping that Lan would know where her husband was. Lan mumbled something in reply and hung up. In other words, he was to blame. But amazingly, three or four years later he received a high honour – the Cross of St Michael and St George, the third highest decoration given for foreign service. His career was not hurt at all.'

Three days later, the *Dolmatova* entered the Bay of Gallipoli. The captain told Kim: 'There's a rather strange ship on the horizon. You should take cover.'

The ship *was* strange. Kim had never seen a round ship like that. It was bristling with antennae.

The passenger from Riga was led deep into the hold and hidden. After a while the captain sent someone to tell him that everything was all right and he could come out. The strange ship had circled the *Dolmatova* three times and left. The manœuvre was unusual. But what it meant and why it had been done neither the captain nor his secret passenger knew. However, there seemed to be no consequences from the circling.

They travelled without stop and were soon in the Marmora Sea. But there was a hold-up at the entrance to the Bosphorus. The two ships ahead of the *Dolmatova* were stopped. So were the two behind. The captain was told from the shore that there was a tanker foundering ahead. It was very dangerous to try to pass it.

Kim told the captain: 'I lived in Istanbul for almost three years and I never heard of a tanker losing control. This tanker must have special reasons.' The captain chuckled.

They spent three anxious hours not moving. The captain was in touch with Odessa. At last he told Kim that Odessa gave orders to proceed ahead and go around the tanker. The Turks were told that the *Dolmatova* took all responsibility for damage and would not bring any claims.

'Is it dangerous?' Kim asked.

'Yes,' replied the captain. 'But orders are orders. Let's go.'

They passed around the tanker safely. Half an hour later they were in the Black Sea. 'Well, now you can say that we're home,' the captain said. Kim really did feel at home. And he went to bed.

They were still far from Odessa. It was very cold that winter and the sea had frozen. Kim was awakened at six in the morning. The captain let him know that a friend was on board who wanted to see him. Kim was surprised; after all, they hadn't reached Odessa yet. But there were three men from Odessa on board.

They were his colleagues. Kim was nervous. How would they greet him? What would they say? After all, defection is a failure.

A bottle of Cognac appeared on the table. Kim thanked them and said: 'I don't know if I will be able to be of use to my homeland. I was able to flee here. But I don't know if I'll be of any use.'

The senior man, who spoke English well, said something that Philby never forgot.

'Listen, dear Kim, every intelligence officer knows that once counter-intelligence takes an interest in you, it is the beginning of the end. Counter-intelligence has been interested in you since 1951 – and not through any fault of yours, as far as we know. Now it is 1963. You've led them around by the nose for twelve years. So what are you worried about?'

35

LUCKY KIM?

Moscow welcomed Kim Philby with January cold and the touching attentions of his colleagues.

The attention was expressed not only in trying to give him comparatively comfortable living arrangements and a course of treatment but – and this was most important for him – they soon gave him the opportunity to work, to feel *needed* in the work that he had considered his *main* work since 1934.

But first came adaptation. The greatest difficulties were not related to the climate, or the unfamiliar language (he was given a Russian teacher), or the imperfections of the lifestyle, but with the security set-up for Kim. This was practically the first problem that he had to discuss and settle with his colleagues from the KGB. However, he talked to me about them with humour.

The question came up the very first day in Moscow. Three men from the KGB administration came to greet the spy in his Moscow apartment ('in the Russian tradition,' Philby said and gestured, tossing back a shot of vodka). Their first request was to describe in as much detail as possible the whole history of his work in the Middle East in the last four years (apparently, since they renewed contact with him). Then they discussed security measures.

'We cannot predict how SIS and its friends will react. But we must be prepared for any extreme steps from them.'

Kim somehow did not believe that British or American secret services would try to kidnap him or kill him. When his guests asked his opinion on the probability of their taking extreme measures, Kim replied: 'One chance in a thousand.'

'One chance in a thousand is too much not to pay attention,' they replied decisively. They asked him to avoid any new contacts in the future, especially with foreigners. Therefore, he had to stay out of restaurants and crowded places like the Bolshoi Theatre and so on.

'Are you trying to say that I can't meet anyone at all?' Kim asked.

They replied very seriously, perhaps expecting a protest from him. 'Yes. Ideally, yes.'

Kim just laughed. 'My God! What bliss! I had so many contacts! Journalists, diplomats, the secret service . . . I was always surrounded by people, people, and more people! How wonderful to get away from them all for a bit!'

He did in fact need to rest from the many years of constant tension. A lifetime of alertness is hard. Naturally, every spy eventually develops an autopilot, Kim told me, which automatically warns him of danger. But even the autopilot does not let the nerves rest completely, since it is made up of them. However, now, in Moscow, he could allow himself to relax and to be alone.

The next morning, in a state of blissful peace, he went for a walk. The street was empty – just a few passersby, a few cars. The snow crunched underfoot. He knew the letters of the Russian alphabet. He walked along and read the signs, mumbling the Russian words whose meaning he did not know. But suddenly the Russian letters formed a German word: 'PARIKMAKHERSKAYA'. He remembered that he needed a haircut. He crossed the street and opened the door under the Russo-German sign.

There were five or six people in the small vestibule, reading newspapers and magazines. The barbers were at work in the next room. Kim took off his coat, hung it up, took a free chair, trying not to attract attention. He glanced at the other men and decided that, based on their clothing, there were no foreigners among them. Thanks to his friends, he was dressed like a Muscovite already. He picked up a copy of *Pravda* from the table and started looking at Khrushchev's photograph on the front page. No one seemed to pay particular attention to him: just a man reading *Pravda*, what was unusual about that? (Donald Maclean later once told him: 'A nation that reads *Pravda* is invincible.') About a quarter of an hour passed. From time to time Kim took sidelong looks at his neighbours in the waiting room: everyone was calm, no one was interested in him.

Suddenly the door was pushed open and a large man in a fur-lined jacket strode into the room. He came in and said something in a loud, aggressive voice standing in the doorway. To Kim's surprise, everyone in the vestibule turned to look at him. The large man repeated the words, which Kim did not know, and everyone looked at Kim again.

Kim was upset.

What had he done, Lord? Just yesterday he had been asked not to attract attention, and now look – this man was searching for him. He might be blowing his cover. He had to leave. He did not lose his aplomb. He looked at his watch, pretended to be late for something, put the newspaper back on the table, got dressed . . . But as soon as he started to leave, the large man, who had already hung up his jacket and taken the chair next to Kim's, put his hand on Kim's arm and said something else in Russian. Kim managed a weak smile, shook his head in puzzlement, and quickly went out. Then he followed all the rules he had learned from the KGB and SIS. He walked one block, turned quickly into an alley, slowed down to see if he was followed. Then he walked up to a shop window and stared at the dusty glass, which made it hard to see across the street: nothing suspicious. He should have taken a taxi then for a few blocks and then changed to another. But there was no taxi nearby, no cinema, either. The metro station was far away. So he just looped around through alleys and lanes. He made sure that his pursuers had got lost or given up. Then, cautiously, he went home.

Later that day the man from the KGB charged with helping him get settled came to see him. Kim told him that he must have committed a terrible error, but he didn't know what.

'What happened?' the colleague asked tensely.

Kim told him about the barbershop with all the details.

The KGB man scratched his head as he mulled it over and then said: 'I know what the man said. When he came in and saw the waiting customers, he asked: "Who's last?" And everyone looked at you. He repeated the question. And everyone looked at you again. The man was aggressive and loud. When he saw that you were leaving, he tried to stop you to find out who was the person ahead of you.'

The KGB man laughed in relief. And Kim relaxed.

There was one occasion when the KGB got what they considered serious information that an attempt on Philby's life was planned in the next few weeks. They discussed the problem. They decided to limit Philby's public appearances even more and to assign a bodyguard to him. But Kim could not get used to having a constant guard and suggested a different approach to his colleagues: to arrange a trip in Central Asia for him for the next three months.

In 1988 he told me that the trip had left him with two contradictory sensations: on the one hand, enormous pleasure, and on the other, horror. The first was due to what he had seen during the trip. The second was related to the gigantic, enormous amounts of food and drink that he was forced to consume in those three months.

'Russian hospitality, multiplied by Eastern hospitality, has created a monster,' Kim said. 'A man who hasn't lived through that hasn't lived!'

But the security measures, even though they created some difficulties and limited his contact with people, had some advantages as far as Kim was concerned. He could always get out of unwanted meetings by blaming security.

I must add that the KGB's concern was not totally unfounded. According to Phillip Knightley, the West did not overlook that 'one chance in a thousand'. In his book, *Masterspy*, he describes SIS and the CIA studying photographs made by satellite and U2s of the Moscow buildings with Maclean's apartment – they were looking for a way to kidnap the former 'Homer'.

The early months of Kim's life in Moscow were filled with meetings with the administration on all levels. They wanted to meet the legendary man, to hear interesting stories from his heroic life as a spy, to have a glass of Cognac with him. I think they were drawn to him by ideological curiosity too: here was a man who remained true to his ideals, those ideals in which they had for the most part (and the higher up the more so) had stopped believing long ago and mentioned only in speeches. Career specialists may have been interested in learning how this brilliant man, of whom it was said that if he had not worked for the KGB he could have been director of SIS, Foreign Secretary, even Prime Minister of England, had remained true all his life to a decision made in his youth, and had never betrayed it or defected, even though there was no benefit to him in staying true. Wasn't it curious? The administration, naturally, did not ask such questions, but they observed him and tried to draw conclusions.

It was a period of spy romanticism. The Soviet public had only recently heard about the brilliant Soviet spy Richard Sorge. They learned about him quite accidentally, only because Khrushchev liked watching foreign movies at his dacha at night and he was shown a foreign film called 'Who Are You, Dr Sorge?' Khrushchev asked if the hero was based on a real prototype, and if so, what his real name was. His aides made inquiries. It turned out there had been a real prototype. And his name was Richard Sorge.

'Then why don't we know anything about him?' Khrushchev demanded in surprise.

He was not impressed by the answer: secrecy. How could there be secrecy if he had been captured in Japan, tried and executed? How could there be secrecy, if the whole world could watch a movie about him and only the Soviet people know nothing about their own hero? Soon afterwards Richard Sorge was awarded the title of Hero of the Soviet Union.

In those years another Soviet spy became famous: Rudolf Ivanovich Abel. Vadim Kozhevnikov quickly wrote a novel about him, *Shield and Sword*, describing his work against Nazi Germany. There was nothing about his work in America either in novels or the newspapers. So Philby's arrival in Moscow came at a time of a romantic attitude towards spies.

He was not exiled to Kuibyshev, like Maclean and Burgess. He was given a good apartment, and an even bigger and better one when Eleanor came to Moscow. He was not forced to work as an English teacher, but allowed to get down to real work right away.

At a small but solemn ceremony he was given a Soviet passport – after he had been asked if he wanted one. He accepted the passport proudly and said that it was a great honour for him. At the same ceremony he was informed that the Central Committee of the Communist Party had awarded him a life pension.

'I was stunned,' Kim told me. 'I had assumed that I would be paid for my work, and instead, I got a pension. I spoke up. And they told me: "You worked for thirty years. You can rest a little." Then I discovered that the pension was much more than I needed. I talked to my colleague – a little naively, perhaps – about that, too. "I can't spend the whole pension. I'm putting the rest in the bank, I don't need that much. You can pay me much less." And he responded in a very capitalist way. "Listen, the decision has been taken, the sum is mentioned in all the paperwork. Changing it will take a lot of work and time. Drop it. Take what you're supposed to get." And ever since then I've been collecting that big pension and needing nothing.

'Of course, my children visit from England, and that's an additional expense. But even so, I have more than enough. I once compared my life with the fate of former Soviet spies who had defected to the West. The usual practice of the SIS and the CIA was to suck out everything they knew, find them a job, shake their hand, and say, "So long, we have nothing to do with each other any more." After that, they were on their own. But they had no profession with which to earn money. They couldn't take up law, or medicine, or anything at all. They couldn't open up their own business, either. They didn't have the experience, or the connections, or the capital. In that sense, my situation is quite different. I feel like a member of a big family. The people who meet me, wherever it may be, treat me with great courtesy and hospitality. Too much so. There's a rather large group of spies like me in Moscow. Burgess, Maclean, Abel, Lonsdale. I never met Abel. But I saw Lonsdale often. He came to our house, full of energy and enthusiasm, and would start talking about something. He would talk non-stop for an hour or more then look at his watch: "Oh, I'm late, I must run!" He would leave. He was always in a hurry, full of ideas, always busy. He had very good English and a beautiful wife: a charming, efficient man, apparently full of health and strength. But one day he was out picking mushrooms with his wife outside Moscow, bent over, and died of a heart attack.'

Gradually, people grew accustomed to the spy. He was shown off to all the administration – in the Centre and locally. He told me frankly that he had got sick of being shown off all the time. Eventually, the level of these meetings dropped to field agents, and that meant to practical work, which was what Kim wanted more than anything else.

There is no need to give a detailed story about Kim Philby's work in Moscow. Anyone can easily imagine how valuable he was to the Centre. First of all, he brought his observations and thoughts gathered over many years of working with SIS and the CIA, a huge layer of information that he could not have passed over to the Centre when he was in the field. Besides which – and this was probably most important – he was the personification of the vast experience that helped them analyse any situation 'from the inside'. His amazing ability to predict the development of events and to calculate the optimum solution delighted his Soviet colleagues. He had a unique knowledge of Western intelligence services and Western political life, and also an almost superhuman intuition.

His advice and counsel to illegals heading off to work abroad were worth more than hundreds of textbooks. His lectures at the

espionage school brought his students into an almost tangible world
of espionage with its dangers, and clashes of minds and wills. His
charm, kindliness and humour, as well as his reputation as 'the
superspy of the twentieth century' (which was not yet known fully
and was developed by each student as his imagination carried him),
turned every lecture into an event, increasing his popularity among
the 'spy youth'.

Once he spoke to a group of field agents at the KGB club. His
lecture was part of the birthday celebration for Felix Dzerzhinsky,
founder of the Soviet Secret Police. There were 500 officers in
the audience. Kim talked about how to plan your work and as
an example talked about the five-year plan he had developed for
himself before leaving for Istanbul as the SIS chief in Turkey and
how, as a 'diligent Marxist', he planned to follow it – especially
since the 'big boss' at SIS called the plan 'marvellous' and made it
Philby's main task in Turkey. 'We at SIS,' he had said, 'will do
everything to help you.' But when Philby arrived in Istanbul, he
was showered with telegrams from London: 'Must find out location
of 12th Bulgarian Division', 'Urgent need data on harvest potential
in Romania' and so on. Finally, his five-year plan was shunted aside
by the daily hassles.

Then Kim smiled and added that he was certain that this could
never have happened at the KGB, where planned work was the basis
of everything. The response of the 500 agents in the audience was
a roar of laughter.

He felt the sincere respect for him, even love, and he knew that
the Centre undoubtedly needed him.

Philby's personal life was much more complicated. Before the
summer of 1963 the British government made no official statements
about Philby. It was only in July that it admitted that Philby was in
Moscow.

Eleanor did not move to Moscow from Beirut, as Philby had
hoped. Confused and hurt by her husband's totally unexpected
action, she gave herself totally into the hands of the SIS. When
Petukhov called to give her news from Philby, she refused to
meet him and told the SIS chief about his call. Since Kim had
once presented his Soviet colleague to her as a correspondent of a
German wire service, she could recognise him from a photograph

shown her by SIS people in Beirut. Under their influence, she was afraid to go to Moscow straight from Lebanon as Kim wanted, and she went back to London first. It was only in September 1963 that she flew to Moscow.

At Vnukovo airport she was met by Kim and his 'curator', who had run Kim from the Centre for many years. She was taken through the VIP lounge and they all went to Kim's new apartment, large and well-furnished by Moscow standards, given to him especially to receive his wife.

But their former relationship was not re-established. Eleanor discovered that the husband she loved also had work to which he was more faithful than to her, consistently faithful throughout his life; and he had not told her about it.

As for Kim, he was very unhappy that she had told SIS everything she knew and had turned in Petukhov, who was, as Kim told her in Moscow, his personal friend and one of 'our' most valuable agents in the Near East.

Eleanor wrote about this in her book, *The Spy I Loved*, and there is no need to go into the disintegration of their relationship here. I will say that a factor that apparently played a role here was the KGB's suspicions of her dealings with the SIS after Kim left Beirut. The KGB (and she felt that Kim shared this feeling) had no guarantee that her 'cooperation' had ended. Her husband interrogated her professionally, following the Skardon method – he asked her the same question many times, setting traps. Finally, she asked her husband: 'What is more important in your life: me and the children or the Communist Party?' Without hesitation, Kim answered: 'The Party, of course.' That came as a shock to her. 'Before then,' she wrote, 'I had never met a truly dedicated Communist before. Kim very rarely mentioned his political convictions and I had always thought that we shared the same views.'

She kept waiting for him to take her aside, put his hand on her shoulder and tell her about his convictions, about what was dearest to him in the world, to what he had devoted his life. But it did not happen. Kim did not feel he had anything to justify.

She took a long trip to the United States, where she spent five months. In Moscow, meanwhile, Philby's friendship with Melinda Maclean grew warmer. The Maclean marriage, according to Kim, had fallen apart back in 1948 in England. Things did not improve in Moscow, where Melinda moved with the children. Melinda felt free. So did Kim once things got worse with Eleanor.

Eleanor eventually had to leave Moscow. It happened on 18 May 1965. In the letter she left Kim to be opened after her departure she wrote that if Kim changed his mind, she would return to him, but she could live only where Melinda Maclean was not. Philby did not change his mind.

Sergei, Philby's runner at the Centre, saw Eleanor off at the airport with a bouquet of tulips. 'If you ever need help,' he said, 'come to the Soviet Embassy in any country and tell them who you are. They'll do everything possible for you.'

Eleanor was very touched.

She died in the USA in 1968. In his book Phillip Knightley quotes what she wrote not long before her death: 'I remember him as a tender, intelligent and sentimental husband . . . He betrayed many people, me among them. But men are not always masters of their fate. Kim had the guts, or the weakness, to stand by a decision made thirty years ago, whatever the cost to those who loved him most, and to whom he too was deeply attached.'

To her last days, she would not hear anything bad about her former husband.

Life in Moscow went on. In the late sixties, after a series of articles about Philby in the British press, it was decided in Moscow that it would be a good idea for Philby to write his own book: he could talk about himself and the work of Western intelligence services much better than his Western biographers. Thus came *My Silent War*.

The Western reader is probably familiar with the furore Philby's book caused and the flood of books on the superspy that followed in the West. There were many details in his book that are dear to the British and American reader, and it was intended for that audience, an audience that belonged to the political and intelligence establishment, and the establishment in general. That is understandable – Philby came from the establishment, and he wrote for his circle of people. His way of thinking suited theirs. His bourgeois nature did not differ from theirs. His habits, his favourite whisky, his woollen tie and tweed jacket in a houndstooth check were bred by them, like the bulldog and the English Afghan hound.

That is why 'his silent war' elicited such an explosion of emotions, passions, misunderstandings and distrust and the desire to learn all the details. People were as astonished as if an English bulldog turned out to be a German or Russian shepherd and – even worse – bit the calf of its master who had been breeding loyalty in it for centuries. It was as bewildering as finding out that an English Afghan is in secret cahoots with the hares.

In Russia the book did not create a stir. It did not have a secret radio transmitter, a lovely mistress in an attic, or chase scenes with shooting and car crashes. There may be a connection between the publication of Philby's book and his first major depression after his arrival in Moscow, and a new wave of drinking that began in the late sixties. Much has been written about that long depression having been brought on a by a new period of KGB distrust of Kim.

I asked Yuri Ivanovich Modin, one of the most talented Soviet runners of agents ('Soviet colleagues', as Philby called them), about this. I have already introduced the reader to him and mentioned that after the war he ran Burgess, Blunt, Cairncross and Maclean, that is, four of the 'five' in London.

He joined the service in 1943, just after his twentieth birthday. He knew English and had finished two years at a military academy, where, as he admits, he was taught discipline. There were not many people in the intelligence service, only six or seven in the entire English department. Sometimes there were even fewer as people went off to the front, often as volunteers. The ones remaining had to do the work of three. Young Modin did everything he was assigned. That was a lot and he very quickly knew everything that was happening in the English area. He read the residence reports, archival material, and wrote memos for his bosses. He was introduced through the files to everyone he later worked with, and not only the famous five. He uses the term very conditionally and says: 'There were plenty of agents there.'

'I'll tell you how it happened,' he told me. 'There was so much espionage information coming out of England that we could barely handle it at the Centre. We had to give priority to someone. So we chose five of the most valuable ones. The make-up of those five changed from time to time, depending on the effectiveness or workplace of an agent at a specific time. For instance, I never included

Cairncross in the "five", even though he was a very valuable agent and stood out.

'There weren't enough field agents to work with all the spies in London. They sent in counter-intelligence officers. But they weren't suited for the work. A counter-intelligence officer treated an agent like a subordinate: I demand that you do as I tell you. But in espionage,' Modin went on, 'you have to be gentle and humane. The way Maly and Stefan worked.'

In the late forties there was a major Soviet counter-intelligence officer working in England, who had done very well during the war. He was assigned Cairncross. But he couldn't work out a relationship with him. They had to find someone else to handle Cairncross. Modin was in the London residence by then. Since in 1947 Cairncross was not of great value as an agent, he was assigned to young Modin: let him get in some practice. Unexpectedly, things went well.

Modin knew that Cairncross had worked very well during the war. In his opinion, he was the most valuable source on German military plans. He warned them well ahead of time about the Nazi tank invasion near Kursk and Belgorod. He sent several concrete reports: the direction of the strikes by various military groups, the use of the air force etc. But the most important information he gave them was the thickness of the armour on the new German Tiger tanks. The Russian anti-tank guns could not pierce it. The Germans kept the data on the new machines top secret. But thanks to Cairncross, Moscow learned the secret a few months before the battle at at Kursk, and by then the USSR created anti-tank shells of the right power. John Cairncross was one of the people who helped the victory in the great tank battle near Prokhorovka and saved the lives of tens of thousands.

Modin told me (in April 1993) that Cairncross was eighty years old and living in poverty. He had appealed to the KGB to help an old agent who had done so much in the victory over fascism, but he did not receive a reply.

After his experience and success with Cairncross, Modin was given Burgess, Blunt and Maclean to supervise as well.

Philby was in Turkey then and Modin never did work with him personally. But through Burgess, who met Philby then, Modin received many reports from Philby to be passed to Moscow. So they knew each other through hearsay. The reader already knows what Modin did in the critical days for Kim Philby and his friends in London.

It was Modin's opinion that there was no distrust of the former 'Sonny' in the KGB while Philby was in Moscow. The reason for their problems was much simpler. As the leadership of the KGB changed, the people who worked with Philby changed. Some were smarter, some stupider, some more pleasant, others more indifferent. For some he was the symbol of loyalty to ideals and they were in awe of him. Others treated him simply as an assignment. Some saw the power of his intellect and valued his experience, knowing that he could be of great benefit to the cause. Others saw him as a museum piece. In other words, it was the human factor at work, which Kim talked about with me in the late eighties. But then, in the late sixties, he saw ulterior motives and deeper reasons in random occurrences. This caused him pain and led to his depressions. Perhaps he continued unconsciously to idealise the Centre, thinking that collective reason was always logical and rational, and had the big picture always in mind. It goes without saying, of course, that the attitude of the people who worked with him directly was shaped in great part by their bosses. If the bosses paid no attention to Philby, the people around him cooled towards him, too. If the bosses were suddenly interested in his opinion, the subordinates flooded him with work.

'It was not explained by a change in policy or doubts in his loyalty,' Modin said. 'He was just assigned the wrong people sometimes.'

I kept remembering what Modin had said in explanation of Burgess's unexpected departure to Moscow with Maclean, a departure that ruined the careers of Kim Philby and Anthony Blunt. 'It just happened.'

And in Moscow, it just happened, too.

Kim's bouts of depression were also influenced by his personal life (you could not call his life with Melinda happy) and by the disillusionment he felt coming into contact with many aspects of 'real socialism'. This is what Modin told me about Philby's relationship with the ideas of socialism.

'I've thought about this a lot. What can I tell you? All of them – Philby, Maclean, Burgess, Blunt and Cairncross – were quite different in personality. The first three were from the upper classes, Cairncross from the lower class. But they all believed that life in this world could be changed for the better. It could be organised in a rational way and made worthy of man . . . They all saw the miners' strikes in England, the Depression years. Philby saw fascism in Germany, he saw workers shot without trial in Austria. This formed their conviction that the world could be and must be changed, that people without their share could and must feel like real people.

'I'm not even talking about the influence of their professors on them. But among the instructors at Cambridge and among the students there were many people who believed in the Communist restructuring of the world. They believed whole-heartedly in it.

'It was for that cause that Philby, Burgess, Maclean and the others worked. They did not work for Russia. They worked for the idea of world revolution, whose vanguard by historical caprice was tied geographically to Moscow. And they were shocked by the quality of life in the USSR. They were certain that it was the fault not of the ideas but of the people executing the ideas. People are not immortal, others would come and do a better job. But the ideas of a scientific reorganisation of life in this world to make it just would not vanish. They would live for ever.'

I asked Modin if it were true that Maclean had called Kim a 'double agent' – working for the KGB and SIS – when Maclean was in Moscow. Modin had heard that. He himself did not believe in Kim's being a double agent. As for Maclean, he might have said that because he was angry about Melinda. And secondly . . .

Here Modin stopped in thought and then continued with a smile, which, I had noticed, was often used to soften harsh words.

Secondly, Modin felt that there could have been a basis for such rumours. What basis? No one had ever studied Philby's philosophy thoroughly. He was an amazing phenomenon. Everyone loved him. The members of the Anglo-German Society, the people around him in Franco's Spain, at *The Times*, his wives, his colleagues at SIS and the CIA, and almost everyone who ran him for the KGB. He was on wonderful terms with everyone. He managed to convince everyone of his decency, his professional competence, his absolute honesty in his work. They liked him, they praised him at Goebbels' Ministry of Propaganda, at SIS, at the CIA and at the KGB. Everything Philby did, he did seriously and with talent. SIS had so much respect for him that they refused to believe that 'their Philby', slated to be head of SIS, could be a KGB agent.

'You mean he could have worked honestly for both sides?' I asked. 'Honestly lead a double life?'

'He could.'

'Without being a double agent?'

'Without being a double agent.'

Modin continued the thought. 'I think only one correction is necessary in this unique story, and it does not contradict what I just said, but adds a stroke to the picture of Philby's psychology. I cannot rule out that with his charm, intelligence and ability to influence people, he mocked us and them, the KGB and the SIS – feeling that he was above them all.'

'He lived his own third life?'

'If you like. And there's nothing surprising about that. After all, he had a wonderful sense of humour.'

A high-placed KGB officer who had run Philby for the Centre told me how after a few glasses of Cognac in Moscow he asked: 'Tell me, Kim, did you give us all the information you thought valuable to us?'

Kim laughed. 'Of course not, I'm not suicidal! Sometimes I had extremely important information in my hands, but I couldn't get it to you because I was afraid that Moscow would not use it carefully enough, and SIS would figure out I was the source. That would have been not only a personal failure for me, but the failure of a major cause – the KGB would have immediately lost a valuable agent.'

His position changed sharply for the better in the early seventies. This change coincided with two events – personal and work-related. Kim met Rufina Ivanova, a young woman of Russian-Polish extraction, at the house of George Blake. He fell in love at first sight, she responded and they soon married. She was his lucky star to the end of his life.

The work-related event was that Yuri Andropov became chairman of the KGB almost at the same time. The new chairman and his people changed Kim's life. He was needed again, and he was needed for extremely important work. He was brought back from oblivion and showered with assignments. His depression vanished.

These two events were probably the last to confirm yet again Kim's certainty that he was lucky.

In 1986, at a congress of the Writers' Union of the USSR, I was elected secretary for foreign affairs. I did not hold the post long – just eighteen months: I preferred creative work. But in that time I

managed to do a few good deeds, I feel. The first was an invitation to
Graham Greene to come to Moscow. The hardline Writers' Union
had been in conflict with him for three decades because Greene had
openly criticised the USSR both for the invasion of Hungary and
the tanks in Czechoslovakia. I adored Greene, in which I was far
from alone, because he had millions of fans in the USSR. For them
(and for myself, I admit), I did everything possible first of all to
persuade the leaders of the Writers' Union to drop the stupid old
grudges and send Greene an invitation to come to the Soviet Union;
and secondly, to persuade Greene by telephone to do the same and
accept the invitation.

The Writers' Union leaders did not resist very hard: perestroika
was beginning, and they had long training in determining the
direction of political winds quickly and surely. As for Greene, I
saw that he was dying to see our country, which he had never
visited, and he asked only one question: was the editor of a popular
Moscow newspaper, which had published an insulting article about
him fifteen years earlier, retired now?

I learned about the article when I was working on the invitation
to Greene, and so I could tell him that while the editor was still
at the newspaper, I had reason to assume that today he had
completely different views on Greene. Greene sniffed and said
he would appreciate not having to meet that editor while he was
in Moscow. I promised.

But after that question came another, of a completely opposite
character. Could I arrange a meeting with Kim Philby, for whom
Greene had 'old good feelings – we worked at the same institution
during the war'. I promised that, too. But while I would have no
trouble keeping my first promise, the second turned out to be
rather difficult. As I later learned, there had been many requests
for a meeting between Philby and Greene, but the KGB had always
refused.

I went to see Alexander Yakovlev, who had not only returned
by then from his 'exile' as Ambassador to Canada, but was already
Secretary of Ideology of the Central Committee, and an influential
secretary, one of the 'architects of perestroika' and a personal friend
of General Secretary Mikhail Gorbachev. I told him Greene's
request.

'What idiots!' Yakovlev said, picked up the hot line, and got
permission. Right away, I told Kim, who knew about Greene's

request. I told Greene about the meeting at Sheremetyevo Airport, in the VIP lounge over the first shot of icy Stolichnaya that we had with the charming Yvonne, the writer's French secretary and friend. The happy news called for a second glass.

The next evening I drove Greene and Yvonne to the Philby house. Greene was silent in the car. I thought he was nervous. Yvonne looked out at Moscow streets curiously. The Philbys lived in the centre of Moscow next to Pushkin Square in a small, quiet back street where the sounds of traffic did not reach. The house was not impressive looking, and the entryway – like most in Moscow – was dark and dirty. But the lift worked well. We went up to the right floor, and we were met by Kim and Rufina. I had been in that cosy and tastefully furnished apartment with the books that did not fit in Kim's study and spilled out to all the other rooms and the hall. I was used to everything there – except for Kim.

We were greeted not by the usual Kim Philby – Soviet citizen, Moscow intellectual, like so many of my friends – whom I knew well. We were met by an Englishman, English to the marrow of his bones. I can't quite explain what gave me the feeling: either his suit, or his first words to Greene, or the gesture with which he invited his guests into the living room, which was also the dining room. Maybe it was just seeing the two of them together. I don't know. But I was seeing two Kims simultaneously – the one I knew and a different one.

Rufina seated us in the living room. Kim gave Greene and me an interrogative look and nodded at a bottle of Stolichnaya. Having obtained our silent agreement, he poured. We drank and then I said I had things to do and left: I wanted to leave the two old men alone together.

Later each of them told me about how worried he had been before the meeting. What if they had nothing to say to each other? What if after so many years they did not have anything in common to discuss?

They had worried in vain. Both were very pleased with their first evening. My wife and I invited them – with Rufina and Yvonne – to our house. Our daughter and son were there in order to see such marvellous guests. Our friend, the poet Andrei Voznesensky, and his Zoya, whose praises he sang in his poem 'Oza', came too. A few other writers and their wives completed the guest list. The party was noisy and happy, like all Moscow tables. Philby and Greene sat next to each other. They kept up with everyone's drinking. They laughed at the jokes like everyone else. They told interesting stories. But they were two Englishmen. I was struck by the strength of the national root that grew twice, thrice as pronounced in Kim when he was with his friend Graham Greene.

A few months later Greene and Yvonne returned to Moscow – he was taking part in an international assembly of people in the arts and sciences invited by Gorbachev. It was winter. I drove Philby and Greene to the snowy countryside, to the wooden house, smelling of resin, of my friend the artist Oleg Vukolov. We were joined by Serge Mikoyan, with whom I became friends in our student days at the Institute of International Relations. Then we all moved to his house. We sat by the fireplace and talked about all sorts of things. Once again, I was taken by the transformation of Kim Philby, even though nothing about him had *seemed* to change.

Kim talked about reading Turgenev, Tolstoy and Dostoevsky long before he had read a single page of Marx. That had created a romantic attitude in him towards Russia which had prepared a 'positive attitude towards Marx'. His first book by a Soviet writer in English translation was something he read in the early thirties. It was Sholokhov's *Quiet Flows the Don*. He also read Arsenyev's *Dersa Uzala* – he brought it up because he had recently seem Kurosawa's film based on the book. After 1934 he stopped reading any Soviet literature. He considered *The Quiet American* Greene's best work. There is a marvellous phrase in it, spoken by the main character about the American, Pile: 'He is absolutely convinced of his righteousness and absolutely indifferent.' He added that this was very accurate and that 'any conviction should leave a chink for doubts, for the possibility of thinking that you're wrong. Otherwise a conviction can turn into a fanatical inquisition.'

Greene listened with interest, adding pine cones to the fire from time to time.

Five years earlier, on his seventieth birthday, Kim decided to write a will. The Soviet colleague who helped him asked about his preference for burial.

'My answer,' Philby told me, 'was that I had only one idea on the subject. I didn't care in the least whether my body would be put in the ground or cremated. It makes no difference to me. The only thing I want is to be buried in the Soviet Union. And that no one moves my body to England, no matter who expresses a desire for it – children, friends, government, or anyone else. The USSR is my country, my homeland. I chose it. I knew it back in Vienna in 1934 . . . Sometimes during my travels [after 1963 he went to many cities in the USSR, and visited Eastern Europe and Cuba] I am asked if I miss my homeland. And I always reply, how can I miss it? I am in my homeland, the homeland I chose for myself . . . My children understand and respect that. The two younger ones may have preferred me to be with them. But my oldest daughter and, of course, my oldest son, support me. My second son, perhaps, has doubts about my rightness . . . My grandchildren come to visit with pleasure. And it gives me pleasure to see them. I give them presents, I buy lots of things for them. They like it here. I know that they don't live a real life here. But that's understandable. During the days of the empire, British families were large – five or six children. Three or four would leave England for Australia, Canada, India. They visited home every two or three years, no more than that. For England it is normal for various family members to live in various countries. And to die there.'

Philby was 'buried' many times, morally and even physically. In June 1985 the Associated Press reported from London that Philby was in a Moscow hospital with cancer of the stomach and that his days were numbered.

In late May 1986, President Reagan, speaking at a dinner at the Washington Hilton for veterans of the US strategic services, said: 'In particular I am thinking of a man who is the symbol of much of what is bad and corrupt in our world; how sleepless must be Kim Philby's nights in Moscow when he sees the new focus, energy and activity of the West, especially the rebirth of our intelligence services. How profoundly he and others like him must be aware that the people they betrayed are going to be victors in the end.'

Kim Philby's nights were in fact sleepless, but not necessarily for the reasons mentioned by Ronald Reagan. He occasionally suffered from insomnia, and that weakened his heart. The doctors had diagnosed tachycardia a long time before. About once a year, when his heart problems worsened, he would spend a few days at the KGB hospital, where they restored his heart into condition.

The last time, he grew ill in the usual way. He was sick for several days. But he refused to call the doctor: it would go away, it would pass. It had gone away on its own so many times before. But his heart continued to be painful. His spells came hard on the heels of the flu he had had. Worst of all, he had not slept for almost a month. He paced the room. Insomnia. That always led to heart inadequacy. When he got really bad, Rufina Ivanova called the doctor herself. They gave him an ECG and sent him straight to the hospital, to intensive care. He had been there before, but never for more than three days. This time, he was there for five days. Maybe they were waiting for a private room to be free, Rufina Ivanova told me hopefully on the telephone.

'His favourite pastime is making tea,' she said. 'A real English tea. It's a ritual that he follows precisely, almost like a Japanese tea ceremony. Yesterday he told me that he wants to make tea. I was so happy. That means he's getting better. And he is more cheerful. His cheeks are rosy again. And now the tea. It's a good sign. I'm bringing him an electric tea kettle and tea today.'

A few days later, on 1 May 1988, he died,[1] in his sleep before dawn, the way heart patients die.

The funeral was at the KGB club, where he had lectured to 500 KGB officers about his 'five-year plan' in Turkey. Now there were many more people – agents, counter-intelligence officers and staff of many other departments. The line of mourners who had come to say a final farewell to the legendary man extended out onto the street, weaving around the Gastronom next to the club. Passersby looked at it in amazement.

I asked Ivan Afanasyevich to arrange for me to be allowed inside. He did.

People walked passed the coffin, sincerely mourning Philby: people from one of the oldest professions, enveloped in secrecy, treachery, mind games, cruelty, heroism, morbid paranoia, torments of conscience, the triumph of victory and the bitterness of defeat and disappointment. He was one of its most brilliant representatives, perhaps the most brilliant in its history.

I placed a flower by his coffin.

He was buried in Moscow's Kuntsevo cemetery with the highest

---

[1] *When I discussed Philby's health with him in 1988, he told me that he had arrhythmia, an irregular heartbeat, not usually a serious condition. It now appears that he had tachycardia, a rapid beat, the most common cause of which is a failing heart. If there was a post mortem, the Russian authorities have not released any details. (PK)*

state honours. His gravestone said: 'Kim Philby 1.01.1912–11.05.1988.' There was a gold star next to the dates. Perhaps he would have preferred 'Lucky Kim' as the inscription? He departed, in many ways still a mystery.

Three and a half years later, the country to which he had devoted his life ceased to exist.

INDEX